*Drift Toward Dissolution*

# *Drift Toward Dissolution*

THE VIRGINIA SLAVERY DEBATE OF 1831–1832

Alison Goodyear Freehling

Louisiana State University Press
Baton Rouge and London

Designer: Patricia Douglas Crowder
Typeface: Palatino
Typesetter: G&S Typesetters, Inc.
Printer: Thomson-Shore
Binder: John Dekker & Sons


**Library of Congress Cataloging in Publication Data**

Freehling, Alison Goodyear.
   Drift toward dissolution.

   Bibliography: p.
   Includes index.
   1. Slavery—Virginia.   2. Virginia—Politics
and government—1775–1865.   I. Title.
E445.V8F73          975.5′03          82-6517
ISBN 0-8071-1035-3                    AACR2

*To my father, Frank Henry Goodyear*
*and to the memory of my mother,*
*Alison Harrison Goodyear (1912–1966)*

# Contents

# Illustrations

# Preface and Acknowledgments

The drama of the 1832 Virginia slavery debate began with a heretofore obscure black named Nat Turner. In appearance, the thirty-one-year-old Turner of Southampton County, Virginia, was but an ordinary slave, yet the insurrection he led in the dark of night on August 23, 1831, had an extraordinary effect. Blacks' massacre of fifty-five whites in this remote "Southside" Tidewater district so convulsed white Virginia society as to provoke unprecedented public debate on emancipation in the 1831–1832 house of delegates. For two weeks early in January, 1832, legislators debated, with open doors, the future of slavery in Virginia. The debate touched the very foundations of Virginia's political, economic, and social order. Assaults on slavery and demands for abolition also filled front pages of Virginia newspapers during and after the legislative session, as whites throughout the commonwealth confronted the "tragedy of Southampton."

That Virginians should so publicly and vigorously weigh emancipation was a momentous historical event, for Virginia in 1832 was not only the nation's largest slaveholding state, but one whose preeminence during the American Revolution and early decades of the republic still carried singular influence and prestige. Yet Joseph C. Roberts' brief study, the *Road from Monticello*, published four decades ago, provides historians of the Old South with their fullest and most current knowledge of Virginia's most explosive internal battle over slavery.

While slighting the contents of the 1832 slavery debate, historians have unanimously accepted Roberts' interpretation of the event as a major turning point in Virginia—and southern—history. At this moment, traditional accounts maintain, Virginia repudiated the antislavery tenets of her revolutionary generation and embraced instead the Deep South's proslavery philosophy. For a brief, single instant, white Virginia, traumatized by Nat Turner, broke the "seal of silence" enveloping slavery. Nonslaveholding western legislators allegedly alone proposed emancipation. The slaveholding eastern majority allegedly easily defeated such motions and thereafter gagged all internal discussion of slavery. With the publication, late in 1832, of Thomas R. Dew's comprehensive proslavery defense, *Review of the Debate in the Virginia Legislature*, the classic analysis concludes, Virginians everywhere closed ranks behind slavery as a perpetual "positive good" and linked Virginia's destiny to the slaveholding lower South. As Joseph C. Roberts' title implies, Virginians thus took the road from Thomas Jefferson's Monticello southward to John C. Calhoun's South Carolina, and onward to William L. Yancey's Montgomery.

In providing a more detailed look at this dramatic episode in Virginia history, I hope to demonstrate that the 1832 Virginia slavery debate was not an isolated aberration, but rather part of an ongoing contest between a white community irrepressibly divided by slavery. The struggle for political power, begun soon after adoption of the 1776 Virginia Constitution and continuing throughout the antebellum era, centered on slavery. Again and again, as democratic reformers challenged aristocratic conservatives for control of Virginia's government in 1829, 1850, 1861, a fundamental question recurred: Is slavery compatible with majority rule? Or must Virginia, to safeguard slavery, forever deny white men equal political rights?

Just as the drive for constitutional reform involved the relationship between slavery and political democracy, so the 1832 debate on emancipation questioned the compatibility of slavery and economic democracy. Such a multisided assault on slavery was not, as traditional studies like Charles H. Ambler's *Sectionalism in Virginia from 1776 to 1861* suggest, confined to western Virginia. Although abolitionism was admittedly more widespread west of the Blue Ridge, a considerable bloc of east Virginians also favored white-basis representation in 1829 and immediate or future emancipation in 1832. Eastern antislavery sentiment centered in the western Piedmont and major Tidewater cities and, especially in the case of nonslaveholding urban whites, contributed an additional class dimension to Virginia abolitionism.

Public demands for abolition did indeed subside east of the Blue Ridge after 1832, and during this same period the Valley also adopted a more conservative posture. But traditional accounts ignore the escalating antislavery clamor in Virginia's vast Trans-Allegheny where, particularly in populous "Panhandle" and northwest regions, whites increasingly resented slaveholders' hegemony. Rather than a rigid east-west confrontation, quickly and easily resolved in 1832, battles over slavery in antebellum Virginia were a continuing, complex phenomenon involving geography, demography, class, and race.

The crucial 1832 slavery debate mirrored the inability of either abolitionists or conservatives to win this battle. As standard interpretations repeat, the house of delegates rejected *immediate* emancipation legislation; more significantly, however, a controlling coalition of antislavery delegates also rejected *perpetual* slavery and approved instead a declaration of *future* abolition once public opinion concurred. Like Virginia's 1830 and 1851 constitutions, this antislavery compromise was more a "temporary patchwork" than a final resolution. But as 1832 Virginia conservatives feared, and 1832 Virginia abolitionists applauded, such public proclamation of slavery as an "evil," and emancipation as a pledge, kept alive Thomas Jefferson's dream of peaceful abolition in the "march of time."

Thomas R. Dew's *Review* of the 1832 debate likewise assumed that slavery *in Virginia* would slowly disappear. Far from identifying Virginia's interests and destiny with the slaveholding Deep South, as historians have heretofore maintained, Dew instead urged development of an urban-industrial society akin to the free-soil North. Such process, he affirmed, would make slave labor increasingly unprofitable and, over the years, rid the "Old Dominion" of slavery and blacks. Neither Dew nor any other 1832 Virginia conservative, either within or without the legislature, defined slavery as a perpetual "positive good."

Rather than a closed proslavery society, antebellum Virginia remained, as in 1832, a "house divided." Although the legislature never again voted on emancipation, Virginians continued to debate representation, suffrage, taxation—issues that, all recognized, involved the fate of slavery. Time and again whites compromised, postponed to preserve the commonwealth. But in 1861, civil war precluded further compromise. At that moment, tenuous bonds connecting slaveholding and non-slaveholding regions shattered, and Virginia became, irrevocably, two separate societies.

A study of Virginia's 1832 legislative debate can no more be "mere political history" than it can end in 1832. Political tensions evident among state leaders mirrored economic and social tensions in Virginia society as a whole. So, too, the "patchwork" compromises, the perennial political quest for a "middle ground" between slaveholding and nonslaveholding interests, highlight the paralysis of a social world torn apart by slavery, an issue Virginians could neither silence nor resolve. In the end, whites' irresolution allowed outsiders to determine Virginia's destiny. The Old Dominion, ever Hamlet-like, drifted toward dissolution.

In undertaking this study of Virginia's irresolution, I have received advice and encouragement from many persons. Librarians at Duke University, the Library of Congress, the Southern Historical Collection, University of Virginia, Virginia Historical Society, Virginia State Library, West Virginia University, and William and Mary College were particularly helpful in locating manuscripts, newspapers, and other relevant materials for a sophomoric graduate student. My typist, Catherine Grover of Johns Hopkins University, cheerfully waded through countless yellow legal pads to prepare the original dissertation and final book. John Shy of the University of Michigan kindly assumed direction of a Ph.D. project well outside his own field of interest and offered valuable criticism of both its style and content. Joel Williamson of the University of North Carolina contributed many perceptive suggestions toward making the dissertation into a book.

On a different, more personal level, I would like to thank my two young children, Alison and Bill, for keeping me ever mindful of the multisided dimensions of daily life. Finally, and most importantly, I would like to thank William W. Freehling for his numerous readings of, and suggested improvements on, my drafts; and for his willingness to share parenting and household duties while I undertook this historical odyssey. His ongoing encouragement and support, professional and emotional, has made my work on antebellum Virginia a delight and a challenge from the start.

*Drift Toward Dissolution*

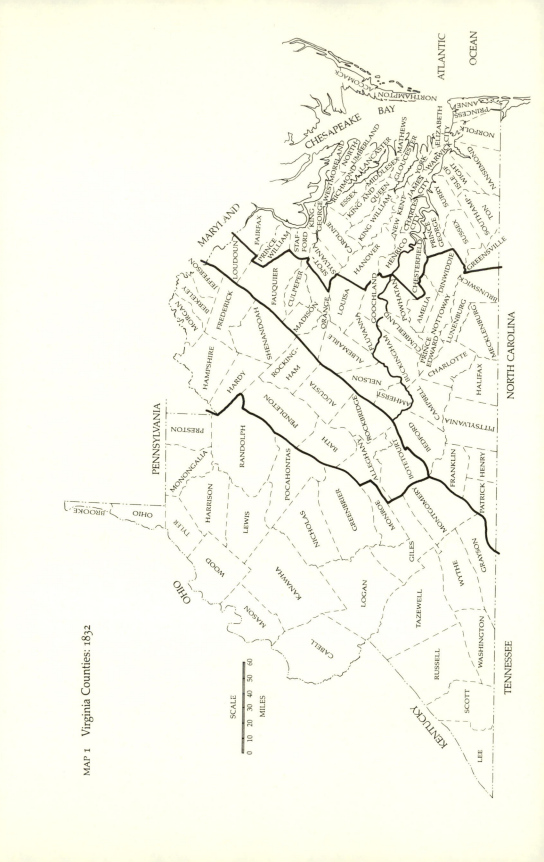

MAP 1   Virginia Counties: 1832

# I / "General Nat"

The mid-August sun cast an uncommon, bluish light over south-eastern Virginia; a dense morning fog covered the countryside. The bluish hue continued throughout most of the day, giving way to a silvery-white tint by late afternoon. As the sun set, a small black spot passed over its surface, and for several hours after twilight brilliant masses of red vapor illuminated the western horizon. Later that night, the moon gave off a strange, bluish color.

Next morning, the sun again rose with a bluish hue, turning to silver and then to green before disappearing beneath the horizon. For a day or two following the peculiar appearance of the sun, an unusually oppressive, sultry air hung over the region. An eerie, death-like calm prevailed. The weird atmosphere alarmed the local population. The better educated feared for the health of the country; the more ignorant expected the end of the world.[1]

For one Southampton County resident, the solar eclipse signaled not his own doom, but a supernatural command to begin his mission. Just as the black spot had passed over the silvery-white surface of the sun, so would Nat Turner and fellow blacks pass over the earth, slaughtering white enslavers.[2]

Born the property of Benjamin Turner of Southampton County, Virginia, October 2, 1800, Nat Turner was in August, 1831, nearly thirty-one years old. In appearance he was rather commonplace: about five and a

1. Norfolk and Portsmouth (Va.) *Herald*, August 19, 1831; Richmond *Constitutional Whig*, August 22, 1831.
2. "The 1831 Text of the Confessions of Nat Turner," in John Henrik Clarke (ed.), *Ten Black Writers Respond* (Boston, 1968), 102–104.

half feet tall, between 150 and 160 pounds, complexion "bright black," but not mulatto. His shoulders were broad, his eyes large, his nose flat, his hair thin. A trim, dark beard covered his upper lip and the tip of his chin. A small scar was visible above one of his temples, another on the back of his neck.[3]

But if Turner possessed no unusual physical traits to set him apart from fellow blacks, he had from early childhood felt himself an uncommon slave. When only three or four years old, he sensed that he had supernatural powers. God had chosen him to carry out a divine purpose on earth.

As he grew to manhood, his intense religious conviction, combined with a natural intelligence and inquisitive mind, reinforced early impressions that he had "too much sense" to be a slave. Fellow bondsmen, persuaded of Turner's superior judgment and divine inspiration, esteemed him as a prophet. Sometime during the year 1825, Turner had a vision of "white spirits and black spirits engaged in battle, and the sun was darkened, the thunder rolled in the Heavens, and blood flowed in streams." Soon afterward he underwent a profound religious experience. The Holy Ghost, he believed, had entered his soul, freeing him from all sin.

Nearly three years later, on May 12, 1828, the Holy Spirit again visited Turner, commanding him to take up the yoke of Christ and "fight against the Serpent, for the time was fast approaching when the first should be last and the last should be first." The Spirit cautioned Turner to conceal his purpose from all men until a sign appeared in the heavens. Thus, for almost three more years, Turner harbored his insurrectionary designs until a solar eclipse in February, 1831, convinced him of divine interposition. At that time he revealed his plan to four trusted slave accomplices, all from nearby farms. The five black insurgents agreed to commence their righteous "work of death" and liberation on July 4, birthdate of white America's affirmation of liberty and equality for all men. But Turner, falling ill at that time, determined to await a further sign. On August 13, 1831, the portentous eclipse appeared. Accordingly, on August 20 Turner arranged to meet his four slave allies the following day in woods behind the house of his current master, Joseph Travis.[4]

3. John Floyd Executive Papers, September, 1831, Virginia State Library, Richmond.
4. "The 1831 Text of the Confessions of Nat Turner," 99–105.

Travis' farm was in a remote region of southern Southampton, near the village of Cross Keys. Less than thirty miles from the North Carolina border, the area was, like most "Southside" Tidewater counties, sparsely populated and exclusively agricultural. White families cultivated potatoes, corn, beans on small, isolated farms. Most owned only a few slaves; yet in 1830, Southampton's slave population outnumbered whites 7,756 to 6,573. If the county's 1,745 free blacks were included, blacks comprised nearly 60 percent (59.1 percent) of Southampton's total population. With whites living far apart, with blacks outnumbering whites almost three to two, and with the major population centers of Norfolk and Richmond each eighty miles away, conditions for servile insurrection were auspicious.[5]

When Nat Turner arrived at the designated spot on August 21, he found that two more slaves had joined the original conspirators. Restating his plan, Turner determined to strike in dead of night while whites lay fast asleep. The uprising would begin at Joseph Travis' house and proceed swiftly to Jerusalem, county seat of Southampton, about ten miles north of Cross Keys. Blacks would gather guns, horses, as well as new recruits, along the way. Once at Jerusalem, a village of only 175 people, Turner would seize sizeable supplies of arms and ammunition stored there before continuing his attack.[6]

After a substantial dinner of pork and apple brandy, "General Nat" and his six accomplices made their way to Travis' home. A few hours past midnight, they ascended a ladder and climbed through an open window. Axing all five members of the sleeping family to death, the insurgents then seized guns and powder, saddled horses, and rode quickly to the next residence. Before news of the uprising reached local officials, fifty-five whites, almost all women and young children, lay mangled along the twenty-mile radius traversed by Turner's forces. Decapitated bodies of several victims were hurled into fireplaces. Others were left in the open, to be devoured by dogs and vultures.[7]

Few escaped the carnage. Those who did manage to flee spread the

---

5. Henry I. Tragle, *The Southampton Slave Revolt of 1831: A Compilation of Source Material* (Amherst, Mass., 1971), 14–15.

6. "The 1831 Text of the Confessions of Nat Turner," 105.

7. Richmond *Constitutional Whig*, August 29, 1831. Estimates of whites killed vary from fifty-five to sixty-three. Fifty-five is the "official" number listed in the September 26, 1831, Richmond *Constitutional Whig*.

alarm throughout the district. Couriers were dispatched from Cross Keys and Jerusalem the morning of August 22, bringing news of servile insurrection to the cities of Richmond, Norfolk, and Petersburg, and to the town of Smithfield in neighboring Isle of Wight County. As reports of butcheries circulated, white families in the immediate locale left their homes to seek shelter in Jerusalem.

Slave insurgents encountered their first resistance the afternoon of August 22, almost twelve hours after the attack at Travis' house. In a corn-field only three miles from Jerusalem, "General Nat's" band, numbering about fifty, ran into a small group of Southampton militia. These local white volunteers, soon reinforced by better-armed troops from Jerusa-lem, succeeded in dispersing the rebels. In the exchange of gunfire, sev-eral blacks were killed. Many others fled in panic. About twenty followed "General Nat" to the home of Dr. Simon Blunt. Arriving shortly after daybreak on August 23, Turner's forces met an immediate barrage of gun-fire from both whites and slaves stationed inside the house. Insurgents retreated and scattered in all directions.[8]

Reports of the Southampton uprising reached Governor John Floyd's office in Richmond just as Turner and his followers were making their final stand. At daybreak, August 23, the governor received a public no-tice from a Southampton resident declaring that a considerable military force would be necessary. As Floyd heard the news, pressing questions must have crossed his mind: Was the revolt confined to slaves in the im-mediate vicinity of Jerusalem, or was the conspiracy widespread? Who were the principal leaders? Of immediate concern, how many troops should be dispatched to meet the emergency? A distraught Floyd cursed the "wretched and abominable Constitution" which prevented his tak-ing official action without consulting the governor's council. Why, at such a dire moment in Virginia history, must he wait? Why were no councilors in Richmond?[9]

All morning, Floyd made arrangements to suppress the insurrection. Orders were dispatched for men, arms, ammunition, and all available horses and wagons were pressed into service to transport requested ma-

8. Richmond *Constitutional Whig*, September 5, 1831; "The 1831 Text of the Confessions of Nat Turner," 109–10.

9. Charles H. Ambler (ed.), *The Life and Diary of John Floyd* (Richmond, 1918), 155.

tériel. By the time Floyd had completed preparations, one councilor had arrived. He advised the governor to "do everything necessary." A few hours after this "vain, foolish ceremony," two Richmond units began the eighty-mile march to the scene of rebellion. Along with troops, Governor Floyd sent emergency supplies of arms and ammunition for local militia. Throughout the day, he continued to forward military equipment to counties bordering Southampton.[10]

By August 25, three days after the uprising began, nearly three thousand troops from nearby Virginia and North Carolina counties were on their way to Southampton. United States forces stationed at Norfolk Navy Yard also aided in suppressing the insurrection. Brigadier General Richard Eppes commanded troops sent to the immediate vicinity of Jerusalem. Brigadier General William Henry Brodnax directed militia from counties adjoining Southampton, as well as a cavalry unit ready for action if conditions required.[11]

The first official communiqué from the scene of the rebellion reached Richmond on August 25, when General Eppes informed the governor that troops sent were more than sufficient. A second dispatch, dated August 28, declared the danger in Southampton over and all insurgents, except the leader Nat Turner, killed or captured. Forty-eight blacks awaited trial in the county jail. Numerous others, suspected by local whites of participating in the massacre, were indiscriminately shot and decapitated before Richmond units arrived. Only the presence of outside troops prevented a more extensive slaughter of both innocent and insurgent blacks. The conspiracy, Eppes reported to Floyd, was not widespread. Slaves in neighboring counties apparently had no prior knowledge of insurrection.[12]

Reports of the suppression of Southampton rebels failed to calm the white population of southeastern Virginia. As news of the uprising spread, hysteria swept the region. Rumors of slave revolts in neighboring counties of Virginia and North Carolina intensified the panic. Early newspaper accounts, estimating "General Nat's" forces to include 150 to

10. Council Journal, 1831–32, in Virginia State Library, Richmond; Ambler (ed.), *The Life and Diary of John Floyd*, 155.

11. John Floyd Executive Letter Book, 1830–34, Virginia State Library, Richmond; William S. Drewry, *Slave Insurrections in Virginia* (Washington, D.C., 1900), 81–84.

12. Richmond *Enquirer*, August 30, 1831.

400 blacks, further inflamed public sentiment.[13] Amidst the terror and confusion, whites left homes in large numbers, seeking refuge in other counties or assembling in local shelters for mutual protection. Public hovels were filled with women and children who, alone and unprotected, had fled in the night without food, clothing, or funds. Unwilling to return home while husbands and sons were away in the militia, they slept on the floor in crowded heaps. The city of Norfolk resembled an armed camp. Two or three hundred men guarded the courthouse and prison each night, and another one hundred citizens patrolled streets on horseback.[14]

Similar alarm spread to regions of eastern Virginia far from the vicinity of Jerusalem. Patrols were out nightly in every community, searching cellars and other dark nooks for suspicious blacks. Local male residents prepared shelters for women and children in event of servile attack.[15]

The Southampton uprising particularly affected one white resident of the western Piedmont town of Charlottesville, near the Blue Ridge Mountains. Although well removed from the scene of rebellion, Jane Randolph, wife of Thomas Jefferson's grandson, confided that "the horrors that have taken place in Southampton have aroused all my fears . . . and indeed . . . increased them to the most agonizing degree. . . . My most torturing imagination had never conjured up anything so terrifick as this unpitying and horrible slaughter, and the very excitement and appalling precautions which it is thought necessary to take even up here, added to vague and I believe false rumours . . . keep up my fears." During the day, Jane conceded, she felt somewhat more assured. But "by night my fears return in full force, and there is no scene of horror that my imagination does not conjure up." Jane, in the last stages of pregnancy, urged her husband, Thomas Jefferson Randolph, to sell their plantation and emigrate to the free-soil town of Cincinnati. Whites in

13. Lynchburg *Virginian*, August 29, 1831; Norfolk (Va.) *American Beacon*, August 30, 1831; Richmond *Constitutional Whig*, September 5, 1831.
14. Virginia Legislative Petitions, Greenville County, 1831–32, Virginia State Library, Richmond; William Campbell to Col. Baldwin, September 4, 1831, in #1441, Alderman Library, University of Virginia; Helen Read to Louisa Cocke, September 17, 1831, Mrs. M. F. Robertson to Louisa Cocke, September 24, 1831, both in Cocke Family Papers, Alderman Library, University of Virginia.
15. Virginia Trist to Nicholas P. Trist, September 25, 1831, in Trist Family Papers, Southern Historical Collection, University of North Carolina.

slaveholding communities, she insisted, were never safe from black assassins.[16]

As similar fears aroused other white Virginians, requests for arms flooded the governor's office. Many came from Tidewater counties bordering Southampton, others from northern Tidewater and western Piedmont counties far from the immediate locale. Residents in these areas reported a "marked degree of insubordination" among local slaves in the aftermath of the Nat Turner uprising. Incendiary northern writings circulating among blacks aggravated the spirit of rebellion, "and" Amherst petitioners emphasized, "we know not the Hour when it may extend to our county."[17]

Although insecurity pervaded the entire white community of eastern Virginia, the greatest number of arms applications came from southeastern Piedmont counties below the James River. This district, part of Virginia's "Southside," was in 1831 the heart of the state's tobacco-growing, slaveholding economy, with slaves in almost all counties outnumbering whites by more than three to two. Such dangerous disproportion of blacks to whites prompted William O. Goode, from Mecklenburg County's Committee of Safety, to declare the situation there "critical if not perilous." Many of the county's 12,117 slaves lived along the Roanoke River "sufficiently contiguous to assemble in bodies of four or five hundred in a few hours." Without additional muskets, Mecklenburg's 7,471 whites could not defend themselves. Colonel Asa Dupuy from nearby Prince Edward County echoed Goode's fears, reporting recent "collections of negroes" in the town of Farmville, "larger than usual, with apparent dispositions to remain in bodies around the streets." The "great proportion" of slaves in the vicinity of Danville, Benjamin Cabell of Pittsylvania County likewise reported, had caused the town's "white inhabitants" to "feel themselves unsafe. . . . Intelligence brought . . . from the city of Raleigh, North Carolina," Cabell informed the governor, left "little . . . doubt that the Southampton insurrection was a branch only of a plan, long since laid," with "extensive ramifications." The "butch-

16. Jane Randolph to Sarah Nicholas, undated, in Edgehill-Randolph Papers, Alderman Library, University of Virginia.
17. John Floyd Executive Papers, September-December, 1831; David S. Garland to John Floyd, October 6, 1831, in John Floyd Executive Papers.

eries in Southampton . . . and, more recently . . . the atrocities" report-
edly "perpetrated" in counties of North Carolina near Danville necessitated "prompt . . . protection to lives and property." The "damnable
spirit of fanaticism engendered by northern publications," Cabell protested, pervaded the entire country.[18]

All through September and October, Governor Floyd sent arms and
ammunition to eastern Virginia communities in an attempt to restore
tranquillity. Newspaper editors also sought to allay public alarm by cor-
recting earlier exaggerated reports of insurrection. The official description of the Southampton uprising appeared in the September 5, 1831,
Richmond *Constitutional Whig*. Widely reprinted throughout the state,
the *Whig* account portrayed the suspected slave leader, Nat Turner, as a
"preacher and . . . pretended Prophet," acting solely upon the "impulse
of revenge against . . . whites, as enslavers of himself and his race." At
no time during the insurrection did Turner's forces number over forty or
fifty men, nor did black insurgents ever pose a real threat to white control. Rebels had fled in confusion after initial encounter with Southampton militia. "Another such insurrection," the *Whig* warned, would
result in "extirpation of the whole black population in the quarter of the
State where it occurs."

Yet as weeks passed, with Nat Turner still at large, disquieting questions remained. What was the origin and extent of the conspiracy? Was
it confined to Southampton, or did Turner expect a concerted uprising of
slaves in adjoining counties? Was seizure of Jerusalem his "ulterior purpose"? With rumors afloat of Turner preaching in Richmond, Petersburg, and Brunswick, was he now plotting another insurrection some-
where in east Virginia?

Trials of suspected insurgents, begun at Southampton County Courthouse on August 31, provided few answers. Testimony offered by slave
witnesses at almost daily sessions throughout September was disturb-
ingly ambivalent. Seemingly, no plans had existed for a general uprising, yet blacks in neighboring counties had evidently known of impending insurrection in Southampton. Even more disquieting, black

18. W. O. Goode and E. B. Hicks to John Floyd, undated, in *The Speech of James
McDowell, Jr. (of Rockbridge) in the House of Delegates of Virginia, on the Slave Question* (Rich-
mond, 1832), 27; Asa Dupuy to John Floyd, September 19, 1831, Benjamin Cabell to John
Floyd, September 20, 1831, both in John Floyd Executive Papers, September-October, 1831.

witnesses declared that "General Nat" should have murdered "all the whites long ago. Negroes had been punished long enough."[19]

Events surrounding the Southampton massacre remained shrouded in uncertainty. Finally, in mid-October, Virginia newspapers reported that a local slave had seen Nat Turner in the immediate vicinity of the insurrection. For two more weeks the rebel leader eluded capture, but on October 30 a local poor white, armed with a gun, found Turner's underground hideout near the Travis farm. Carrying only a small, light sword, Turner surrendered without resistance.[20]

The following morning Turner was taken to Jerusalem, and before being confined to the county jail he admitted to planning and leading the Southampton insurrection. His trial was set for November 5. Prior to the hearings, the slave leader unveiled the origin and design of his conspiracy to a local white lawyer. In the "Confessions" that resulted from the three-day interrogation, Nat Turner emerged as a religious zealot motivated to insurrection by a sense of divine mission. The original conspiracy, he avowed, involved only four slaves, all from the immediate vicinity of Cross Keys. He had formulated no plans for a general uprising.

Turner affirmed the validity of his "Confessions" during his trial. Offering no further defense, he was unanimously found guilty of "conspiring to rebel and make insurrection." Jeremiah Cobb, chief magistrate of Southampton County Court, sentenced the slave to be hanged on Friday, November 11.[21]

Nat Turner was executed about one o'clock that Friday. Exhibiting "utmost composure," he declined to address the large crowd assembled in Jerusalem for the occasion. As he faced death, still defiant, "not a limb nor a muscle was observed to move."[22]

Yet not even "General Nat's" passing could restore confidence to Virginia's slaveholding communities. For events in Southampton had only rekindled fears, long dormant, that any slave, in any neighborhood, might be a Nat Turner. The greatest danger, white Virginians recog-

19. Southampton County Minutebook, 1830–35, pp. 72–131, Virginia State Library. Slave witnesses all referred to Nat Turner as "General Nat."

20. Richmond Constitutional Whig, October 24, November 3, 1831; Norfolk and Portsmouth (Va.) Herald, November, 2, 4, 1831; Richmond Enquirer, November 8, 1831.

21. Southampton County Minutebook, 1830-35, pp. 121–23; "Condemned Slaves, 1831–34," in Auditor's #153, Virginia State Library.

22. Lynchburg Virginian, November 21, 1831.

nized, was not of *general* insurrection, but of *individual* acts of violence. Slave domestics could always poison whites' food, murder sleeping slaveholders and their families. Locked doors and bolted windows could not protect against insurgent blacks within the house.

Was there, then, white Virginians shuddered, no security? Could nothing be done to rid slaveholding Virginia of the eternal anxieties, the ever-suspected perils? Must the specter of Southampton forever stalk the land?

# II / Of Virginia's Lands and Peoples in 1830

The "Southside" Virginia planter dismounted his chestnut mare and strolled across the lawn to his Georgian mansion. Before reaching the portico, he turned and looked out over his James River plantation. There, in early twilight, strong-bodied blacks gathered up their tools and trudged wearily toward the slave quarters. When the last field slave had disappeared from view, the planter entered the house and greeted his wife. Moments later, a well-dressed black domestic appeared, carrying two glasses of brandy. As they sipped their drinks before the fire, the couple recounted the day's activities and chatted about forthcoming social events. In the midst of their conversation, a second black servant arrived to announce dinner. Seated at a polished mahogany table, set with English china and silver, the east Virginia aristocrats awaited their evening meal.

Many miles westward, across both the Blue Ridge and Allegheny mountains, a white Virginia yeoman likewise concluded his day's labor. As he walked toward the family log house, he spotted his son still at work in the garden. Inside, his wife bustled about the kitchen preparing dinner. A stack of home-sewn clothes lay atop the table. After greeting his wife, the farmer went back out to feed the cattle and hogs. He returned soon afterward with his son and sat down to supper. When the meal ended, the wife got up from the rough-hewn table and rinsed off wooden plates and utensils. The Trans-Allegheny family chatted briefly about the next day's chores before retiring early to bed.

The "Southside" planter and Trans-Allegheny yeoman in antebellum times were both Virginians, the first from the heart of the state's slaveholding section, the second from the heart of her nonslaveholding section. But though both inhabited a single commonwealth, the topography, soil, and climate of their regions showed little similarity. Likewise, the values, institutions, and interests of their societies so diverged as to constitute separate peoples. As such, the two symbolize some of the polarities of Virginia's white society before the Civil War, a society so rent by conflict as to preclude peaceable resolution.

The territory comprising antebellum Virginia consisted of two planes, sloping in opposite directions and separated by a narrow valley. The eastern plane sloped upward from the Chesapeake Bay to the Blue Ridge Mountains. The western plane sloped downward from the Allegheny Mountains to the Ohio River.[1]

The Equalization Act of 1782 divided the commonwealth into four major sections: Tidewater, Piedmont, Valley, and Trans-Allegheny. Intended to achieve greater equity in land taxation, such apportionment simply recognized the state's natural geographic divisions.[2] The Tidewater, Virginia's easternmost section, stretched from the Atlantic coastline westward to the falls, or rapids, of the Potomac, Rappahannock, York, and James rivers. These numerous tidal rivers and bays divided the Tidewater into five principal regions. The northernmost peninsula, known as the "Northern Neck," lay between the Potomac and Rappahannock rivers; the "Middle Peninsula" between the Rappahannock and York; and "The Peninsula," site of Virginia's original colonial settlement, between the York and James. South of the James River to the North Carolina border was known as the "Southside," whereas Accomack and Northampton counties, separated from the rest of the Tidewater by the Chesapeake Bay, comprised the "Eastern Shore."[3]

The Tidewater was generally a flat, lowland region, in some areas marshy. Although the soil was often sandy and poor, lands along the many rivers were rich and fertile, well suited to intensive agriculture. The climate, for the most part, was mild, with summer months uncomfortably hot and humid.

1. George E. Moore, *A Banner in the Hills: West Virginia's Statehood* (New York, 1963), 13.
2. Frederick Neely, "The Development of Virginia Taxation, 1776–1860" (Ph.D. dissertation, University of Virginia, 1953), 50.
3. Joseph C. Robert, *The Tobacco Kingdom: Plantation, Market, and Factory in Virginia and North Carolina, 1800–1860* (Durham, N.C., 1938), 15–16; Edmund S. Morgan, *American Slavery, American Freedom: The Ordeal of Colonial Virginia* (New York, 1975), 410.

Beginning immediately west of the Tidewater Fall Line, Virginia's Piedmont section continued to the eastern base of the Blue Ridge Mountains. In contrast to the flat Tidewater, the Piedmont was generally a broad, rolling upland plateau, with scattered hills and ridges in westernmost counties. The soil in most areas was fertile, particularly along river bottoms, and in counties near the Blue Ridge consisted of a rich, dark red clay. Like the Tidewater, the climate was mild, but not so hot and muggy in upland areas.[4]

The Tidewater and Piedmont together comprised antebellum Virginia's eastern plane; the Trans-Allegheny comprised her western. Unlike eastern Virginia, which bounded slaveholding Maryland on the north and slaveholding North Carolina on the south, Trans-Allegheny Virginia shared borders with both slaveholding and nonslaveholding states. The southern Trans-Allegheny adjoined slaveholding Kentucky on the west and slaveholding Tennessee on the south, but the northern Trans-Allegheny, particularly the region known as the "Panhandle" in the extreme northwestern corridor, bordered free-soil Pennsylvania and Ohio.

In contrast to the Tidewater's flat lowlands and the Piedmont's rolling uplands, Virginia's Trans-Allegheny was a rugged, mountainous district, traversed its entire length by narrow, parallel valleys separated from each other by equally narrow, parallel ranges of the lofty Alleghenies. The soil, though rocky, was quite fertile and in many areas contained rich deposits of coal, natural gas, iron ore, and salt. The climate was generally cool and moist, more variable than that of the eastern plane.[5]

Between Virginia's two great planes lay the Valley, a long, narrow corridor bordered on the north by the Potomac River and on the south by the Trans-Allegheny. Separated from the east by the gentle Blue Ridge Mountains and from the west by the more elevated Alleghenies, the Valley combined characteristics of each of Virginia's major planes. In some areas the terrain was rough and mountainous, the soil rocky. In others, long, picturesque valleys nestled between mountain ridges.

4. Robert, *Tobacco Kingdom*, 16; Joseph Martin (ed.), *A New and Comprehensive Gazeteer of Virginia and the District of Columbia* (Charlottesville, 1836), 112–32.
5. Virgil A. Lewis, *West Virginia: Its History, Natural Resources, Industrial Enterprises, and Institutions* (Charleston, W.Va., n.d.), 6–10, 192, 250–84.

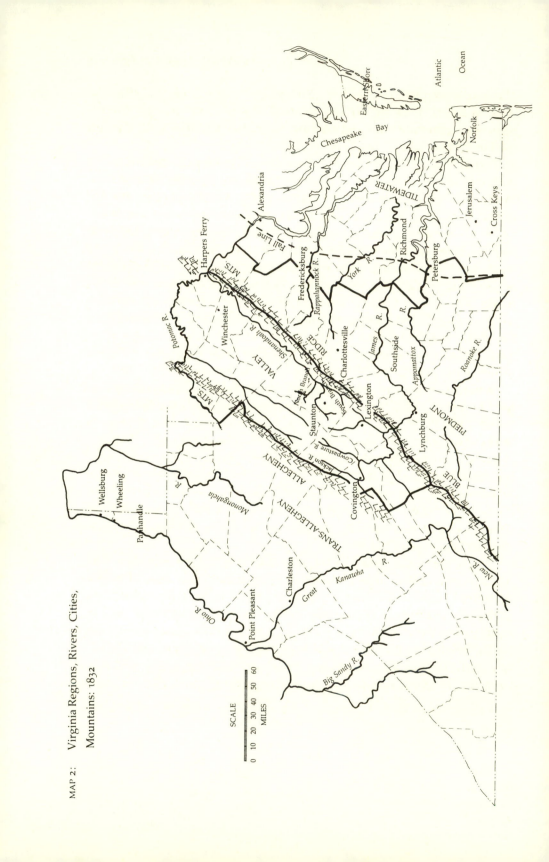

MAP 2: Virginia Regions, Rivers, Cities, Mountains: 1832

These lush bottomlands, bordering on quiet-flowing rivers and streams, boasted a rich, black soil, among the most fertile in all Virginia. The climate was generally cool and variable in higher altitudes and, though warmer in the valleys, rarely oppressive.[6]

Just as eastern and western planes sloped in opposite directions, so principal rivers of eastern and Trans-Allegheny Virginia flowed contrarily. Following the natural inclination of the Atlantic plateau, the Potomac, Rappahannock, and York rivers, with their branches and tributaries, all flowed in a southeasterly direction across the upper Piedmont and Tidewater into the Chesapeake Bay. So, too, the Roanoke River, the most southerly of major eastern waterways, wound southeastward across "Southside" Piedmont and northern North Carolina into Albemarle Sound. The mighty James River also flowed eastward from its head west of the Blue Ridge Mountains to its mouth in the Chesapeake Bay. Traversing the central Piedmont and Tidewater for a distance of almost 350 miles, the James, with its branches and tributaries, was the principal commercial artery of eastern Virginia before the Civil War.

Whereas Tidewater and Piedmont rivers flowed southeastward to the Chesapeake Bay, Trans-Allegheny waterways flowed northwestward to the Ohio River. The Monongahela, Little Kanawha, and Big Sandy rivers of northwestern and western Trans-Allegheny were all tributaries of the Ohio. Likewise, the Great Kanawha, formed by the junction of the New and Gauley rivers in North Carolina, traversed the central Trans-Allegheny in a northwestward direction to join the Ohio at Point Pleasant. Navigable for its entire length of about ninety-eight miles, the Great Kanawha was the principal commercial artery of Trans-Allegheny Virginia before the Civil War.

The rivers of the Valley of Virginia flowed both east and west. The scenic Shenandoah, with its North and South branches, wound northeastward to enter the Potomac at Harpers Ferry. Some forty miles south of the Shenandoah in the middle Valley, the Cowpasture and Jackson rivers joined near the town of Covington to form the eastward-flowing James. The New River in the southwest Valley, conversely, was a tributary of the Great Kanawha. Valley waterways thus connected with central arteries of both eastern and Trans-Allegheny Virginia. But the James

6. Henry Howe, *Historical Collections of Virginia* (Charleston, S.C., 1852), 334–41, 448, 460.

and Great Kanawha remained disconnected. As the major routes of commerce in the early nineteenth century, these divergent river systems reinforced the natural geographic isolation of Virginia's eastern and western planes. Whereas Tidewater and Piedmont trade flowed eastward to the Atlantic Ocean, Trans-Allegheny trade flowed westward to fast-developing markets of the Ohio and Mississippi valleys.[7]

As early as the 1770s, such prominent Virginians as George Washington had proposed schemes to join the James and Great Kanawha and, thereby, link the state's disparate sections into a single economic unit. Connecting Virginia's major rivers would not only strengthen political and social ties within the commonwealth but it would also enable the state to compete with Maryland, Pennsylvania, and New York for the burgeoning western trade. Construction of a continuous transportation route from the Atlantic Ocean to the Ohio River, proponents urged, was as vital to Virginia's internal unity as to her continued power and influence within the nation.

Initial internal improvements projects, undertaken by the privately owned James River Company from 1785 to 1820, involved construction of a canal around the falls of the James above Richmond to Westham. The seven-mile canal, completed in 1795, allowed boats from inland regions to unload and load articles at Richmond, thereby opening up important trade channels between the Piedmont and Tidewater. With completion of the Richmond-Westham canal, the company began improvement of navigation on the James River from Westham through the Blue Ridge Mountains to Crow's Ferry in Botetourt County, a distance of 220 miles. This project, completed in 1808, enabled proximate Piedmont and Valley regions to ship products down river to Richmond, and then around the falls to the navigable Tidewater portion of the James.

Dissatisfaction with the limited undertakings of the James River Company prompted the Virginia General Assembly in 1820 to transform the internal improvements concern into a state-owned, state-operated enterprise. As a private corporation, the company had been primarily involved with improvement of the river bed and removal of obstructions

7. Virginia Board of Immigration, *Virginia: A Geographical and Political Summary* (Richmond, 1876), 8–10; Wayland F. Dunaway, *History of the James River and Kanawha Company*, Columbia University Studies in History, Economics, and Public Law, CIV (New York, 1922), 21–22.

on the James River. As a state agency, the company's original goal was construction of a canal paralleling the James from Richmond to Covington.

During this period of exclusive state control, the dream of uniting Virginia's eastward- and westward-flowing rivers made little headway. From 1823 to 1832, the James River Company built a seven-mile canal through the Blue Ridge Mountains and improved navigation of the Great Kanawha River. The refusal of the general assembly to appropriate adequate funds for internal improvements, however, seriously impeded progress on the Richmond-Covington water route. Delegates from those areas of eastern, particularly Tidewater Virginia, which would not directly benefit from the central canal, increasingly opposed legislative appropriations for this costly undertaking. As a result of such short-sighted, local rivalries, work on Virginia's major internal improvements project consisted only of enlarging the existent Richmond-Westham canal and extending it to Maiden's Adventure Falls in Goochland County, thirty miles above Richmond. Throughout the first three decades of the nineteenth century, then, the Trans-Allegheny remained commercially isolated from the Tidewater and Piedmont, an isolation that would have crucial consequences for the subsequent three decades of Virginia history.[8]

The peoples of Virginia's eastern and western planes were as disparate as the lands they inhabited. Whites who first settled the Tidewater peninsula between the York and James rivers were Englishmen of Anglican faith. Drawn to the New World primarily by desire for immediate profit, these colonists early turned to cultivation of tobacco as the principal export crop in trade with England. With little knowledge of farming techniques, they developed a system of soil-depleting, single-crop agriculture based on large plantation units and black slave labor.

As constant tobacco cultivation robbed the soil of fertility, Tidewater planters abandoned worn-out fields and migrated to new, virgin lands. By the mid-seventeenth century, Virginia's tobacco culture had already spread from original sites along the York and James rivers onto lowland areas along the Rappahannock and Potomac. By the early eighteenth

8. Dunaway, *History of the James River and Kanawha Company*, 10–28, 44–58, 86–87; Linn Banks to Joseph Good, February 26, 1831, in Miscellaneous Letters File, Virginia Historical Society, Richmond.

century, descendants of old Tidewater families had pushed beyond the Fall Line into the central and western Piedmont counties of Hanover, Goochland, Albemarle, Orange, and Culpeper. And just prior to the American Revolution, tobacco production expanded rapidly south of the James River, particularly to the south and west of the town of Petersburg. Here, in such counties as Mecklenburg, Lunenburg, Brunswick, Charlotte, and Nottoway, soon were concentrated most of Virginia's large plantations, her largest slaveholders. Here, too, by 1830, slaves generally comprised between 60 percent and 70 percent of the total population and outnumbered whites by more than three to two. Although tobacco continued to be cultivated in older Tidewater and western Piedmont regions, the "Southside" Piedmont had, by the early nineteenth century, become the center of the state's tobacco-growing plantation economy.[9]

As the old Tidewater families spread westward across the Piedmont, they brought with them the values and institutions of colonial Virginia society. Intrinsic to this planter aristocracy was a deep sense of family pride, a consciousness of privileged birth and social responsibility. From earliest colonial days, prominent Tidewater gentry had governed all aspects of their society, serving as members of the house of burgesses and council of state, as militia commanders, justices of the peace, vestrymen of the Anglican church. So, too, such eminent Tidewater and Piedmont statesmen as George Mason, Edmund Pendleton, Patrick Henry, George Washington, James Madison, and Thomas Jefferson were leaders in the struggle for American independence and in the creation and direction of the new republic. This dominance of eastern Virginia planters both within and without the state would continue throughout the early decades of the nineteenth century. While Tidewater and Piedmont aristocrats were writing America's Declaration of Independence, her Constitution, and controlling the presidency and judicial branch of the federal government, they concurrently adopted a state constitution that assured their disproportionate political power at home. The 1776 constitution, incorporating the old colonial principles of freehold suffrage and county

9. Richard H. Shryock, "British Versus German Traditions in Colonial Agriculture," *Mississippi Valley Historical Review*, XXVI (1939), 44–45; Avery O. Craven, *Soil Exhaustion as a Factor in the Agricultural History of Virginia and Maryland, 1606–1860*, University of Illinois Studies in the Social Sciences, XIII (Urbana, 1926), 30–64; Robert, *Tobacco Kingdom*, 3–6.

representation, allowed slaveholding easterners to control all three branches of Virginia's government long after more democratic tenets had prevailed in other states.[10]

The qualities of pride and leadership characteristic of Virginia's slaveholding aristocracy were as evident at home on the plantation as in the political realm. By the mid-eighteenth century, the Carters, Harrisons, Byrds, Lees, and many other old Tidewater families had built stately brick mansions overlooking the James, Potomac, Rappahannock, and York rivers. Inside these dignified dwellings, ancestral portraits and family coats of arms were prominently displayed. Fine china and silver, mahogany furniture, books, wines, silks and satins were all imported from England and brought directly up river inlets to plantation wharves. Foremost among the virtues of Virginia's planter aristocracy were hospitality, courtesy, decorum. The great families took pride in setting their tables with extravagant amounts of food and wine, and in entertaining guests for extended periods. Fox hunting, gambling, and cockfighting were favorite pastimes of the Virginia gentleman. Gracious manners and elegant dress marked both the gentleman and his lady, along with such essential social accomplishments as dancing and music.[11]

Although the code of Virginia's eastern aristocracy required an appearance of leisure, realities of plantation life belied such notion. For underlying the elegance of the plantation mansion was the institution of Negro slavery. Of the state's 469,755 slaves in 1830, 416,318, or 88.6 percent, lived east of the Blue Ridge. Tidewater slaves outnumbered whites 185,457 to 167,001, comprising 48.6 percent of that section's total population. The proportion of slaves in the Piedmont was even higher, comprising 51.1 percent of that section's total population and outnumbering whites 230,861 to 208,656. Piedmont counties like Amelia, Brunswick, Buckingham, Lunenburg, Mecklenburg, Nottoway, Powhatan, and Prince Edward in the eastern and central "Southside" had by 1830 the largest slave percentages of any region of the commonwealth. Indeed,

10. Louis B. Wright, *The First Gentlemen of Virginia: Intellectual Qualities of the Early Colonial Ruling Class* (San Marino, Calif., 1940), 64–70; Robert E. and B. Katherine Brown, *Virginia 1705–1786: Democracy or Aristocracy?* (East Lansing, Mich., 1964), 225–27; Charles S. Sydnor, *Gentleman Freeholders: Political Practices in Washington's Virginia* (Chapel Hill, N.C., 1952), 73–106.

11. Paul Wilstach, *Tidewater Virginia* (Indianapolis, 1929), 75–93; Edmund S. Morgan, *Virginians at Home: Family Life in the Eighteenth Century* (Williamsburg, Va., 1952), 43–75.

throughout east Virginia, only four counties—Franklin and Patrick in the southwest Piedmont, Loudoun in the northwest Piedmont, and Accomack on the Tidewater "Eastern Shore"—had less than 40 percent slaves. (See Appendix, Tables I, II.)

Inside the master's house on large Tidewater and Piedmont plantations, trusted "black domestics" cooked, cleaned, laundered, sewed, and raised the planter's children. Outside in fields, "common working negroes"[12] cultivated the tobacco which was the principal source of the slaveholder's wealth. Elsewhere on the estate, skilled slave artisans worked as carpenters, blacksmiths, weavers, and tanners, fashioning the buildings, tools, and coarser clothing used by the plantation community. Blacks also tended the cattle, hogs, and sheep raised for meat, hides, and wool.[13]

As governors of this self-sufficient society, the plantation master and mistress worked long, active hours supervising farm and household concerns. The planter, often aided by a white overseer, directed the labor of field slaves and artisans; his wife managed house servants, cared for the sick, and planned meals for frequent guests. The paternalistic concept of slavery aspired to by Virginia aristocrats defined blacks as part of the "family," as dependents who must be properly fed, clothed, and ministered to when ill. This familial view demanded diligent attention to the needs of numerous slaves and, consequently, infringed upon the ease of the patriarch and his lady. Nevertheless, paternalism was as integral to the code of the Virginia gentleman as was leisure, for it allowed him to represent slavery in Virginia as a mild, benevolent institution unlike the harsh, exploitative system of the Deep South.[14]

Although the heart of eastern Virginia was rural in 1830, towns had gradually developed, most on or near falls of tidal rivers. Of these principal urban centers, Alexandria and Fredericksburg were in the northern Tidewater, the first on the falls of the Potomac in Fairfax County proximate to the District of Columbia, the latter on the falls of the Rappahannock in Stafford County. Richmond, the state capital since 1779, was just above the falls of the James on the Tidewater's westernmost edge,

12. John Hartwell Cocke to [?], September 23, 1831, in Cocke Family Papers. This letter includes an excellent description of the slave hierarchy on a large Virginia plantation.
13. Morgan, *Virginians at Home*, 52.
14. Robert, *Tobacco Kingdom*, 17–20; Morgan, *Virginians at Home*, 42–43.

whereas Norfolk, the other major Tidewater town, was at the mouth of the James on Chesapeake Bay. Petersburg and Lynchburg were the most important towns in Piedmont Virginia. Both located in the tobacco-growing "Southside," Petersburg was on the falls of the Appomattox River in Dinwiddie County, just twenty-three miles south of Richmond. Lynchburg was on the south bank of the James in Campbell County, not far from the eastern base of the Blue Ridge Mountains.

During the colonial and early national periods, Norfolk was Virginia's leading town, a major commercial entrepôt not only for eastern Virginia, but for the entire Chesapeake Bay region. When, by the mid-eighteenth century, the size of English tobacco ships prevented their going directly up tidal rivers to plantation wharves, Tidewater planters instead shipped tobacco in hogsheads down the James to Norfolk for export to England. With the gradual diversification of Virginia agriculture, planters also sent barrels of flour, wheat, and corn to Norfolk for export to the West Indies. In conjunction with this lucrative trade, Norfolk soon developed a prosperous shipbuilding industry. The town's mercantile interests suffered disastrous consequences during the American Revolution, however, when both British and American troops set fire to almost all the warehouses, shops, and residential buildings. Prosperity returned for a brief period following the Revolution, but events surrounding the War of 1812, particularly Jefferson's embargo policy and the British blockade of Chesapeake Bay, again paralyzed Norfolk's economy. By 1830, Virginia's principal seaport had for the most part recovered from desolation and, though surpassed by New York as the nation's leading entrepôt, aspired to become, once again, a bustling commercial center.[15]

If Norfolk's ample harbor and proximity to the Atlantic Ocean promoted her early rise as a leading export-import center, Virginia's Fall Line and "Southside" towns initially developed as points of transfer for produce from upcountry regions. Before the American Revolution, Lynchburg, Petersburg, Richmond, and, to a lesser extent, Fredericksburg, were important centers for marketing tobacco from nearby plantations. With abundant water power furnished by river falls, these Tidewater and Piedmont towns gradually established manufacturing as well as commercial enterprises. During early decades of the nineteenth cen-

15. Thomas J. Wertenbaker, *Norfolk: Historic Southern Port* (Durham, N.C., 1931), 26–67, 91–103, 114–70.

tury, manufacture of tobacco became an important business, particularly in Petersburg and Richmond, along with such secondary industries as flour, cotton, and paper milling. Thus, although the most rapid industrial growth would occur in years after 1835, already by 1830 a prosperous commercial-manufacturing class had emerged in eastern Virginia.[16] These enterprising merchants and industrialists, who tended to be of Scottish or Irish rather than of English origin, comprised an urban aristocracy whose interests were often at odds with those of the rural elite. More nationalistic in outlook, these urban Virginians generally favored vigorous programs of federal and state internal improvements, and high protective tariffs, to encourage commerce and domestic manufacturing. Most Tidewater and Piedmont planters, conversely, opposed extensive internal improvements and supported low tariffs as beneficial to agricultural interests.[17]

Although town gentlemen may have differed with country gentlemen over such issues as internal improvements, federal tariffs, and states' rights, the life-style of eastern Virginia's urban elite in many ways mirrored that of the wealthy planter. Like their rural brethren, prosperous urban merchants, manufacturers, lawyers, and doctors prided themselves on dignified living, abundant hospitality, gracious manners. Town houses, though built on a smaller scale than grand plantation mansions, nevertheless were elegant, spacious residences, often with an acre or two of property. Most wealthy urban families owned one or more household slaves who cooked, cleaned, laundered, and gardened. So, too, town gentry imported fine clothing, furniture, china, and silver from England, drank foreign wines, and served lavish, delectable meals to frequent guests. Dancing, gambling, and horse racing were favorite forms of entertainment, and during "Race Week" in the spring and fall, country gentlemen flocked to town to join in the rounds of races, parties, and balls.[18]

16. Wilstach, *Tidewater Virginia,* 27; Robert, *Tobacco Kingdom,* 55–72; Edward A. Wyatt, "Rise of Industry in Antebellum Petersburg," *William and Mary Quarterly,* XVII (1937), 1–8, 14–28.

17. Margaret C. Cabell, *Sketches and Recollections of Lynchburg* (Richmond, 1858), 12, 84–89, 279–98; Wyatt, "Rise of Industry in Antebellum Petersburg," 10–13; Kathleen Bruce, *Virginia Iron Manufacture in the Slave Era, 1800–1860* (New York, 1931), 259–73.

18. Morgan, *Virginians at Home,* 85–87; Wertenbaker, *Norfolk,* 14–15; Samuel Mordecai, *Virginia, Especially Richmond, in By-Gone Days: Being Reminiscences and Last Words of an Old Citizen* (Richmond, 1860), 177–79.

Nor were common social patterns the only bond between town and country gentlemen. Despite oft-divergent interests, urban-industrial growth created vital links between east Virginia's mercantile-manufacturing and plantation economies. Urban merchants and manufacturers depended on products of plantation agriculture for commercial transactions, as well as for raw materials used in tobacco factories and other processing industries. Even more important, entrepreneurs and planters alike looked to a common institution as the basis of their prosperity. Particularly in the tobacco factories of Richmond, Petersburg, and Lynchburg, slaves comprised the principal source of skilled and unskilled labor. In the early nineteenth century, urban manufacturers owned most black factory hands, but as industries expanded in the last three decades before the Civil War, hiring of blacks from nearby plantations would become an increasingly prevalent practice. This system of slave-hiring, usually based on annual contracts between entrepreneur and planter, fostered an ever-greater interdependence between Tidewater and Piedmont towns and countryside. With slavery becoming as characteristic of factories as of plantations, east Virginia's white elite, urban and rural, would have an equally direct economic stake in the "peculiar institution."[19]

More independent of plantation slaveholders were white artisans, mechanics, and tradesmen who occupied the urban social rung just beneath wealthy merchants, manufacturers, and professionals. Whereas rural Tidewater and Piedmont communities trained slaves as carpenters, blacksmiths, bricklayers, and shoemakers, in urban centers skilled white craftsmen performed many of these essential jobs. Norfolk's shipbuilding industry attracted numerous white ship's carpenters and joiners, riggers, and sailmakers. So, too, white cabinetmakers, printers, coopers, tanners, and weavers established small businesses in all major east Virginia towns.

Like merchants and manufacturers, east Virginia's white artisans and mechanics looked to commercial-industrial growth to expand economic opportunities. Unlike the urban elite, they generally owned no slaves and had no direct ties to plantation agriculture. Indeed, in cities like

19. Wyatt, "Rise of Industry in Antebellum Petersburg," 9–11; Richard C. Wade, *Slavery in the Cities: The South, 1820–1860* (New York, 1964), 33–36, 42–43; Robert, *Tobacco Kingdom*, 197–98; Bruce, *Virginia Iron Manufacture*, 231–35; David R. Goldfield, *Urban Growth in the Age of Sectionalism: Virginia, 1847–1861* (Baton Rouge, 1977), 130–33.

Richmond, Norfolk, and Petersburg, skilled white workers everywhere competed for jobs with slaves and free blacks, a competition that not only aroused racial resentment against black slaves, but also class hostility toward white slaveowners. Thus when rural Tidewater and Piedmont legislators repeatedly blocked internal improvements appropriations in the early nineteenth century, nonslaveholding urban whites swelled reformers' ranks to protest slaveholders' economic and political hegemony.[20] Far from being monolithic and harmonious, white Tidewater and Piedmont Virginia was in 1830 a complex, discordant society characterized by sometimes similar, sometimes dissimilar interests between urban and rural elite, and by more deep-rooted class rifts between democratic white artisans and aristocratic white planters.

A final major component of east Virginia society, both urban and rural, were free blacks. With 47,349 free blacks in 1830, Virginia had the second largest number in the nation. Just as slaves were overwhelmingly concentrated in the Tidewater and Piedmont, so 41,006, or 86.6 percent, of the state's free blacks lived east of the Blue Ridge. If free blacks were a visible social factor throughout the slaveholding east, however, they were particularly conspicuous in the Tidewater. There 28,980 free blacks comprised 13.5 percent of the Tidewater's total black population, 7.6 percent of the total population. The Piedmont's 12,026 free blacks represented 5 percent of that section's total black population, 2.7 percent of the total population. Throughout the antebellum period, Virginia and Maryland alone of the large slaveholding states contained such significant proportions of free blacks, a class that turned topsy-turvy the coincidence between color and caste.[21] (See Appendix, Table I.)

Free blacks generally worked as seasonal farmhands in rural regions, and as boatmen, fishermen, and oysterers along rivers and coastal areas. However, difficulties of finding employment in plantation communities, where slaves monopolized skilled and unskilled jobs, led ever larger numbers of free blacks to migrate to urban centers. There, a willingness

20. Wertenbaker, *Norfolk*, 14–18, 102. Divisions between east Virginia's slaveholding and nonslaveholding whites will be more fully discussed in subsequent chapters.
21. U.S. Census Office, *Fifth Census; or Enumeration of the Inhabitants of the United States, 1830. To Which is Prefixed a Schedule of the Whole Number of Persons Within the Several Districts of the United States, Taken According to the Acts of 1790, 1800, 1810, 1820* (Washington, D.C., 1832), Tables [10]–[11].

to accept lower wages and longer hours, combined with a temperament regarded by employers as more obedient and docile than whites', made free blacks valued laborers. In towns like Petersburg, Richmond, and Norfolk, where free blacks constituted, respectively, 24 percent, 12 percent, and 10 percent of the total population in 1830, most worked as unskilled day laborers in factories, mills, and shipyards, and as domestics, laundresses, and stevedores. Many, though, were skilled artisans and mechanics, competing with white craftsmen for jobs as carpenters, bricklayers, blacksmiths, shoemakers, coopers. The most prosperous group were barbers, a profession virtually monopolized by urban free blacks throughout the antebellum South and, consequently, shunned by whites as "nigger work."[22]

Although many free blacks were hardworking, respected members of their communities, many others were unemployed and destitute, forced by poverty to resort to petty theft and crime. State codes, adopted in 1801 and applicable only to free blacks, required free blacks to register in counties or towns where they resided and prohibited their going elsewhere to seek employment, or for any other purpose.[23] Such proscription reflected whites' fears of free blacks as potential organizers of slave rebellion. At the same time, by severely limiting free blacks' job opportunities, it reinforced the stereotype of this class as indolent and parasitical. Tidewater and Piedmont free blacks, then, were at once industrious and indolent, prosperous and indigent, valued by white employers and resented by white workers, esteemed as docile and feared as insurgent. Above all, they were, throughout the antebellum era, an "anomalous population" in a society where white skin connoted freedom, and black skin, slavery.

Across the Alleghenies, in Virginia's westernmost section, a very different society had evolved by 1830, a society whose life-style and values were more akin to nonslaveholding northern and western states than to the slaveholding Tidewater and Piedmont. Neither the rugged terrain nor the variable climate of the Trans-Allegheny was well suited to plan-

---

22. John H. Russell, *The Free Negro in Virginia 1619–1865*, Johns Hopkins University Studies in Historical and Political Science, XXXI (Baltimore, 1913), 13–15, 146–51; Ira Berlin, *Slaves Without Masters: The Free Negro in the Antebellum South* (New York, 1974), 218–29; Wertenbaker, *Norfolk*, 139–41.

23. Russell, *The Free Negro in Virginia*, 155–69.

tation agriculture. More important than topography or climate in pro-scribing the slaveholding economy of Virginia's eastern plane, however, were the attitudes of whites who peopled the western plane. Unlike Tidewater colonists, early Trans-Allegheny settlers were mostly of German or Scotch-Irish, rather than English, origin. Attracted by cheap, abundant lands, hardy emigrants came across the mountains from northern Virginia and western Maryland, and southward from Pennsylvania and New York, in the years just before the American Revolution and settled along the Monongahela River in the northwest Trans-Allegheny. By the late 1770s, settlements extended westward to the Ohio River and, immediately after the Revolution, expanded rapidly in regions south of the Great Kanawha River in the central Trans-Allegheny.[24]

By heritage and training, these Germans and Scotch-Irish were farmers and artisans, accustomed to diversified, largely self-sufficient husbandry and proficient as carpenters, cabinetmakers, blacksmiths, weavers, tanners. Their remoteness from established population and trade centers reinforced such independent traditions and values and fostered a life-style antithetical to that of eastern planters.

On their hilly acres, early Trans-Allegheny families built simple log cabins, grew vegetables and fruits, and raised a few hogs, cattle, and sheep for food and clothing. Most supplemented their standard diet of pork, hominy, and milk with wild game—turkey, deer, elk, bear—that abounded in the woods. The men fashioned crude, wooden furniture, household utensils, and farm tools, while the women wove coarse linsey cloth for shirts and dresses and tanned leather for breeches and shoes. They were hardworking, self-reliant people, white yeomen and hunters with little distinction in wealth or social status and imbued with an egalitarian outlook at odds with the aristocratic culture of the slaveholding east.[25]

Completion of the National, or Cumberland, Road to the "Panhandle" town of Wheeling in 1818 began a new era of development for Vir-

24. Moore, *Banner in the Hills*, 14–15; Joseph Doddridge, *Notes on the Settlement and Indian Wars of the Western Parts of Virginia and Pennsylvania from 1763 to 1783, inclusive, together with a Review of the State of Society and Manners of the First Settlers of the Western Country* (Reprint; Parsons, W.Va., 1910), 80–81; Charles H. Ambler and Festus P. Summers, *West Virginia: The Mountain State* (2nd ed.; Englewood Cliffs, N.J., 1958), 54, 103.

25. Doddridge, *Notes on the Settlement and Indian Wars*, 88–111.

ginia's Trans-Allegheny. The opening up of this heretofore isolated region to stagecoach travel attracted growing numbers of northern, New England, and foreign-born immigrants to northwest Virginia. Between 1810 and 1830, the white population of the Trans-Allegheny grew from 104,391 to 183,854, an increase of 76.1 percent. Accompanying this population surge were the development of commercial agriculture, particularly livestock grazing and grain growing, and the burgeoning of new industries based on the area's abundant natural resources. As transportation facilities improved, farmers began raising sheep, cattle, hogs, corn, wheat, and oats for market. In northwestern counties, with their numerous flocks of sheep and rich deposits of coal, wool manufacture and coal mining were leading industries by 1830. The town of Wheeling, situated on the eastern bank of the Ohio River just sixty-six miles south of Pittsburgh, soon became the most populous as well as the most important industrial and commercial center, not only for northwest Virginia, but for the entire Trans-Allegheny. Surrounded by coal fields, which furnished cheap fuel for manufacturers; convenient to markets in the Ohio Valley, Pittsburgh, and Baltimore; and with a plentiful supply of both skilled and unskilled white laborers, Wheeling during the first three decades of the nineteenth century established several large flour mills, paper mills, saw mills, and glass-manufacturing plants in addition to major wool and coal-mining enterprises.[26]

Like east Virginia's mercantile-manufacturing class, Wheeling merchants and industrialists generally favored extensive internal improvements and high protective tariffs. But unlike tobacco manufacturers of Richmond, Petersburg, and Lynchburg, wool and coal manufacturers of the northwest Trans-Allegheny did not depend either on products of plantation agriculture or on slave labor. Nonslaveholding white farmers raised the sheep, corn, and wheat used in wool and flour mills. Nonslaveholding whites comprised the principal labor force in factories and coal mines. Throughout the "Panhandle" and northwest Trans-Allegheny, slaves were a negligible social factor in 1830. Of a total population of 15,584 in the "Panhandle" county of Ohio, where Wheeling was located, only 360, or 2.3 percent, were slaves. In Brooke County, just north of Wheeling, slaves numbered 228, or 3.2 percent of the total popula-

26. Ambler and Summers, *West Virginia*, 125–29; Lewis, *West Virginia*, 192, 328–29.

tion, and in both Monongalia and Tyler, the two counties just south of Wheeling, slaves constituted 2.6 percent of the total population.[27] (See Appendix, Table I.)

Free blacks were an even smaller component of society in the "Pan-handle" and northwest Trans-Allegheny. Free blacks in Ohio County numbered only 195, or 1.3 percent of the total 1830 population. In Brooke, Monongalia, and Tyler, they comprised less than 1 percent.[28] Economically, socially, and geographically, then, the northwest Trans-Allegheny formed an unnatural connection with Virginia's eastern plane. Its trade flowed northward and westward to free-soil markets; its peoples were overwhelmingly nonslaveholding whites whose democratic, enterprising values more closely reflected free-soil than slaveholding communities.

Elsewhere in Virginia's Trans-Allegheny, nonslaveholding whites also predominated, but proportions of slaves were larger than in the "Pan-handle" and northwest. Nonslaveholding white yeomen settled the fertile Kanawha Valley in the central Trans-Allegheny and, like farmers in northwestern counties, gradually shifted from self-sufficient agriculture to commercial grain growing and livestock grazing. During early decades of the nineteenth century, the Kanawha Valley also developed an important salt-mining industry. Begun in 1807 along the Great Kanawha River near the town of Charleston, salt mining had expanded by 1830 to include seventy major saltworks. The Kanawha Valley saltworks, located mostly in Kanawha and Greenbrier counties, produced more salt than any region in the nation. Salt manufactured there was shipped on the Great Kanawha to the Ohio River and subsequently distributed throughout the Ohio Valley for use in curing and preserving meats, and for household purposes.[29]

Like the wool and coal-mining interests of the Wheeling region, Kanawha salt manufacturers favored extensive internal improvements and high protective tariffs. But whereas industries in the northwest Trans-

27. Ambler and Summers, *West Virginia*, 129–30; Charles H. Ambler, *Sectionalism in Virginia from 1776 to 1861* (Reprint; New York, 1964), 118–21; U.S. Census Office, *Fifth Census*, Tables [10]–[13].
28. U.S. Census Office, *Fifth Census*, Tables [10]–[13].
29. Lewis, *West Virginia*, 229–42, 359–61; Robert S. Starobin, *Industrial Slavery in the Old South* (New York, 1970), 24–25.

MAP 3: Density of Slave Population in Virginia: 1830

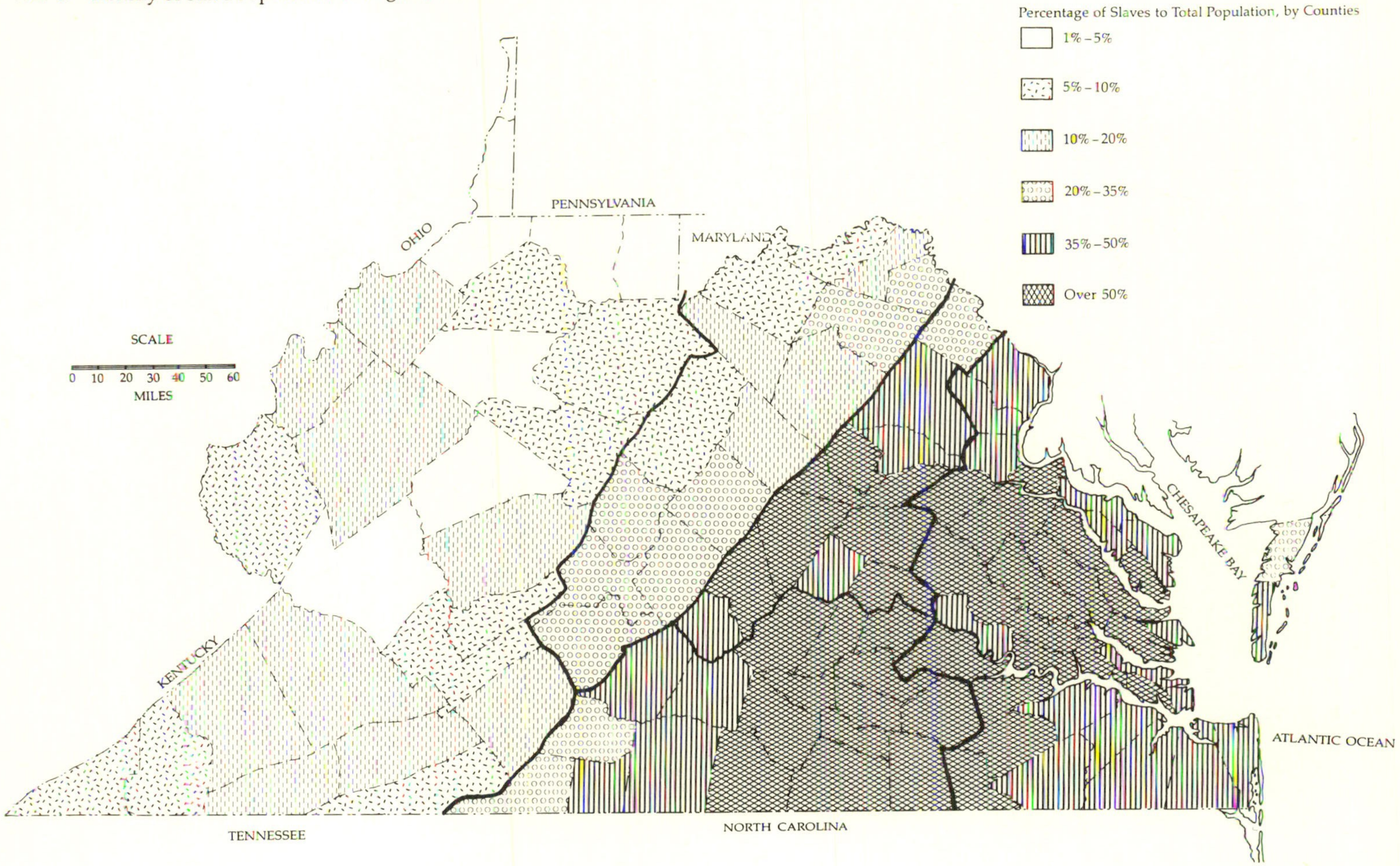

Percentage of Slaves to Total Population, by Counties

- 1%–5%
- 5%–10%
- 10%–20%
- 20%–35%
- 35%–50%
- Over 50%

SCALE

0 10 20 30 40 50 60

MILES

OHIO

PENNSYLVANIA

MARYLAND

KENTUCKY

TENNESSEE

NORTH CAROLINA

CHESAPEAKE BAY

ATLANTIC OCEAN

Allegheny relied almost exclusively on white labor, Kanawha salt mines used slaves. By 1830, the seventy major saltworks employed 440 slave laborers and 200 slave coopers. The ratio of slaves in Kanawha, consequently, was the highest west of the Alleghenies, comprising 18.4 percent of the total population. In nearby Greenbrier County, slaves in 1830 constituted 12.9 percent of the total population, also one of the largest concentrations of slaves in the entire Trans-Allegheny.[30] (See Appendix, Table I.)

Several counties in southeastern and southwestern Trans-Allegheny likewise had considerable slave populations by 1830. In Montgomery, just across the Blue Ridge Mountains from Virginia's southwest Piedmont and not far from North Carolina, slaves comprised 16.5 percent of the total population. Similarly, slaves in nearby Tazewell, Wythe, and Washington counties, all bordering on or proximate to slaveholding Kentucky and Tennessee, represented, respectively, 14.3 percent, 17.2 percent, and 16.4 percent of the total. Although such slave percentages were high for the Trans-Allegheny, they in no way approximated the 40–70 percent slave ratios characteristic of all but a handful of Tidewater and Piedmont counties. Of the total Trans-Allegheny population of 204,117 in 1830, slaves numbered 18,665, or just 9.1 percent. Equally significant, although the Trans-Allegheny contained 26.5 percent of Virginia's whites by 1830, only 4 percent of the state's slaves and 3.4 percent of her free blacks resided west of the Alleghenies.[31] Such divergent black-white ratios in eastern and Trans-Allegheny Virginia would play a crucial role in escalating debates over slavery during the antebellum period. (See Appendix, Table I, II.)

Just as the Valley was geographically a "middle ground" between Virginia's eastern and western planes, so its population displayed characteristics of both eastern and Trans-Allegheny society. Whites first came to Virginia's picturesque Valley in 1732, when German families from York and Lancaster counties in Pennsylvania migrated southward and settled near the present towns of Winchester and Stephensburg in Frederick County. This southwesterly movement of Germans from Pennsylvania, Maryland, New Jersey, and New York continued throughout the colonial

30. Starobin, *Industrial Slavery in the Old South*, 24–25; U.S. Census Office, *Fifth Census*, Tables [10]–[13].
31. U.S. Census Office, *Fifth Census*, Tables [10]–[13].

era and for several decades following the American Revolution. The great majority of early German immigrants settled in the northern Valley, particularly in Frederick, Shenandoah, and Rockingham counties. From there they spread westward across the mountains into valleys of the South Branch of the Shenandoah and helped form the counties of Hardy, Hampshire, and Pendleton. Some, too, pushed eastward through the Blue Ridge Mountains and occupied sparsely inhabited regions of Virginia's western Piedmont.

During the same period, numerous Scotch-Irish families also came to the Valley. Like the Germans, most Scotch-Irish migrated southwestward from the Middle Colonies. In the 1750s, however, considerable numbers came directly from Scotland and northern Ireland. The majority settled in Augusta and Rockbridge counties in the middle Valley, but some crossed the Blue Ridge Mountains and settled in the western Piedmont. This movement of nonslaveholding German and Scotch-Irish into counties along the eastern base of the Blue Ridge would contribute to more progressive, democratic attitudes in Virginia's western Piedmont than in older-settled counties of the Tidewater and southeastern Piedmont.[32]

Like later Trans-Allegheny settlers, Germans and Scotch-Irish who peopled the Valley and western Piedmont were mostly small farmers and artisans attracted to the region by the abundance of cheap, fertile lands. The Germans, particularly, were fine, experienced farmers accustomed to individual, diversified agriculture and dependent on their own labor to construct farm buildings, wagons, and tools. On their small, well-cultivated holdings, they built modest log cabins for their families and grew wheat, oats, hay, and corn for cattle, horses, sheep, and hogs. The barn was the largest and best-constructed building on German farms, providing shelter for livestock during the winter and storage for hay and grain.[33]

In contrast to the soil-depleting, single-crop agriculture of Tidewater English colonists, Valley Germans and Scotch-Irish adopted such prac-

32. Samuel Kercheval, *A History of the Valley of Virginia* (2nd ed.; Woodstock, Va., 1850), 40–61, 154–61; John W. Wayland, *The German Element of the Shenandoah Valley of Virginia* (Charlottesville, 1907), 20–23, 52–53, 83–94; Lewis C. Gray, *The History of Agriculture in the Southern United States to 1860* (2 vols.; Washington, D.C., 1933), II, 90–92.

33. Gray, *History of Agriculture*, II, 122; Wayland, *The German Element of the Shenandoah Valley*, 190–95; Kercheval, *History of the Valley*, 134-37.

tices as crop rotation and deep plowing to conserve the soil. Not concerned with making large, immediate profits from farming, these settlers also differed from Tidewater Englishmen in eschewing all forms of privilege and pretension. Valley whites were an industrious, frugal, democratic people who dressed in homespun clothing, made their own furniture, baked their own bread, and raised their own vegetables. Unlike slaveholding Tidewater and Piedmont communities which disparaged manual labor as "nigger work," Valley Germans and Scotch-Irish were proud of working with their hands. Often at harvest time, mothers and daughters toiled long hours alongside the men, haying and harvesting the grain.[34]

Such values of industry and democracy, joined to a tradition of independent farming and craftsmanship, were major obstacles to the extension of slavery west of the Blue Ridge. The strong religious convictions of early Valley settlers were an additional barrier. Most of the Scotch-Irish were Presbyterians, whereas the Germans belonged to numerous religious sects, especially Lutheran, German Reformed, Mennonite, Dunker, and United Brethren. Unlike the Anglican church of eastern Virginia, whose views on slavery generally reflected those of wealthier slaveholding members, Valley churches in the late eighteenth century firmly opposed slavery. Great Awakening revivalism, proclaiming the spiritual equality of all men, had little impact on the Anglican church but intensified antislavery persuasions of Valley churchgoers.[35] Heritage, customs, and religion thus combined to arrest the early march of slaves, plantations, and aristocratic modes across the Blue Ridge. Instead, a society of nonslaveholding white yeomen, artisans, and mechanics evolved, a democratic, essentially middle-class structure which, like Virginia's later-settled Trans-Allegheny, was more akin to the free-soil North and West than to the slaveholding Tidewater and Piedmont.

As generations passed, natural and man-made forces eroded the strong antislavery convictions of early Valley settlers, for unlike the mountainous Trans-Allegheny, fertile Valley bottomlands were well

34. Wayland, *The German Element of the Shenandoah Valley*, 195–201; Kercheval, *History of the Valley*, 134-37; Shryock, "British Versus German Traditions in Colonial Agriculture," 46–48.

35. Wayland, *The German Element of the Shenandoah Valley*, 110, 128–31, 179–83; Morgan, *Virginians at Home*, 81–82; Wesley Gewehr, *The Great Awakening in Virginia, 1740–1790* (Durham, N.C., 1930), 26–27.

suited to slave labor. And whereas Trans-Allegheny rivers all flowed westward away from east Virginia markets, the Shenandoah, Potomac, and James provided Valley farmers natural access to Richmond and Norfolk. Turnpikes, canals, and railroads constructed during the early nineteenth century established further commercial ties between the Valley and east Virginia. With expansion of commercial livestock grazing and grain growing, the Valley towns of Staunton in Augusta County and Winchester in Frederick County became prosperous trade centers. Turnpike roads from Staunton and Winchester led east and west, north and south, linking the Valley economy with not only east Virginia markets but Baltimore, Pittsburgh, and western regions as well. Winchester, residence of many eminent Valley lawyers and doctors, had also, by the late 1820s, established railroad connections with Harpers Ferry at the juncture of the Shenandoah and Potomac rivers.[36]

While internal improvements projects carried Valley agricultural products eastward, the process of assimilation, or "Americanization," slowly undermined cultural and religious traditions of Valley Germans and Scotch-Irish and, over the years, compromised their antislavery beliefs. From 1800 to 1830, the Valley's slave population grew from 18,058 to 34,772, an increase of 92.3 percent. During the same period, the Valley's white population increased from 106,323 to 134,791, or only 26.8 percent.[37]

Yet despite increasing slave ratios, the Valley slave interest in no respect approached that of eastern Virginia. Slaves in 1830 comprised 19.9 percent of the total Valley population, compared to 51.1 percent in the Piedmont and 48.6 percent in the Tidewater. Moreover, just 7.4 percent of all Virginia slaves lived in the Valley, whereas 88.6 percent lived east of the Blue Ridge. Significantly, too, the highest concentration of Valley slaves was in Jefferson and Frederick. These two northern Valley counties, where slaves represented, respectively, 30.9 percent and 28.5 percent of the total populations, had originally attracted a considerable English population. Descendants of old Virginia families, these Englishmen brought with them across the Blue Ridge Mountains the values and institutions of aristocratic Tidewater society. Almost one-third (32.8 per-

36. Kercheval, *History of the Valley*, 309–18.

37. Shryock, "British Versus German Traditions in Colonial Agriculture," 49–50; U.S. Census Office, *Fifth Census*, Tables [10]–[13].

cent) of the Valley's 34,772 slaves in 1830 lived in these two "old Virginia" counties.[38] (See Appendix, Table I.)

Elsewhere in the Valley, though slavery did make inroads in the early nineteenth century, whites generally resisted extension of large slave-holding plantations and aristocratic social modes. Those farmers who did own slaves owned only a few and worked alongside them in the fields. Similarly, though the Valley had developed socially prominent families like the Campbells, Prestons, and McDowells by 1830, such elite shared the more progressive, democratic values of their community rather than the conservative, aristocratic attitudes of most Tidewater and Piedmont gentry.[39] Valley society in 1830 thus more closely resembled Virginia's nonslaveholding Trans-Allegheny than her slaveholding eastern plane. Yet at the same time the Valley had significant commercial ties to east Virginia and twice as many slaves as the state's remote western district.

Virginia at the close of the first three decades of the nineteenth century was a complex, heterogeneous society, a region of extremes both in lands and in peoples. Her vast territory, stretching from the Chesapeake Bay to the Ohio River, encompassed flat lowlands and towering mountains, rural plantations and urban factories, aristocratic slaveholders and democratic nonslaveholders. She had, at once, the largest number of slaves in the Union, and a section where slaves were less than 10 percent of the population. Perhaps more than any other state, Virginia mirrored polarities within the nation as a whole. Her "Southside" Tidewater and Piedmont area, with its large tobacco plantations and huge slave populations, was most akin to the Deep South. Her vast Trans-Allegheny, especially the "Panhandle" and northwest, was socially and economically more compatible with the free-soil North and West. Other areas of Virginia—the Valley, western Piedmont, major Tidewater and Piedmont towns—belonged to neither the free-soil North nor the slaveholding Deep South. Rather, they resembled a "half-way house" between the two extremes. Whites in this "middle" Virginia generally shared enterprising, progressive values of "Yankee" communities; yet many, concurrently, had a substantial interest in the South's "peculiar institution."

38. Howe, *Historical Collections of Virginia*, 334–41; Wayland, *The German Element of the Shenandoah Valley*, 93, 186.
39. Thomas P. Abernethy, *Three Virginia Frontiers* (Reprint; Gloucester, Mass., 1962), 58–60.

Although there were at least three "Virginias" in 1830, the state government suggested instead a homogeneous white society of aristocratic, rural gentry. The system of county representation and freehold suffrage incorporated in the 1776 constitution assured the Tidewater disproportionate influence in all three branches of government and disenfranchised the majority of Virginia's adult white males. As population swelled in western Piedmont, Valley, and Trans-Allegheny counties in post-1776 decades, whites there increasingly protested undemocratic apportionment in both houses of the general assembly. Growing numbers of nonfreeholding whites from all sections of the commonwealth likewise protested landed suffrage qualifications. The movement for constitutional reform, begun even as Virginia adopted her original constitution, culminated first in the 1829–1830 constitutional convention when reformers from both sides of the Blue Ridge challenged conservative easterners for control of the state government.

# III / "A Temporary Patchwork of a Constitution"

"Time and trial," Thomas Jefferson wrote in *Notes on the State of Virginia* just five years after Virginia formed her first government, "have discovered very capital defects" in the 1776 constitution. The thirty-seven-year-old Jefferson, serving as governor of a war-torn Virginia during the closing days of the American Revolution, particularly attacked freehold suffrage and county representation. The "majority of the men in the state" who fought and paid taxes, he protested, were denied the right to vote. Just as unrepublican, with each county having "equal representation in the House of Delegates regardless of white population," "every man" in tiny Warwick County had as much political influence as "17 men" in populous Loudoun. Accordingly the Tidewater, with approximately 19,000 "fighting men," controlled 71 of 149 seats in the lower house, whereas the Piedmont, Valley, and Trans-Allegheny, with more than 30,000 "fighting men," together had only 78 seats.

Senate representation, Jefferson continued, was even more unequal. There the Tidewater, with twelve of the state's twenty-four arbitrarily drawn senatorial districts, controlled half the upper house. Although the Tidewater was four members short of a majority in the lower house, the proximity of its representatives to the "seat of government," Jefferson maintained, assured their more frequent, punctual attendance. Thus, with only a little more than one-third of the state's white population, Virginia's easternmost section exercised majority power in both branches of the general assembly. And since the general assembly elected, by joint ballot, Virginia's governor, governor's council, and principal judicial officials, Tidewater freeholders in effect controlled all three branches of the state government. Jefferson urged fellow Virginians to call an immediate convention to adopt a constitution based on the republican principles of the Revolution.[1]

Thomas Jefferson was not the only white Virginian to protest his state's undemocratic government. For rather than reforming colonial laws, the Virginia Constitution, approved by a Tidewater-dominated legislature June 29, 1776, simply continued freehold voting requirements of the 1736 Suffrage Act, as well as equal county representation for the house of delegates. Regarding land as the requisite symbol of permanent attachment to the community, the 1776 constitution limited suffrage to adult white males who had owned, for one year prior to the election, one hundred acres of unimproved land, or twenty-five acres with a house, or a house and lot in town. Furthermore, only those who met such freehold qualifications could serve as members of the Virginia General Assembly. An equally flagrant denial of democracy, the 1776 constitution allowed each county two representatives in the house, and each district one senator, both without regard to white population. To base voting and office holding on ownership of land, and representation on counties and districts, everywhere violated the principle of equal political rights for white men. These transgressions against republicanism particularly offended Virginians like Thomas Jefferson, James Madison, and others who were prominent national spokesmen in the struggle for American independence. Such members of Virginia's landed aristocracy, slaveholders from eastern sections of the state, were early leaders of the movement to democratize suffrage and representation in the years before the War of 1812.[2]

Expecting the general assembly to call a convention, Jefferson, in the summer of 1783, drafted a revised state constitution. The draft, published as an appendix to *Notes on the State of Virginia*, proposed extension of suffrage to all adult white males who, for one year prior to the election, had been "resident in the county," or had owned "therein real property" of a certain value, or had been enrolled in the militia. With Virginia's tax-

1. Thomas Jefferson, *Notes on the State of Virginia*, ed. William Peden (Chapel Hill, 1954), 118–20.
2. Julian A. C. Chandler, *The History of Suffrage in Virginia*, Johns Hopkins University Studies in Historical and Political Science, Series 19, VI–VII (Baltimore, 1901), 28–29; Julian A. C. Chandler, *Representation in Virginia*, Johns Hopkins University Studies in Historical and Political Science, Series 14, VI–VII (Baltimore, 1896), 25.

paying and fighting men eligible to vote, Jefferson then recommended that representation in the house of delegates be based on the number of qualified voters in each county. Senatorial districts should also be reapportioned "from time to time" and one senator chosen "for every six delegates" a district was entitled to elect. Such reforms in suffrage and representation, Jefferson believed, would provide a more just, "republican organization" for the government of Virginia.[3]

Jefferson's friend, James Madison, was the principal sponsor of a bill, introduced in the house of delegates in May, 1784, calling for a constitutional convention. Although the general assembly defeated this proposal, legislators at the subsequent 1785 session approved a suffrage bill reducing freehold requirements from one hundred to fifty acres of unimproved land. As land ownership was rather widespread in late eighteenth-century Virginia, such property qualification allowed between 40 and 50 percent of the state's adult white males to vote. With more than half disenfranchised, however, the 1785 act in no way approximated the virtually universal white manhood suffrage proposed by Thomas Jefferson.[4]

As white population swelled in western Piedmont, Valley, and Trans-Allegheny counties in the decades after American independence, the refusal of the Tidewater-dominated legislature to call a convention aroused growing antagonism. Demands for constitutional reform intensified following the War of 1812, influenced as much by general equalitarian tendencies of Jacksonian America as by specific changes in the character of Virginia's white population. With nonslaveholding and slaveholding states alike democratizing suffrage in the early nineteenth century, Virginia's freehold qualification came under escalating moral attack within and without the commonwealth. To uphold her self-proclaimed heritage as the birthplace of republicanism, critics charged, Virginia must abandon landed suffrage and recognize instead the principle of equal rights for white men.[5]

Demands for voting reform continued the traditional Jeffersonian

3. Jefferson, *Notes on the State of Virginia*, 209–12.
4. William W. Hening (ed.), *Virginia Statutes at Large, 1619–1792* (Richmond, 1823), XII, 120–23; Chilton Williamson, *American Suffrage from Property to Democracy 1760–1860* (Princeton, N.J., 1960), 224, 230.
5. Williamson, *American Suffrage from Property to Democracy*, 224–26.

moral condemnation of freehold suffrage as contrary to revolutionary ideals. In the years after 1815, however, as cities like Richmond and Wheeling expanded industrial-commercial activities, a new class of white Virginians joined the older generation of landed aristocrats to protest freehold suffrage. In ever-greater numbers, nonfreeholding urban artisans, mechanics, and laborers from all sections of the commonwealth petitioned the general assembly to democratize suffrage. Eastern and Trans-Allegheny merchants and industrialists likewise urged suffrage reform as a means of increasing the state's white industrial population. Only if Virginia renounced her landed property qualification, reformers everywhere insisted, could she both halt emigration of her own nonfreeholders and attract white workers from other states. With nonfreeholders comprising about 45 percent of adult white males in cities like Richmond by 1829,[6] such class attack on freehold suffrage represented a more powerful force than earlier moral protests by a minority of Virginia's landed aristocracy.

Although agitation for suffrage reform was statewide in the early nineteenth century, the movement to democratize representation gained more widespread support in western than eastern Virginia. Yet despite greater Valley and Trans-Allegheny clamor, a considerable bloc of western Piedmont, as well as a few northern Tidewater counties, also favored republican apportionment of the general assembly. The struggle for equal political representation was not a rigidly east-west confrontation, as traditional studies like Charles H. Ambler's *Sectionalism in Virginia from 1776 to 1861* suggest.[7] Rather it was an effort by progressive, under-represented counties in all sections of Virginia to end the disproportionate legislative influence of the conservative Tidewater. The over-representation of the Tidewater, protested by Thomas Jefferson as early as 1781, became, by the nineteenth century, the transcendent issue in demands for a constitutional convention. Much more than to suffrage extension, reform-minded Virginians looked to equalization of political power to achieve an enterprising state government.

Again and again, at the start of the nineteenth century, reformers pe-

6. *Ibid.*, 228–29.
7. Ambler, *Sectionalism in Virginia*; George E. Moore, "Slavery as a Factor in the Formation of West Virginia," *West Virginia History*, XVIII (1956), 5–89, provides a more contemporary restatement of Ambler's standard thesis.

titioned the general assembly for a constitutional convention. Just as persistently, the house of delegates rejected such proposals. In 1815, Valley and Trans-Allegheny counties sent petitions calling for a popular referendum on the convention issue. The house said "no."[8]

Angry reformers organized mass meetings throughout western Virginia during the summer of 1816, the largest and most significant being held in the Valley town of Staunton. Convening August 19, delegates from twenty-four western, and twelve eastern, counties drew up a memorial decrying "existing inequality of representation in the two houses of the General Assembly." All twelve Valley, and twelve of nineteen Trans-Allegheny counties, attended. Of the "reform" eastern counties, ten were in the western Piedmont, most directly bordering the Blue Ridge Mountains. The two Tidewater counties of Fairfax and Prince William adjoined, or were proximate to, both the western Piedmont and the District of Columbia.[9]

Staunton reformers looked to the 1810 census to justify demands for legislative reapportionment. Although Virginia's white population had increased from 442,115 to 561,534 during the period 1790 to 1810, the growth rate *among* the state's major sections had sharply diverged. Of the 119,419 additional whites, the Trans-Allegheny gained 70,161, or 58.8 percent of the total; the Valley, 19,445, or 16.3 percent; the Piedmont, 25,729, or 21.5 percent; and the Tidewater 4,084, or just 3.4 percent. Together, then, Virginia's two western sections accounted for three-fourths of the white population increase. East of the Blue Ridge, the Piedmont also gained large numbers of whites; but here, the growth rate *within* the section was markedly uneven. White population in all southeastern Piedmont counties either declined or stagnated, whereas in the northern and western Piedmont, particularly the tier of counties stretching from Loudoun in the northwest to Patrick in the southwest, whites rapidly increased. Significantly, the ten western Piedmont counties attending the 1816 Staunton convention accounted for more than 60 percent of the section's white population gain in the 1790–1810 period.

Like the southeast Piedmont, all Tidewater counties, including the

8. Chandler, *History of Suffrage in Virginia*, 25–27.
9. Chandler, *Representation in Virginia*, 25; "Memorial of the Staunton Convention to the Legislature of the State of Virginia," *Niles' Weekly Register*, September 7, 1816, pp. 17–25.

two represented at Staunton, either lost white population or gained only small numbers in the decades from 1790 to 1810. Despite a decline, however, whites in both Fairfax and Prince William in 1810 far outnumbered those in most eastern and southern Tidewater counties. With representation in the house of delegates based on counties rather than population, Fairfax's 6,626 whites and Prince William's 5,733 might well protest a system that allowed them each just two members, while the first-settled Tidewater counties of York, James City, Elizabeth City, and Warwick, with a *combined* white population of 5,648, had a total of eight.[10]

In a state "boasting of the pure republican character of its institutions," Staunton reformers proclaimed, it was time to end such overrepresentation of Virginia's "eastern and southern sections."[11] Despite the westward shift of population, whites in older-settled Tidewater and Piedmont counties still controlled both branches of the general assembly. In the 1815–1816 house, the Tidewater had seventy-five, the Piedmont fifty-eight, the Valley twenty-four, the Trans-Allegheny forty-two delegates. Had representation mirrored 1810 white population, the Tidewater would have fifty-six, the Piedmont sixty-eight, the Valley thirty-eight, and the Trans-Allegheny thirty-seven.[12] The Valley and western Piedmont would gain most from republican apportionment; the Tidewater would suffer most. Trans-Allegheny representation would also decline, but despite present loss, Virginia's westernmost section urged democratization of representation to sap the political power of conservative eastern bastions, and to establish a republican basis for future legislative reapportionment.

If the system of county representation in the house violated fundamental republican tenets, the "inequality of representation" in the senate, Staunton delegates charged, was "still more apparent." There the Tidewater, with only 28.2 percent of the state's white population in 1810, elected twelve of twenty-four members, whereas the Valley and Trans-Allegheny, with, respectively, 19.3 percent and 18.6 percent of Virginia's whites, had but two senators each. Democratic apportionment would give the Tidewater just seven senators, the Valley five, the Trans-

10. U.S. Census Office, *Fifth Census*, Tables [10]–[13].
11. "Memorial of the Staunton Convention," 20.
12. Earl Gregg Swem and John W. Williams, *A Register of the General Assembly of Virginia and of the Constitutional Conventions* (Richmond, 1918), 90–92.

Allegheny four. The Piedmont, with eight members in the 1815–1816 senate, would also have eight in a republican government.[13]

Virginia must act at once, Staunton reformers urged, to assure the "just rights" of her white majority. Government by a minority, especially a "minority inhabiting a particular section of the state" was "pernicious to the general interests." Let the general assembly, then, call an immediate convention apportioned on white population. Only if "every part" of Virginia received its due "weight," would "excitements existing" in the commonwealth "be allayed" and the constitution assured of "durability."[14]

The convention movement received important additional support in the summer of 1816. In a July 12 letter to a leading Valley reformer, Thomas Jefferson again labeled the 1776 Virginia Constitution a "gross departure . . . from genuine republican canons" and endorsed Staunton delegates' demands for equalization of representation in both branches of the general assembly. Jefferson went beyond the Staunton memorial, however, in once again urging extension of suffrage to all adult white males who paid taxes or served in the military, and for popular election of Virginia's governor and judges. Laws and institutions, Jefferson wrote from his beloved western Piedmont retreat, Monticello, must "keep pace with the times." The present generation of Virginians, like the "one preceding," had a "right to choose . . . the form of government . . . most promotive of its own happiness."[15]

Neither the Staunton memorial nor Jefferson's widely circulated letter moved the general assembly to call a convention. The 1816–1817 legislature could not, however, completely ignore widespread clamor for reform. Following defeat of the convention bill, conservative easterners agreed to reapportion senate districts on 1810 white population. By equalizing representation in one branch of the general assembly, conservatives hoped, this February, 1817, act would quell agitation for more sweeping democratization of Virginia's government.[16] To further appease reform-

13. "Memorial of the Staunton Convention," 20; U.S. Census Office, *Fifth Census*, Tables [10]–[13]; Swem and Williams, *Register of the General Assembly of Virginia*, 92.

14. "Memorial of the Staunton Convention," 20–21.

15. Paul Leicester Ford (ed.), *The Writings of Thomas Jefferson* (New York, 1905), XII, 3–17.

16. Virginia, *Acts and Joint Resolutions of the General Assembly of the Commonwealth of Virginia, 1816–17* (Richmond, 1817), 7–15.

minded Virginians, conservatives also supported creation of a Board of Public Works to allocate increased state funds for internal improvements.[17] In return for such eastern acquiescence in senate reapportionment and state internal improvements, both of particular interest to the Valley and Trans-Allegheny, western representatives agreed to the first reassessment of lands throughout the commonwealth since 1782. Such reassessment, designed to raise rates on Valley and Trans-Allegheny lands to current market value, met conservatives' demands for a more equitable distribution of state taxes between Virginia's eastern and western sections.[18]

Conservatives' efforts to quash the convention movement proved ineffectual. Agitation for constitutional reform, temporarily quieted by senate reapportionment, revived during the Panic of 1819. Amidst severe economic depression, conservative easterners once more blocked legislative appropriations for internal improvements.[19] The 1820 census, revealing continued rapid growth of white population in the western Piedmont, Valley, and Trans-Allegheny since 1810, and stagnation or decline in the Tidewater and southeastern Piedmont, added to reformers' ire. Resentment now centered on inequality of house representation. There, in years since the 1816 Staunton convention, Tidewater and Piedmont strength had remained virtually unchanged, with the Tidewater still having seventy-five delegates, the Piedmont increasing from fifty-eight to fifty-nine. Proliferation of new counties west of the Blue Ridge had boosted Valley membership from twenty-four in 1815–1816 to twenty-eight in 1824–1825. Trans-Allegheny representation had expanded most rapidly, from forty-two to fifty-two delegates. Had house apportionment reflected 1820 white population, the Tidewater would have had just fifty-six, the Piedmont sixty-eight, the Valley forty-three, and the Trans-Allegheny forty-seven delegates.[20] As on the eve of the 1816 reform convention, then, Virginia's extreme eastern and western sections were

17. Virginia, *Acts and Joint Resolutions of the General Assembly of the Commonwealth of Virginia, 1815–16* (Richmond, 1816), 35–39.

18. Virginia, *Acts and Joint Resolutions of the General Assembly, 1816–17*, pp. 7–15; Neely, "Development of Virginia Taxation," 137–39.

19. Chandler, *Representation in Virginia*, 27; Robert P. Sutton, "The Virginia Constitutional Convention of 1829–1830: A Profile Analysis of late-Jeffersonian Virginia" (Ph.D. dissertation, University of Virginia, 1967), 60–61.

20. Swem and Williams, *Register of the General Assembly of Virginia*, 113–15.

both over-represented; the western Piedmont, and particularly the Valley, continued to be under-represented. While the Tidewater resisted, the over-represented Trans-Allegheny again joined the drive for white-basis apportionment to augment reformers' present political power and, above all, to assure increased Trans-Allegheny representation in future legislatures. For as white population in the Tidewater, Piedmont, and Valley had grown, respectively, 1.6 percent, 2.5 percent, and 14.3 percent from 1810 to 1820, west of the Alleghenies the growth rate was 30.6 percent. Expecting such demographic patterns to continue, the Trans-Allegheny was willing to sacrifice present house strength for an anticipated escalating share of legislative power in post-1820 decades.[21] (See Appendix, Table III.)

Although equality of house representation remained reformers' chief priority, suffrage extension assumed growing importance during the 1820s. East of the Blue Ridge, as cities like Richmond and Lynchburg attracted ever larger numbers of white artisans and laborers, these urban nonfreeholders swelled reform ranks to protest their disenfranchisement. Rival political editors Thomas Ritchie of the Democratic Richmond *Enquirer* and John Hampden Pleasants of the Richmond *Constitutional Whig* also endorsed suffrage reform and lent powerful support to the convention cause.[22] With eastern Virginia cities allied to the western Piedmont, Valley, and Trans-Allegheny, the movement for constitutional reform increasingly transcended sections.

Amidst mounting clamor, an aging Thomas Jefferson once more attacked the 1776 constitution, this time in an April 27, 1824, public letter to the Richmond *Enquirer*. Both freehold suffrage and county representation, Jefferson reiterated, "prostrate" the principle of equal political rights. With nonfreeholders comprising more than half of Virginia's adult white males,[23] to deny them "any participation in . . . self-government" is "an usurpation of the minority over the majority." To give "every citizen of Warwick as much weight" in the house as "twenty-two equal citizens

21. U.S. Census Office, *Fifth Census*, Tables [10]–[13].

22. "Virginia Convention," *Niles' Weekly Register*, March 15, 1824, p. 179; Sutton, "Virginia Constitutional Convention of 1829–1830," 59–62.

23. Figures furnished for the 1829–30 convention showed that 44,325, or 56.6 percent, of Virginia's 78,265 adult white males paying *state* taxes on real or personal property were eligible to vote under freehold qualifications. However, if another 18,000 adult white males paying county levies, but not state taxes, are included in the total, the 44,325 freeholders represented only 46 percent of Virginia's adult white males, compared to 51,940 nonfreeholders (54 percent).

in Loudoun" was even more undemocratic. Most other states, Jefferson noted, had corrected such constitutional defects; Virginia, birthplace of republicanism, must do the same.[24]

Again resisting the reform tide, the 1824–1825 general assembly rejected a bill proposing a popular referendum on the convention issue. Angered at legislative disregard of public opinion, reformers responded to a call by Loudoun County to reassemble at Staunton. There, in July, 1825, delegates from traditional eastern and western reform counties, plus the cities of Richmond and Lynchburg, unanimously endorsed democratization of representation and suffrage.[25] Before the legislature convened, reformers circulated petitions throughout the state to promote a constitutional convention. Conservative easterners, alarmed at the accelerating reform tempo, published counter-memorials urging "friends of the constitution" to oppose revolutionary "conventionizing schemes . . . with all their might."[26]

Again in 1825–1826 and 1826–1827, the general assembly denied reformers' demands. Finally, in January, 1828, in the face of rising public outcry, legislators agreed to a popular referendum on the convention question at April, 1828, elections. Only "persons qualified to vote . . . under existing laws," however, would be eligible to participate.[27] With nonfreeholders barred from voting, conservatives anticipated, reformers might well meet defeat.

Virginia's freeholders dashed conservatives' hopes. Despite the undemocratic nature of the referendum, the convention measure passed 21,896 to 16,632.[28] Voting followed established reform-conservative patterns. Almost three-fourths (74.1 percent) of the Tidewater freeholders disapproved a constitutional convention, the largest negative vote of any section of the state. Analyzed by counties, all but four voted "no." Yet despite these anticonvention majorities, results of even the Tide-

24. Richmond *Enquirer*, quoted in *Niles' Weekly Register*, March 15, 1824, p. 179.

25. Chandler, *Representation in Virginia*, 28–29; Sutton, "Virginia Constitutional Convention of 1829–1830," 62–63.

26. Benjamin Watkins Leigh to George C. Dromgoole, August 22, 1825, in George C. Dromgoole Papers, Duke University Library, Durham, N.C.

27. Sutton, "Virginia Constitutional Convention of 1829–1830," 65–69; Virginia, *Acts and Joint Resolutions of the General Assembly of the Commonwealth of Virginia, 1827–28* (Richmond, 1828), 18.

28. Virginia, *Journal of the House of Delegates of the Commonwealth of Virginia, 1828–1829* (Richmond, 1829), 50. All subsequent analyses of sectional and county voting are from this official "Vote on the Convention Question."

water referendum might give conservatives pause. For more than 25 percent of Tidewater freeholders, assumedly among the staunchest "friends of the constitution," endorsed reform. Furthermore, though only Fairfax, Prince William, and the two "Eastern Shore" counties of Accomack and Northampton approved a convention, Stafford and Spotsylvania, just south of Prince William and including the town of Fredericksburg, cast, respectively, 44 percent and 38 percent "yes" votes, both strong reform minorities. Major Tidewater cities also evidenced significant proconvention sentiment. Norfolk freeholders voted 144 to 102 in favor of a convention, whereas Richmond, with 90 "yes" and 92 "no" votes, was virtually divided. Had nonfreeholders participated in the referendum, conservatives recognized, Richmond and other Tidewater urban centers would have more strongly endorsed reform.

Returns from the Piedmont proved much more disquieting. Despite conservatives' pleas for unity within Virginia's "planting country," 45 percent of Piedmont freeholders approved a convention. Just as Tidewater reform sentiment was concentrated in northern counties and in urban centers, so all nine Piedmont counties casting proconvention majorities either bordered or were near the Blue Ridge Mountains. A tenth western Piedmont county, Thomas Jefferson's Albemarle, with 163 "yes" votes and 166 "nos," was, like Richmond, virtually divided. Eastern and southeastern Piedmont counties, in contrast, joined the southern Tidewater in voting overwhelmingly against constitutional reform.

West of the Blue Ridge, both the Valley and Trans-Allegheny returned large proconvention majorities. As the Valley would gain most from democratization of house representation, freeholders there cast the highest proportion of "yes" votes—87.8 percent—of any section of the commonwealth. The Trans-Allegheny, which, conversely, would lose present strength from democratic reapportionment, nevertheless voted 76.6 percent in favor of a convention. "Panhandle" and northwestern counties most strongly approved, whereas the six counties voting "no" were all in southwestern and central Trans-Allegheny. Rather than a clear-cut east-west contest, then, the 1828 freehold referendum revealed schisms within each major section except the Valley. The Piedmont divided sharply along east-west lines; the Tidewater and Trans-Allegheny, though less markedly, divided along north-south lines. Equally significant, although the Valley and Trans-Allegheny together cast 67.3 percent of the "yes" votes, without the support of "reform" freeholders in Virginia's two eastern sections, the convention proposal would not have passed.

Following the freeholders' mandate, the 1828–1829 general assembly debated how to organize the convention. Controversy at once developed over the crucial issue of apportioning representation. Uncompromising reformers demanded white population alone. Hard-line conservatives proposed a variety of schemes. A few urged the existent system of equal county representation; others advocated "federal numbers," the principle governing apportionment in the United States House of Representatives whereby slaves counted as three-fifths a person. Conservatives' favorite plan, however, was the so-called mixed basis, apportioning delegates on "white population and taxation *combined*."[29] Since slaves were a major source of taxable property in Virginia, conservatives argued, such principle would best protect eastern slaveholding interests against western antislavery tendencies. Conservatives' insistence on representation for slaves, whether as persons (federal numbers) or as property (mixed basis), would grow ever more strident once the constitutional convention began. Indeed the relationship between slavery and political power, already basic to preconvention legislative clashes, would become the paramount issue of the 1829–1830 convention. Although ostensibly a question of representation, the contest for democracy in Virginia was, in fact, a contest over slavery.

Neither white-basis reformers nor mixed-basis conservatives had adequate power to carry their favorite proposals in the general assembly. Instead, legislators finally adopted a "compromise" introduced by western Piedmont reformer, William Fitzhugh Gordon. As Gordon's plan provided, the February, 1829, act authorized freeholders from each of the twenty-four senate districts to elect four convention delegates. By such principle, the Tidewater would have twenty-eight, the Piedmont thirty-two, the Valley sixteen, and the Trans-Allegheny twenty representatives.[30]

Gordon's apportionment, excluding slaves and taxation as compo-

29. Chandler, *Representation in Virginia*, 31; Sutton, "Virginia Constitutional Convention of 1829–1830," 70–71; William M. Rives to John C. Rutherfoord, August 10, 1828, in John C. Rutherfoord Papers, Duke University Library, Durham, N.C.; George C. Dromgoole to Edward Dromgoole, December 6, 1828, in Edward Dromgoole Papers, Southern Historical Collection, University of North Carolina, Chapel Hill.

30. Virginia, *Acts and Joint Resolutions of the General Assembly of the Commonwealth of Virginia, 1828–1829* (Richmond, 1829), 17–21.

nents of representation, was seemingly a concession to white-basis reformers. In fact, however, this legislative "compromise" was more favorable to conservative interests. As in the 1828 referendum, Virginia's nonfreeholders could not vote for convention delegates. Even more undemocratic, existing senate districts reflected *1810* white population, thus depriving huge numbers of new whites in the western Piedmont, Valley, and particularly the Trans-Allegheny, of any representation. Had apportionment followed estimates of 1829 white population furnished the general assembly, as white-basis reformers demanded,[31] Tidewater representation would have declined from twenty-eight to twenty-three delegates, the Piedmont from thirty-two to twenty-eight. Conversely, the Valley would have increased from sixteen to nineteen representatives, the Trans-Allegheny from twenty to twenty-six. By stripping western Virginia of nine members and assigning them instead to conservative Tidewater and Piedmont districts, Gordon's apportionment thus reduced reformers from an almost-majority to an apparently overwhelmed minority. The struggle to democratize Virginia's government seemed doomed to defeat even before the convention began. (See Appendix, Table IV.)

Huge crowds filled Richmond's public square the morning of October 5, 1829. Some, hoping to catch a glimpse of the many illustrious Virginians elected to the constitutional convention, waited outside the capitol. Others entered the building at once and hurried toward the hall of the house of delegates where the convention would assemble. About noon, the packed gallery began to buzz with excitement as surviving giants of Virginia's revolutionary generation gathered in the hall below. Exchanging salutations, former Presidents James Madison and James Monroe, former Chief Justice John Marshall, former United States Senator John Randolph, and current United States Senators John Tyler and Littleton Tazewell took their seats alongside such distinguished state leaders as Governor William Giles, Benjamin Watkins Leigh, Philip Doddridge, Chapman Johnson, and Abel Upshur. A little after midday, Madison called the delegates to order and nominated his old friend, James Monroe, to preside. Unanimously approved, the feeble, aging

31. Virginia, *Journal, Acts and Proceedings of a Convention Held in the Commonwealth of Virginia, 1829–1830* (Richmond, 1830), No. 14, n.p.

Monroe was conducted to the president's chair by John Marshall. As the constitutional convention got underway, a mood of anxious anticipation filled the chamber.[32]

During the first week of the convention, delegates organized committees to consider reforms in the executive, legislative, and judicial branches. James Madison was appointed chairman of the all-important legislative committee, responsible for initial debate on the explosive representation issue.[33]

The legislative committee met behind closed doors in the senate chamber. There the seventy-nine-year-old Madison, impeccably attired in an olive-green coat, white cravat, and black pantaloons, presided at the head of a long table. The other members, with one exception, gathered around the table. Only John Randolph sat apart, in a far corner of the room, his eyes riveted to the eastern portion of a map of Virginia hung on a nearby wall.[34]

For two weeks the committee debated representation. Reformers aligned behind "Panhandle" delegate, Philip Doddridge, in demanding the white basis. Conservatives looked to "Southside" Piedmont representative, Benjamin Watkins Leigh, to champion the mixed basis of white population and taxation combined. Democratic apportionment would give the Tidewater thirty-two, the Piedmont forty, the Valley twenty-six, and the Trans-Allegheny thirty-six representatives in a 134-member house of delegates. The mixed basis would increase Tidewater membership to forty-one and the Piedmont to forty-six, whereas the Valley would have twenty-four, and the Trans-Allegheny just 23, delegates. Conservatives' apportionment thus would particularly benefit the Tidewater, as well as large slaveholding counties in the southeastern Piedmont, but it would deal a disastrous political blow to the nonslaveholding Trans-Allegheny. Virginia's westernmost section contained 26.5 percent of the state's whites in 1830, but paid only 9.2 percent of the state's total taxes. The Valley, in contrast, contained 19.4 percent of Virginia's whites and

32. Hugh Blair Grigsby, "The Virginia Convention of 1829–30," *Virginia Historical Reporter*, I (1854), 17.
33. Virginia, *Proceedings and Debates of the Virginia State Convention of 1829–1830* (Richmond, 1830), 9.
34. Grigsby, "Virginia Convention of 1829–30," 20; Hugh Blair Grigsby, "Sketches of Members of the Constitutional Convention of 1829–1830," *Virginia Magazine of History and Biography*, LXI (1953), 331.

paid 14.8 percent of the taxes. Valley house representation accordingly would be almost the same under either the white or mixed basis.[35] Such differential levels of population and taxation, reflecting the higher land values and greater slave interest of the Valley, would ultimately produce divergent attitudes toward the new state constitution in Virginia's western sections.

Despite an east Virginia majority of fifteen to nine on the legislative committee, members finally voted, 13 to 11, in favor of the white basis for the house of delegates. Equally momentous, the committee resolved, by the same margin, that a census of Virginia's population be taken in 1831, 1845, and "at least once in every twenty years" thereafter to assure democratic representation in both present and future legislatures. As in the 1828 convention referendum, easterners provided crucial support to Valley and Trans-Allegheny reformers. Although all six Tidewater committee members voted "no," four of nine Piedmont representatives, all from districts near the Blue Ridge, joined the nine westerners in recommending republican apportionment in the house.[36]

Madison presented the report to the convention on October 24. John Green, a conservative Piedmont member of the legislative committee, at once moved to substitute "white population and taxation combined" as the basis of house representation. On October 27, Benjamin Watkins Leigh rose to defend Green's mixed-basis amendment.[37]

Although long a prominent Richmond lawyer, the forty-eight-year-old Leigh represented in the convention the "Southside" Piedmont district of his birth. Renowned as a champion of conservative eastern interests, Leigh had served in the Virginia House of Delegates and, as befit his brilliant legal reputation, had been selected to compile the 1819 Re-

35. U.S. Census Office, *Fifth Census*, Tables [10]–[13]; Virginia, *Journal, Acts and Proceedings of a Convention, 1829–1830*, No. 15. Tax percentages are for the year 1828, the latest state revenue figures computed by the auditor's office, October 20, 1829, for use by the 1829–30 convention.

36. George C. Dromgoole to Edward Dromgoole, October 18, 1829, in Edward Dromgoole Papers; Merrill D. Peterson (ed.), *Democracy, Liberty, and Property: The State Constitutional Conventions of the 1820's* (Indianapolis, 1966), 275; Virginia, *Proceedings and Debates of the Virginia State Convention of 1829–1830*, p. 22. The four western Piedmont reformers were: James Madison of Spotsylvania-Louisa-Orange-Madison; Charles F. Mercer of Loudoun-Fairfax; George Townes of Franklin-Henry-Patrick-Pittsylvania; and James Pleasants of Albemarle-Amherst-Nelson-Fluvanna-Goochland.

37. Virginia, *Proceedings and Debates of the Virginia State Convention of 1829–1830*, pp. 39, 53.

vised Code of Virginia. In appearance, Leigh was "uncommonly striking . . . a small, very graceful man" despite a thick-soled shoe worn on his lame leg. Glossy, black hair covered his temples; as he spoke, his dark eyes sparkled with excitement. Leigh's heart, one sympathetic observer remarked, "was with by-gone times." He "dwelt on the glory of Virginia before the Revolution" and seemed all his life "to cherish the prejudices of the old cavalier." Intent on defending "all that was good and beautiful" in Virginia's noble past, the "Southside" aristocrat denounced the white basis as the "most crying injustice ever attempted in any land." Those who uphold the rights of property, as well as men, to political representation, Leigh warned reformers, would never submit to a plan which "puts the power of controlling the wealth of the State into hands different from those which hold that wealth." Given the "circumstances and condition of this Commonwealth," representation of "numbers alone" would lead to "rapine, anarchy, and bloodshed." He challenged reformers to justify their jacobinical principle.[38]

Valley delegate John R. Cooke accepted Leigh's angry challenge. The American Revolution, Cooke affirmed, enshrined "*sovereignty of the people*" and "*equality of men*" as the "deep foundations of our Republic." Virginia's own Declaration of Rights confirmed "those great principles," proclaiming "*the right of the majority*" the "essential character" of republican government. Exigencies of war, however, required framers of the 1776 state constitution to retain the "*aristocratic* features" of county representation and freehold suffrage established during the colonial period. To attempt a "new distribution and arrangement of political power" amidst this crisis would have been "unwise and impolitic." Yet even as early as 1781, Cooke noted, "*one* statesman, at least,—Mr. Jefferson—," urged Virginians to correct "the inconsistency" between "theoretical principles" and "practical regulations" by equalizing representation and suffrage.

"From that time on," the Valley delegate avowed, "the spirit of reform has never slept." At last, "after a struggle of fifty years," the "friends of liberty" seem "on the eve" of establishing a government based on major-

38. Hugh R. Pleasants, "Sketches of the Virginia Convention of 1829–30," *Southern Literary Messenger*, XVII (1851), 148, 149; *Dictionary of American Biography*, VI, 152–53; Grigsby, "Virginia Convention of 1829–30," 95–100; Virginia, *Proceedings and Debates of the Virginia State Convention of 1829–1830*, p. 53.

ity rule. In "apportioning representation, or political power . . . on *the people* only," and not on wealth or counties, the white basis would give "practical effect" to principles espoused by Virginia's revolutionary generation. Conservatives' mixed basis, in contrast, would repudiate democracy and substitute instead government by that "most odious, pernicious, and despicable of all aristocracies—an aristocracy of wealth." To make *"property* and *people"* equal "elements of representation," Cooke protested, would give the *"few,* who are *rich,* a control over the *many,* who are *poor,"* and thus "dilapidate the very foundations of our free institutions."[39]

Opening debate between conservatives and reformers had centered on the relationship between wealth and power. Yet in references to "numbers alone," "circumstances" of Virginia, representation of "property," "aristocracy of wealth," neither Leigh nor Cooke had exposed the real issue underlying such rhetoric. The subsequent, much lengthier exchange between conservative Abel P. Upshur and reformer Philip Doddridge would define, in ever more acrimonious tones, what Leigh and Cooke had already implied.

Abel P. Upshur was born June 17, 1790, at Vaucluse, the family's Northampton County plantation on the Tidewater "Eastern Shore." A descendant of an old Virginia slaveholding family, he began college at Yale in October, 1805, but transferred to Princeton after the first session. At Princeton, young Upshur was an outspoken proponent of students' rights to associate together and to petition college officials for redress of grievances. His participation in the College Hall riots of March, 1807, and subsequent refusal to renounce his beliefs, prompted his dismissal from Princeton prior to graduation. The resolute rebel thereupon returned to Virginia, entered the office of a prominent Richmond lawyer, and was admitted to the bar in 1810. Upshur's devotion to democracy was short-lived. Elected to the house of delegates in 1812, and again from 1824 to 1827, the former student rebel became one of Tidewater Virginia's leading conservatives, just as tenacious a proponent of the status quo as he had once been of college reform. Now a judge of the Virginia General Court, he represented at the 1829 convention the district com-

39. Virginia, *Proceedings and Debates of the Virginia State Convention of 1829–1830,* pp. 54–62.

prising the "Eastern Shore" counties of Accomack and Northampton, as well as the small Tidewater counties of Mathews, Middlesex, and Gloucester. Conservatives would hail his two-day defense of the mixed basis as one of the most masterful analyses of their position.[40]

Upshur began by acknowledging reformers' basic premise. "As a general proposition," he admitted, "in free Governments, power ought to be given to a majority . . . of *persons only.*" But, the Tidewater conservative quickly continued, democratic representation required "identity of interests" among members of the political community. The interests of Virginia's white population were "different and *distinct*"; and, he emphasized, the "difference between us arises from property alone." Throughout "Eastern divisions of the State," slaves constituted an "interest of imposing magnitude . . . almost the whole productive labor . . . and full half the wealth" of the Tidewater and Piedmont. West of the Blue Ridge, slaves were of "secondary consequence . . . absorbed" by westerners' "predominant interest" in internal improvements. Such dichotomy of interests, Upshur predicted, would not disappear. Instead it would intensify in future generations as slaves became an ever-smaller percentage of the western population. Westerners' "rooted antipathy" to slavery, their "habits . . . of personal industry and . . . exertion" would discourage widespread use of slave labor. Moreover, the proximity of many areas of western Virginia to nonslaveholding Ohio and Pennsylvania would "forever render" slave property there "precarious and insecure." The "moral sentiment of these States," the Tidewater aristocrat declared, "is against slavery. . . . That influence" would reinforce western Virginians' own hostility to "this species of property." Equally subversive, it would encourage slaves themselves to run away.[41]

"For far distant times," then, slaves must remain the *"peculiar* property" of eastern Virginia, the *"peculiar* interest" of a white minority inhabiting a particular section of the commonwealth. Consequently, in a government based on "white population alone," Upshur insisted, *"our* property . . . is exposed to peculiar impositions, and therefore, to peculiar hazards." The sole "danger" slaveholders could "reasonably ap-

40. Claude H. Hall, *Abel Parker Upshur Conservative Virginian, 1790–1844* (Madison, Wis., 1964), 7–15, 17–32, 42–45.
41. Virginia, *Proceedings and Debates of the Virginia State Convention of 1829–1830*, pp. 70–71, 74–76.

prehend" was "oppressive and unequal taxation." As his colleague Leigh had already warned, Virginia's slaveholding white minority could not give her nonslaveholding white majority "power to tax us at their will and pleasure." Already, slaves represented "30 percent of the whole revenue derived from taxation." And what "more ready source" of taxable property existed to finance westerners' "roads and canals" than Tidewater and Piedmont slaves? "*Our* property," Upshur accordingly insisted, "demands *that kind of protection* which flows" solely from "possession of power. . . . Constitutional guarantees," adopted by present-day Virginians, could not adequately protect slaveholders' "peculiar rights and interests" from possible "oppression . . . in time to come. . . . No paper guarantee was ever yet worth anything unless . . . a majority of the community were interested in maintaining it." Since white Virginians' interests everywhere conflicted, slavery could only be secure if "*property*" had equal weight with "persons" in apportioning house representation. Whether it be "true as a *general proposition* . . . that property is entitled to influence in Government," Upshur concluded in Burkeian tones, "*it is true as to us.*"[42]

Slavery in Virginia, conservatives like Leigh and Upshur unabashedly affirmed, was now, and would always be, incompatible with white-basis democracy. As nonslaveholding Valley and Trans-Allegheny whites increasingly outnumbered Tidewater and Piedmont slaveholders, slave property would become ever more vulnerable to oppressive taxation to promote majority interests. To protect slavery, then, the government of the commonwealth must forever remain in the hands of a propertied, sectional minority. At stake in the contest for political power, conservatives agreed, was the future of slavery in Virginia.

As Upshur concluded his address, "Panhandle" reformer Philip Doddridge angrily responded. Born May 17, 1773, in Bedford County, Pennsylvania, the muscular, thick-set Doddridge was descended from one of the original Trans-Allegheny Virginia families. About a year after his birth, Doddridge's Scotch-Irish parents migrated southwestward from Pennsylvania and settled on four hundred acres in the remote

---

42. *Ibid.*, 74–76. Taxes on slaves represented 27.1 percent of Virginia's total revenue in 1828. Of the revenue derived from slaves, the Piedmont paid 49 percent; the Tidewater, 39.8 percent; the Valley, 7.5 percent; and the Trans-Allegheny, 3.7 percent.

"Panhandle" region of northwest Virginia. Following his father's death in 1791, Philip and his older brother Joseph were sent to study at Jefferson Academy in Canonsburg, Pennsylvania. Upon graduation, both brothers settled in the "Panhandle" town of Wellsburg in Brooke County. There the younger Doddridge practiced law and, in 1815, was elected to the Virginia House of Delegates. A brilliant, impassioned orator, he soon became, both within and without the legislature, the west's leading spokesman for constitutional reform and was, in part, responsible for the 1817 senate reapportionment.[43] Currently a member of the United States House of Representatives, Doddridge represented at the convention the "Panhandle" and northwest district including the industrial-commercial center of Wheeling. This area of the Trans-Allegheny, Virginians everywhere acknowledged, included the state's most uncompromising proponents of white-basis democracy.

Echoing Valley reformer John R. Cooke, Doddridge first denounced conservatives' mixed basis as a repudiation of Virginia's Declaration of Rights. But whereas Cooke had alluded to government by an "aristocracy of wealth," rule by the "*few, who are rich*," Doddridge was unfeignedly blunt. To apportion power on white population and taxation, he charged, was no more than a "flowery disguise" for representation of slaves. Judge Upshur had just admitted, the Trans-Allegheny reformer observed, that "but for the possession of great masses" of slaves by the minority in eastern Virginia, "majority government would be safe." Solely to protect slave property, then, Tidewater and Piedmont slaveholders demanded "power to govern the State, that is . . . to rule the majority. Such doctrine, Doddridge protested, "looks to the perpetual slavery" of western Virginia. While conservatives affirmed that the "great mass of slave property" must always be in the east, they also acknowledged that a majority of whites would soon reside west of the Blue Ridge. Distrustful of swelling nonslaveholding western majorities, the slaveholding eastern minority would seek ever greater representation to shield their property from "rapacious" taxation. The principle that slaveholders, "however small their numbers," must possess "all the powers of Government" thus "admits of no relaxation . . . because the weaker

43. Doddridge, *Notes on the Settlement and Indian Wars*, 272–81; Peterson, *Democracy, Liberty, and Property*, 331–32; Grigsby, "Virginia Convention of 1829–30," pp. 63–64.

the minority . . . the greater . . . their fears and desires for power. . . . So long as you hold political dominance over me," Doddridge boldly addressed conservative easterners, "I am a slave."[44]

Not for long, however, could eastern slaveholders "impose a yoke" on western Virginians. If present growth rates continued, "within thirty years" the Trans-Allegheny would contain more than half the state's present white population, while the east, "oppressed by the increasing weight" of its black population, would stagnate. By then, Doddridge warned, Valley and Trans-Allegheny whites would be "sufficiently strong and powerful to burst asunder any chain by which you . . . attempt to bind them." Those who demanded "equal political rights" for white men, the Trans-Allegheny republican concluded, demanded "no new thing." The "plain English" of Virginia's Declaration of Rights asserted the right of a "majority of numbers alone" to "alter or amend the Constitution." Furthermore, the 1817 senate reapportionment "equalized representation on the basis of white population." Gentlemen who demanded representation for slave property, who thereby exalted minority rule, were, in contrast, "proceeding on a principle never before recognized in the Colony or State." Despite the "injustice" accorded the west in apportioning convention delegates, he hoped that, at last, the "cause of the people will triumph" in Virginia.[45]

During early stages of debate, Doddridge's hopes seemed well founded. For though white- and mixed-basis spokesmen alike depicted a rigid demarcation between a democratic west and an oligarchic east, such rhetoric ignored the considerable bloc of eastern reformers from districts bordering or near the Blue Ridge. In initial voting on representation, thirteen Piedmont representatives would ally with the thirty-six westerners to defeat conservatives' schemes. But as the convention atmosphere grew more acrimonious and delegates on both sides threatened state dismemberment, several western Piedmont reformers would desert the white-basis principle. As representatives of districts with both large white *and* slave populations, these eastern moderates hoped to find a "middle ground" between democracy and slavery, a compromise representation harmonizing the interests of all white Virginians. Com-

44. Virginia, *Proceedings and Debates of the Virginia State Convention of 1829–1830*, pp. 83, 86, 87–88.
45. *Ibid.*, 87, 81–82, 89.

mitted above all to the integrity of the commonwealth, "middle ground" Piedmont reformers would hold the balance of power throughout the 1829–1830 constitutional convention.

James Monroe, representing the long-standing reform district of Loudoun-Fairfax, was one of the earliest advocates of compromise. "I am satisfied," the venerable former president declared, "that if no such thing as slavery existed, that the people of our Atlantic border would meet their brethren of the west upon the basis of . . . free white population." To abolish slavery, however, would produce "perfect confusion." A "different colour" would preclude incorporation of the more than four hundred thousand eastern slaves into Virginia society. Nor could freedmen be "removed beyond the limits of the Union" without federal aid. Given the "particular circumstances" of the commonwealth, then, some compromise was necessary between "rights of man" and rights of property. Let the house of delegates, the aged statesman accordingly resolved, be apportioned on the white basis, the senate on the mixed basis. Such "arrangement" would allow the senate an "immediate check" on legislation originated by the "popular branch," and thereby assure "reasonable protection for property."[46]

Monroe's proposal for a democratic house and an aristocratic senate met with immediate rebuff from intransigent conservatives. He regretted to disagree with the "venerable gentleman from Loudoun," Benjamin Watkins Leigh declared, but there was, nevertheless, a crucial difference in the "principle of representation" for house and senate. He would be "content," the "Southside" Piedmont conservative conceded, to endorse a white-basis senate, as the 1817 Reapportionment Act had provided, but he could never approve white-basis apportionment for the house. That branch of the general assembly had exclusive power to originate tax measures. The upper branch, conversely, could neither originate nor amend "*money bills*" but could only accept or reject those "sent up by the House." To protect "interests of property," Leigh resolutely resolved, "*the House of Delegates, the tax-giving branch*" must be apportioned on the mixed basis. Leigh's willingness to apportion the senate, but not the house, on white population typified conservatives' fear that in any "serious conflict" over taxation the lower legislative branch would prevail.

46. *Ibid.*, 149–51.

With the house "representative of *numbers*" and the senate "of *property*," as Monroe's plan proposed, the senate would never possess sufficient "moral and political energy" to resist "unjust or excessive" revenue bills. As the "more numerous body, more intimately connected with the people," the house would at once raise the "odious cry" of "aristocracy of wealth." The senate, "disheartened and impotent," would soon yield. Thus in Virginia, Leigh challenged Monroe, the house was the "proper representative of the interests of property."[47]

Oppressive taxation of slaves was not the only danger posed by majority rule. Westerners who attributed Virginia's economic decline to slavery, Leigh continued, might also promote abolition legislation. "I wish, indeed," the "Southside" conservative admitted, "that I had been born in a land where . . . negro slavery is unknown. No . . . I misrepresent myself. . . . I shall never wish that I had been born out of Virginia—but I wish, that Providence had spared my country this moral and political evil." In the absence of such Providential blessing, the slaveholding east must resist, "to the bitter end," any "transfer of power" to the nonslaveholding west. "In every civilized country under the sun," Leigh philosophized, "there must be some who labour for their daily bread." Trans-Allegheny Virginians who "tend the herds and dig the soil, who have neither real nor personal capital of their own," could never have adequate "political intelligence" to participate in government. Although superior in "intellectual power" and "moral worth" to Tidewater and Piedmont slaves, such propertyless white "day-labourers" occupied the "same place *in political economy*." Yet white-basis reformers demanded full representation for "peasantry of the mountains" while opposing any representation for "slave labourers" of the east. Slaveholding planters of eastern and southern Virginia, Leigh angrily reiterated, would never submit to the "grinding tyranny" of the "peasantry of the west." Better to separate the state than to "give power over property to numbers alone . . . in the revenue-giving" lower house.[48]

Murmurs of indignation ran through the convention. "Peasantry" indeed! The "rank aristocracy" of Leigh's remarks, the "cold, taunting manner" of his delivery, dismayed opponents as well as many friends.[49]

47. *Ibid.*, 159, 171–72.
48. *Ibid.*, 172–73, 156–58.
49. Peachy Harrison to Gessner Harrison, November 4, 1829, in Gessner Harrison Papers, Alderman Library, University of Virginia.

Most offensive was the fiery Leigh's demand for representation for black slaves while denouncing equal political rights for white men. Leigh's position epitomized, in its starkest form, the dilemma confronting slaveholding Virginia. Negro slavery, conservatives concurred, required white aristocracy and, accordingly, precluded white democracy.

Yet even as Leigh fought to protect slave property from majority rule, he did not pronounce slavery *per se* a "positive good." Like other conservatives, he opposed legislative infringement on slaveholders' rights, whether by oppressive taxation or, more direct, by abolition legislation. At the same time, he decried slavery as a "moral and political evil" and wished it had never existed in Virginia. Such stalwart defense of property rights, combined with an apologetic tone toward slavery as an institution, foreshadowed conservatives' posture during the 1831–1832 house debate on emancipation and, indeed, typified the nature of Virginia "pro-slaveryism" throughout the ensuing decade.

Reformers looked to Valley representative Chapman Johnson to rebut Leigh's oligarchic doctrines. Born in Louisa County in the central Piedmont, Johnson had been a classmate of Leigh's at William and Mary College. Although Johnson later moved to Augusta County in the middle Valley, where he lived for twenty years, the two men remained close friends and served together in the Virginia General Assembly. Like Leigh, Johnson revered the old Virginia Constitution and initially supported his friend's anticonvention campaigns. Unlike the "Southside" conservative, however, Johnson recognized "defects" in the original government, especially "inequality of representation." Johnson accordingly represented Augusta County at the 1816 Staunton reform convention and voted for the 1817 Senate Reapportionment Act. When a majority of freeholders approved a constitutional convention in the 1828 referendum, Johnson abandoned his earlier opposition and urged Virginians everywhere to obey the popular will. Although he was, at the time, a well-established Richmond lawyer, he agreed to represent former Valley constituents at the 1829–1830 convention.[50] Feelings of "divided allegiance," Johnson admitted, prompted him to attempt to "mediate" between east and west in this "contest for political power."[51]

In his role as mediator, Johnson declared he could best serve the wel-

50. Grigsby, "Virginia Convention of 1829–30," 84–91; Grigsby, "Sketches of Members of the Constitutional Convention of 1829–1830," 326–27.
51. Virginia, *Proceedings and Debates of the Virginia State Convention of 1829–1830,* p. 257.

fare of "all parts of the community" by opposing the mixed basis and proposing instead that the house be apportioned on "qualified voters." He had, Johnson addressed many lifelong eastern friends, "insuperable objections" to the principle that "property must possess . . . power." To "admit this principle into our republic" would tend toward "aristocracy or oligarchy" and contravene the doctrines of majority rule and equality of all men proclaimed in Virginia's Declaration of Rights.[52]

Representation of property not only contravened democracy. It also, paradoxically, posed a graver danger to slavery than majority rule. "Let it once be openly avowed and adopted as a principle of your Constitution," Johnson warned conservatives, "that the price . . . the Western people must pay for the protection of your slaves, is the surrender of their power in the Government, and you render that property hateful to them in the extreme, and hold out to them the strongest of all possible temptations to make constant war upon it." If deprived of equal representation, westerners would not resort to "acts of violence or disloyalty." Rather they would seek allies in the very "bosom" of eastern society. There, Johnson declared, they would find "many and ardent" nonslaveholding white artisans and laborers, who, forced to compete for jobs "in common with the slave," resented slaveowning aristocrats. With extension of suffrage, these newly enfranchised, "discontented" easterners would join the "whole Western country" to end minority rule, not by "civil war or bloodshed," but by the "peaceful remedy" of legislative petitions "earnestly pressed and long persevered in" by Virginia's burgeoning white majority. A constitution combining the mixed basis with more democratic suffrage thus could not long protect slave property. In less than ten years the legislature would again "be compelled" to yield to "the force of public opinion" and call another convention. By then, the inevitable surrender of minority power might "come too late." Bonds uniting Virginia might be forever severed.[53]

Why not instead, Johnson urged conservatives, base representation on "qualified voters" and "judiciously" define the "Right of Suffrage" so as to assure "safe, enduring protection for property." Let voting qualifications be "fixed so low," the Valley reformer proposed, that the "industrious of all classes, professions, and callings "may acquire the requisite

52. *Ibid.*, 265, 293–94.
53. *Ibid.*, 283–84.

property, "real or personal," in a "few years of persevering labor; but so high" as to disfranchise the "habitually idle." Representation based on such democratic, yet "prudent," suffrage requirements would give "equal political power" to all white men having "'common interest with, and attachment to, the community'" as Virginia's Declaration of Rights proclaimed. "Aristocratic distinction" would be eliminated, sectional animosities allayed, and property rights "permanently" secured. If these arguments failed to persuade conservatives, Johnson offered further assurances that his representation plan would not endanger slavery. Comparing the "quantity of mountain and arable land" on each side of the Blue Ridge and "their capacity to sustain population," he doubted whether a majority of qualified voters would ever reside in western Virginia. As his friend Benjamin Watkins Leigh had already remarked, there were many propertyless white industrial and agricultural laborers in the Trans-Allegheny who would be denied political representation under Johnson's proposed suffrage basis.[54]

But should political power someday transfer to a western majority, eastern slaveholders need not fear oppressive taxation or other unjust legislation. Challenging Abel Upshur's assumption that slavery must forever remain the "peculiar interest" of eastern Virginia, Johnson predicted that during the next twenty years, demand for slave labor would multiply rapidly west of the Blue Ridge. In every decade from 1790 to 1820, he correctly observed, slave population had increased at a faster ratio in both the Valley and Trans-Allegheny that in either eastern district.[55] Slavery's westward march would accelerate over the next twenty years as tobacco culture shifted from worn-out "Southside" plantations onto fertile Valley lands. Already many Valley farmers in Rockbridge and Botetourt had turned to cultivation of tobacco, and the slave population of these middle Valley counties had, respectively, increased almost 33.3 percent, and more than 100 percent, in the last nine years. Tobacco growing would further spread in the "rich and populous counties of Frederick and Jefferson" in the northern Valley, where slaves "at this

54. *Ibid.*, 284, 280–81.
55. Between 1790 and 1820, slaves in the Tidewater increased from 157,910 to 176,496, or 11.8 percent; in the Piedmont, from 119,539 to 205,501, or 71.9 percent; in the Valley, from 12,870 to 29,785, or 131.4 percent; and in the Trans-Allegheny, from 2,308 to 13,366, or 479.1 percent. Of Virginia's 425,148 slaves in 1820, however, 381,997, or 89.8 percent, resided in eastern Virginia. U.S. Census Office, *Fifth Census*, Tables [10]–[13].

time" comprised nearly one-third of the population. Thus by 1850, Johnson avowed, whites in these and "many other" Valley counties would have "so strong an interest" in slavery as to "insure their cooperation in its protection." Even in a republican government, then, "power will abide with slaveholders." Virginia's circumstances, Johnson once more cautioned conservatives, do not require representation for slave property. Far safer to promote "feelings of affection and . . . justice" by granting west Virginians political equality than to attempt to "impose" the odious mixed basis on a long-discontented people.[56]

Johnson's bold address exposed a crucial flaw in conservatives' position. To deny equal representation to white men as a necessary consequence of slavery would not only heighten hostilities *between* east and west Virginia; it would also intensify antislavery feelings among non-slaveholding whites *within* east Virginia. As the 1829–1830 convention itself evidenced, Tidewater and Piedmont conservatives could not forever resist the reform tide. Rather than exacerbate sectional and class antagonisms, then, conservatives might more wisely seek to ally non-slaveholding white Virginians by conceding time-worn demands for political equality. Johnson's argument that "prudent" democratization of suffrage and representation would best protect slaveholders' interests foreshadowed arguments of the prominent Tidewater politician, Henry Wise, at the 1850–1851 Virginia constitutional convention. Majority, not minority rule, these reformers contended, was most compatible with slavery.

When Johnson concluded his nine-hour speech, he glanced quickly around the convention hall. There, conspicuously placed, the tall, skinny John Randolph was derisively opening his English hunting watch. Although Randolph had not yet addressed the convention, the renowned conservative orator exerted "extraordinary influence" over "all members." Opponents writhed under his disdainful glances. Conservatives seemed emboldened by his approving nods. Gallery spectators likewise followed every gesture, noticed every expression on his boyish countenance. "He was," one observer remarked, "like the musical director in the midst of an immense orchestra."[57]

56. Virginia, *Proceedings and Debates of the Virginia State Convention of 1829–1830*, p. 282.
57. Grigsby, "Virginia Convention of 1829–30," 55; Pleasants, "Sketches of the Virginia Convention of 1829–30," 303.

Of all convention delegates, John Randolph best epitomized the traditional east Virginia aristocrat. Born on a "Southside" Tidewater plantation in June, 1773, he was descended on both sides from prominent, old Virginia families. Delicate and effeminate in appearance, he had, from birth, a fitful, brooding personality, an "uncontrollable temper." Like Benjamin Watkins Leigh, Randolph revered the elegant lifestyle of colonial Tidewater planters. He was fond of horses, guns, dogs. His slaves rode purebred horses. A deep attachment to the soil and to aristocratic social order supported his inveterate belief in government by landed gentry. The "character of the *real* gentleman," he once advised his nephew, "is the most respectable amongst men. It consists not of plate, and equipage, and rich living . . . but in *truth*, courtesy, bravery, generosity, and learning."[58]

Randolph bitterly resisted the democratic tendencies of postrevolutionary America. He labeled the equalitarian philosophy of the Declaration of Independence a "pernicious falsehood" and opposed universal white manhood suffrage. He decried Virginia's abolition of entail and primogeniture as destructive of the aristocratic way of life. Throughout his political career, he stubbornly adhered to states' rights and strict construction of the federal Constitution. As the old colonial order eroded, Randolph became increasingly gloomy and eccentric. He drove through the east Virginia countryside in an old-fashioned English coach drawn by four imported English thoroughbreds. Ever defiant of the times, he affirmed in a distinct, high-pitched voice, "I am an aristocrat. I love liberty. I hate equality." He came to the constitutional convention determined to hold back equality in his beloved commonwealth.[59]

Unprecedented crowds packed the gallery, lobby, and convention hall on November 14 in anticipation of Randolph's response to Chapman Johnson. Every delegate was in his seat. As the famed conservative rose, a sudden hush fell over the audience. Randolph seemed ill at ease at the start of his two-hour speech, but his confidence quickly returned as friends and spectators cheered his "biting sarcasm." Resting his left hand on a cane, he shook his long, bony right forefinger defiantly at oppo-

58. William Cabell Bruce, *John Randolph of Roanoke, 1773–1833* (New York, 1922), 3; Hugh A. Garland, *The Life of John Randolph of Roanoke* (New York, 1860), 12; Russell Kirk, *John Randolph of Roanoke* (Chicago, 1964), 100, 163–64, 198.

59. Kirk, *John Randolph of Roanoke*, 36–44, 100, 159–64, 28.

nents. "We are told," the Tidewater conservative addressed Chapman Johnson's plan, that representation based on "prudent" suffrage would best safeguard slaveholders' rights. But "surely gentlemen know," he retorted, that "once this principle is in operation, the waters are out . . . there is an end to the security of all property in the Commonwealth." Restrictions on suffrage could never be maintained. Instead, "King Numbers" would soon "regulate all things." A "bare majority" would have power to tax slave property *"ad libitum,"* with the "strongest temptation . . . to do it."[60]

What "degree of infatuation," then, Randolph angrily demanded, had led one of Virginia's "great slave-holding and tobacco-planting districts" to unite with westerners in support of the white basis? "I would not have believed," he reproached western Piedmont reformers, that the "real danger" to slavery should "spring from . . . the tobacco-grower and slave-holder of Virginia" who would "lend his aid" to reduce "his brethren," and himself, to political "bondage." When the "people of those districts" understood the "real question," they would sooner "force ratsbane down their throats" than adopt a constitution with white-basis representation.[61]

He was "not at war with the Bill of Rights." Its declarations served as "lights and guides" in establishing political institutions. Statesmen, however, must adapt abstract principles to particular societies. Is there "any country on earth," Randolph echoed fellow conservatives Upshur and Leigh, "where circumstances have a more important bearing than . . . in Virginia?" More than half of east Virginia's population were slaves. Those who ignored such "circumstances," who sought to "divorce property from power" in the tax-laying house of delegates, were "stark mad." He would "not give a button" for the mixed basis in the senate. "Twenty-four gentlemen upstairs" could never resist 120 "below." As a "practical man," he would go only for "solid security," for representation of property, as well as persons, in the house. Adopt the white basis by a narrow majority, Randolph warned reformers, and the "tocsin of civil war"

60. Grigsby, "Virginia Convention of 1829–30," 53; Pleasants, "Sketches of the Virginia Convention of 1829–30," 148; Virginia, *Proceedings and Debates of the Virginia State Convention of 1829–1830,* pp. 317–19.
61. Virginia, *Proceedings and Debates of the Virginia State Convention of 1829–1830,* pp. 315–16.

would be sounded. Slaveholding Virginia would never tamely submit to the "monstrous tyranny" of "King Numbers!"[62]

Randolph's assault on the white basis paralleled Benjamin Watkins Leigh's assertion that democracy and slavery could not coexist. Yet whereas Leigh had decried nonslaveholding Trans-Allegheny "peasantry" as the gravest threat to slavery, Randolph seemed more alarmed by eastern slaveholders' own disloyalty to the "peculiar institution." His denunciation of western Piedmont reformers dramatized crucial divisions within east Virginia's *slaveholding* community, divisions as ominous to slavery as sectional and class antagonisms already detailed by Leigh and Chapman Johnson. So, too, Randolph's warnings of "civil war" augured possible convulsive dismemberment of the commonwealth should a revised constitution incorporate majority rule.

The vote that followed Randolph's address confirmed his fear of easterners' disloyalty. Despite the "Southsider's" upbraiding, thirteen western Piedmont delegates joined the thirty-six westerners to defeat the mixed basis by a 49–47 margin. Representatives from Loudoun-Fairfax and from Albemarle-Amherst-Nelson-Fluvanna-Goochland, both long-standing reform districts in the northern and western Piedmont, voted unanimously against conservatives' undemocratic house apportionment. Of the five other eastern reformers, three represented the Campbell-Buckingham-Bedford district, two the Franklin-Patrick-Henry-Pittsylvania district.[63] Although both latter districts were south of the James River, both also bordered or were near the Blue Ridge Mountains and had traditionally evidenced more republican attitudes than the eastern and southeastern Piedmont. Moreover, the Campbell-Buckingham-Bedford district included the manufacturing-commercial town of Lynchburg, whose population typified the progressive outlook of urban centers throughout Virginia.

Immediately following defeat of the mixed basis on November 14, Benjamin Watkins Leigh moved that apportionment in the house of delegates, like that in the United States House of Representatives, be based on white population plus three-fifths of the slaves. Compared to the

---

62. *Ibid.*, 317–21.
63. *Ibid.*, 321. Fairfax County is technically in the northern Tidewater but was part of the senate district comprising Loudoun County in the northwest Piedmont. Thus I have, for purposes of analysis, considered Fairfax as part of the western Piedmont reform bloc.

mixed basis, Tidewater representation in a 134-member house would decline from forty-one to thirty-eight, while Piedmont representation would increase from forty-six to forty-eight. West of the Blue Ridge, Valley strength would decline from twenty-four to twenty-one; the Trans-Allegheny would increase from twenty-three to twenty-seven. Overall, then, apportionment on white population and three-fifths slaves would result in a shift of only one delegate from eastern to western Virginia. White-basis representation, in contrast, giving the Tidewater thirty-two, the Piedmont forty, the Valley twenty-six, and the Trans-Allegheny thirty-six house members, would effect a significant transfer of power, particularly from the slaveholding eastern and southeastern Tidewater and Piedmont to the nonslaveholding Trans-Allegheny. With federal numbers as unfavorable to republicanism as the mixed basis, the same coalition of eastern and western reformers rejected, 49 to 47, conservatives' second proposal.[64] (See Appendix, Table V.)

The convention was deadlocked. Conservatives could not carry their favorite schemes giving disproportionate power to slaveholders, nor could reformers secure democratic representation in both branches of the general assembly. The balance of power rested with those western Piedmont moderates who, like James Monroe, favored the white basis in the house, but not in the senate. In hopes of ending the stalemate, delegates turned in late November to compromise plans formulated by western Piedmont moderates from the Albemarle-Amherst-Goochland district. Reformers rallied behind former Governor James Pleasants' proposal to apportion the house on 1830 white population, with provision for future reapportionment, and the senate on federal numbers. Conservatives backed William Fitzhugh Gordon's plan to base both house and senate on 1820 white population, but without any principle of future reapportionment. Pleasants' compromise would give the Tidewater thirty-two, the Piedmont forty, the Valley twenty-six, and the Trans-Allegheny thirty-six delegates in a 134-member house. Gordon's would give the Tidewater thirty-six, the Piedmont forty-two, the Valley twenty-five, and the Trans-Allegheny thirty-one. Gordon's 1820 population basis thus would strip western Virginia of six representatives, assigning them instead to conservative eastern counties. (See Appendix, Table V.)

Gordon's senate apportionment, conversely, was slightly more favor-

64. *Ibid.*, 341–42.

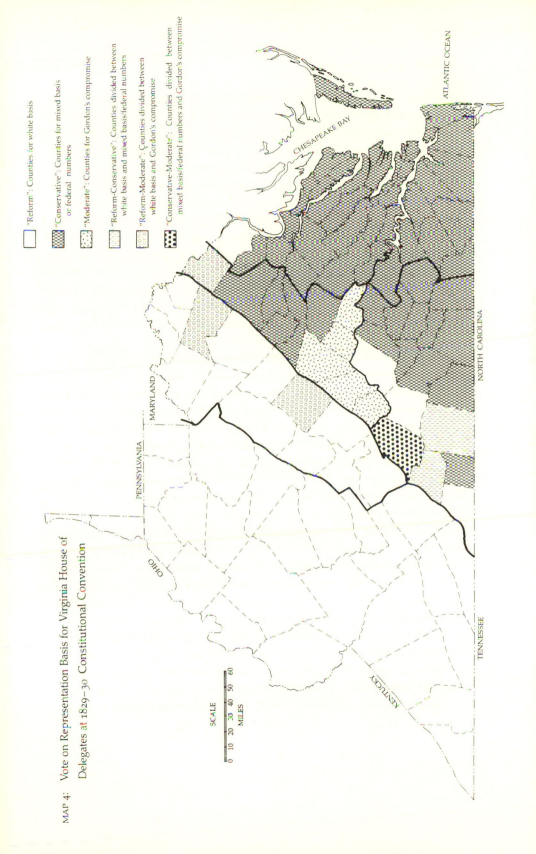

MAP 4:  Vote on Representation Basis for Virginia House of
        Delegates at 1829–30 Constitutional Convention

"Reform": Counties for white basis

"Conservative": Counties for mixed basis or federal numbers

"Moderate": Counties for Gordon's compromise

"Reform-Conservative": Counties divided between white basis and mixed basis/federal numbers

"Reform-Moderate": Counties divided between white basis and Gordon's compromise

"Conservative-Moderate": Counties divided between mixed basis/federal numbers and Gordon's compromise

ATLANTIC OCEAN

CHESAPEAKE BAY

NORTH CAROLINA

MARYLAND

PENNSYLVANIA

OHIO

KENTUCKY

TENNESSEE

SCALE

0  10  20  30  40  50  60

MILES

able to the west. A thirty-two-member senate based on 1820 white population would have eight Tidewater, eleven Piedmont, six Valley, and seven Trans-Allegheny representatives. Pleasants' federal-numbers senate would have nine Tidewater, eleven Piedmont, five Valley, and seven Trans-Allegheny members. A white-basis senate of eight Tidewater, ten Piedmont, six Valley, and eight Trans-Allegheny members would, however, most benefit reform interests. There, unlike Gordon's senate, majority power would lie with western Piedmont, Valley, and Trans-Allegheny districts. (See Appendix, Table VI.)

Far more intolerable to white-basis reformers than Gordon's present compromising of democracy was his failure to provide for future reapportionment of political power. To freeze representation on 1820 white population would assure a permanent conservative majority, both in the crucial house of delegates and in the senate. Fixed apportionment would be especially disastrous to Virginia's rapidly growing Trans-Allegheny, where whites already comprised 26.5 percent of the state's 1830 white population, yet would have, under Gordon's plan, just 23.1 percent of house members. Despite objections to three-fifths representation for slaves, reformers preferred a federal-numbers senate and white-basis house, now and in the future, to perpetual apportionment of both legislative branches on the 1820 census.[65]

Each side denounced opponents' concessions. A "Government of numbers in opposition to property," "Southsider" John Randolph protested, was "rank Jacobinism." He "nailed his colours to the mast"; he would "go down" rather than surrender to a "tyrannous" white-basis house. Adopt majority rule, and "in less than twenty years," legislation would be "brought into the House . . . for the emancipation of every slave in Virginia." Eastern slaveholders, he warned, would never endure such political "vassalage." A separation of the state would result. Philip Doddridge, in turn, delivered his *"ultimatum."* He would "yield" federal numbers in the senate, the Trans-Allegheny leader declared, only if opponents "yield us" the white basis in the house, with provision for "periodical" reapportionment to "meet our future growth in population." This was the "last step he could take with a view to compromise." If

65. *Ibid.*, 361–62, 455; Peterson, *Democracy, Liberty, and Property*, 278–79; U.S. Census Office, *Fifth Census*, Tables [10]–[13].

eastern "oligarchs" continued to resist a democratic house, further debate was futile. He would determine within a few days whether to quit the convention.[66]

Shortly after this acrimonious exchange, uncompromising reformers forced a vote on the naked issue of a white-basis house. Three delegates from the Albemarle-Amherst-Goochland district, who earlier had allied with reformers to defeat both a mixed-basis and federal-numbers house, now joined conservatives to vote first against the white basis, and then for compromise. Committed to the 1820 population basis for house and senate, these western Piedmont moderates regarded Gordon's diluted democracy as the most viable "middle ground" between slaveholding and nonslaveholding Virginians, the plan best suited to preserve the present integrity of the commonwealth. With such defection from reformers' ranks, the convention rejected, 50 to 46, a white-basis house and approved, by the same margin, apportionment on the 1820 census.[67]

White-basis proponents suffered a far worse calamity the following day when delegates defeated Doddridge's proposal for "new apportionment," the house on white population, the senate on federal numbers, "after the year 1841, and every *twenty* years thereafter." On this critical issue of future democratization of house representation, twelve of the thirteen original western Piedmont reformers joined the thirty-six westerners to support Doddridge's amendment. But the shift of William Fitzhugh Gordon to conservative ranks, a shift the former white-basis advocate felt "reluctantly compelled" to make as author of the 1820 population plan, sounded the initial death knell of democracy at the 1829–1830 convention. By a tie 48–48 vote, delegates determined that white Virginians would not, either now or in the foreseeable future, have equal representation. Instead, both branches of the general assembly would be frozen on population figures already a decade old.[68]

White-basis reformers were incensed. Adoption of Gordon's plan without Doddridge's amendment, Valley delegate Peachy Harrison wrote his son, "fixes the political inferiority" of western Virginia "both for ourselves and our posterity." He "feared the consequences" should

66. Virginia, *Proceedings and Debates of the Virginia State Convention of 1829–1830*, pp. 501–502, 556–57, 858, 570–72.
   67. *Ibid.*, 667–68.
   68. *Ibid.*, 667, 690.

conservative easterners "force" this principle on the west "without their consent" and "without any fair scheme of future apportionment. . . . For the present," Harrison noted, Gordon's 1820 population basis did "full justice" to the Valley and western Piedmont. But it stripped Trans-Allegheny whites of both present and future political equality. His "Panhandle" constituents, an irate Doddridge concurred, would never ratify a constitution without a *"just . . . rule of future apportionment."*[69]

For two more weeks, Trans-Allegheny reformers struggled to secure an "equitable principle" of future representation. However, on January 12, 1830, the convention for the final time rejected a resolution, introduced by "Panhandle" delegate Alexander Campbell, to reapportion both house and senate on white population alone "in the year 1841, and every __ years thereafter." Delegates then narrowly approved James Madison's plan for future reapportionment of the general assembly if a two-thirds majority of each house concurred. Madison's amendment doused reformers' flickering hopes. Never, Alexander Campbell bitterly remarked, would "two-thirds" of both house and senate assent to white-basis reapportionment. With slaveholding easterners assured of legislative control, white-basis reformers had lost the contest for equal representation at the 1829–1830 convention.[70]

Reformers also lost the battle for white-basis suffrage, a battle that once again pitted conservative slaveholding bastions of southern and eastern Virginia against more populous, progressive regions on both sides of the Blue Ridge. Delegates who championed representation for slave property generally also championed freehold suffrage. Likewise, those who urged apportionment on white population alone urged universal white manhood suffrage. Although alignments followed traditional patterns, however, slavery was not as intrinsic to the suffrage question as to the contest for equal representation. Debate focused instead on the relationship between land and political power. Yet if delegates argued more about land than slaves, a similar principle was at stake: Would Virginia recognize equal political rights for white men? Or would she con-

---

69. Peachy Harrison to Gessner Harrison, December 5, 19, 28, 1829, all in Gessner Harrison Papers; Virginia, *Proceedings and Debates of the Virginia State Convention of 1829–1830*, p. 681.

70. Virginia, *Proceedings and Debates of the Virginia State Convention of 1829–1830*, pp. 849–51.

tinue to grant special political privileges to a propertied white minority? Because the issue of property rights was fundamental to both, the rhetoric of the suffrage debate closely paralleled delegates' exchanges on the white- versus mixed-basis of representation. Reformers denounced freehold voting qualifications as "aristocratic" and "oligarchic" and demanded that Virginia at last effect republican tenets of her own bill of rights. Conservatives countered with epithets of "despotism" and "license and anarchy" and argued that, in Virginia, freehold suffrage *was* republican.

A memorial from Richmond nonfreeholders, introduced by John Marshall during the first week of the convention, outlined reformers' general position. Although nonfreeholders were a majority of the city's adult white males, Richmond petitioners protested, because they did not own "a certain portion of land," they had been "passed by, like aliens or slaves, in measures involving their future political destiny." To base suffrage on landed property created an "odious distinction among members of the same community" by denying white artisans, mechanics, and laborers their "rightful equality" and vesting "all power" in a "favored class." Although opponents maintained that any industrious Virginian could acquire the amount of land necessary to vote, those whom "fortune or inclination have engaged in other than agricultural pursuits" did not find it "easy or convenient" to purchase a freehold.

Freehold suffrage not only contravened democracy; it also "greatly augmented" the "danger of abuse" to landholders' rights. Echoing Chapman Johnson's arguments against the mixed basis of representation, Richmond nonfreeholders warned that continued disenfranchisement of Virginia's urban white artisans and laborers, as well as her "commercial and manufacturing classes," would intensify present "angry conflicts" between freeholding and nonfreeholding whites. Throughout the commonwealth, nonfreeholders "feel with full force their degraded condition." They would not continue to "acquiesce" in a "privileged order" founded on the "patrician pretensions of the landholder." Just as white-basis representation would best protect slave property, so white-basis suffrage would provide the "safest check" on any "abuse" of landed property.[71]

71. *Ibid.*, 25–31.

Delegates from the Trans-Allegheny "Panhandle," the western Piedmont, and the Tidewater "Eastern Shore" led the fight for universal suffrage on the convention floor. All followed Richmond nonfreeholders in attacking freehold voting as a repudiation of republicanism, and many went beyond political abstractions to urge suffrage extension on practical grounds. Freehold suffrage, "Panhandle" reformer Eugenius Wilson declared, inhibited growth of white population by discouraging migration from other states and encouraging emigration of "many of Virginia's most valuable sons" to lands beyond the Ohio River. There, in those "splendid regions of the West," the "mechanic, the merchant," the nonfreeholding farmer, barred from the polls in their native state by this "odious restriction," could "enjoy the rights of freemen." Of the "twenty-four states that form the Federal Family," Loudoun delegate Richard Henderson added, "*Virginia alone, proscribes and brands, with utter political opprobium, the far greater part of her sons.*" All other states, slaveholding and nonslaveholding alike, had abandoned freehold qualifications in favor of democratic age and residency requirements, or a simple tax-paying basis. Consequently Virginia, once the "first State of the Union," Thomas Bayly of Accomack lamented, had "fallen . . . to that of the third." Already white population in neighboring Ohio was "greater than that of the renowned and *once powerful* Commonwealth of Virginia." To prevent her further decline in power and prestige, Virginia must adopt "liberal and republican" voting qualifications. Extend suffrage, the Tidewater "Eastern Shore" reformer proclaimed, and "you will fill all parts of your State," particularly western Virginia, with a "more dense" white population.[72]

Suffrage extension was essential not only to augment white population and, thereby, bolster Virginia's national influence; it was also, eastern and western reformers alike argued, crucial to the state's domestic security. Virginia's population, Richard Henderson of Loudoun gravely remarked, included "four distinct classes—the freeholder, the non-freeholder, the free negro, and the slave. May not occasions arise," the western Piedmont democrat warned in a not-so-veiled allusion to slave insurrection, "when the common weal will loudly call for the united exertions of your white population?" Equally ominous to white Virginians, "Pan-

72. *Ibid.*, 353–56, 374–75. North Carolina still retained freehold qualifications in voting for members of the state senate, but not for the house. Virginia was the only state retaining a freehold basis for both legislative branches.

handle" delegate Charles Morgan declared, was the crisis "fast approaching" all slaveholding states—a "crisis truly alarming . . . when freemen will be needed—when every man must be at his post" to defend southern rights against the free-soil North. Whether to confront hostile blacks within the state, or hostile whites without, Virginia must bind her entire white population in "chords of common affection." Admit the state's nonfreeholders to "equal participation in their political rights," Henderson addressed conservatives, and "such principles" would "happify this community." Cling to "aristocratic" freehold qualifications, and "antipathies" already existent among white Virginians would be intensified. "When we disfranchise one class of men . . . to secure any property or privilege we possess," Alexander Campbell of Brooke concurred, "we endanger that very property and . . . privileges, more by such disfranchisements, than we protect them. . . . It is the nature of man to hate, and to attempt to impair and destroy, that which . . . degrades him in his own estimation."[73]

Western Piedmont delegate Lucas Thompson offered a final corollary to reformers' contention that democratic suffrage would best harmonize the interests of all white Virginians. Of "any state in this Union," the Amherst County reformer declared, Virginia seemed particularly suited to extend suffrage "with safety." Unlike many free states, she had "no overgrown cities—no overgrown manufactory establishments." Even more important, whereas free states had enfranchised large numbers of propertyless white laborers, a class regarded "by others" as "dangerous voters," Virginia instead had "upwards of four hundred thousand slave" laborers entitled to no political rights. Conservatives' arguments to the contrary, universal white manhood suffrage had not produced "tumults," "civil discord," or invasion of property rights in nonslaveholding states. Much less, then, need slaveholding Virginia fear such consequences.[74]

Those parts of the commonwealth bordering states with democratic suffrage, reformers noted in conclusion, favored suffrage extension in Virginia. The "South-West," joining Tennessee and Kentucky; the "North-West," joining Ohio and Pennsylvania; the "North-East," joining Maryland—"freeholders in these districts," Thomas Bayly of Accomack declared, were "all anxious" to democratize voting. Only in the "centre

73. *Ibid.*, 360, 382, 361, 390.
74. *Ibid.*, 417–19.

of the State," and "to the South, on the North Carolina line," "Panhandle" delegate Charles Morgan reiterated, did nonfreehold suffrage "meet with opposition." Reformers everywhere urged "Southside" "anti-reformist gentlemen" to abandon their principle of landed qualifications. "For the safety and preservation . . . of those very interests" that freehold proponents upheld, suffrage extension was "indispensable."[75]

Like white-basis reformers, proponents of democratic suffrage unanimously challenged the principle that property, whether slaves or land, must possess political power. The mixed basis, federal numbers, freehold suffrage—all these proposals, reformers argued, contravened republicanism and, accordingly, were more inimical to slaveholding and landholding interests than majority rule. In urging conservatives to equalize representation, Valley reformer Chapman Johnson had raised the specter of a class alliance between disaffected easterners and westerners in a "constant war" on slave property, a "war" that transcended sections to pit Virginia's nonslaveholding white majority against her slaveholding white minority. So, too, in urging democratization of suffrage, Richard Henderson and Lucas Thompson of the western Piedmont had joined "Panhandle" reformer Alexander Campbell to warn that landed voting qualifications would heighten similar class antagonisms between nonfreeholding and freeholding whites. Only if Virginia abandoned her time-worn, aristocratic government would antipathies toward privileged property interests subside. Majority rule was essential to minority rights!

Rather than a weakened, divided commonwealth, reformers at the 1829–1830 constitutional convention evoked a resurrected, united republic, burgeoning with industrious, harmonious whites. Such vision heralded that of antislavery legislators during the 1831–1832 house debate on emancipation. Whereas 1829 suffrage reformers attributed Virginia's declining national influence and stagnant white population to freehold voting, however, just two years later abolitionist legislators would directly blame slavery. Virginia abolitionists of 1831–1832 would, further, reject Lucas Thompson's contention that black man's slavery provided ideal conditions for white man's democracy. Ironically, this argument for suffrage extension, rebuffed by antislavery Virginians, would

75. *Ibid.*, 374, 381, 385, 390.

become a central theme of conservatives in Virginia and the Deep South in post-1832 decades.

Reformers' insistence that democratic suffrage would best protect landed property interests failed to persuade hard-line conservatives. Just as mixed-basis delegates argued that transfer of political power to Virginia's nonslaveholding majority would lead to oppressive taxation of slaves, so proponents of freehold voting charged that extension of suffrage to nonfreeholders would lead to oppressive taxation of land. The "landholders of Virginia," Benjamin Watkins Leigh summarized conservatives' position, paid "almost the whole revenue of the State." They owned "all the real property of the Commonwealth" and "almost all . . . the taxable personal property." That "class of men," who thus had "the greatest stake in society," had to "be entrusted with the political powers of the State." Put government in the hands of nonfreeholders, who paid "little or nothing" in taxes and who had "no necessary community of interest" with the landed class, the "Southsider" maintained, and freeholders might "be ground to dust and ashes."[76]

While upholding the "*principle* of . . . freehold qualifications" to protect landed interests, Leigh and other conservatives denied that such principle was "aristocratic." Any man "with honest labour and persevering industry," Leigh declared, could acquire the requisite amount of land to vote. Freehold suffrage excluded only the "veriest paupers and drones in the community, whom all agree upon excluding." Furthermore, the freehold basis implemented the republican tenet of Virginia's own bill of rights, according suffrage to " 'all men, having sufficient evidence of permanent common interest with, and attachment to, the community.'" Only "ownership of the soil of the country," Tidewater conservative Philip N. Nicholas expanded on Leigh's argument, assured such "*permanent* interest and attachment. . . . Personal property . . . horses, cattle, or slaves . . . is fluctuating. . . . It can be removed, and . . . enjoyed as well in one society as another." Virginia, then, conservatives concurred, must retain "substantial and permanent" landed qualifications to safeguard property against any "extremes of democracy" enacted by "transient" nonfreeholders.[77]

76. *Ibid.*, 399–401. Taxes on lands and lots represented 41.4 percent of Virginia's total revenue in 1828.

77. *Ibid.*, 400–402, 364, 393–96.

Conservatives' eulogies to the "republican" character of freehold suffrage ignored the fact that nonagricultural Virginians might not choose to acquire land simply to be eligible to vote. As the memorial of Richmond nonfreeholders confirmed, urban white laborers, artisans, merchants, manufacturers did not find it either "easy or convenient" to purchase a freehold and resented their disenfranchisement by such restrictions. Similarly, hosannahs to the "permanency" of land disregarded the essentially "transient" nature of real property. In a society as mobile as early nineteenth-century America, a man might just as readily sell his land as his slaves, horses, or cattle. Ownership of "the soil" thus afforded no more fixed "attachment to the community" than other forms of property. Amidst the equalitarian spirit of Jacksonian America, when states north, south, and west of Virginia had all abandoned freehold suffrage, conservatives were hard pressed to defend this visible vestige of aristocratic government.

As in the debate on representation, neither conservatives nor reformers could carry their favorite principles. Rejecting both the freehold basis and universal white manhood suffrage, delegates adopted instead a complex compromise enfranchising existent freeholders, as well as all adult white males owning lands or lots worth twenty-five dollars, or leasing land at a twenty-dollar annual rent for five years or more, or who were tax-paying, housekeeping heads of families.[78] Approximately 44,325, or 56.6 percent, of Virginia's adult white males paying *state* taxes on real or personal property had voted before 1830 under freehold provisions of the 1776 constitution. Extension of suffrage to leaseholders and householders would add about 8,000 new voters, thereby enfranchising 66.9 percent of the state's tax-paying adult white males. Another 25,940, who would have been eligible to vote under reformers' simple tax-paying basis, would still be excluded.[79] Although Virginia thus abrogated ownership of a fixed quantity of land as the sole criterion for voting, suffrage requirements of the 1830 constitution fell far short of reformers' goals.

78. *Ibid.*, 854.

79. Williamson, *American Suffrage from Property to Democracy*, 234; Philip Doddridge to "Constituents," March 1, 1830, p. 5, MSS 2 D6615al, Virginia Historical Society, Richmond. Doddridge noted that another 18,000 adult white males who paid county levies, but not state taxes, would also remain disenfranchised under the new constitution. These latter would also have been disenfranchised under a tax-paying basis, but not under universal white manhood suffrage. If these 18,000 are included as "nonvoters," 45.6 percent of Virginia's adult white males remained disenfranchised under the 1830 constitution.

Nat Turner, the Virginia slave whose insurrection in August, 1831, triggered the legislative debate on emancipation.

John Floyd, governor of Virginia during the 1831–1832 slavery debate and an important behind-the-scenes "lobbyist" for abolition.

George Catlin's painting of the 1829–1830 Virginia Constitutional Convention, which includes many of the Virginians involved in the 1831–1832 slavery debate. *Courtesy of the Virginia Historical Society*

Benjamin Watkins Leigh, champion of conservative eastern Virginia during the 1829–1830 constitutional convention. *Courtesy of the Virginia Historical Society*

James McDowell, a leading member of the 1831–1832 Virginia House of Delegates and later governor of Virginia. *Courtesy of the Virginia State Library*

Thomas R. Dew, author of "Review of the Debate in the Virginia Legislature of 1831–1832." *Courtesy of the College of William and Mary in Virginia*

Whites who favored sweeping democratization of Virginia's government found little consolation in the outcome of the 1829–1830 constitutional convention. New principles of representation and suffrage were admittedly more republican than the old system of county representation and freehold suffrage. Yet representation based on 1820 white population, without a viable method of future reapportionment, seemed particularly to doom the state's burgeoning Trans-Allegheny section to permanent political inequality. So, too, disfranchisement of almost a third (33.1 percent) of Virginia's adult white male taxpayers was antithetical to "one man, one vote." The convention further rejected reformers' demands for popular election of Virginia's governor and judges, retaining instead the existent system of election by joint ballot of the general assembly.[80] Although Virginia in 1830 took a few hesitant steps toward democracy, the state's new constitution represented more a perpetuation of John Randolph's beloved "aristocracy."

On January 14, 1830, delegates adopted the revised constitution by a 55–40 margin. Of the 55 "yes" votes, easterners cast 54. Only one westerner, Valley delegate John R. Cooke of Frederick County, voted for passage. Conversely, of the 40 "no" votes, westerners cast 34, easterners 6. Analyzed by sections, the Tidewater and southeastern Piedmont unanimously approved, whereas the entire Trans-Allegheny and all but one Valley representative disapproved. The western Piedmont was more divided. Of the six easterners voting against the new constitution, three represented the resolute reform district of Loudoun-Fairfax; two, the district comprising Campbell-Buckingham-Bedford, counties south of the James River but bordering or near the Blue Ridge and including the town of Lynchburg; and one, the district comprising Spotsylvania-Louisa-Orange-Madison, counties bordering or near the Blue Ridge and including the town of Fredericksburg.[81]

Other western Piedmont districts, traditionally allied with the Valley and Trans-Allegheny, deserted inveterate reformers. Delegates from Albemarle-Amherst-Goochland and Franklin-Patrick-Henry-Pittsylvania, both strong "reform" regions at the 1816 and 1825 Staunton conventions and at the start of the 1829 constitutional convention, voted

80. Virginia, *Proceedings and Debates of the Constitutional Convention of 1829–1830*, p. 822.

81. *Ibid.*, 832. Philip Doddridge was absent; his later vote against the 1830 constitution would make the margin 55–41.

unanimously for the half-way democracy of the 1830 constitution. With large white and slave populations, and without major urban centers, these western Piedmont counties found the 1820 population principle, giving *their* region full political representation, an acceptable compromise to the undiluted white man's democracy championed by nonslaveholding westerners.

At April, 1830, elections, newly enfranchised voters ratified the constitution by a 10,492 majority.[82] The Piedmont returned the largest positive vote, with 92.2 percent of qualified whites, and *all* counties, "Southside" as well as western, strongly approving. Under the old system of equal county representation, the Piedmont, with 30.0 percent of the state's 1830 white population, had had only 27.6 percent of house seats. Under the 1820 population basis, the Piedmont would now have 31.3 percent of house members, with populous western Piedmont counties gaining the additional delegates.[83] (See Appendix, Table V.)

In contrast to the Piedmont, Tidewater legislative representation would decline from 35 percent to 26.9 percent of house members. Yet despite relative loss of power, the Tidewater, with just 24.1 percent of the state's whites by 1830, still had four more delegates than justified by democratic apportionment. And with representation frozen for the foreseeable future, the new constitution would perpetuate the disproportionate strength of both sections of eastern Virginia. Assured of slaveholders' political ascendancy, the Tidewater thus joined the Piedmont in voting heavily for ratification, with 86.4 percent of qualified whites, and all but two counties, approving.[84] Of the 26,055 votes in favor of the 1830 constitution, the Piedmont and Tidewater together accounted for 20,071, or 77 percent. (See Appendix, Table V.)

West of the Alleghenies, attitudes dramatically differed. There, 83.9 percent of qualified voters rejected Virginia's new government, with twenty-four of twenty-six counties disapproving. Only two southwestern

82. *Ibid.*, 903. All subsequent analysis of sectional and county voting is from this "Entire Official Poll on the New Constitution of Virginia."

83. U.S. Census Office, *Fifth Census*, Tables [10]–[13]; Swem and Williams, *Register of the General Assembly of Virginia*, 126–28. All subsequent percentage figures for voters and house members are from these same sources.

84. Lancaster and Warwick, both of which lost separate representation in the house as a result of merger with other small Tidewater counties, were the only eastern Virginia counties disapproving the 1830 constitution.

Trans-Allegheny counties, Lee and Washington, bordering slaveholding Kentucky and Tennessee, ratified a constitution that reduced present Trans-Allegheny strength from 24.3 percent to 23.1 percent of house seats and precluded future reapportionment. Comprising 26.5 percent of the state's whites by 1830 and anticipating more rapid future population gains than other, already-settled sections, Virginia's nonslaveholding Trans-Allegheny deeply resented this seemingly permanent denial of democracy by the slaveholding east. In a public letter to his constituents shortly before the vote on ratification, "Panhandle" reformer Philip Doddridge labeled the 1830 constitution a "political compact for the slavery of us and our children." Representation based on 1820 white population, without future reapportionment, sealed the "political vassalage" of the Trans-Allegheny "under the yoke of that Eastern oligarchy . . . we have so long been endeavoring to shake off." He urged constituents to reject a government perpetuating the "preponderance of our Eastern aristocracy" and the "degradation, present and future," of the Trans-Allegheny.[85] Sharing Doddridge's wrath, Virginia's westernmost district cast 11,189, or 71.9 percent, of the 15,563 votes against the new constitution.

Whereas eastern Virginia heavily endorsed, and the Trans-Allegheny heavily opposed the 1830 constitution, the Valley was less resolute. Of all sections of the state, the Valley gained most from reform of representation, increasing its strength in the house of delegates from 13.1 percent under the old county system to 18.7 percent under the 1820 population basis. At the same time, since the Valley contained 19.4 percent of Virginia's total 1830 whites, it had one less delegate than was justified by republican apportionment. (See Appendix, Table V.)

Acknowledging greater equalization of their political power, 3,842, or 64.7 percent, of Valley voters, and nine of fourteen counties, ratified Virginia's new government. Yet despite an almost two-thirds positive majority of both whites and counties, voting patterns revealed a sharp divergence of opinion within the Valley. Of the nine counties ratifying, eight—Augusta, Botetourt, Frederick, Hampshire, Jefferson, Rockingham, Rockbridge, and Shenandoah—had large white populations and thus particularly benefited from legislative reapportionment. Equally sig-

85. Doddridge to "Constituents," March 1, 1830, pp. 5–6.

nificant, seven of these nine counties bordered the Blue Ridge, just across the mountains from Piedmont Virginia. In contrast, all five counties rejecting the 1830 constitution—Bath, Berkeley, Hardy, Pendleton, and Morgan—had relatively small white populations. All also bordered the Alleghenies, just across the mountains from Trans-Allegheny Virginia.

Slavery was a further determinant of Valley voting. Of the nine counties approving, six had more than 20 percent slaves. Of the five counties opposing, only one, Bath, had more than 20 percent slaves. Furthermore, the three counties with the highest percentages of slaves—Botetourt (25.3 percent), Frederick (28.5 percent), and Jefferson (30.9 percent)—all ratified, whereas the two counties with the lowest percentages of slaves —Pendleton (7.9 percent) and Morgan (5.7 percent)—both rejected.

Numbers of whites, numbers of blacks, geography—all three affected Valley attitudes toward Virginia's new government. All three also tended to draw the Valley closer to east Virginia and, consequently, to divide the state's formerly allied western sections. Not anticipating huge gains in white population in post-1830 decades, large, already-populous Valley counties near the Blue Ridge found the 1830 constitution adequately republican to assure their future political equality with the Tidewater and Piedmont. So, too, much of this eastern tier of Valley counties already had a considerable interest in slavery and, like the east, sought to safeguard their property from any "extremes of democracy." Expansion of internal improvements in the years after 1830 would strengthen bonds between the Valley and east even now evident in voting on ratification. Likewise, the isolation of the Trans-Allegheny, already apparent in that section's resolute rejection of the 1830 constitution, would intensify in later decades as Virginia, and the nation, faced escalating crises over slavery. Again and again, both within and without the state, the same, explosive question central to Virginia's 1829–1830 debate on representation would recur: Could slavery and white-basis democracy coexist? Or would slaveholders, to protect their "peculiar property," forever demand disproportionate political power?

Virginia, in 1830, held back white-basis democracy and opted instead for slaveholders' political ascendancy. Ratification of the new constitution did not, however, resolve the angry conflict between slaveholding and nonslaveholding whites. With the Trans-Allegheny ablaze with discontent, Virginia's new government was indeed a "temporary patch-work of a Constitution, to be torn to pieces" as future generations of nonslaveholding whites relentlessly pressed for political equality.[86] Yet even as Virginia now adopted her controversial new constitution, the state faced another ominous crisis over slavery.

86. Virginia, *Proceedings and Debates of the Constitutional Convention of 1829–1830*, p. 570.

# IV / A Legacy of Emancipation

Early in January, 1830, Governor William B. Giles sent a confidential communiqué to the Virginia House of Delegates. The mayor of Richmond, the governor informed legislators, had just forwarded an antislavery pamphlet entitled *David Walker's Appeal*, along with a letter from David Walker to Thomas Lewis, a Richmond free black. Walker, a free black born in North Carolina but now living in Boston, had mailed Lewis thirty copies of his *Appeal* with instructions to distribute them among local blacks.[1] Citing Christianity, nature, and the Declaration of Independence, Walker declared that "white Americans" had no right to "reduce" blacks to the "wretched state of *slavery*." Jesus Christ, not white slaveholders, was the only "Master" blacks must obey. God, Walker prophesied, would soon send a "mighty" Negro general to deliver blacks from "cruel" bondage. Blacks must support this divinely appointed leader. They must prove to "white Americans" that "we are MEN . . . not *brutes*." Twelve courageous blacks, "well armed for battle," could "kill . . . fifty whites." Better to die gloriously fighting for liberty, Walker exhorted fellow blacks, than "to be a slave to a tyrant."[2]

Upon learning of the circulation of this abolitionist tract, Governor Giles continued, the mayor acted immediately to prevent its further dissemination among Richmond blacks. At present, however, he had se-

---

1. William B. Giles to Linn Banks, January 7, 1830, in Virginia Executive Communications, Box 37, Virginia State Library, Richmond.
2. Charles M. Wiltse (ed.), *David Walker's Appeal in Four Articles; Together with a Preamble to the Colored Citizens of the World, but in Particular, and Very Expressly, to those of the United States of America* (New York, 1965), 16–20, 25–26.

cured only twenty of the thirty copies. "In my judgment," the "South-side" Piedmont governor concluded his secret communiqué, "increasing" circulation of "insurrectionary pamphlets and speeches amongst the people of colour . . . requires" the general assembly to consider this "extremely delicate and interesting subject," whether "with open, or closed doors."[3]

The legislature, deliberating behind closed doors, took no immediate steps to counter Walker's *Appeal*. At the following session, however, shortly after another Bostonian, William Lloyd Garrison, began publication of his virulent antislavery journal, *The Liberator*, the Virginia General Assembly banned all assemblages of free blacks for educational purposes. The April 7, 1831, act also prohibited whites from teaching slaves to "read or write."[4] The growing circulation of incendiary northern literature among free blacks and slaves clearly worried white Virginians.

Four months later, Nat Turner confirmed such fears. God, one white Virginian commented, had had no hand in the Southampton insurrection. But "those agents of the *black gentleman*, the editors of the 'Liberator' and 'Walker's pamphlet,' may" have.[5]

Governor John Floyd likewise held Garrison, Walker, and other "Northern incendiaries" responsible for the Nat Turner uprising. But he also blamed white Virginians. During recent years, Floyd remarked in a November, 1831, letter to South Carolina Governor James Hamilton, while "Yankee" agitators intensified their antislavery campaign, Virginians were "resting in apathetic security." Laws governing slaves and free blacks "became more inactive." Whites, particularly the "most respectable . . . females," taught "negroes to read and write" so that they "might read the Scriptures." Many of these "pious" ladies became "tutoresses in Sunday schools and . . . distributors" of northern religious tracts proclaiming the spiritual equality of all men. Virginians further allowed "large assemblages of negroes" where "black preachers" read "incendiary publications of Walker, Garrison, and Knapp of Boston," and congregations sang "songs and hymns of a similar character. . . . I am

3. Giles to Banks, January 7, 1830.
4. Virginia, *Acts Passed at a General Assembly of the Commonwealth of Virginia, 1830–1831* (Richmond, 1831), 107–108.
5. Nicholas P. Trist to Joseph Coolidge, Jr., October 27, 1831, in Ellen Wayles Coolidge Correspondence, Alderman Library, University of Virginia.

fully convinced," Floyd avowed, that "every black preacher . . . east of the Blue Ridge" knew of the "intended rebellion" in Southampton. To quash the "spirit of insubordination" in the immediate future, the governor informed Hamilton, he would recommend in his annual message laws confining slaves to masters' estates, prohibiting slaves and free blacks from preaching, and removing all free blacks from Virginia.

If Floyd looked to rigid curbs on blacks' mobility to lessen the likelihood of another Southampton, such proscription, the governor believed, was only a partial, temporary expedient. For in his letter to Governor Hamilton, Floyd went beyond laws consolidating slavery to outline a plan for gradual emancipation. Virginia's annual "surplus revenue," he advanced, might be used "for slaves, to work for a time upon our Rail-Roads, etc., etc., and then sent out of the country." State-financed colonization of slaves would be "preparatory, or rather . . . the first step to emancipation. This last point," Floyd reassured the South Carolina governor, "will of course be tenderly and cautiously managed, and will be urged or delayed as your State and Georgia may be disposed to cooperate."[6]

Writing in his diary just two days later, Floyd was more resolute. "Before I leave this Government," he confided in his entry for November 21, "I will have contrived to have a law passed gradually abolishing slavery in this State, or at all events to begin the work by prohibiting slavery on the West side of the Blue Ridge Mountains."[7] Floyd, who had succeeded "Southsider" William B. Giles as Virginia's first governor under the recently adopted 1830 constitution, was also the state's first governor from west of the Alleghenies. Born April 24, 1783, near present-day Louisville, Kentucky, then still part of Virginia, Floyd as a young man had journeyed northward to study medicine at the University of Pennsylvania in Philadelphia. Receiving his M.D. degree in 1804, he returned to Virginia and practiced medicine in Botetourt County in the southernmost Valley. After the War of 1812, Floyd moved to Montgomery County in the southeast Trans-Allegheny and from 1817 to 1829 served in the United States House of Representatives. Elected governor the following year, the forty-eight-year-old Montgomery County resident, himself the

6. John Floyd to James Hamilton, Jr., November 19, 1831, in John Floyd Papers, Library of Congress.
7. Ambler (ed.), *The Life and Diary of John Floyd*, 170.

owner of twelve taxable slaves in 1831, now seemed determined to use Nat Turner as a catalyst to abolish rather than to strengthen slavery in Virginia.

Leading Virginia newspapers echoed Governor Floyd's conviction that Virginians must act promptly and vigorously to prevent another Southampton. "There seems to be a . . . general wish," the Richmond *Constitutional Whig* affirmed, "that the approaching legislature . . . take the subject" of Virginia's black population "into serious and solemn consideration. . . . That which was deemed too delicate to mention before . . . occurrences in Southampton is now freely and unreservedly canvassed." The *Whig* urged legislators to determine constituents' views on slavery before the general assembly met, so that "when the time for action arrives, they may not, as is too often the case, do nothing for fear of doing wrong."[8]

Editors east of the Blue Ridge proposed a variety of schemes. "Southside" journals urged immediate, "general arming" of militia units. "The mere sight of arms in the hands of the militia," the Lynchburg *Virginian* avowed, "would strike terror into the minds of the slaves, while their unarmed condition absolutely invites insurrection." Tidewater and Piedmont newspapers similarly called for rigorous enforcement of recent laws against black assemblages and slaves' instruction. To proscribe "all means of *concert* and *conspiracy*," the Richmond *Enquirer* outlined, slaves must "not learn to read and write—they must not be permitted to wander from their respective plantations, particularly after dark—nor attend black preachings—nor hold any unlawful meetings." Slaves, the *Enquirer* added, "should be as kindly treated as possible—but no indulgence should interfere with the necessary authority."[9]

Valley editors joined the eastern press in supporting yet a third course of action. Removal of the "Free People of colour," the Martinsburg *Gazette*, Norfolk and Portsmouth *Herald*, and Richmond *Enquirer* all concurred, was "vital" not only to the "peace and welfare" of white Virginians, but also to free blacks themselves. "We are gratified to learn," *Herald* editors reported, that "as soon as transportation can be afforded them," one hundred free blacks from Southampton County desired to

8. Richmond *Constitutional Whig*, November 17, 1831.
9. Lynchburg *Virginian*, September 8, October 6, 1831; Richmond *Enquirer*, October 25, 1831.

emigrate to Liberia. Others, "we hope," will "follow their example" until all this "unfortunate population" enjoys "real freedom" in the "land of their fore-fathers" instead of the "demi-slavery" of free blacks in America. "*In what way*" such large-scale colonization of Virginia's free blacks could be "accomplished," the *Enquirer* however acknowledged, is a "problem of delicate and difficult solution."[10]

Arming white militia, restricting blacks' mobility, prohibiting slaves' education—all these proposals by the Virginia press mirrored Governor Floyd's intended public call for consolidation of slavery in his forthcoming annual message. But whereas Floyd had urged gradual abolition only in private letters and diaries, the editors of east Virginia's two leading journals publicly proposed that the commonwealth go beyond effectual "government of slaves" to strike at slavery itself. Once "slaves are so well governed" as to remove serious threat of insurrection, Thomas Ritchie of the Democratic Richmond *Enquirer* demanded, "shall we stop there?" Could not some plan be "firmly and deliberately introduced, for striking at the roots of the evil . . . for reducing surely but quietly, the number of our slaves?" The federal government, the states'-rights Ritchie avowed, had no right to finance "emancipation of a single slave, or . . . exportation of a single freedman. What can be done by . . . State authority" and by the "munificent spirit of individuals," however, is a "very different question." Like colonization of free blacks, Ritchie reiterated, gradual emancipation and colonization of slaves "will require all our caution and wisdom."

Although often at odds with Ritchie over national politics, on the issue of slavery in Virginia, John Hampden Pleasants of the Richmond *Constitutional Whig* echoed his rival's call for thorough "deliberations" of the "great questions forced upon public attention" by Southampton. Virginians everywhere recognized, Pleasants affirmed, "that something ought to be, and must be done. It is not the non-slaveholder, or the visionary Philanthropist, or the fanatic, who says this, but the mass of slave-holders themselves. It is *their* question, "the National Republican editor agreed with Ritchie, "and we are glad that it . . . receives their intense consideration." Neither the *Enquirer* nor the *Whig* offered any specific plan to "lessen . . . the appalling evils" of slavery before the

10. Martinsburg (Va.) *Gazette*, October 20, 1831; Norfolk and Portsmouth (Va.) *Herald*, October 5, 1831; Richmond *Enquirer*, October 25, 1831.

1831–1832 general assembly convened. Each insisted, however, that the fate of slavery in Virginia must rest with Virginians themselves, not with the federal government or with northern "fanatics."[11]

Petitions pouring into the general assembly from all sections of the commonwealth testified to widespread public desire for prompt, resolute action on slavery in the aftermath of the Nat Turner uprising. Most memorials simply urged removal of Virginia's free blacks. Others demanded either state or federal-financed colonization of free blacks *and* manumitted slaves. A few called for gradual emancipation and colonization of all Virginia slaves.[12] Formidable tasks awaited the 1831–1832 legislature.

Although Nat Turner abruptly ended whites' regime of "apathetic security" toward blacks, Virginians had anguished over slavery long before Southampton. The Virginia House of Burgesses in 1772 requested the British king's "paternal assistance in averting" a "most alarming . . . calamity." Importation of African slaves, colonial legislators protested, "hath long been considered as a trade of great inhumanity." Continued encouragement might "endanger the very existence of your Majesty's American dominions." Four years later, Virginia justified rebellion against England partly on grounds of the king's persistent refusal to end the African slave trade. The preamble to the 1776 constitution, unanimously adopted by a Tidewater-dominated legislature, denounced "*George* the third" for "prompting our negroes to rise in arms among us, those very negroes, whom, by an inhuman use of his negative, he hath refused us permission to exclude by law." In October, 1778, the newly independent state prohibited the African trade and freed any slave hereafter "so imported into this Commonwealth."[13]

In conjunction with protests against the African trade as inhumane and as promoting an "alarming" increase of slaves, Virginians enacted rigid laws to control blacks already in the colony. At the close of the colonial era, slaves and free blacks could not vote, bear arms, or testify at

11. Richmond *Enquirer,* October 25, 1831; Richmond *Constitutional Whig,* November 17, 1831.
12. Virginia Legislative Petitions, 1831–32, Virginia State Library, Richmond.
13. Journal of the Virginia House of Burgesses (1772), in James Curtis Ballagh, *A History of Slavery in Virginia* (Baltimore, 1902), 22; Virginia, *Journal, Acts and Proceedings of a Convention Held in the Commonwealth of Virginia, 1829–1830,* No. 3, p. 5; Hening (ed.), *Virginia Statutes at Large,* IX, 471–72.

trials involving whites. Slaves committing capital crimes were denied trial by jury. As starkest testimony to whites' distrust of blacks, any slave or free black convicted of "conspiring to rebel or make insurrection," or plotting murder, or administering "any medicine whatsoever" would "suffer death without benefit of clergy."[14] Whether plotting mass uprisings against all whites, or individual acts of violence against particular whites, slaves and free blacks, colonial Virginians assumed, were a hostile, dangerous population.

Although independence produced little change in laws for "effectual government" of slaves, the natural rights ideology of the American Revolution and religious equalitarianism of the concomitant Great Awakening did heighten Virginians' hostility to slavery itself. Increased antislavery sentiment in turn effected dramatic revision in the state's manumission policy. Colonial laws prohibited emancipation of slaves "except for some meritorious services, to be adjudged" by the governor and his council or, after 1777, by the legislature.[15] To encourage private manumissions, the general assembly in May, 1782, abrogated existent restrictions and instead authorized slaveholders to free any blacks under forty-five years of age, either by last will and testament or, during "his or her . . . lifetime," by "any . . . written instrument" of emancipation. The following year, the legislature freed all slaves who had served in the revolutionary army. Those who have "contributed towards the establishment of American liberty and independence," Virginia's 1783 act proclaimed, "should enjoy the blessings of freedom as a reward for their toils and labours."[16]

Imbued with ideals of freedom, Virginia slaveholders responded to the revised manumission policy with the most widespread emancipation of slaves in the state's antebellum period. Between 1782 and 1790, Virginia's free black population burgeoned from approximately 2,800 to 12,766. By 1800, free blacks numbered 20,124, and by 1810, 30,570. During this high-tide of private manumissions, free blacks thus increased more than tenfold, jumping from 4.2 percent of Virginia's entire black population in 1790 to 7.2 percent by 1810.[17] As the first slaveholding

14. Hening (ed.), *Virginia Statutes at Large, 1619–1792*, VI, 104–105.
15. Helen Catterall (ed.), *Judicial Cases Concerning American Slavery and the Negro* (Washington, D.C., 1926), I, 72.
16. Hening (ed.), *Virginia Statutes at Large*, XI, 39–40, 308–309.
17. U.S. Census Office, *Fifth Census*, Tables [10]-[13].

southern state to legitimize private antislavery action, Virginia led the way for similar voluntary manumission laws in upper South states from Delaware to North Carolina during the years 1782 to 1801.[18] Such policy not only sanctioned individual antislavery sentiment; equally crucial, it recognized masters' rights to dispose of private property at will. By authorizing slaveholders to effect emancipation, Virginia's 1782 manumission law at once satisfied Americans' zeal for liberty *and* for property, thereby resolving conflicts between rights of man and rights of property inherent in revolutionary ideology.

During this era of widespread private manumissions, more radical antislavery Virginians also urged state action to emancipate *all* Virginia slaves. As in the movement to facilitate individual manumissions, Quakers and Methodists led agitation for general emancipation. Throughout the 1780s and early 1790s, religious groups petitioned the general assembly to enact compulsory abolition. "Liberty," a 1786 petition proclaimed, "is the birthright of mankind, the right of every rational creature." Slavery was contrary both to principles of Christianity and of American democracy.[19]

Alarmed by widespread antislavery agitation, conservative "Southside" Virginians petitioned the general assembly in the 1780s to "utterly reject" all abolition petitions. Just as antislavery petitions appealed to Christianity and to natural-rights philosophy to urge emancipation, so opponents of emancipation looked to the Bible and to revolutionary ideology to justify slavery. Both the Old and New Testaments, "Southside" memorialists avowed, recognized ownership of slaves. "Sacred rights of property" affirmed by Viriginia's bill of rights further precluded legislative "wresting" of slaveholders' "most valuable and indispensable Article of . . . Property, Our Slaves." Legislative abolition not only contravened Christian and natural-rights doctrines; it was also, "Southsiders" insisted, inimical to the welfare of all Virginians, white and black. To emancipate a "vast Multitude" of "unpropertied, revengeful . . . Banditti" would result in "Rapes, Murders, and Outrages" against whites,

18. Winthrop D. Jordan, *White Over Black: American Attitudes Toward the Negro, 1550–1812* (Chapel Hill, 1968), 347.
19. Stephen B. Weeks, *Southern Quakers and Slavery* (Baltimore, 1896), 201–13; Russell, *The Free Negro in Virginia,* 57; Virginia Legislative Petitions, Frederick County, 1786, Virginia State Library, Richmond.

"Famine and Death" to blacks, and "final Ruin" to the commonwealth.[20]

At the same time that they denounced general emancipation, "Southside" conservatives similarly protested the "partial emancipation of Slaves" resulting from Virginia's liberal manumission policy. Already, petitioners declared in 1785, individual acts of emancipation had been "productive of a very great and growing evil." Many of the state's burgeoning free black population had "been guilty of Thefts and Outrages, Insolences and Violences, destructive to the Peace, Safety, and Happiness of Society." To curb further increase of this dangerous class, the general assembly had to "immediately and totally" repeal the 1782 act "empowering . . . Owners of slaves to liberate them."[21]

Neither petitions for legislative emancipation nor those against voluntary manumission altered Virginia's official posture toward slavery in the late eighteenth century. If legislators failed to effect abolition, they also refused to abrogate slaveholders' right to emancipate. Private manumissions continued unabated, producing ever larger numbers of free blacks, as Virginians carried out individual antislavery convictions but resisted legislative interference with slave property.

While Quakers and Methodists agitated for, and "Southside" slaveholders against, emancipation in the late eighteenth century, several prominent Virginians formulated specific schemes to rid the commonwealth of slaves. As early as 1779, Thomas Jefferson, Edmund Pendleton, and George Wythe, as members of a committee to revise and codify state laws, had drafted an amendment to a "Bill concerning Slaves" providing for the emancipation and eventual colonization of all Virginia slaves born after a certain date.[22] The committee intended to introduce this *post-nati* emancipation plan to the general assembly but ultimately decided to withhold it. Public opinion, Jefferson explained, years later, "would not yet bear the proposition."[23]

More audacious in proposing general emancipation was Jefferson's friend and contemporary, St. George Tucker. Born in Bermuda in 1752, Tucker had come to Virginia before the Revolution to study philosophy and law at William and Mary College. He settled in Williamsburg and,

20. Frederika Teute Schmidt and Barbara Ripel Wilhelm, "Early Proslavery Petitions in Virginia," *William and Mary Quarterly,* XXX (1973), 138–41.

21. *Ibid.*, 138, 140.

22. Julian P. Boyd (ed.), *The Papers of Thomas Jefferson* (Princeton, N.J., 1950), II, 470–72.

23. Ford (ed.), *The Writings of Thomas Jefferson,* I, 67–68.

after the war, became a judge of the general court, a distinguished professor of law at William and Mary, and, finally, judge of the federal circuit court of Virginia.[24]

Tucker's desire to rid Virginia of slavery prompted him to inquire as to how "our sister State," Massachusetts, had accomplished abolition. In a January, 1795, letter to Jeremy Belknap, secretary of the Massachusetts Historical Society, Tucker noted that "as soon as the Revolution took place," Virginia prohibited "importation of slaves" and permitted "voluntary emancipation of them by their masters." Although the state had initiated such steps to partially "eradicate" slavery, the William and Mary professor however lamented, "difficulties" involved in "wholly exterminat[ing] . . . the evil" had inhibited introduction "in the legislature" of a "general emancipation" plan. He hoped that Virginia might "learn" from the "example" of Massachusetts "what methods are most likely to succeed" in abolishing slavery.[25] Belknap's reply convinced Tucker that the two states faced radically different circumstances. Whereas the ratio of slaves to whites in Massachusetts was, at most, one to forty, in Virginia the ratio was nearly two to three. Equally difficult, the huge majority of slaves lived in the Tidewater and Piedmont. East Virginia slaveholders would thus "almost exclusively . . . bear . . . the dangers and inconveniences of any experiment" in general emancipation, as well as a disproportionate "diminution of property."

Underlying dilemmas of sheer numbers of Virginia slaves and their disparate sectional concentration was the formidable stumbling block of race. If, as Belknap had reported, Negrophobia was "discernable" in Massachusetts with its "very small" slave population, "how much stronger" must "this prejudice" be in Virginia. Here, "every white man felt himself born to tyrannize" and regarded blacks "as of no more importance than . . . brute cattle." To banish such "deep-rooted, nay, almost innate prejudices," Tucker admitted, was "perhaps, beyond the power of human nature to accomplish." Tucker himself hesitated to affirm black's innate inferiority. Yet like antislavery Virginians of his own and later generations, the William and Mary professor assumed that "general opinion" of blacks' "mental inferiority" and "aversion" to their color precluded a

24. Percy W. Turrentine, "The Life and Works of Nathaniel Beverly Tucker" (Ph.D. dissertation, Harvard University, 1950), 32–41.
25. St. George Tucker, "Queries Relating to Slavery in Massachusetts," in *Collections of the Massachusetts Historical Society*, Series 5, III (1877), 379–80.

harmonious, biracial society. "If it be true," Tucker theorized, "that either nature or long habit have depraved their faculties so as to render them, in their present state, an inferior order of beings, may not an attempt to elevate" blacks "depress" whites? Even more convulsive, "full incorporation" of freedmen might "generate" racial warfare ending in "extermination" of one or the other race.[26]

Tucker's association of emancipation with racial amalgamation and racial violence typified the posture of both Virginia abolitionists and Virginia conservatives throughout the antebellum period. Although he opposed incorporation of emancipated slaves, Tucker, however, differed from most Virginia abolitionists in also opposing compulsory colonization of freedmen, whether within or without the United States. "Mr. Jefferson," he noted, proposed forcible deportation of blacks to resolve racial dilemmas of emancipation. Such proposal notwithstanding, to remove the almost three hundred thousand Virginia slaves, Tucker insisted, was an "undertaking" too great and costly for either the state or federal government. Colonization was not only impracticable; it was also inhumane. Blacks, ill-prepared for responsibilities of freedom, would suffer "hardships" and "destruction" in unfamiliar lands. "If humanity plead for their emancipation," Tucker contended, "it pleads more strongly against colonization."[27]

If blacks could be neither incorporated nor deported, what course could be pursued? A "large majority" of Virginia slaveholders, Tucker held, would "cheerfully concur in any feasible plan" of abolition. In a third letter to Belknap, the optimistic professor outlined a proposal for gradual emancipation in Virginia, which, he hoped, would lay the "foundation of universal freedom" in the United States.[28] An expanded version of Tucker's plan, *A Dissertation on Slavery: With a Proposal for the Gradual Abolition of It, in the State of Virginia*, appeared in 1796.

"America," Tucker began, "hath been the land of promise to Europeans," but the "Vail of death to millions of the wretched sons of Africa. . . . Whilst we were offering up vows at the shrine of Liberty," proclaiming that "all men are by nature *equally free* and *independent* . . . we were imposing upon our fellow men, who differ in complexion . . . a

26. *Ibid.*, 405–406, 407–408.
27. *Ibid.*, 407–408.
28. *Ibid.*, 418.

slavery ten thousand times more cruel" than British tyranny. "Surely it is time," he urged, to transcend that "partial system of morality which confines rights and injuries to particular complexions." Not just republican principles, but also the "safety and security" of slaveholders, require removal of this "stigma." Already, Tucker acknowledged, the enormity of Virginia's slave population made emancipation a difficult, dangerous undertaking. Yet if Virginia now had three hundred thousand slaves, by 1830 the number would double. In one hundred years, there would be two million. Unless Virginians began at once to abolish slavery, he warned, they would entail an ineradicable "curse" upon future generations. But although the magnitude of slavery necessitated present action, at the same time it prohibited immediate emancipation. As the "recent history of the French West Indies exhibits," Tucker alluded to ongoing slave rebellion in St. Domingo, "to turn loose a numerous . . . and enraged" horde of blacks would endanger white Virginians. Forcible deportation, conversely, would jeopardize the welfare of blacks.[29]

As a viable "middle course," Tucker proposed gradual emancipation and voluntary removal. Every female slave born after a certain date would be emancipated, and freedom transmitted to her male and female offspring. As compensation to slaveholders for costs of upbringing, emancipated blacks would serve their former masters until the age of twenty-eight. At that time, each freedman would receive twenty dollars, two suits of clothes, a hat, a pair of shoes, and two blankets. Having provided blacks freedom, money, and clothing as the first stage of his abolition scheme, Tucker then proposed to *encourage* their emigration from Virginia. Let us, he advised white Virginians, prohibit freedmen from holding public office; from voting; from keeping or bearing arms; from marrying whites; from serving as jurors or witnesses in cases involving whites; from becoming lawyers, executors, or trustees; and from owning land. Moreover, as long as they remain in the state, compel them to labor, lest they become idle, degraded "banditti." Such harsh political, economic, and social proscriptions, the Williamsburg professor admitted, "may appear to savour strongly of prejudice." But given the virulent Negrophobia of whites, any practicable abolition must include removal of emancipated slaves. He proposed to induce blacks to seek

29. St. George Tucker, *A Dissertation on Slavery with a Proposal for the Gradual Abolition of It, in the State of Virginia* (Philadelphia, 1796), 7–8, 96, 103, 77, 82–85.

happiness in more "congenial," unsettled territories of Louisiana and Florida. "Voluntary" emigration would eliminate a major stumbling block to general emancipation.[30]

Race was not the only obstacle to abolition of slavery in Virginia, for emancipation also involved property rights. Slaveholders who viewed blacks as part of the "brute creation," Tucker recognized, would contend that they "possess a *property* in an *unborn* child." Those who denied that their "fellow creatures" were "by nature *free,* and *equal*" would demand full compensation for emancipated slaves.[31] Respect for private property, Tucker conceded, was as inherent to Virginians as antipathy to blacks. Slaves' status as both persons and property dramatized, in its starkest degree, the incongruity between revolutionary ideals of liberty on the one hand, and property on the other.

Tucker's "solution" to racial dilemmas of emancipation involved uncompromising repression of freedmen. Provisions barring newly freed blacks from owning land and compelling them to work were harsher than the existent proscription of free blacks. Reducing freedmen to a state of *de facto* slavery, Tucker believed, would prompt them to leave Virginia. Such "solution" differed little from the compulsory colonization that Tucker decried. Each assumed that removal of blacks was a *sine qua non* of emancipation.

If Tucker "solved" the dilemma of what to do with Virginia's emancipated slaves, he offered no solution to the similarly crucial issue of compensation. Slaveholding Virginians, he conceded, could not be compelled to surrender private property. He could only hope, the idealistic professor avowed, that the "voice of reason, justice and humanity" would someday triumph over slaveholders' "sordid avarice" and "unfeeling tyranny." Then masters who now opposed uncompensated, *post-nati* emancipation would recognize that property rights to present slaves "cannot extend to those *not in being.* . . . No man," Tucker concluded, "can in reality be *deprived* of what he doth not possess."[32]

Tucker's emancipation proposal required the ascendancy of Enlightenment values among Virginia slaveholders, the subordination of property rights to human rights. Whereas uncompromising 1832 Vir-

30. *Ibid.,* 88–93.
31. *Ibid.,* 94–95.
32. *Ibid.,* 95.

ginia abolitionists would urge legislative confiscation of *post-nati* slaves, Tucker looked instead to slaveholders' voluntary surrender of future off-spring to accomplish abolition. Given the acknowledged Negrophobia of Virginia society—whites' repression of free blacks, their view of slaves as "brute cattle"—such reliance on the "voice of reason, justice, and humanity" seems unrealistic, naïve. Moreover, given Americans' deep-rooted attachment to private property, to anticipate slaveholders' general acceptance of uncompensated emancipation seems similarly utopian. Amid the widespread individual manumissions following the 1782 act, however, perhaps Tucker could expect a "large majority" of Virginia slaveholders to "cheerfully concur" in his antislavery scheme. Yet even Tucker could not wholly transcend that "partial system of morality which confines rights" to whites and "injuries" to blacks. For Tucker's general emancipation, like Virginia's 1782 manumission policy, rested ultimately on white men's will. The initial step—emancipation—required slaveholders' consent, thereby affirming masters' rights to control blacks' destiny. The second step—removal of freedmen—likewise assumed white men's "rights" to impose such harsh "injuries" on blacks as to compel their emigration from Virginia. Voluntarism applied only to whites, coercion only to blacks.

Tucker dedicated his *Dissertation on Slavery* to the Virginia General Assembly, "to whom it belongs to decide upon the expediency and practicability" of gradual abolition. He sent copies to both houses in November, 1796, with the request that his emancipation plan be presented in the "manner deemed most respectful to the honourable body." The house tabled the proposal without discussion. The senate thanked Tucker for his *Dissertation* and expressed the hope that some day "Liberty in our country shall be inseparable from life." Legislative response rested with this "civil acknowledgement."[33]

In a despondent letter to Belknap early in 1797, Tucker confessed he had misjudged Virginia public opinion. Opposition to abolition was more virulent than he had imagined. No legislator had even read his proposal; "nobody could explain its contents." Slaveholders' self-interest

33. St. George Tucker to the Speaker of the Senate of Virginia, November 30, 1796, in Tucker-Coleman Papers, Earl Gregg Swem Library, William and Mary College; Ludwell Lee to St. George Tucker, December 5, 1796, in Mary H. Coleman (ed.), *Virginia Silhouettes: Contemporary Letters Concerning Negro Slavery in the State of Virginia* (Richmond, 1934), 4–5; Tucker, "Queries Relating to Slavery in Massachusetts," 428.

had silenced the Enlightenment "voice of reason," and property rights had vanquished human rights. Perhaps one day, Tucker surmised, "actual suffering . . . will open the oppressors' eyes" to the evils of slavery. "Till that happens," he had abandoned hope of effecting emancipation.[34] In forwarding his comprehensive emancipation plan to the general assembly, Professor Tucker pursued a bolder course toward slavery than most Virginians of his generation. Likewise, in publicly urging abolition, he displayed greater optimism regarding Virginians' desire for present antislavery action. With the refusal of both house and senate to discuss his proposal, however, Tucker reluctantly accepted Thomas Jefferson's view that public opinion would not yet tolerate general emancipation.

Thomas Jefferson never emulated his friend St. George Tucker in proposing emancipation to the Virginia legislature. Unlike Tucker, whose career as professor-judge allowed a relative aloofness from political affairs, Jefferson was at the center of revolutionary politics. Such role, the Virginia statesman firmly believed, precluded public endorsement of, or active participation in, antislavery activities. "I have most carefully avoided every public act or manifestation on that subject," Jefferson explained, upon refusing to endorse an antislavery poem in 1805. "Subscription" to an abolitionist tract such as this would not only be "injurious" to its cause but, more importantly, would "lessen my powers of doing . . . good in the other great relations in which I stand to the publick. . . . Should an occasion ever occur in which I can interpose with decisive effect, I shall certainly know & do my duty with promptitude & zeal."[35] For Jefferson and fellow Founding Fathers, establishment of the new nation—of a republic for white men—was always of greater priority than the persistent, but subordinate, goal of freedom for blacks.

Despite a reluctance to publicly promote emancipation, Jefferson remained a lifelong opponent of slavery and thus dramatized—perhaps more than any other Virginian of his times—the tension between revolutionary ideas and the realities of Negro bondage. As author of America's Declaration of Independence, Jefferson proclaimed the "inalienable rights" of all men to "life, liberty, and the pursuit of happiness." Yet as owner of nearly ten thousand acres of land in Virginia's western Piedmont, he depended on the labor of more than 150 slaves. The "tranquil

34. Tucker, "Queries Relating to Slavery in Massachusetts," 428.
35. Ford (ed.), *The Writings of Thomas Jefferson,* VIII, 351–52.

pursuits" of science, philosophy, and the arts, which Jefferson professed "my supreme delight"; his fondness for fine wines, fancy clothes, French cuisine, purebred horses; his cultivated life as a Virginia planter-aristocrat all rested on slavery. During Jefferson's frequent absences from Virginia, field slaves worked under supervision of an overseer cultivating tobacco and other crops which were the source of the master's wealth. Jefferson also owned numerous household slaves, coachmen, grooms, and skilled black artisans involved in building and maintaining the plantation community. A French nobleman, visiting Monticello in June, 1796, noted Jefferson's reliance on slaves for all aspects of plantation life. "As he can not expect any assistance from the two small neighboring towns," the Frenchman observed, "every article is made on his farm: his negroes are cabinetmakers, carpenters, masons, bricklayers, smiths, etc. The children he employs in a nail factory, which yields already a considerable profit. The young and old negresses spin . . . the clothing of the rest." Jefferson, the French visitor commented, was a kind, indulgent master. "His negroes are nourished, clothed, and treated as well as white servants could be."[36]

Jefferson's elegant life-style necessitated large expenditures for books, wines, foods, clothes. At the same time, the declining fertility of Monticello's once-rich soil, due partly, perhaps, to frequent reliance on overseers, meant lower agricultural profits. "Ten years' abandonment" of his plantations to the "ravages of overseers," Jefferson lamented upon his return to Monticello in 1794, had produced a "degree of degradation far beyond what I had expected." More than a decade later, burdened with accumulating debts, Jefferson turned over financial-farm management to his grandson, Thomas Jefferson Randolph. "I am indeed an unskillful manager of my farms," he wrote his son-in-law in 1816, "and sensible of this from its effects . . . I have ceded the entire direction . . . to better hands."[37]

Dwindling income did not affect Jefferson's taste for aristocratic living, and such persistent self-indulgence had deleterious consequences for Monticello's blacks. At times, mounting expenses forced Jefferson to hire out or to sell some of his slaves. Although he disliked both practices as subjecting slaves to possible "ill usage" by less benevolent masters,

36. Sarah Randolph, *The Domestic Life of Thomas Jefferson* (New York, 1871), 323, 238.
37. *Ibid.*, 229, 364.

Jefferson preferred hiring. "Hiring," he asserted, "will be temporary only," whereas selling entailed slaves' permanent departure from the familial environs of Monticello. Another factor, more practical than humanitarian concern for blacks' welfare, governed Jefferson's reluctance to sell his slaves; he needed their labor to pay "debts due from the estate."[38]

In the end, then, despite his inveterate hostility to slavery, Jefferson lived surrounded by slaves, slaves he could not afford to emancipate either during his lifetime or by last will and testament. As a slaveholding Virginia aristocrat, he fell far short of the Enlightenment ideals he espoused. Indeed, in failing to act on private antislavery convictions, Jefferson fell far short of many fellow Virginia planters who, consistent with the state's liberal manumission policy, voluntarily freed their slaves.

If Jefferson was less bold than Tucker in proposing general emancipation, and less resolute than other antislavery planters in manumitting his own slaves, such shortcomings do not, as several recent studies have argued, mean that Jefferson's abolitionism was inconsequential.[39] On the contrary, his published and private writings, as well as the specific legislation he did introduce, all indicate his lifelong opposition to slavery and his anticipation of its "ultimate extinction" both in Virginia and in the nation.

Jefferson first openly attacked slavery in his 1774 pamphlet, *A Summary View of the Rights of British America*. There, the thirty-one-year-old Virginia patriot denounced the African slave trade as contrary to the natural rights of man and to colonists' desire to abolish slavery in America. In his draft of the Declaration of Independence two years later, Jefferson again decried the African trade. Due to protests from South Carolina and Georgia, however, the Continental Congress expunged this antislavery clause. Primarily concerned with securing the allegiance of all states to the newly launched American republic, Jefferson acquiesced in such amendment of his Declaration.[40] His efforts to incorporate antislavery provisions in his own state's constitution met similar rebuff. Not

38. Ford (ed.), *The Writings of Thomas Jefferson*, IV, 416–18.
39. Recent studies affirming Jefferson's ambivalence toward slavery include Robert McColley, *Slavery and Jeffersonian Virginia* (Urbana, 1964); David Brion Davis, *The Problem of Slavery in the Age of Revolution, 1770–1823* (Ithaca, N.Y., 1975); and John Chester Miller, *The Wolf by the Ears: Thomas Jefferson and Slavery* (New York, 1977).
40. Miller, *The Wolf by the Ears*, 6–17.

long after adoption of the revised Declaration of Independence, the 1776 Virginia convention rejected Jefferson's constitutional draft barring further importation of African slaves into the commonwealth. Although the legislature prohibited the practice in 1778, such provision against the foreign slave trade never became part of the Virginia Constitution as Jefferson had proposed.

In the summer of 1783, Jefferson, expecting the general assembly to call a convention to reform Virginia's government, drafted another constitution. This time his antislavery proposals went beyond prohibition of "any more" slave importations to include abolition of slavery itself. Published as an appendix to *Notes on the State of Virginia* in 1785, Jefferson's constitution provided for emancipation of all slaves born in Virginia after December 21, 1800.[41] At the same time that he urged equal representation and suffrage for white men, then, the master of Monticello also urged liberty for *post-nati* blacks. In rejecting the convention bill, the Virginia legislature once more rebuffed Jefferson's efforts to implement, at least in part, the ideals of the American Revolution.

Despite legislative resistance, Jefferson never abandoned the hope, and expectation, that Virginia would someday abolish slavery. Indeed, Jefferson, and contemporaries like St. George Tucker and James Madison, assumed that their beloved commonwealth would be the first southern state to initiate emancipation. "In Maryland," Jefferson wrote in 1785 while serving as minister to France, "I do not find such a disposition" to act against slavery "as in Virginia." Virginia "is the next state to which we may turn our eyes for the . . . spectacle of justice in conflict with avarice & oppression: a conflict wherein the sacred side is gaining daily recruits."[42]

Like antislavery Virginians of his own and future generations, Jefferson's dream of abolition did not include incorporation of emancipated blacks. In *Notes on the State of Virginia*, which contained Jefferson's only published proposal for abolition during his lifetime, the realistic Virginian affirmed that viable *post-nati* emancipation required removal of freedmen "beyond the reach of mixture." "Deep-rooted prejudices" against blacks' color, as well as widely held assumptions of blacks' mental inferiority, Jefferson believed, would forever prevent their acceptance

41. Jefferson, *Notes on the State of Virginia*, 209, 214, 286–87.
42. Ford (ed.), *The Writings of Thomas Jefferson*, IV, 82–83.

as equals in white society. And at the same time that he wished to "vindicate the liberty of human nature," Jefferson shared, to some degree, the Negrophobia of contemporary white Virginians. An ineradicable "difference of color" between whites and blacks, he maintained, accounted for a "greater or less share of beauty in the two races." Jefferson left no doubts as to which "color" he found "superior." "Are not the fine mixtures of red and white," he avowed, "preferable to that eternal monotony . . . that immovable veil of black which covers the emotions of the other race?"[43]

Convinced of blacks' inferior "beauty," Jefferson was less resolute as to their mental inferiority. Like his friend St. George Tucker, he hesitated to assert *innate* deficiencies in blacks' "faculties of reason and imagination." In Virginia, the master of Monticello acknowledged, blacks appeared "much inferior" to whites "in reason," and "dull, tasteless, and anomalous . . . in imagination." Yet "great allowances" must be made for "differences of condition, of education, of conversation, of the sphere in which they [blacks] move." On balance, however, although Jefferson recognized slavery's deleterious influences on blacks' intellectual development, he surmised, "as a suspicion only," that blacks "perhaps" were "inferior" to whites "in the endowments of . . . mind." Such "conjecture," he reiterated, "must be hazarded with great diffidence" and, before being verified, required "further observation."[44]

Jefferson never abandoned his "suspicion" of blacks' intellectual inferiority. Nor did this suspicion ever give way to "fixed opinion." As regards the "grade of understanding" allotted blacks "by nature," he wrote twenty-five years after publication of *Notes on the State of Virginia,* "it was impossible for doubt to have been more tenderly or hesitatingly expressed. . . . Nothing was or is farther from my intentions, than to enlist myself as the champion of a fixed opinion, where I have only expressed a doubt." "Whatever be their degree of talent," Jefferson once more alluded to his hopes for blacks' liberty, "it is no measure of their rights."[45] Jefferson might question blacks' equality, but not their right to freedom.

Whites' racial prejudices were not the only stumbling block to incorporation of freedmen. As a consequence of "injuries . . . sustained" un-

43. Jefferson, *Notes on the State of Virginia,* 143, 138.
44. *Ibid.,* 139–40, 143.
45. Ford (ed.), *The Writings of Thomas Jefferson,* IX, 262, 246–47.

der slavery, Jefferson believed blacks also harbored ineradicable resentments toward whites. With emancipation, "new provocations" would combine with "ten thousand recollections" of past injustices to intensify blacks' hatred of whites. In Virginia, then, mutual antagonisms between the races would forever preclude a harmonious, biracial society. Any attempt to incorporate freedmen would convulse society and "probably . . . end" in "extermination of . . . one or the other race." Peaceful abolition of slavery, Jefferson accordingly maintained in *Notes on the State of Virginia* and in all subsequent writings on emancipation, required an unprecedented "second effort." Upon reaching a "certain age"—females eighteen, males twenty-one—*post-nati* Virginia slaves "should be colonized" in a "proper place." Already skilled in "tillage, arts, or sciences," freedmen should be "sent out" with "arms," household and handicraft implements, "domestic animals," and other supplies necessary to a "free and independent people." Virginia would protect this fledgling colony until blacks had "acquired strength" to defend themselves. At the same time, the state would encourage immigration of an "equal number of white inhabitants" to replace deported blacks.[46]

Historians who attribute Jefferson's failure to manumit his slaves, and to introduce emancipation legislation, to half-hearted abolitionism further attribute his compulsory colonization plan to callous disregard of blacks' welfare. Jefferson, in contrast, assumed that *post-nati* emancipation and colonization would benefit all Virginians, white and black. Convinced of the incompatibility of the two races, he looked to gradual removal of freedmen to avoid widespread social convulsions. Gradual immigration of white laborers to east Virginia would prevent similar economic dislocations associated with general emancipation and, concomitantly, accomplish the homogeneous white society Jefferson envisioned. Over the years, then, Virginia would be rid of slavery *and* of blacks. Of corresponding concern to Jefferson, blacks would also be rid of the twin shackles of slavery *and* of white racism. Colonized in a "proper place," blacks would enjoy not just liberty, but an equality forever denied them in Negrophobic Virginia.

Colonization to Jefferson and other Virginia emancipators of the revolutionary period was thus, at once, a realistic response to white men's racial prejudices and an idealistic venture to achieve greater human dig-

46. Jefferson, *Notes on the State of Virginia*, 137–38, 143.

nity and opportunity for blacks. In urging separate societies for the two races, Jefferson did not transcend the Negrophobia of his slaveholding Virginia community—or of the entire American nation. He did, however, remain dedicated to universal freedom. Colonization seemed the only viable means of fulfilling such dream for blacks. For without provisions for removal of freedmen, Jefferson foresaw, white Virginians would never effect abolition. Applauding the "gradual emancipation" principles of the newly established American Colonization Society, Jefferson, in 1817, termed colonization the "corner stone" of the "complete retirement" of blacks from Virginia and their realization of "freedom and safety . . . elsewhere." Such "proposition," the aging patriarch declared, would be "equally desirable and welcome to us as to them."[47]

For the rest of his long life, Jefferson privately advanced the *post-nati* emancipation and colonization plan publicly outlined in *Notes on the State of Virginia.* "The only practicable plan I could ever devise," he wrote thirty years later, "is stated under the 14th quaere of the Notes on Virginia, and it is still the one most sound in my judgment." Although Jefferson would not again promulgate his antislavery views, he persistently urged more youthful Americans to carry out peaceful abolition "in the march of time." Just as the revolutionary generation had forged a republic for whites, so America's "younger generation," nurtured in "principles of liberty," must accomplish freedom for blacks. "This enterprise," Jefferson wrote the young Virginian Edward Coles in 1814, "is for the young; for those who can follow it up, and bear it through to its consummation." Virginia's youth had not yet "made . . . the progress I had hoped" toward emancipation, and thus Coles's "solitary voice" amidst the "general silence" on slavery was most "welcome." He advised the western Piedmont slaveowner to "come forward in the public councils" of Virginia to "inculcate" antislavery principles "softly but steadily. . . . Associate others in your labors," and when abolition had gained sufficient support, "press the proposition perseveringly until its accomplishment. It is an encouraging observation," the Enlightenment statesman affirmed, "that no good measure was ever proposed, which, if duly pursued, failed to prevail in the end."[48]

Jefferson's advice to Edward Coles crystallized the author's inveterate

47. Ford (ed.), *The Writings of Thomas Jefferson,* X, 76–77.
48. *Ibid.,* IX, 515–16, 477–79.

posture toward emancipation. To peacefully abolish slavery in a state like Virginia, where the "disease . . . is incorporated with the whole system," Jefferson repeatedly avowed, "requires time, patience, and perseverance." The "revolution in public opinion which this cause requires is not to be expected in a day, or perhaps in an age. . . . There is a snail-paced gait for the advance of new ideas on the general mind, under which we must acquiesce." Ill-timed efforts to hasten emancipation would only "rivet still closer the chains of bondage, and retard the moment of delivery" for oppressed blacks. Jefferson elaborated on his gradualist approach to emancipation in an 1815 letter to David Barrow. "Unhappily," the antislavery Virginian acknowledged, the plan of *post-nati* emancipation and colonization outlined in *Notes on Virginia* involved "long and difficult preparation" for slaveowners and slaves. "By reflection, and . . . by . . . energies of conscience," masters must first transcend "self-interest" and acknowledge "rights of others." Once "justice" so vanquished "avarice," and masters emancipated *post-nati* slaves, freedmen must then be "prepared . . . for self-government and for the honest pursuits of industry and social duty."[49]

As an exponent of Enlightenment faith in the inevitability of progress, in man's ever advancing moral sense, Jefferson most often anticipated that slaveholders would someday favor emancipation. Accompanying his affirmation of human benevolence, however, was a portentous warning. Black men's liberty, Jefferson assumed, was inevitable. "Nothing is more certainly written in the book of fate than that these people are to be free. . . . The hour of emancipation is advancing, in the march of time. . . . It will come. . . . It is still in our power to direct the process of emancipation and deportation peaceably and in . . . slow degree," he asserted in his 1821 *Autobiography*. "If, on the contrary," America waited too long, Jefferson cautioned that emancipation would not be gradual and peaceful, but sudden and violent. While he extolled the "hour" of peaceful emancipation, he "shuddered" at the foreseen alternative. Successive slave uprisings in St. Domingo, where blacks gained their freedom by massacring whites, persistently intruded on Jefferson's abolitionist dream and lent increased urgency to his "admonition" that the nation "rise and be doing."[50]

49. *Ibid.*, 515–16, 168–69; IV, 184–85; IX, 515–16.
50. *Ibid.*, I, 68; X, 292.

If Jefferson palled at the specter of blacks, not whites, "direct[ing] the process of emancipation," he likewise anguished over the prospect of slavery dissolving his beloved republic. Such prospect loomed large during the years 1819–1821, as the slaveholding South contested the non-slaveholding North over admission of Missouri to the Union. As Jefferson confronted the shattering of the republic his generation had struggled to create, concern for the Union more strongly than ever outweighed his antislavery convictions. Defending the South's right to extend Negro bondage to Missouri, the Virginia patriarch further resurrected the time-worn theory that extension of slavery would promote not only blacks' "happiness," but also abolition. Because their financial loss would be less, small slaveholders would more likely emancipate future offspring than masters owning large numbers of blacks.[51]

Jefferson's resurrection of the dubious "diffusion theory" of slavery evidenced a strained attempt to reconcile two increasingly irreconcilable objects—preservation of the Union and gradual abolition of slavery. Yet even as Jefferson defended Missouri's admission to the Union as a slave state, he more fervently hoped the "threatening" crisis would galvanize the nation to abolish slavery. "Amidst this prospect of evil," Jefferson wrote Joseph Gallatin in December, 1820, "I am glad to see one good effect. It has brought the necessity of some plan of general emancipation and deportation more home to the minds of our people than it has ever been before." Jefferson was particularly glad to report that, in Virginia, "our governor has ventured to propose" abolition to the 1820–1821 general assembly. "This will probably not be acted on at this time," he informed Gallatin, "nor would it be effectual." To devote only "one-third of the revenue of the state" to emancipation-colonization, as Jefferson's son-in-law, Governor Thomas Mann Randolph had suggested, "would not reach one-tenth of the annual increase" of Virginia's slaves. "My proposition," Jefferson briefly described his *post-nati* emancipation-deportation scheme, would appropriate state revenue, "charitable contributions," and federal funds. "Proceeds of the land office," he concluded, would be "quite sufficient" to transport Virginia freedmen to St. Domingo at a "proper age."[52]

51. *Ibid.*, X, 158.
52. *Ibid.*, 177–78.

Contrary to such recent studies as John C. Miller's *The Wolf by the Ears*, then, the Missouri crisis did not transform Jefferson from an opponent of slavery to an "orthodox," proslavery southerner bent on perpetuation and expansion of the "peculiar institution." Instead, as the sectional conflict over slavery threatened to destroy the republic, the revolutionary patriarch pronounced emancipation-colonization a more urgent necessity. The "firebell in the night" must not herald the final "knell of the Union." It must rekindle America's commitment to gradual abolition.

Jefferson's 1824 letter to Jared Sparks, three years after the Missouri crisis, further reveals the aging Virginian's continued support of the antislavery plan sketched in his 1785 *Notes on the State of Virginia*. In elaborating on how emancipation-colonization might be effected, Jefferson again looked to slaveholders' "voluntary surrenders" of *post-nati* blacks as the initial step. Since the "estimated value of new-born" slaves was "so low, (say twelve dollars and fifty cents)," Jefferson wrote Sparks, masters would "probably" yield their property "gratis." Voluntary emancipations would avoid "violation of private right" and, by eliminating "six hundred millions of dollars" in compensation, would leave "only the expense" of raising and removing *post-nati* slaves.[53]

Having eliminated the stumbling block of property rights, Jefferson then more fully described the colonization scheme he had only alluded to in his December, 1820, letter to Gallatin. The federal government, Jefferson wrote Sparks, could appropriate funds from sale of public lands, ceded mostly by slave states, to meet costs of "nurture" and transportation. Such revenue was more than "sufficient" to finance bringing up *post-nati* slaves with their mothers "a few years"; teaching them "industrious occupations" as wards of the state; and, at a "proper age," deporting them beyond the United States. Estimating the "whole annual increase" of slaves in America to be sixty thousand, fifty vessels could carry off that number "every year" whereas older blacks, still enslaved, would "die off in the ordinary course of nature." This gradual process, Jefferson affirmed, would rid the nation of both slavery and blacks in half a century. As to a "particular asylum" for freedmen, Jefferson at the end of his life preferred St. Domingo (Haiti) to Africa. Not only would

53. *Ibid.*, 289–93. All further quotes from Jefferson's 1824 letter are from this source.

costs of transporting blacks to nearby St. Domingo be considerably less; but the "country and climate" also seemed more "friendly to human life and happiness." The population of this newly independent black republic, Jefferson further remarked, was "of that color only." Geographically, politically, socially, St. Domingo seemed a congenial locale for emancipated American slaves to establish themselves as a "free and independent people."

Emancipation-colonization of future offspring of the South's "million and a half" slaves, Jefferson thus insisted in his final summation on slavery, was still within white Americans' "control." His proposal for large-scale federal participation in abolition, he recognized, "involves some constitutional scruples." So, too, separation of slave children "from their mothers . . . would produce some scruples of humanity." Yet in each instance, Jefferson believed that the "object" to be realized—freedom for all *post-nati* blacks from the oppressions of slavery and white racism— "justified . . . amendment of the constitution, the whole length necessary," as well as dissolution of present slave families. But, the aged patriarch again admonished, if America's younger generation were to "enjoy a beatitude forbidden my age," the nation must begin the process of gradual emancipation at once, lest slaves multiply so rapidly as to preclude peaceful accomplishment of Jefferson's plan.

Just as Jefferson's writings reveal a lifelong commitment to emancipation, so various acts he initiated or supported evidence his desire to doom slavery to "ultimate extinction." As William W. Freehling argues in his article, "The Founding Fathers and Slavery,"[54] both the Northwest Ordinance of 1787 and congressional abolition of the African slave trade in 1808 weakened slavery's capacity to survive in nineteenth-century America. The first, outlawing Negro bondage in territories north of the Ohio and east of the Mississippi rivers after 1800, considerably limited slavery's geographic domain. As one of Virginia's delegates to the Continental Congress in 1784, Jefferson had drafted a more radical ordinance, prohibiting slavery in *all* territories, north *and* south of the Ohio River. Had the Congress adopted Jefferson's version, slavery would have been outlawed not only in Indiana and Illinois, but also in Alabama and Mississippi. Jefferson, significantly, was the sole Virginia delegate—and one

54. William W. Freehling, "The Founding Fathers and Slavery," *American Historical Review*, LXXVII (1972), 81–93.

of only two southern delegates—to vote for such sweeping exclusion of slavery.[55] Even as the nation began, southerners overwhelmingly upheld their constitutional right to extend slavery to the national domain. Yet if Jefferson and his generation had to compromise to achieve sectional harmony, the half-way ban on slavery effected by the 1787 Northwest Ordinance made the institution "peculiar" to the South at the start of the nineteenth century and, accordingly, put the South at a disadvantage in the ensuing sectional contest for power.

Whereas the Northwest Ordinance circumscribed slavery's geographic boundaries, abolition of the African slave trade sharply curtailed importations of black laborers to the Deep South in the decades after 1808. Congressional prohibition of the African trade, effected during Jefferson's presidency, carried out the compromise enacted at the Constitutional Convention in 1787. Jefferson regarded outlawing of foreign slave importations as one of the major accomplishments of his presidency, a "long stride toward the inevitable abolition of slavery."[56] Jefferson's prognosis proved correct. Deprived of African slaves, Deep South planters would purchase ever larger numbers of blacks from border South states like Delaware, Maryland, and Virginia. Over the years, sale of blacks to the Deep South would reduce relative numbers of slaves in the border South. As percentages of slaves declined, loyalty to the "peculiar institution" also declined, ultimately prompting the border slave states of Delaware, Maryland, Kentucky, and Missouri to side with the free-soil Union rather than with the slaveholding Confederacy.[57] Amidst this final crisis over slavery, Virginia, like the nation, would split asunder, her vast Trans-Allegheny region joining the Union as the free-soil state of West Virginia, her other sections reluctantly joining the Confederacy. Both the Northwest Ordinance and abolition of the foreign slave trade, then, pushed slavery inexorably southward, fostering the Deep South's growing anxiety about border South commitment to slavery and, concomitantly, producing a sense of "claustrophobia" which drove more extremist southerners to secession.

Jefferson always believed his own words and deeds—like those of his revolutionary compatriots—would lead the nation slowly, but irre-

55. Miller, *The Wolf by the Ears*, 27–29.
56. *Ibid.*, 146.
57. Freehling, "The Founding Fathers and Slavery," 88–89.

sistibly, to emancipation. Although his generation did not accomplish this task, their insistence that slavery was an evil, and the partial steps they did take to undermine that evil, began the process that would end in black men's freedom. The inalienable right of all men to liberty proclaimed in the Declaration of Independence would become an ideal toward which the nation aspired in the decades after Jefferson's death. If slaveholders' moral sense ran aground on shoals of economic interest and sectional politics, the principle that slavery was morally wrong would become a cardinal tenet of northern society, at first of a small group of northern abolitionists and ultimately of leading northern politicians. The Republican party's crusade against slavery in the territories would link Jefferson's view of slavery as an evil with his racist vision of an American republic for white men. The conviction that slavery and democracy were, like blacks and whites, fundamentally incompatible would consummate Jefferson's dream of universal freedom, not gradually and peaceably as he had hoped, but suddenly and violently as he had feared.

Within his own Virginia, Jefferson's conviction that slavery was an evil to be abolished "in the march of time" would likewise persist throughout the antebellum era. In its most dramatic manifestation—the 1832 legislative debate on abolition—Jefferson's favorite grandson, Thomas Jefferson Randolph, would "come forward in the public councils" to propose a *post-nati* emancipation plan largely modeled on that of his beloved grandfather. Although legislators did not effect Randolph's scheme, the slavery issue would remain at the fore of state politics in post-1832 decades and lead, finally, to separation of the commonwealth. For both Jefferson's republic and his state, slavery was indeed a "firebell in the night," sounding the temporary "knell of the Union" and the perpetual "knell" of Virginia.

Jefferson's legacy on slavery includes numerous shortcomings, numerous inconsistencies. He urged voluntary emancipation of *post-nati* slaves but failed to free many of his own. He urged Virginia's "young men" to promote abolition but declined to use his own influence publicly to forward the antislavery cause. He so revered property rights as to preclude government confiscation of *post-nati* slaves, yet he expected slaveholders to subordinate their property interests to justice for blacks. And at the same time that he urged slaveholders to elevate human rights of blacks, he proposed forcible colonization of freedmen to achieve his ideal white republic. Yet the blots on Jefferson's antislavery slate—and on the antislavery slate of America's revolutionary generation—cannot obliterate the more powerful impact of both his words and, in several instances, his deeds on the later course of antebellum history. He would "not live to see" his antislavery sentiments "consummated," Jefferson wrote just two weeks before his death on July 4, 1826, but "they will not die with me." [58]

The specter of black insurrection that long troubled Jefferson's emancipationist dream was "brought home" in part to white Virginians even as the nineteenth century began. Late in August, 1800, Gabriel, a twenty-four-year-old slave blacksmith on Thomas Prosser's Henrico County plantation near Richmond, conspired with local blacks to attack the city at night, burn buildings, massacre whites, and seize arms and ammunition from the magazine and penitentiary. With Virginia's capital paralyzed and state officials, including Governor James Monroe, murdered, Gabriel and fellow insurgents would then lead a mass uprising of slaves throughout the surrounding countryside and in the nearby town of Petersburg "to fight the White people for Freedom." Slave informants and adverse weather foiled Gabriel's plot. At least two Henrico County slaves warned their master of impending revolt in time for Governor Monroe to call out local militia, alert nearby towns, place guards at the penitentiary, magazine, and capitol, and declare a state of siege. On the day of attack, torrential rains also washed out a strategic bridge, cutting off slaves' planned access to Richmond. [59]

Whites demanded prompt, rigorous reprisals against suspected slave insurgents, and in the immediate aftermath, large numbers of blacks from Henrico, Hanover, and Chesterfield counties were arrested and tried. About twenty slaves, found guilty of "conspiracy and insurrection," were hung at the Richmond gallows between mid-September and mid-October, 1800. Another twenty were acquitted or pardoned due to

58. Merrill D. Peterson, *Thomas Jefferson and the New Nation* (New York, 1970), 1001.
59. William P. Palmer, Sherwin McRae, and H. W. Flournoy (eds.), *Calendar of Virginia State Papers and Other Manuscripts Preserved in the Capitol at Richmond* (Richmond, 1890), IX, 140–47, 164–65, 134; Stanislaus M. Hamilton (ed.), *The Writings of James Monroe* (New York, 1903), III, 201–204, 239–41; 207, 234–35; Gerald W. Mullin, *Flight and Rebellion: Slave Resistance in Eighteenth-Century Virginia* (New York, 1972), 150–54.

insufficient evidence. The acknowledged leader, Gabriel, was captured aboard a schooner in Norfolk harbor after a month-long search. Brought to Richmond on September 27, tried on October 6, and convicted on October 7, the slave insurgent awaited execution in defiant silence. "He seemed to have made up his mind to die," Governor Monroe observed, "and to have resolved to say little on the subject of the conspiracy."[60]

Writing his friend, Thomas Jefferson, shortly after the aborted uprising, Monroe reported that testimony of suspected black rebels "clearly proved" a "plan of . . . insurrection . . . of considerable extent. . . . It is unquestionably the most serious and formidable [slave] conspiracy" against whites' lives and property Virginia has "ever known." Moved by such evidence and by widespread public alarm, the governor urged the general assembly to "weigh with profound attention this most unpleasant incident. . . . What has happened may occur again at any time, with more fatal consequences, unless suitable measures be taken to prevent it. Unhappily while this class of people exists among us," Monroe acknowledged, "we can never count with certainty on its tranquil submission. The fortunate issue of the late attempt should not lull us into repose."[61]

As an immediate response to the Gabriel conspiracy, the 1800–1801 general assembly provided for an armed guard of about one hundred men, stationed at the doors of the capitol building, to defend Richmond and its residents.[62] At subsequent sessions, legislators tightened laws governing Virginia's entire black population, slave and free. A January, 1804, act outlawed nighttime assemblages of slaves. "If not restrained," legislators resolved, the heretofore "common practice" of large gatherings of slaves "at meeting houses and places of religious worship, in the night . . . may be productive of considerable evil to the community."[63]

Hanging of rebel slaves, posting of armed guards at the capitol, rigid proscription of blacks—all represented, at most, short-run expedients to

60. Palmer, McRae, and Flournoy (eds)., *Calendar of Virginia State Papers*, IX, 140–44, 148–50, 154–58, 164; Herbert Aptheker, *American Negro Slave Revolts* (New York, 1963), 219–22; Hamilton (ed.), *The Writings of James Monroe*, III, 213.

61. Hamilton (ed.), *The Writings of James Monroe*, III, 208–209, 232.

62. Robert R. Howison, *A History of Virginia, From Its Discovery and Settlement by Europeans to the Present Time* (Richmond, 1848), II, 393.

63. Samuel Shepherd (ed.), *The Statutes at Large of Virginia, from October Session 1792, to December Session, 1806, Inclusive* (Richmond, 1836), III, 108.

dangers posed by Virginia's burgeoning black population. Confronted with the stark, if thwarted, reality of servile insurrection in their own capital, and with actual scenes of recurrent black uprisings on the island of St. Domingo, Virginians in the years after 1800 began to search for long-run, lasting solutions to their state's racial dilemmas.

Most Virginians prescribed the remedy of colonization. Late in December, 1800, the Virginia General Assembly, meeting behind closed doors, resolved that Governor James Monroe correspond with President Thomas Jefferson concerning purchase of territory outside Virginia "whither persons obnoxious to the laws or dangerous to the peace of society may be removed." Complying with such request, Monroe wrote Jefferson in June, 1801, as to the possibility of acquiring lands either in vacant western territory of the United States or "without the limits of the Union." The resolution of the Virginia legislature, Monroe informed his friend Jefferson, "was produced by the conspiracy of the slaves which took place in this city [Richmond] and neighborhood last year." The subject was "of great delicacy and importance," the governor stressed, "one which, in a peculiar degree, involves the future peace, tranquility, and happiness of the good people of this Commonwealth."[64]

In agreeing to cooperate with the Virginia General Assembly, President Jefferson indicated that the West Indies offered a more desirable colonization site than United States territory. Affirming his vision of an all-white American republic, Jefferson explained in his November, 1801, reply to Monroe, that a homogeneous population, "governed by similar laws," would someday cover the North American continent. He could not "contemplate with satisfaction, either blot or mixture in that surface." The United States, Jefferson, as always, anticipated, would in future years be rid of slavery and blacks. The West Indies, in contrast, were "inhabited already by a people of their own race and colour" and had "climates congenial with their natural constitution." Of all these islands, the president asserted, St. Domingo seemed the "most promising." Blacks there had established *de facto* sovereignty and "have organized themselves under regular laws and government." If Jefferson and fellow Virginians feared St. Domingo as promoting an insurrectionary

64. Philip Slaughter, *The Virginian History of African Colonization* (Richmond, 1855), 1–2.

spirit among Virginia slaves, they also heralded the emerging black republic as a congenial locale for colonizing Virginia blacks. "Africa," Jefferson concluded, "would offer a last and undoubted resort, if . . . others more desirable should fail us."[65]

As the 1801 Jefferson-Monroe correspondence illustrates, removal of insurgent slaves was Virginia's foremost priority just after Gabriel's conspiracy. By the following year, Monroe approvingly informed President Jefferson, colonization resolutions of the Virginia General Assembly "embraced . . . two descriptions of negroes." The first comprised slaves who committed "certain enumerated crimes." For those guilty of conspiracy and insurrection, the legislature "preferred" deportation to Africa, or to "Spanish or Portuguese settlements in South America." The second type of colonist, the governor continued, "respects free negroes and mulattoes, including those who may hereafter be emancipated. For these," the general assembly did not propose a "particular region or country." Colonization of Virginia's free blacks and manumitted slaves, the governor concluded his February, 1802, letter, was a "policy equally wise and humane," both "to ourselves and the people who are the object of it." He hoped the president would "be so good as to . . . promote" Virginia's efforts "in these . . . respects."[66]

Jefferson concurred that Africa, particularly the "British establishment at Sierra Leone," would be a "proper place" to send "insurgent negroes." The settlement there is "composed of negroes," formerly inhabitants of the southern states . . . who were carried over to England during the revolutionary war." Should the Sierra Leone company "permit us to . . . take mercantile objects . . . affording . . . commercial profit," Jefferson suggested, the west African colony "might then" also become an "asylum . . . for freed negroes and persons of colour" already free. Without "mercantile operations . . . to defray . . . expenses of transportation . . . so distant a colonization" might be too costly. The West Indies or South America, the president concluded, may provide "other suitable places" should Sierra Leone "be unattainable."[67]

United States' purchase of Louisiana in 1803 momentarily shifted Vir-

65. *Ibid.*, 3–4.
66. Virginia, *Journal of the House of Delegates of the Commonwealth of Virginia, 1801–1802* (Richmond, 1802), Doc. 10, p. 1.
67. *Ibid.*, 1–2.

ginia's search for viable colonization sites away from Africa and the West Indies to vast, new territory beyond the Mississippi River. St. George Tucker, in an anonymous 1803 pamphlet, was one of the first to propose that Virginians "entice" blacks "who have already, or may hereafter obtain . . . freedom, through . . . benevolence of their masters" to "remove" to these sparsely settled western lands. The "southern parts of Louisiana bordering upon the gulph of Mexico," Tucker maintained, "lie under a climate more favourable to the African constitution than any part of the United States." General emancipation of Virginia's slaves was still an "utopian idea." But "at least, it may be advisable," Tucker expressed hopes for widespread private emancipations, to encourage manumitted slaves to leave the commonwealth.[68]

Thomas Jefferson, in a December, 1803, letter to Virginia Governor John Page, likewise suggested Louisiana as a more immediate possibility than St. Domingo. Acting on the president's proposal, the 1804–1805 general assembly resolved that Virginia's congressional representatives seek to obtain part of the Louisiana territory for colonization of the state's free blacks, manumitted slaves, and those who may "hereafter become dangerous to the public safety."[69] The 1805 resolutions were Virginia's last official act on colonization until 1816. As antagonisms between America and England intensified, Virginians momentarily abandoned all search for viable asylums. And by the end of the War of 1812, rapid settlement of the Louisiana Territory would preclude further consideration of that region. If interest in Louisiana was short-lived, however, interest in colonization was not. With the return of peace, Virginia would renew her commitment to the colonization policy already outlined in the period 1800–1805.

As Virginians searched for colonization sites in early years of the nineteenth century, the state took concurrent steps to curb the growth of its free black population. Although no free blacks were found guilty of participation in Gabriel's conspiracy, the aborted rebellion heightened Virginians' ever present fears of this class as potential inciters and leaders of enslaved black brethren. Efforts to limit numbers of free blacks had begun well before 1800, however, and involved more than fear of

68. "Sylvestris" [St. George Tucker], *Reflections on the Cession of Louisiana to the United States* (Washington, D.C., 1803), 25–26.
69. Slaughter, *The Virginian History of African Colonization*, 5–6.

recurrent slave insurrection. As early as the mid-1780s, "Southside" conservatives had protested the rapid increase of free blacks resulting from private acts of emancipation and urged repeal of slaveholders' right to manumit.

Antipathy to free blacks was equally common to Virginia abolitionists. In a society stratified by color, where white skin connoted freedom and black skin, slavery, Virginians of all persuasions believed *free* blacks a dangerous anomaly, a class whose very presence symbolized whites' loss of racial control.[70] Antislavery Virginians like St. George Tucker and Thomas Jefferson had always coupled emancipation with removal of freedmen. Incorporation of large numbers of emancipated blacks would promote racial amalgamation, racial warfare, and other evils which, Virginia's revolutionary-era abolitionists agreed, loomed larger than the evil of slavery itself.

Although Virginia emancipators urged removal of freedmen to resolve dilemmas of race, the state's 1782 manumission law allowed blacks to remain. Such inconsistency seemed more dangerous in the aftermath of Gabriel's conspiracy, as whites' misgivings about a rapidly expanding free black population intensified. Growing hostility to free blacks in turn sparked extensive debate on the "*policy* of emancipating slaves" during the 1804–1805 and 1805–1806 sessions of the general assembly.[71]

As in the mid-1780s, opponents of Virginia's 1782 manumission act called for total prohibition of private emancipations. "The law formerly in existence," as "Southside" Piedmont delegate Thomas Robertson referred to the colonial policy of emancipation solely by legislative act, had forbidden manumission by individual slaveowners. "We only propose to restore it." He urged repeal of private manumission as "necessary" to limit further increase of "dangerous" free blacks, "not because I am less friendly to the rights of men," but because "emancipation was destructive to the happiness of the state." Williamsburg representative James Semple likewise declared voluntary manumission contrary to the general welfare of white Virginians. Noting that Virginia already had "20,000 free blacks among us," he raised the specter of servile in-

70. Jordan, *White Over Black*, 578.
71. Richmond *Argus*, January 17, 1806. Winthrop D. Jordan very kindly made available his microfilm copy of the *Argus* during my work on Virginia's manumission debate. All subsequent quotes for and against the 1782 manumission act are from this microfilm.

surrection and racial intermixture if private emancipation continued. When free blacks become "more numerous," the Williamsburg delegate warned, "they will furnish the officers and soldiers around whom the slaves will rally." Freedmen will also "continue to mix with the whites as they have already done," so that "I know not what kind of people the Virginians will be in one hundred years." Although "we cannot now avoid the evil of slavery," the conservative Semple avowed, prohibition of "partial emancipation" would avoid the evils of a burgeoning free black population.

Whereas opponents attacked private manumission on grounds of expediency, proponents upheld Virginia's 1782 law on grounds of principle. John Love of Fauquier County in the northwest Piedmont contended that the "right of property in a slave was the same as that in a horse, or other personal thing." To deny slaveowners the "power of emancipation" thus would "sacrifice" a "most important principle . . . the right to dispose of property freely." Dabney Minor of Orange County expressed greater concern for human rights of black slaves than for property rights of white slaveholders. Repeal of Virginia's liberal manumission law, the western Piedmont delegate proclaimed, was "destructive of liberty." Legislators "have no right to do a moral wrong," to "contravene" the "great principle . . . of the bill of rights which declares that 'all men are by nature free.'" He did not advocate "a general emancipation of slaves. . . . *That*," Minor declared, "would tend to the injury of the country" and most likely "could not be done." He hoped, however, that delegates would not "shut against this unfortunate race . . . the only door through which they can enter the sacred ground of liberty." He further hoped, Minor now argued on behalf of slaveholders' moral sense, that "if emancipation of his slaves would produce momentary comfort to the conscience of a dying man," legislators would not "deprive" masters of the right to manumit.

At the same time that Minor pronounced repeal of private manumissions a "moral wrong" both to black slaves and white masters, he also challenged opponents' contention that prohibition of "partial emancipation" would afford whites greater security. To deny blacks even a "small avenue . . . to escape to liberty and happiness," the western Piedmont emancipator argued, would augment, not lessen, dangers of servile insurrection. "Fixed in the deepest state of damnation, despair without hope," Virginia slaves "will prefer death to existence." The "door" of private antislavery action must therefore be left open, Minor urged fellow legislators, to protect rights and interests of all Virginians.

Virginia's debate on private manumission, published in part in the January 17, 1806, Richmond *Argus,* was a forerunner of the much lengthier, more explosive debate on general emancipation during the 1831–1832 general assembly. Like 1831–1832 conservatives, delegates opposed to individual antislavery action in 1805–1806 did not proclaim slavery a positive good. Instead they adopted an apologetic tone, acknowledging slavery as an "evil," but an evil that had no remedy. Emancipation, whether "partial" or general, would only promote greater evils associated with a growing population of "dangerous" free blacks.

If arguments against emancipation were similar in 1806 and 1832, arguments for emancipation were not. Rather than appeals to slaves' natural rights and slaveholders' moral sentiments, 1831–1832 Virginia abolitionists would primarily assert economic and social rights of nonslaveholding whites. Furthermore, insistence on slaveowners' property rights would, by 1831–1832, be a central tenet of Virginia conservatives, not of Virginia emancipators. Whether positions persisted or changed, however, slavery remained an explosive issue in Virginia, both before and after 1832.

Legislators rebuffed efforts to repeal the 1782 manumission act in 1804–1805, and again in 1805–1806. Following their second defeat, proponents of repeal changed strategy. Unable to effect absolute prohibition of private manumissions, conservatives now pursued the far more accepted policy of removal of freedmen from Virginia as a condition of emancipation.[72] This revised legislation retained the principle of slaveholders' "right to dispose of property freely" but required all slaves so emancipated to leave the state within twelve months or forfeit their right to freedom.[73] Amendment of Virginia's 1782 act thus ended the dichotomy between whites' antipathy to incorporation of freedmen and the realities of widespread incorporation. The 1806 manumission act brought Virginia's antislavery policy in line with antislavery beliefs.

Historians have cited the 1806 manumission act as a waning of Vir-

---

72. Jordan, *White Over Black,* 575.
73. Shepherd (ed.), *The Statutes at Large of Virginia,* III, 251–53.

ginia abolitionism, the "abandonment," as Winthrop Jordan affirms in his comprehensive study, *White Over Black,* "of the last vestige of emancipation." "More than any event," Jordan continues, it "marked the reversal" of the strong antislavery tendencies of the revolutionary generation and was the "key step . . . onto the slippery slope which led to Appomattox and beyond."[74]

Rather than repudiating earlier antislavery persuasions, however, Virginia's 1806 manumission act embraced principles of revolutionary emancipators like St. George Tucker and Thomas Jefferson. Hostility to free blacks, coupling of emancipation with removal, not incorporation, of freedmen, had always been central to Virginia abolitionism. In years after 1800, as St. Domingo and Gabriel's conspiracy heightened fears of servile insurrection, misgivings about 1782 provisions for manumission-without-removal intensified. Intent on checking growth of free blacks, Virginians in 1806 thus qualified, but did not revoke, slaveholders' right to emancipate. Admittedly, emigration requirements did restrain private manumissions. Masters concerned with slaves' welfare were reluctant to emancipate without any place for blacks to remove, particularly when the following year Maryland, Delaware, Kentucky, and subsequently, Ohio, North Carolina, Missouri, and Tennessee all denied permanent residence to free blacks from other states.[75] Yet, amidst Virginia's notoriously lax enforcement of emigration provisions, private manumissions, though less frequent, did persist. Moreover, even as Virginia moved to *curb* manumission-without-removal, she concurrently moved to *promote* manumission-with-removal by accelerating the search for black asylums outside the United States. Far from reflecting new proslavery zeal, the 1806 manumission act instead complemented the 1805 colonization resolutions of the Virginia General Assembly; both were consistent with age-old racist beliefs that abolition of slavery in Virginia required an unprecedented "second effort."

Virginia's commitment to colonization, interrupted by the War of 1812, revived immediately afterward. Resolutions adopted behind closed doors by the Virginia General Assembly in December, 1816, now looked to Africa, rather than St. Domingo or Louisiana, as the most desirable

74. Jordan, *White Over Black,* 574–77.
75. Russell, *The Free Negro in Virginia,* 71–72.

asylum for blacks "now free" and for "those who may be hereafter emancipated within this commonwealth."[76]

Revival of colonization sentiment within Virginia provided the principal impetus for establishment in Washington, D.C., of the American Colonization Society. Organized in December, 1816, the society held its first meeting on January 27, 1817, and elected Bushrod Washington of Virginia as president. As stated in its constitution, the society's major purpose was "to colonize, with their consent" America's "free people of colour . . . on the coast of Africa. . . . Many causes, which can never be realized here," the society's founding members proclaimed, "will operate in Africa to develop the talents, invigorate the faculties, and dignify the purposes of the people of colour." While operating as a private agency, the society concurrently sought to cooperate with federal and state governments to effect voluntary removal of free blacks.[77]

"Slavery," the society's constitution continued, "is untouched by any direct operations of the Society. . . . It does not interfere . . . in any way with the rights or the interests" of slaveholders. It believes that slavery can only be abolished by . . . consent of the slaveholders," not by any action of the "General Government." While avoiding "direct" antislavery activities, however, the society hoped "its *moral influence*" would "safely, extensively, and effectually" promote "voluntary emancipation." African colonization, the constitution proclaimed, "shows how this evil may be removed" consistent with slaves' welfare and masters' rights. Demonstration of the practicability of removing free blacks would encourage slaveholders to manumit and, thereby, ultimately accomplish "a great and good end by virtuous means." "It affords me no little satisfaction," the prominent Virginia colonizationist Charles Fenton Mercer wrote in April, 1818, "that our native state has taken the lead in the humane enterprize . . . of wiping from the character of our institutions the only 'blot' which stains them." Another leading antislavery colonizationist, William Mayo Atkinson of Petersburg, Virginia, echoed Mercer's sentiments. "I have no doubt that emancipation without emigration," Atkin-

76. Virginia, *Acts and Resolutions of the General Assembly of the Commonwealth of Virginia, 1816–1817*, No. 1, p. 200.
77. Philip J. Staudenraus, *The African Colonization Movement 1816–1865* (New York, 1961), 31; American Colonization Society, *The African Repository and Colonial Journal* (Washington, D.C., 1831), VII, 193–96.

son wrote the secretary of the American Colonization Society in November, 1831, "would utterly ruin the State. . . . Hence I must oppose it . . . by all gentlemanly and Christian means. Hence, too, one reason of my zeal for colonization, as indispensable to that other indispensable measure [emancipation.]" Although colonization also found support among conservatives who wished to strengthen slavery, theirs was not the leading impulse behind Virginia's commitment to removal of free blacks during the first three decades of the nineteenth century. Colonization, Virginian and other founders of the American Colonization Society anticipated, was a crucial first step toward emancipation. Once the nation surmounted obstacles of race, abolition could gradually and peaceably proceed.[78]

During the early 1820s, Virginia cities and counties from the Tidewater to the Trans-Allegheny established auxiliary colonization societies. The most influential, the Richmond and Manchester Society, included among its membership many of the state's leading citizens. John Marshall was president; James Madison, James Monroe, John Tyler, and James Pleasants were vice-presidents.[79] At its January, 1825, meeting, the Richmond auxiliary reported that during the past year, 105 Virginia free blacks had emigrated to Africa under auspices of the American Colonization Society and settled in the recently acquired colony of Liberia. "It is now shown to the most skeptical," Richmond colonizationists affirmed, that with additional state and federal funds, the American Colonization Society could establish a "permanent and flourishing colony . . . in Africa, to which, in the course of years, all . . . free persons of colour, now in the United States, and those who may be hereafter emancipated, may be transported."[80]

Although colonization was more popular in Virginia than in any

78. American Colonization Society, *The African Repository and Colonial Journal*, 200–206; Charles Fenton Mercer to John Hartwell Cocke, April 19, 1818, in John Hartwell Cocke Papers, Alderman Library, University of Virginia; William Mayo Atkinson to Ralph R. Gurley, November 10, 1831, in Early Lee Fox, *The American Colonization Society 1817–1840*, Johns Hopkins University Studies in Historical and Political Science, Series 38, III (Baltimore, 1919), 28–29.
79. Staudenraus, *The African Colonization Movement*, 107; Slaughter, *The Virginian History of African Colonization*, 11–12.
80. Virginia Colonization Society Minute Book, 1823–1859, pp. 17–19, Virginia Historical Society, Richmond.

other state, not all Virginians approved. Opponents, centered in large slaveholding counties south of the James River, viewed colonization as an insidious abolitionist plot. Like Deep South slaveholders, these "Southside" Piedmont conservatives denounced colonizationists as "mischievous intermeddlers, whose principles and designs were calculated to disturb . . . relations of master and servant, and jeopardize the peace and tranquillity of society."[81] Whereas other conservative Virginians supported removal of free blacks to consolidate slavery, conservative opponents feared any colonization was but a stepping stone to emancipation.

Even among antislavery Virginians who provided the principal impetus to colonization, attitudes toward federal cooperation differed. Some urged generous congressional appropriations to aid the American Colonization Society; others feared federal support would arouse slaveholders' animosity and, thereby, damage the society's "moral influence." The American Colonization Society, these latter Virginians maintained, must rely solely on state funds and private contributions to remove free blacks. "One of the strongest recommendations of the Colonization Society," the "Southside" antislavery colonizationist William Atkinson declared in a July, 1827, letter to the society's secretary, "has always been the *indirect*, but powerful influence I thought it would exert on the very existence of . . . slavery." Now, the Petersburg lawyer noted "with deep regret," because of the "application *made last winter . . . to Congress for aid* . . . the enemies of the Society in this part of Virginia . . . are increasing in number and violence. . . . If the Society . . . perseveres in making application to Congress," Atkinson cautioned, it risks "alienating all their friends in the Southern Atlantic States."[82]

By the late 1820s, the anticolonization sentiment alluded to by Atkinson had become more widespread among eastern Virginians. Although the general assembly continued to appropriate small sums for African colonization, popular support for the project was on the wane. In December, 1828, the Richmond auxiliary reorganized as the Colonization Society of Virginia, a state agency independent of the American Colonization Society. Amidst Virginians' growing states' right scruples, how-

81. *Ibid.*, 46.
82. William Mayo Atkinson to Ralph R. Gurley, July 4, 1827, in Fox, *The American Colonization Society,* 82.

ever, even the autonomous state organization did not meet in 1829 or 1830.[83]

Overnight, in August, 1831, African colonization resurged. Just as Gabriel's conspiracy had sparked initial efforts to remove blacks, so the more convulsive Nat Turner insurrection lent dramatic new urgency to such proposals. Petitions flooding the general assembly after the Southampton uprising mostly urged colonization of free blacks. A few, however, demanded abolition of slavery itself. As St. George Tucker had long ago surmised, whites' "actual suffering" had "opened the oppressors' eyes" to evils of racial bondage. Perhaps now, as Thomas Jefferson had so often hoped, Virginia's younger generation would "come forward in the public councils" to "press" emancipation.

The "hour of emancipation is advancing," Jefferson had warned in his *Autobiography* just ten years before Nat Turner convulsed Virginia. Whether whites would resolve dilemmas of race and property by gradual, peaceful means, or whether blacks would win their own freedom by the "bloody process of St. Domingo," Jefferson somberly noted, was a "leaf of history not yet turned over."[84] In the autumn of 1831, Virginians called upon their legislature to turn over that "leaf."

83. Staudenraus, *The African Colonization Movement,* 178; Slaughter, *The Virginian History of African Colonization,* 18–19.
84. Ford (ed.), *The Writings of Thomas Jefferson,* IX, 478.

# V / "Slavery in Virginia Is an Evil"

Cold, blustery winds blew across Shockoe Hill; light snow fell. Legislators arriving for the start of the general assembly walked briskly toward the capitol building, few noticing the exhibition of John Randolph's purebred horses on the public square. Situated atop Shockoe Hill, Virginia's state capitol commanded a panoramic view of Richmond. Thomas Jefferson, inspired by ancient republics, had modeled the majestic white structure after a classical Roman temple. Massive Ionic columns fronted the building. A handsome portico looked out over vast, sloping terrain. But Jefferson's republican monument faced south, toward large James River slave plantations. Like the slaveholding Roman republic, Virginia's "city on a hill" was built upon a tragic flaw.[1]

Over the years, Virginia's republican edifice, like Jefferson's dream of universal freedom, slowly crumbled. By 1831, the exterior white stuccoing, plastering, and stonework needed renovation. Inside, the hall of the house of delegates also required major improvements. Legislators were surrounded by outmoded relics. Original rows of straight-backed, narrow benches did not adequately accommodate present house members, and although additional circular seats had been nailed to the floor, the small hall precluded providing chairs and writing tables for every delegate. Old stoves no longer effectively heated the room, and fireplaces or Franklin stoves could not be installed without enormous ex-

1. John Hartwell Cocke, Sr., to John Hartwell Cocke, Jr., December 5, 1831, in John Hartwell Cocke Papers; Paul S. Dulaney, *The Architecture of Historic Richmond* (Charlottesville, 1968), 3, 77; E. Griffith Dodson, *The Capitol of the Commonwealth of Virginia at Richmond* (Richmond, 1938), xx, 23; John P. Little, *History of Richmond* (Reprint; Richmond, 1933), 169.

pense.[2] As delegates took their seats in the chilly chamber on December 5, 1831, many must have hoped the "early and severe . . . winter"[3] would not persist throughout the legislative session. "The weather has been so cold," a Richmond visitor remarked, "as almost to freeze ideas ere they reach maturity."[4] Antiquated seating and stoves, frigid temperatures within and without the house—all seemingly conspired to arrest the "advance of new ideas," to suspend the "revolution of public opinion" Jefferson had deemed crucial to emancipation.

In contrast to the patriarchal 1829–1830 convention, unusually large numbers of young, inexperienced men had been elected to the 1831–1832 house. However, several sons and grandsons of Virginia's famed revolutionary generation were among delegates from east of the Blue Ridge: Thomas Jefferson Randolph, grandson of Thomas Jefferson; Thomas Marshall, oldest son of John Marshall; William Henry Roane, grandson of Patrick Henry. Other prominent easterners included "Southsider" William Henry Brodnax, commander of militia units during the Southampton insurrection and active proponent of the American Colonization Society, and William Osborne Goode, who had represented his "Southside" Piedmont district in the house since 1822 and recently at the 1829–1830 constitutional convention. From west of the Blue Ridge, leading delegates included Trans-Allegheny representative William Ballard Preston, son of former Virginia Governor James Preston and nephew of the present governor, John Floyd; Valley representative James McDowell, another of Governor Floyd's nephews who would himself serve as governor of Virginia from 1842–1846; and Charles James Faulkner, a brilliant, young Valley lawyer who would long represent his district both in the Virginia House of Delegates and in the United States House of Representatives.

The rout of republican principles at the 1829–1830 constitutional convention significantly affected apportionment of representation in the 1831–1832 house. The compromise deprived progressive, nonslavehold-

2. Virginia, *Journal of the House of Delegates of the Commonwealth of Virginia, 1830–31* (Richmond, 1831), 108; Virginia, *Acts Passed at a General Assembly of the Commonwealth of Virginia, 1831–32* (Richmond, 1832), 8–9; Virginia, *Journal of the House of Delegates of the Commonwealth of Virginia, 1831–32* (Richmond, 1832), Doc. 7.

3. John Hartwell Cocke, Sr., to John Hartwell Cocke, Jr., December 5, 1831, in John Hartwell Cocke Papers.

4. Charlestown *Virginia Free Press and Farmers' Repository*, December 15, 1831.

ing regions of western Virginia of six seats, assigning them instead to conservative slaveholding counties of the Tidewater and Piedmont.[5] With an eastern majority of twenty-two in the present house, rather than ten in a democratic house, conservatives might well expect to control anticipated legislation on slavery in the aftermath of Nat Turner.

On December 6, Governor Floyd presented his annual message. "The present crisis," Floyd advised legislators, "has inspired the community with a just expectation" of decisive, energetic measures. Delegates must turn first to the "melancholy subject" of Southampton. Negro preachers had incited these "shocking and horrid" barbarities; they must be silenced, and slave religious assemblages must be banned. Slaves must be confined to masters' estates. To guard against "possible repetition" of the Nat Turner insurrection, the governor further recommended that all laws governing Virginia slaves be revised to assure "due subordination."[6]

Concomitant with tightened control over slaves, the general assembly must appropriate annual funds to remove free blacks. This class, Floyd observed, could readily convey incendiary northern pamphlets to slaves. In urging repression of slaves and removal of free blacks, Floyd advanced measures for consolidation of slavery already outlined in his November, 1831, letter to South Carolina Governor James Hamilton. He did not, as he had described in the letter, propose state-financed colonization of slaves as the "first step to emancipation." Neither did he call for gradual abolition of slavery in Virginia, or even its prohibition "west of the Blue Ridge Mountains," the intent he had confided to his diary just two weeks before the general assembly convened. The governor's public silence, however, belied his private intentions. "If I can influence my friends in the Assembly to bring it on," he noted in his diary on December 26, "the question of gradual abolition" would soon be debated. "Eastern members . . . wish to avoid the discusssion," but with support from young Valley and Trans-Allegheny delegates, debate on emancipation "must come." "I will not rest," Floyd concluded his diary entry, "un-

---

5. Swem and Williams, *Register of the General Assembly of Virginia*, 131–33; U.S. Census Office, *Fifth Census*, Tables [10]–[13]. The house declared Valley delegate Henry Byrne, of Morgan County, ineligible because he owned no freehold. With the Valley having twenty-four instead of twenty-five representatives, western Virginia thus had seven fewer house seats than under republican apportionment.

6. Virginia, *Journal of the House of Delegates, 1831–32*, pp. 9–10.

til slavery is abolished in Virginia." Unaware of the governor's private resolve, editors of the Norfolk and Portsmouth *Herald* criticized Floyd's response to the "Southampton tragedy." "We could have wished," the Tidewater journal reproached, "that the Governor had recommended some provision for the gradual extinction of slavery, by however slow a process. . . . There is nothing more sickening to us as a native Virginian, than the idea that our noble State is forever to be saddled with the incubus of slavery."[7]

Following the governor's annual message, the speaker of the house appointed a special committee to consider proposals relating to "insurrectionary movements." Chaired by William Henry Brodnax, the thirteen-member committee included seven Piedmont, three Tidewater, two Valley, and one Trans-Allegheny representative. Of the ten easterners, seven represented "Southside" Piedmont and Tidewater counties, one the "Eastern Shore," and only two the western Piedmont. Furthermore, of the three westerners, one represented Frederick, the Valley county with the largest percentage of slaves west of the Blue Ridge. Selection of the special committee, a leading Valley newspaper rightfully protested, "appears to have been very sectional." Indeed the Piedmont, with but 30.0 percent of Virginia's whites and 31.3 percent of house members, controlled a whopping 53.8 percent of the committee, whereas the Trans-Allegheny, with 26.5 percent of Virginia's whites and 23.1 percent of house members, controlled only 7.7 percent. Tidewater and Valley representation, respectively 23.1 percent and 15.4 percent of the committee, was not as dramatically distorted. Yet with eastern Virginia controlling 76.9 percent of the special committee and the nonslaveholding Trans-Allegheny virtually disenfranchised, abolitionist forces seemed doomed. Slavery, the Valley Martinsburg *Gazette* decried, was not "exclusively an *Eastern* question." To deny western Virginia her just influence on the legislative committee "seems to us an attempt to strangle every project of emancipation at its birth."[8]

During the first week, delegates presented numerous petitions for colonization of free blacks, and for laws barring free blacks and slaves from mechanical trades. All such memorials were referred to the special

7. Ambler (ed.), *The Life and Diary of John Floyd*, 172; Norfolk and Portsmouth (Va.) *Herald*, December 9, 1831.

8. Virginia, *Journal of the House of Delegates, 1831–32*, p. 15; Martinsburg (Va.) *Gazette*, January 5, 1832.

committee. Then on December 14, William Henry Roane of Hanover County introduced a petition from the Religious Society of Friends. "Slavery," the Quaker memorial declared, has "long violated . . . the first principles of our republican institutions and the immutable laws of Justice and Humanity." Abolition of a "system repugnant to the laws of God" and to the "best interests of the Commonwealth" demands "legislative interference." The Friends urged immediate enactment of *post-nati* emancipation and colonization to restore not only the "inalienable rights of . . . the African race," but also the "peace, safety, prosperity and happiness" of white Virginians.[9]

The Quaker memorial provoked heated debate. "Southside" Piedmont delegate William O. Goode moved to reject the antislavery petition. Northern Tidewater representative Charles S. Carter likewise opposed referral of the petition to the special committee, insisting that "discussion of . . . emancipation would be, at present, premature. . . . The Legislature" must not "allow a set of enthusiasts to introduce" a "foreign" subject into its "deliberations" on removal of free blacks.[10]

Other easterners disagreed. Chairman William Henry Brodnax declared that his committee's "jurisdiction" embraced Virginia's entire "black population," slave and free, and accordingly urged full discussion of emancipation. "Some measures to restore confidence and security were necessary," the "Southsider" asserted, when slaveholders "were found to lock their doors at night, and open them in the morning to receive their servants . . . with pistols in their hands." "Is there one man in Virginia," Brodnax demanded, "who does not lament that there was ever a slave in the State. . . . Does any man doubt that Slavery is an evil?" Perhaps this present legislature might enact "an entering wedge, towards ultimate emancipation." Philip Bolling of Buckingham County and John A. Chandler of Norfolk County joined Brodnax in labeling slavery the "most pernicious of all evils," the "greatest curse ever inflicted upon this State." "Best interests of the community," these "Southside" Piedmont and urban Tidewater representatives alike contended, "require . . . consideration of any plan" of gradual abolition.

Another "Southsider," John Thompson Brown of Petersburg, also

9. Virginia Legislative Petitions, Charles City County, 1831, Virginia State Library, Richmond.

10. Richmond *Enquirer*, December 17, 1831.

pronounced slavery an "evil,—the greatest, perhaps, that an angry Providence could inflict on a sinning people." However, Brown challenged Brodnax, Bolling, and Chandler, slavery was "so interwoven" with the "habits and interests" of Virginians, that it "was too late to correct it." But though he doubted the practicability of gradual abolition, the Petersburg delegate differed with fellow conservatives Goode and Carter in favoring thorough debate on emancipation. The "people . . . expected and desired" the general assembly to examine the "whole subject" of slavery to determine whether "anything can or ought to be done." Our "conclusions" will then be "regarded as final and unalterable," and "the subject will sleep forever." If the house "rejected" abolition petitions, the slavery issue "would never be sunk."[11]

Following this initial exchange on slavery, delegates voted 93 to 27 to refer the Quaker memorial to the special committee. Most of those opposed represented large slaveholding Piedmont counties south of the James River. A huge majority of legislators were willing to examine gradual emancipation. "This is an important step," the Richmond *Constitutional Whig* exulted. "The question of remote and gradual abolition is under consideration. . . . Circumstances have subdued the morbid sensitiveness which disallowed . . . public allusion to the topic." Perhaps "posterity" would celebrate December 14 "as a day" comparable in Virginia history to the "Fourth of July."[12]

Petitions concerning slaves and free blacks continued to pour into the special committee. On December 23, northwest Piedmont delegate James McIlhaney presented a memorial from Loudoun County urging the general assembly to commence the "glorious work" of gradual emancipation and *"removal of a race irreconcileably antagonistic to ours."* Virginians would "manfully and cheerfully sustain their representatives in this momentous effort," Loudoun petitioners proclaimed, "and bear, without a murmur, privations . . . incident" to abolition. A week later, the house requested Governor Floyd to transmit all documents and papers relating to the Southampton insurrection; he immediately complied. On January 2, 1832, Valley member Charles J. Faulkner resolved that the special committee recommend to the house "a scheme of grad-

11. *Ibid.*
12. Virginia, *Journal of the House of Delegates, 1831–32,* p. 29, Richmond *Constitutional Whig,* December 16, 1831.

ual emancipation" guaranteeing slaveholders' rights to "*slaves now in esse*, or adequate compensation for their loss." The eastern-dominated committee tabled the resolution.[13]

Pressures for legislative action mounted. "Members begin to talk of debating" gradual emancipation, Governor Floyd noted in his diary on January 9. "Talented young men" from the Valley and Trans-Allegheny "will be fast friends to the measure." East Virginia's most influential journals also urged legislative debate. "We are no fanatics," the Richmond *Enquirer* declared. But "when this dark population is growing upon us . . . and when our whites are moving westwardly in greater numbers than we like to hear of . . . *can we, ought we*, to sit quietly down, fold our arms?" Some "gradual, systematic" measures "ought to be adopted," the *Enquirer* insisted, to reduce "the greatest evil which can scourge our land. . . . If worked by the hands of white men alone," Virginia, "fairest" of all states for "soil, climate and situation combined," might become a "garden spot." The Richmond *Constitutional Whig* endorsed its rival's call for antislavery action. "We will fight by his [Thomas Ritchie's] side in this holy cause," *Whig* editors proclaimed, "to the jeopardy, (if need be) the loss of all. We are no enthusiasts, either," the National Republican organ disassociated its antislavery stand from northern abolitionism. "We despise the sickly philanthropy which at a distance, weeps at what it does not comprehend. We go for the *whites* and the country."[14]

On January 10, William O. Goode inquired as to the progress of the special committee. Chairman Brodnax replied that members were considering two categories of petitions: (1) those relating solely to removal of free blacks and (2) those proposing "gradual extinction of slavery." Because of "numerous details" and "conflicting views," colonization required "much time." Slavery, conversely, "presented only one simple question." Members must determine whether to recommend, at present, gradual emancipation. The committee would report within a week.[15]

13. Virginia Legislative Petitions, Loudoun County, 1831, Virginia State Library, Richmond; Virginia Executive Papers, December, 1831, Virginia State Library, Richmond; Richmond *Constitutional Whig*, January 7, 1832.

14. Ambler (ed.), *Life and Diary of John Floyd*, 172–73; Richmond *Enquirer*, January 7, 1832; Richmond *Constitutional Whig*, January 10, 1832.

15. Wellsburg (Va.) *Gazette*, February 2, 1832.

The intransigent Goode could not wait. The next day he moved to discharge the committee from further consideration of emancipation. The general assembly, the thirty-four-year-old "Southsider" contended, had no right to confiscate private property. The state lacked funds to compensate slaveowners, and asylums to colonize even free blacks. Since the house "could do nothing" to effect abolition, why continue "this farce"? Debate not only created "great anxiety" among Virginia slaveholders; it also, Goode warned, endangered the lives of all whites. Slaves were not an "ignorant herd of Africans," but an "active, intelligent class, watching and weighing every movement of the Legislature, with perfect knowledge of its bearing and effect." Once blacks saw that Nat Turner had "inspired" legislators "with fear," they would seek to "force . . . emancipation upon the State" by "repetition" of "murderous acts." To protect both property and lives, delegates must "arrest" this "untimely," "pernicious" discussion.[16]

As the conservative Goode concluded, western Piedmont representative Thomas Jefferson Randolph promptly introduced a counter-resolution to submit *post-nati* emancipation to Virginia's qualified voters. He did not intend to "throw a fire-brand into the House," the forty-year-old Randolph declared, but rather to allow "the people" to determine slavery's fate. If a majority approved abolition, the legislature would act.[17] Randolph's emancipation plan drew, in part, upon the gradualist tradition of his grandfather, Thomas Jefferson. Let all slaves born on or after July 4, 1840, Randolph proposed, become state property, males at age twenty-one, females at eighteen. Until that time, hire them out so that their labor would "defray" costs of "removal beyond the limits of the United States."

Although Randolph looked to public opinion and *post-nati* principles to effect abolition, his antislavery proposal differed from Jefferson's in one crucial regard. "Emancipation," he observed, was not a "necessary consequence." Slaveholders could sell *post-nati* blacks "beyond the limits" of Virginia before they became state property. Only slaves "detained by their owners in Virginia" would be free, and those not for twenty-eight years hence. His plan, Randolph accordingly boasted, eliminated obstacles of race and property—heretofore "leading objections" to aboli-

16. Richmond *Enquirer*, January 19, 1832.
17. *Ibid.*

tion. Incorporation of freedmen was "forbidden." Emancipated slaves would be immediately colonized without cost to Virginia taxpayers, since "each slave pays his own removal by his hire." Furthermore, slaveholders would "pocket the money" for blacks sold out of Virginia and thus receive full compensation for property. Over the years, the "African will pass away from the wasted lands of Virginia, and from a people whose only curse was to have him thrust upon them."[18] Unlike his grandfather's, then, Randolph's hopes for a free-soil, white Virginia did not necessarily include the concomitant dream of universal freedom. The "love of liberty," the "sympathy with oppression," that Jefferson had hoped would "kindle" the "breast" of Virginia's younger generation[19] was strikingly absent from Randolph's antislavery appeal. Rather than affirming black men's "inalienable right" to liberty, Randolph would allow slaveholders' "avarice" to triumph over "justice," property rights to vanquish human rights. To rid Virginia of the twin "curse" of slavery and blacks, Jefferson's grandson seemed ready to consign thousands of bondsmen to perpetual, forced labor on hot, harsh plantations of the Deep South.

Randolph's public indifference to blacks' welfare belied his private feelings. As a child, he had formed "warmest attachments" to young slaves on his father's Albemarle County plantation. "The manners of well-bred gentlemen," Randolph recalled years later, "were always kind and courteous to slaves." But affection for blacks as persons impaired their value as property. This inherent "double" aspect of slavery, Randolph avowed, "early gave me a disgust to the whole system and made me an abolitionist."[20]

Randolph's relationship with his beloved grandfather strengthened his antislavery feelings. The oldest son of Jefferson's daughter, Martha, and of Thomas Mann Randolph, member of a prominent, old Virginia planter family, T. J. Randolph grew up at Edgehill plantation across the river from Monticello. Jefferson was very fond of Martha and her children, particularly his namesake, Thomas Jefferson, and took a "lively interest" in his grandson's character and education. "Cherish your little

18. *Ibid.*
19. Ford (ed.), *The Writings of Thomas Jefferson*, X, 477–79.
20. Thomas Jefferson Randolph, "Memoirs of his Youth, Slavery, and Thomas Jefferson" (MS in Edgehill-Randolph Papers).

ones for me," he wrote his daughter Martha in 1793, "for I feel the same love for them as I did for yourself when of their age." "We are all well here," Jefferson reported during one of his grandchildren's frequent stays at Monticello. "Jefferson particularly so. He is become the finest boy possible. Always in good humor, always amusing himself, and very orderly."[21] When Randolph was sixteen, Jefferson arranged for him to attend school in Philadelphia to study "Botany, Natural History, Anatomy, and perhaps Surgery." His grandson's education, Jefferson informed the anatomy professor, "has not hitherto been employed to the greatest advantage" due to "frequent change of tutors. . . . But I think he has an observing mind and sound judgment."[22] As to a proposed course of instruction, Jefferson advised Randolph, "it is provident . . . to possess . . . some means by which we can get a living." Since "we have no good surgeons" here in Virginia, "Surgery" would offer "certain . . . emploiment."[23]

Randolph studied science, but did not pursue a medical career. Instead, following his marriage to fellow Virginia aristocrat Jane Nicholas in 1815, Randolph and his bride lived at Monticello for two years and then moved into one of Jefferson's farm houses a mile away. In 1816, Randolph became manager of Monticello and sole executor of his grandfather's estate.[24]

Although he proved an able farm manager, Randolph could not offset Jefferson's mounting debts; overseers and tobacco had exhausted Monticello's once-rich soil. The low productivity of slave labor, Randolph further believed, aggravated his grandfather's economic plight. "Overwhelmed" at the prospect of bankruptcy, Jefferson in February, 1826, bemoaned the "comfortless situation" in "which I may leave my . . . belovèd daughter and her children. . . . Yourself particularly, dear Jefferson, I consider . . . the greatest of the Godsends . . . heaven has granted . . . me. Without you, what could I do under the difficulties now environing me?" "Neither my Mother or Yourself," Randolph re-

21. Edwin Morris Betts and James Adam Bear, Jr. (eds.), *The Family Letters of Thomas Jefferson* (Columbia, Mo., 1966), 113–14, 135–36.
22. Ford (ed.), *The Writings of Thomas Jefferson*, IX, 78.
23. Betts and Bear (eds.), *The Family Letters of Thomas Jefferson*, 375–76.
24. Joseph C. Vance, "Thomas Jefferson Randolph" (Ph.D. dissertation, University of Virginia, 1957), 37–47.

assured the anxious Jefferson, "can ever want comforts as long as you both live. . . . It shall ever be my pride and happiness to watch over you both with the warmest affection and guard you against the shafts of adversity."[25]

At his grandfather's death just five months later, Randolph assumed Jefferson's debts and, as he had promised, gradually paid off creditors. Although he guarded his grandfather against "shafts of adversity," however, he could not so shield Monticello's blacks. To meet pressing debts, Randolph was forced to sell all Jefferson's personal property, including slaves. "Dispersion of his slaves," Randolph recollected long afterward, "was a sad scene. I had known all of them from childhood and had strong attachments to many." He arranged for slaves to be sold in families, but his inability to prevent their sale reinforced Randolph's "disgust" of the "double" aspect of slaves and "deepened . . . abolition feelings."[26] A decade-long experience as Monticello's manager had produced in Jefferson's grandson firm convictions as to slavery's economic and moral shortcomings.

Antislavery sentiments of Randolph's Edgehill household mirrored those of Monticello. While residing with her father in France in 1787, young Martha Jefferson decried transport to Virginia of "algerians" to be "sold as slaves. Good God have we not enough?" Jefferson's elder daughter exclaimed. "I wish with all my soul that the poor negroes were all freed. It grieves my heart" to think that "our fellow creatures should be treated so terribly . . . by many of our countrymen."[27]

Added to T. J. Randolph's mother's moral antipathy was his father's equally inveterate economic hostility to slavery. While governor of Virginia in 1820, Thomas Mann Randolph had decried the "deplorable error of our ancestors . . . in fixing upon their posterity . . . the depressing burthen" of slave labor. Slavery, the governor declared in his annual message, had "deprived" Virginia "of the immense advantages for enlightened agriculture, manufactures and commerce . . . offered by our fertile soil . . . long and deep rivers . . . [and] abundance of miner-

25. Randolph, "Memoirs of his Youth, Slavery, and Thomas Jefferson"; Betts and Bear (eds.), *The Family Letters of Thomas Jefferson*, 469, 472.

26. Randolph, "Memoirs of his Youth, Slavery, and Thomas Jefferson"; Vance, "Thomas Jefferson Randolph," 108–10.

27. Betts and Bear (eds.), *The Family Letters of Thomas Jefferson*, 39.

als. . . . We have been outstripped . . . by states, to which nature has been far less bountiful. . . . It is painful to calculate what *might* have been" Virginia's "general wealth . . . under other circumstances." To "remedy" Virginia's "diseased state," Governor Randolph proposed to use the "whole revenue" derived from slave taxation to purchase and remove young black males and a "double proportion of females" to nearby St. Domingo. Although he pronounced "general emancipation . . . impolitic and dangerous," the elder Randolph hoped to significantly reduce the number of slaves born in Virginia. "Responsibility to posterity" demands present action to halt "startling . . . geometrical progression" of this two-hundred-year-old "evil."[28]

As Jefferson had surmised in his December, 1820, letter to Joseph Gallatin, the Virginia legislature immediately tabled Governor Randolph's antislavery proposal. Neither economic conditions within the state nor the Missouri crisis without had moved Virginians to consider abolition. Twelve years later, public alarm over Nat Turner would transpose legislative "silence" into open debate on the more sweeping abolition plan of Thomas Mann Randolph's son.

Thomas Jefferson Randolph was first elected to the house of delegates in 1831. Soon after the session began, he received a letter from his friend and former Albemarle County neighbor, Edward Coles, urging Randolph to "press . . . the absolute necessity of gradual abolition." Almost two decades before, Coles had similarly appealed to Randolph's illustrious grandfather to lead Virginia's antislavery cause. Jefferson had declined, pronouncing abolition an "enterprise for the young" and inviting Coles to undertake "this salutary but arduous work." Rather than abandon his native state, Jefferson advised Coles in 1814, enter the "public councils" of Virginia to "softly but steadily" promote emancipation.[29]

Coles, in turn, ignored Jefferson's plea. Four years later, the ardent young Virginian sold his Albemarle County plantation and emigrated to free-soil Illinois. There he freed his seventeen slaves and established them as tenant farmers with liberal opportunities to purchase land. As

28. Virginia, *Journal of the House of Delegates of the Commonwealth of Virginia, 1820–21* (Richmond, 1821), 10.

29. Edward Coles to Thomas Jefferson Randolph, December 29, 1831, in *William and Mary Quarterly*, 2nd ser. (April, 1927), 105–107; Ford (ed.), *The Writings of Thomas Jefferson*, X, 477–79. See Chapter IV for fuller discussion of the Jefferson-Coles correspondence.

governor of Illinois in 1823–1824, the former Virginia planter also defeated efforts of slaveowners in southern portions of the state to legalize slavery by constitutional amendment.[30] By emancipating his own blacks and barring Negro bondage from Illinois, Coles resolutely carried out antislavery beliefs. Yet he had turned his back on freedom in Virginia; his withdrawal, as Jefferson had pointedly observed, would "lessen the stock" of Virginians committed to the "difficult work" of emancipation and, thereby, slow the state's long-anticipated march toward universal liberty.[31]

Just as Jefferson had once looked to Coles to champion Virginia abolitionism, so now, "in the existing crisis" produced by Nat Turner, Coles looked to Jefferson's grandson. He was "particularly gratified to find," the Illinois resident wrote Randolph in December, 1831, "that you had inherited the feelings & principles of your illustrious Grand Father. . . . No one of the young generation could be more suitable to lead or could bring more moral and political weight of character to aid the good work than his grandson. . . . Now is the time to . . . step forward" in the Virginia legislature to propose *post-nati* emancipation and colonization. If legislators were reluctant to "assume responsibility" for antislavery measures, let them submit "such a Bill to the people at the next . . . election." If a "majority of qualified electors approved," Coles concluded, emancipation "should become the law of the land."[32]

Randolph "felt no hesitation" in following Coles's advice. Long sensitive to slavery's moral and economic evils, he was, in the aftermath of Southampton, particularly distressed by his wife's lingering anxiety "about the negroes." Late in January, 1832, even as the house concluded debate on abolition, he sought to reassure Jane Randolph that winter was the least likely time for insurrection. Slaves' "enterprise," he wrote his troubled wife, "can not be stirred" in cold weather. Moreover, Virginia was "upon the alert." The militia would be organized and armed that winter to "satisfy the public mind. . . . If I could imagine a possibility of danger," Randolph avowed, "I would be with you without delay. . . . The danger is to our children's children 40 or 50 years hence, not

30. Miller, *The Wolf by the Ears*, 207–208.
31. Ford (ed.), *The Writings of Thomas Jefferson*, X, 477–79.
32. Coles to Randolph, December 29, 1831.

to us."[33] To avert future calamity, Randolph resolved to submit *post-nati* emancipation to present-day Virginia voters.

Randolph's resolution broke the "seal of silence" surrounding slavery. For the first time in Virginia history, legislators, with open doors, began to debate emancipation. At 1804–1805 and 1806–1807 sessions, house members had publicly decried slavery and debated slaveholders' right to manumit. So, too, at the 1829–1830 constitutional convention white-basis reformers had pronounced slavery incompatible with democracy and challenged slaveholders' right to rule. Yet during neither earlier confrontation did Virginia's elected representatives contest the future of slavery *per se*. "Mr. Goode's motion . . . to prevent debate upon the Slave question," Governor Floyd jubilantly recorded in his January 12 diary entry, has "produced the very debate" the "slave party . . . wished to avoid."[34]

Newspapers in urban centers of east Virginia likewise applauded the unprecedented abolition debate. "What is the question of who shall be President—of Banks, of Roads and Canals, of Tariffs—to *this*?" the Richmond *Constitutional Whig* proclaimed. "What philanthropy can calculate the benefits to mankind of Virginia's successful execution of . . . abolition? . . . This year may not see the vast work commenced, nor the next, nor the next. A half century may not see it completed." But "the moment statesmen were permitted publicly to examine the moral foundation, and . . . pernicious effects of slavery, and the Press was unshackled . . . that moment the debate of abolition was registered in the book of fate." The Richmond *Enquirer,* Norfolk and Portsmouth *Herald* and Lynchburg *Virginian* all acknowledged the "mountainous difficulties" of gradual emancipation but, like *Whig* editors, predicted that the "remarkable" public discussion would ultimately doom slavery in Virginia. After a "silence" of twenty-seven years, the *Enquirer* declared, the "bloody massacre" in Southampton has "raised the floodgates of discussion" on slavery. "We now see the whole subject ripped up and discussed, with open doors, and in the presence of a crowded gallery and

33. Thomas Jefferson Randolph to Jane Randolph, January 29, 1832, in Edgehill-Randolph Papers. See Chapter I, pp. 7–8, for Jane Randolph's reaction to the Nat Turner insurrection.

34. Norfolk and Portsmouth (Va.) *Herald,* January 23, 1832; Ambler (ed.), *The Life and Diary of John Floyd,* 174.

lobby." Amidst this "unparalleled event," the *Enquirer* "determined . . . to make one *last appeal*" for emancipation. Virginia has "too long shrunk from agitation of this important subject," *Herald* editors agreed. "The present General Assembly will deserve the thanks of their constituents and the gratitude of posterity . . . for grappling with the monster." Even if legislators did not act now, "they will at least have set the ball in motion." If slavery "can be entirely shaken off in fifty or even one hundred years, it is as much as we should expect." Whether or not the current legislature adopted "efficacious" antislavery measures, the "Southside" Piedmont Lynchburg *Virginian* echoed its Tidewater counterpart, "the day is not distant when Virginia will take the first step towards gradual emancipation. . . . Public sentiment is daily marshalling itself with accumulating force, against continuance of slavery."[35]

Despite frigid weather, Virginians crowded the gallery and lobby of the hall of the house of delegates throughout the two-week debate. "Letters from Richmond inform us," the Martinsburg *Gazette* reported to Valley subscribers, that unparalleled "excitement prevails" in Virginia's capital. The "excitement" of the 1829–1830 convention "bears no comparison" to "the question of . . . abolition."[36]

During early stages, delegates primarily disputed the expediency of public debate and the merits of T. J. Randolph's abolition plan. As in the recent contest over political representation, three major groups— conservative, moderate, and abolitionist—emerged. Conservatives who favored indefinite postponement of emancipation overwhelmingly represented the Tidewater and Piedmont. Abolitionists who favored immediate antislavery legislation mostly represented the Valley and Trans-Allegheny. As in alignments on white versus mixed basis, however, abolitionists also garnered support from western Piedmont delegates and from Tidewater representatives of major cities and proximate counties. Moderates who favored future but not present action on emancipation came from all sections of Virginia except the Trans-Allegheny. With conservatives numbering sixty, and abolitionists fifty-eight, this middle group of four northern Valley, two western Piedmont, and nine urban

35. Richmond *Constitutional Whig*, January 19, 1832; Richmond *Enquirer*, January 12, 19, 1832; Norfolk and Portsmouth (Va.) *Herald*, January 23, 1832; Lynchburg *Virginian*, January 12, 1832.

36. Martinsburg (Va.) *Gazette*, January 26, 1832.

Tidewater delegates would hold the balance of power in the 1831–1832 house.

"Southside" Piedmont representative James H. Gholson presented the initial conservative position. Like William O. Goode of neighboring Mecklenburg County, the thirty-three-year-old Brunswick County delegate decried legislative discussion as dangerous and "useless." "We debate it—the Press debates it—everybody debates it . . . as if the slaves around us had neither eyes nor ears." Furthermore, most Virginians had petitioned only for removal of free blacks, not of slaves. Colonization of this "depraved, dissolute . . . and dangerous" class would "absorb" available state funds for the next decade and thus preclude "undigested and premature action" on emancipation.[37]

Randolph's abolition plan, Gholson moreover protested, was "unconstitutional." The "gentleman from Albemarle" proposed "governmental usurpation" of private property worth "uncalculated millions." He proposed to disregard the "sacred" principles of Virginia's colonial and revolutionary laws, and of the United States Constitution, which legitimized masters' rights to "just compensation" for both existent and *post-nati* slaves. Without such fundamental "maxims," Gholson declared, "there is no civilization, no government." Propertied "minorities" would have no "protection" against the "caprice and pleasure of . . . vindictive majorities." When "distant" generations "discover that the Virginia legislature, in the year 1832," is "solemnly" debating confiscation of private property without compensation, and also whether future slave offspring "is property," the "Southside" conservative avowed, they will "exclaim of us, 'can these be the sons of their fathers?'"

Property rights were not Gholson's only concern. Randolph's *post-nati* principle also endangered lives. "Every slave born" *before* July 4, 1840, and thus denied emancipation, would be "ripe for . . . insurrection." Faced with the "dark and gloomy prospect of perpetual bondage," he would seek to attain that "full and unrestrained freedom conferred" on others, not because of "services or merit," but solely because "they were *born on a different day*." To put "liberty and slavery side by side," as Randolph proposed, would destroy the peace and safety of Virginia's

37. Richmond *Enquirer*, January 21, 24, 1832. All subsequent quotations from Gholson's speech are from these editions of the *Enquirer*.

white community. Randolph's plan would likewise "inspire revolution" among slaves born *after* July 4, 1840. *Post-nati* blacks whose owners intended to sell them outside Virginia before they reached the "designated age" for emancipation would forcibly "resist this attempt." Slaves' "love of freedom" and slaveowners' "love of property" would produce a "desperate struggle" between the two classes and "constant alarm" among white Virginians. "Those who think" Virginia's slaves "dangerous and restless *now*," Gholson warned, should consider the "appalling" consequences of Randolph's proposal.

Turning from specific attacks on Randolph's plan to general condemnation of abolition *per se*, Gholson argued that though "public safety" at times necessitated abolition, slavery in Virginia did not jeopardize the community. Virginia's slaves were a "peaceful, contented" population and, "when well regulated," a "harmless" one. The Southampton "tragedy" had, admittedly, aroused momentary "alarm and excitement." But this "solitary occurrence," the *"one* insurrection" in Virginia history, "was not of such character" as to "destroy" all "sense of security" or "attach suspicion" to all slaves. Nat Turner was an "ignorant, religious fanatic." His insurrection, quickly suppressed, involved "four or five others, of his *immediate neighborhood*" and secured only "forty or fifty adherents" during the course of the "massacre." Public fears had now "subsided." Virginians "again sleep quietly on their pillows" and would probably have enjoyed "uninterrupted repose" if legislators had silenced this "intemperate debate."

He did not intend, Gholson continued, to defend the "morality" of slavery. New England and British merchants had "entailed . . . this curse," "this poisoned chalice" upon Virginia. These same "fanatical miscreants" who "crowded *our* markets with captured Africans" now disseminate "dangerous" publications inciting slaves to "insurrection and blood-shed." Although present-day Virginians could do nothing to remove slavery, they had at least "mitigated its evils." Virginia's slaves were "well fed," "well clothed," and "well treated. In health, but reasonable labour is required of them—in sickness, they are nursed and attended to. . . . They are content to-day, and have no care or anxiety for to-morrow." No other "laboring class," the Brunswick County delegate maintained, had "more happiness and less misery."

Slavery, the "Southside" conservative addressed westerners, was "almost exclusively" an eastern "interest." Western Virginia's "climate, soil, and agricultural pursuits" all "forbid . . . undue growth" of slave labor, which could only exist to any "alarming extent" where plantation agriculture "is predominant." Nor need westerners "fear for their safety from insurrections among *us*." "Lofty mountains" separating east and west Virginia provided an "impregnable barrier" for westerners' "security." Since the Valley and Trans-Allegheny had no "direct interest in this question," they must therefore consult easterners' "feelings" and "prejudices." "Almost to one man," Gholson asserted, east Virginians opposed emancipation. To abolish slavery by "rash and inconsiderate legislation" would bring "bankruptcy and ruin" to Tidewater and Piedmont planters and "blight the happiness" of the entire commonwealth. Abolition "ought never to be publicly discussed," Gholson reiterated, until the "general community" sanctioned "the time, the mode, and the measure" of "such action."

*The sanctity of private property; the rights of a slaveholding minority; fears of a hostile nonslaveholding majority; the peculiar interest of eastern Virginia.* . . . As James Gholson spoke, the voices of Abel Upshur, Benjamin Watkins Leigh, and John Randolph seemed to echo in the hall. Gholson had gone beyond considerations of property rights and republican theory, however, to raise the issue of public safety, and here his antiabolitionist arguments had worn thin. If Virginia slaves were "harmless," why did he fear public debate on emancipation? If slaves had "more happiness" than other laborers, why would they prefer liberty to bondage? The specter of discontented, dangerous rebels continuously intruded upon Gholson's portrait of contented Virginia slaves. Every black, the "Southside" conservative unwittingly assumed, was a potential Nat Turner.

Gholson did not deny slavery's moral shortcomings, but T. J. Randolph's antidote seemed worse than the "poisoned chalice." Uncompensated, *post-nati* emancipation would overturn time-honored tenets of Virginia society and imperil whites' lives. The state could not afford to compensate slaveowners for *post-nati* blacks. Virginia thus could not escape her slaveholding "curse." Slaveowners could only do their utmost to make the "evil" a mild, benevolent institution. Like past generations of conservatives, Gholson reluctantly fled to the towering sanctuary of the status quo, a status quo he did not regard with pride and tranquillity, but with apologies and fears.

Another "Southside" Virginian was not so fatalistic. Declaring his disagreement with both "extreme parties," William Henry Brodnax proposed a "middle ground" between Gholson's position that "nothing can or ought to be done" and Randolph's "monstrous" scheme, so subversive of "private property" rights.[38] Although descended from an old Virginia family, the tall, stately Brodnax had "commenced life with nothing" and had "married a girl in the same situation."[39] Now, at forty-three a successful lawyer and brigadier general of the Virginia militia, he lived with his wife and five children on the 1,626-acre Kingston plantation in Dinwiddie County. Brodnax's plantation "family" also included twenty-six taxable slaves, a number that made him one of the eleven largest slaveholders in the 1831–1832 house.[40] (See Appendix, Table VII.)

Brodnax was a devout Episcopalian and an active "friend" of the American Colonization Society. Already one of the most influential house members, his position as chairman of the special committee lent further weight to his slavery opinions. His residence in the "neighborhood of the Southampton massacre," another zealous Virginia colonizationist informed the American Colonization Society's secretary, "will probably" make Brodnax the "first man in our . . . Legislature." Although a considerable slaveowner himself and a representative of a "Southside" Piedmont county where slaves comprised 55.3 percent of the total population, Brodnax nevertheless determined to act upon personal antislavery beliefs. "My course," he later wrote his brother-in-law, "has brought on me denunciations from various quarters—but compliments and support from many more. My conscience at least approves."[41]

"The time has passed," Brodnax addressed opponents of debate,

38. *The Speech of William H. Brodnax (of Dinwiddie) in the House of Delegates of Virginia, on the Policy of the State with respect to Its Colored Population* (Richmond, 1832), 6–7.

39. William Henry Brodnax to Joseph C. Cabell, February 12, 1821, in Joseph C. Cabell Papers, Alderman Library, University of Virginia.

40. H. F. Turner, "General William Henry Brodnax," *John P. Branch Historical Papers of Randolph-Macon College,* III (1909), 14–18; *National Cyclopaedia of American Biography,* XIX, 228–29; Virginia Personal Property Books, 1831, Virginia State Library, Richmond.

41. William Mayo Atkinson to Ralph R. Gurley, October 14, 1832, in American Colonization Society Papers, Ser. I, Library of Congress; William Henry Brodnax to Robert Walker Withers, February 24, 1832, in William Henry Brodnax Papers, Virginia Historical Society, Richmond.

"when there can be any 'sealed subject' in this country. . . . The spirit of the age will not tolerate suppression." People in other states were demanding "more liberal institutions," and Virginians must not linger on the "skirts" of a departing era. They must remove the "mantle of mystery" long enveloping slavery. All must admit, the general affirmed, that *"slavery in Virginia is an evil . . . a mildew which has blighted . . . every region it has touched. . . .* Originally the first-rated state in the union," Virginia has gradually been "razed to the condition of a third-rate state." No longer did she "lead the councils and dictate the measures of the federal government." And who can deny that slavery is "principally" responsible for desolation of much of Virginia's once-fertile lands and for emigration of "many of her most valuable citizens?"[42]

Although he concurred with the "gentleman from Albemarle" that *"something must* and . . . *can* be done" to abate this "appalling" evil, Brodnax also supported Gholson's view that Randolph's *post-nati* plan was unconstitutional. "Confiscation" of future slave offspring, Brodnax charged, contravened two "cardinal principles" of Virginia's laws and constitution: *"security* of private property" and *"consent"* of property owners, or *"just compensation."* Since the "value of a female slave" included "probability of increase," slaveowners' "inviolable" property rights embraced both existent and *post-nati* blacks. Legislators thus could not force slaveowners to "surrender our property" without "paying . . . us its value." Nor could the general assembly justly submit emancipation to Virginia's qualified voters. To allow Trans-Allegheny and Valley whites, most of whom "own no slaves," to decide "whether *we* shall surrender" *post-nati* property, Brodnax protested, would "bring upon" Tidewater and Piedmont slaveholders the "revolutionary" white basis so "earnestly" opposed at the "late convention." Such popular referendum would "violate" the "compromise . . . given the east . . . principally" to protect slave property. Slaveowners, Brodnax reiterated, *"will not, ought not . . .* submit" to "mere force." Should the legislature or the nonslaveholding majority attempt to "deprive" the slaveholding minority of "any portion of this property . . . without our consent," slaveowners would "burst into atoms the bond" uniting Virginia.[43]

Just as Randolph's "bold experiment" would subvert property rights,

42. *The Speech of William H. Brodnax,* 9–11.
43. *Ibid.,* 12–14, 18–19.

so it would also "corrupt both master and slave." "This plan," Brodnax explained, "pretends" to emancipate, "yet allows" slaveowners "to sell and pocket the value of every . . . *post-nati,* up to the very hour" of "liberation." Masters would have "every inducement to hold . . . young slaves" as long as possible and then, "to evade total" financial loss, sell them outside Virginia. Such "operation," the "Southside" aristocrat objected, would be "of degrading character to the state." Gentleman planters would be "converted" into sordid "negro-traders." Similarly perturbing, slaves who "discovered" their long "hoped-for liberation" so "unjustly" nullified would become "unhappy," "restless" rebels. Even blacks born before the designated time of emancipation would have "strongest temptations to rebel" to realize the freedom withheld solely because of their birthdate. Randolph's *post-nati* emancipation, Brodnax thus adjudged, was at once "immoral" and "degrading" for Virginia slaveholders, "unjust" and "unequal" for Virginia slaves, and "dangerous" to the peace and safety of the entire white community.[44]

Although he repudiated Randolph's "unsound" scheme, "*some* efficient measure" was necessary to halt the "alarming increase" of Virginia's black population. In 1790, there were twenty-five thousand more whites than blacks in eastern Virginia. Now, despite ongoing sales of slaves to the lower South, there were almost eighty-two thousand more blacks than whites. If current trends continued, in forty years blacks would outnumber whites by two hundred thousand. Unless whites acted now to arrest this "onward evil," dangers of insurrection would multiply. Should blacks attempt a "few more" Southamptons, the brigadier general forewarned, whites, with "moral, intellectual, and scientific advantages," would "annihilate" the "whole race."[45]

To avert such "fearful consequences," Brodnax prescribed gradual, systematic colonization, first of Virginia's free blacks, and then of her slaves. Annual removal of six thousand free blacks, the "Southsider" cited estimates of the American Colonization Society, would cost $200,000. Should Virginia "rely exclusively . . . on her own resources . . . to effect this great object . . . abstinence from two or three glasses of toddy at the courthouse" would furnish the thirty-cent tax required of each white. However, Virginia could also use federal funds without vio-

44. *Ibid.*, 15–16.
45. *Ibid.*, 26–28.

lating states' rights principles. The state was *"entitled"* to about $275,000 a year from sales of public lands ceded the "general government." If the state annually deported six thousand free blacks, within ten years all this class "would be removed."

With the "practicability" of colonization "demonstrated," Brodnax proposed, Virginia could "go on" to remove six thousand, or even ten thousand, slaves. Although the state could afford to purchase such numbers "at fair prices," this would only be "necessary" to a "limited extent." More and more slaveholders would "voluntarily surrender their slaves" if the state provided colonization funds. Masters who could not "sacrifice the entire value of their slaves, would cheerfully compromise with the state for half their value." Remove ten thousand slaves annually, Brodnax declared, and "in less than eighty years" there would not be "one single slave or free negro in all Virginia." White immigrants from "other quarters of the world" would fill the "vacuum" created by deported blacks.

As to an "appropriate place," Liberia, the American Colonization Society's colony on the west coast of Africa, afforded a favorable "domain" for Virginia's free blacks. Other African territory could also be readily acquired "almost for a song." In Africa, the zealous colonizationist proclaimed, free blacks could "secure all the rights and privileges of free men." Here, they must forever remain a "distinct and degraded caste," with "none of the rights or privileges, or attributes of free men." Removal of free blacks to the land of "their fathers" would thus be "beneficial to themselves" and "to us" and, unlike Randolph's *post-nati* scheme, might ultimately liberate all Virginia's slaves. This "desirable political object," Brodnax concluded, required "resolute determination and unwavering perseverance." He urged proponents of more radical antislavery action not to "peril everything" by "attempting too much." Nor must "we refuse to do anything because we cannot obtain all we desire." His proposal, the "Southside" moderate believed, would "promote the interests of all, without violating the rights of any."[46]

The Richmond *Enquirer* lauded Brodnax's position. "Mr. Brodnax differs with most of the East," the influential journal approved, "in insisting upon . . . doing something" to abate slavery's "growing evil." He "differs with many . . . western members" in upholding the "inviolabil-

46. *Ibid.*, 29–37.

ity" of slave property. "Not a single slave," the *Enquirer* reiterated Brodnax's principles, "should be taken from its owner, *without his . . . consent or . . . ample compensation for its value.*" This is the "true ground," the "middle ground" between "two ultra parties."[47]

Despite the *Enquirer's* praise, Brodnax's "middle ground" left several issues unresolved. As the general had noted, Liberia contained, at present, only 2,400 settlers. How, then, could this "little colony" annually accommodate 6,000 new blacks? Moreover, even if Virginia could successfully remove her 47,349 free blacks, would African colonization prove practicable for the state's 469,755 slaves? Brodnax had assumed that many slaveholders would "voluntarily surrender" slaves for colonization, or "cheerfully compromise" half their value. Yet his Jeffersonian faith in masters' moral benevolence seemed inconsistent, hollow. For though he looked to voluntary emancipations to effect *his* antislavery scheme, Brodnax argued that under Randolph's plan slaveholders' "interests" would lead masters to sell rather than liberate *post-nati* blacks. If "interests" so governed men's actions, then would not most slaveholders also demand "just compensation" for colonized slaves? Could Virginia afford to purchase 6,000 or 10,000 slaves annually at "fair prices"?

Northern Valley delegate Charles J. Faulkner soon challenged the *"practicability"* of Brodnax's antislavery plan. To insist upon slaveholders' "inviolable" right to "ample compensation," the twenty-five-year-old westerner contended, "is to deny all right of action" on emancipation "now or at any future period." The state could not afford to purchase a "mass of property, valued at ninety millions of dollars. . . . The utmost extremity of taxation would fall far short of an adequate treasury." Nor would slaveholders consent to surrender their property. To rely on voluntary emancipations to furnish the "annual quota" of 6,000–10,000 slaves was "visionary." Although he acknowledged the "pacific spirit" of Brodnax's compensated emancipation, such "compromise," the Berkeley County abolitionist asserted, "seeks . . . to reconcile impossibilities."[48]

In denying the "practicability" of compensated emancipation, Faulkner insisted, he was not "embarking on a crusade against private property" or advocating "wild . . . schemes of abolition." Contrary to Ghol-

---

47. Richmond *Enquirer,* January 24, 1832.
48. *The Speech of Charles Jas. Faulkner (of Berkeley) in the House of Delegates of Virginia, on the Policy of the State with respect to Her Slave Population* (Richmond, 1832), 3–4, 13–15.

son's and Brodnax's claims, property rights were not "absolute" but were instead dependent on the "acquiescence and consent . . . of society." Masters held slaves "not by any law of nature" or "patent from God," but solely by "positive enactments of the state." Once that property "jeopardizes the peace, the happiness . . . the very existence of society," slaveholders' "subordinate" rights must yield to the "GREAT *rights* of the community." Nor could slaveholders demand compensation for "pernicious property." To guarantee masters' rights to existent slaves and to "all . . . born before July 4, 1840," Faulkner insisted, was more than adequate "profit." Confiscation of only the *post-nati*, as T. J. Randolph proposed, represented a "fair and just compromise" between "private rights" and "public safety." Uncompensated *post-nati* emancipation, not Brodnax's compensated, voluntary scheme, was thus the true "middle ground," the "only compromise" compatible with the "safety and resources of the state."[49]

"No gentleman . . . in this hall," Faulkner was "gratified" to note, was an "avowed advocate of slavery." Although all opposed slavery "upon principle," however, *apologists* like Gholson had pronounced slavery in Virginia "harmless" and the *Southampton tragedy* "trifling. That slaves had "attacked—butchered—mangled" sixty-one white Virginians "in a county as well protected as most . . . east of the Blue Ridge," the Valley delegate protested, "does not appear to me . . . petty," but "most momentous." No matter that servile insurrections "rarely occur." That "such an evil *may* occur," at any day, any hour, despite "police vigilance," is "sufficient" proof of slavery's dangers.[50]

Slavery not only imperiled whites' lives; it also contravened the "interests" of Virginia's nonslaveholding majority. Virginia's once-fertile soil was now "barren and desolate." Industry, commerce, and education languished. White "mechanics, artisans, manufacturers . . ., deprived" of jobs by slavery, emigrated to free-soil regions. If any denied slavery's "withering effects," Faulkner challenged, let them "contrast" the "indolence and poverty" of the slaveholding South with the "enterprise" and prosperity of the nonslaveholding North. Must Virginia "droop" and "die," the Valley abolitionist demanded, that slaveholders might "continue to gather [their] *crop* of human flesh?" Must "all interests," "all

49. *Ibid.*, 14–16.
50. *Ibid.*, 21.

rights" be "subordinate" to those of a slaveholding white minority? The "mechanic," the "middle classes," also have "rights—rights incompatible with the existence of slavery."[51]

Public safety and majority interests alike, Faulkner accordingly insisted, "demand" abolition. Although he was willing to "defer" to easterners' "prejudices" as to "details" of emancipation, he could not allow slaveholders to determine whether there should be "*some* scheme of emancipation." Slavery was not, as Gholson and Brodnax had argued, "exclusively an *eastern* question." West Virginia, "more particularly the *Valley*," was "vitally interested" in "arresting the further march of slavery" over the Blue Ridge. Just as east Virginians had once "implored" England to "forbid" further importation of Africans, so now Valley whites determined to check this "growing evil." Heretofore, Faulkner observed, surplus Virginia slaves found a "profitable market" in the Deep South. But with "southern markets" recently "closed," would not western Virginia *"afford the only outlet"* for the *"redundant and overflowing slave population"* of the east? "Uniformity in political views, feelings and interests," the Valley abolitionist acknowledged, would be "extremely desirable"— but not at the cost of Virginia's becoming "one universal slaveholding and slave-destroyed people." Virtuous, independent "yeomanry" west of the Blue Ridge must not "yield" to the "slothful, degraded African." Those "hills and vallies" which now echoed with "songs and industry of freemen" must not be desolated by slavery's "withering footsteps." Before western Virginia would "submit" to the "filth and corruption" of slavery, "violent convulsions must agitate this state."[52]

To arrest slavery's extension over the mountains, Faulkner concluded, he did not propose simply to prohibit "further introduction" of bondsmen into the Valley and Trans-Allegheny. Instead, he urged legislators to remove the "curse of slavery" from the entire state by gradual emancipation and colonization of *post-nati* blacks. Such plan was not "novel" or "monstrous," as opponents had charged, but a "rich legacy" of Virginia's revolutionary generation, a principle sanctioned by the commonwealth's most "illustrious" statesmen. If successful, *post-nati* emancipation would involve a "moral, political and physical revolution in Virginia," a revolu-

51. *Ibid.*, 17.
52. *Ibid.*, 7–8, 9–10. Virginia newspapers reported in November-December, 1831, that Louisiana and Georgia had recently prohibited importation of slaves from other states for sale.

tion "beneficial . . . to every great interest in the Commonwealth." To "forward a revolution so grand and patriotic," the fervent young abolitionist proclaimed, is one of the "proudest incidents of my life."[53]

If Faulkner's support of *post-nati* emancipation carried on antislavery principles of the Jeffersonian era, a more strident tone had crept into his abolitionist appeal. The Jefferson-Tucker generation had largely opposed slavery as a violation of black men's natural rights. Slaveholding aristocrats had led the earlier emancipationist crusade. Now, attacks on slavery came primarily from Virginia's nonslaveholding regions. Traditional humanitarian-moral concerns gave way to pragmatic class interests. Abolition, Faulkner had argued, would expand economic opportunities for nonslaveholding whites; manufacturing and commerce would flourish. Skilled white mechanics and artisans would replace slaves as carpenters, bricklayers, and stonemasons, and industrious white yeomen would till Virginia's soil. A burgeoning, nonslaveholding population would improve educational facilities. Neither aristocratic planters nor "degraded" blacks would trespass upon this middle-class white utopia.

Indeed, Faulkner's abolitionism more closely mirrored antislavery arguments of the 1829–1830 convention than concerns of Virginia's revolutionary emancipators. Antagonisms between slaveholding and nonslaveholding whites, manifest in the struggle for equal representation and suffrage, resurfaced in Faulkner's idyllic portrait of a free-soil Virginia. White-basis reformers had pronounced slavery antithetical to political democracy; abolitionists now declared slavery incompatible with economic democracy. In a Negrophobic society, appeals to equal rights for white men posed a graver threat to slavery than altruistic crusades for blacks.

But although Faulkner echoed 1829–1830 appeals to class "interests," his insistence on the separateness of east and west Virginia reversed the posture of such earlier Valley spokesmen as Chapman Johnson. During debate on political representation, Johnson and other westerners had argued that slavery would gradually spread throughout the Valley. Because eastern and Valley interests would soon coincide, slaveholders did not need to fear majority rule. Now, just two years later, Faulkner acknowledged the already "large slave interest" in some Valley counties but urged *post-nati* emancipation to shield west Virginia from further

53. *Ibid.*, 4, 10–12, 18.

"withering footsteps" of slavery and blacks. Faulkner's warning that nonslaveholding yeomen would resolutely resist slavery's "westward march" paralleled Gholson's notice that slaveholding aristocrats would resolutely resist uncompensated emancipation. This standoff between abolitionists and conservatives exposed a society already dangerously divided over slavery and augured Virginia's final dismemberment less than three decades later. So, too, Faulkner's opposition to the extension of slavery foreshadowed the central tenet of the Free-Soil and Republican parties during the 1840s and 1850s—a principle that in 1860 precipitated secession of the Deep South and led ultimately to the Civil War.

At the conclusion of Faulkner's speech, each group had outlined its initial posture. Conservatives proposed to silence debate and take no action on slavery; moderates favored colonization of free blacks as a stepping-stone to gradual, compensated emancipation; abolitionists urged uncompensated, *post-nati* emancipation and colonization. On January 16, the conservative-dominated special committee chose Gholson's status quo. It is "inexpedient," the committee report resolved, for the house of delegates to "make any legislative enactments for the abolition of slavery."[54]

Western Piedmont representative Archibald Bryce, Jr., acting in the moderate antislavery spirit of William Henry Brodnax, promptly proposed a preamble to the committee report. Virginia, Bryce resolved, should begin at once to colonize free blacks and manumitted slaves. This "first step" toward abating "evils" of a large black population would "absorb" the state's "present means." General "removal of slaves should await more definite development of public opinion."[55] His resolution, the Goochland County moderate explained, was not intended to stifle debate on emancipation. On the contrary, in proposing to commence colonization his preamble sought to "show the world" that Virginians "look forward" to "final abolition of slavery . . . and that we will go on, step by step, to that great end." He hoped, therefore, that all members who favored abolition would support the preamble as an "entering wedge" against slavery. Once state resources and "public opinion" allowed general emancipation, a future legislature might act.[56]

54. Virginia, *Journal of the House of Delegates, 1831–32*, p. 99.
55. *Ibid*.
56. Richmond *Enquirer*, January 17, 1832.

Bryce's preamble, a compromise between conservatives' slaveholding status quo and abolitionists' immediate antislavery legislation, embodied the gradualist emancipation philosophy of the American Colonization Society. Like other antislavery moderates, Bryce expected the removal of free blacks and voluntarily manumitted slaves to demonstrate the practicability of colonization *per se*. Successful execution of this experiment would overcome racial obstacles inherent in general emancipation and, moderates anticipated, persuade growing numbers of slaveholding Virginians to support abolition.

Indeed the Bryce preamble, with its expectation of gradual, peaceful abolition, reflected the antislavery tenets of Virginia's more renowned western Piedmont resident, Thomas Jefferson. Like Bryce, Jefferson had looked to a steady, if "snail-paced," *evolution* of Virginia public opinion to realize the "revolution" of general emancipation. Where slavery was so deeply "incorporated," Jefferson had "unhappily" affirmed, abolition would require "time, patience, and perseverance." Virginia emancipators must "softly," but relentlessly, "inculcate" antislavery principles and, with community support assured, press abolition "until its accomplishment." Heralding the gradual abolitionism of the American Colonization Society, Jefferson had speculated that colonization might "be the cornerstone" of abolishing slavery in Virginia and freeing blacks "elsewhere."[57] Bryce's proposal for immediate colonization and "final abolition" carried on such Jeffersonian persuasions.

Trans-Allegheny abolitionist William Ballard Preston rejected Bryce's antislavery compromise. The house, the twenty-six-year-old westerner instead proposed, should reverse the committee report and proclaim the "expediency" of emancipation legislation. Conservatives' control of the special committee, he charged, had precluded western participation in this crucial debate. But the Valley and Trans-Allegheny would not quietly "submit" to the "voice and will" of the slaveholding east.[58]

As had Valley abolitionist Charles J. Faulkner, Preston attacked conservatives' notions of private property and their portrait of happy, harm-

57. Ford (ed.), *The Writings of Thomas Jefferson*, IX, 168–69, 477–79, 515–16; X, 76–77. See Chapter IV, pp. 101–102, for Jefferson's views on the American Colonization Society.
58. Virginia, *Journal of the House of Delegates, 1831–32*, p. 99; Richmond *Enquirer*, February 9, 1832. All subsequent quotations from Preston's speech are from this edition of the Richmond *Enquirer*.

less Virginia slaves. *"Self-preservation,"* the Montgomery County delegate contended, was a "higher law" than property rights. When "public necessity" for emancipation became "greater than public necessity" for slavery, "this or any subsequent legislature" had "power" to abrogate slaveholders' rights, to declare "what *shall*" or *"shall not* be property" in Virginia. "Happiness," Preston further insisted, "is incompatible with slavery. . . . Love of liberty" is man's "ruling passion; it has been implanted in his bosom by the voice of God, and he cannot be happy . . . deprived of it." If slaves were "white men in oppression," he would rejoice in a "revolution here" to secure God-given rights. But he palled at the prospect of black insurrection.

To remove this "danger from the East" and "prevent" its extension to the west, Preston urged fellow delegates to adopt some plan of gradual abolition more "effective" than the Brodnax-Bryce compromise. Efforts of the American Colonization Society to remove free blacks and manumitted slaves could not accomplish general emancipation. Virginia could never abolish slavery "either now or at any future time," Preston reiterated Faulkner's position, without some "infringement" on property rights. Preston's amendment, with its fresh appeal for gradual emancipation, began a new phase of the slavery debate. Discussion no longer centered on T. J. Randolph's specific abolition scheme, but on the expediency of adopting *any* emancipation legislation. The mood of the house grew angrier, more ominous.

"Southside" Piedmont representatives again carried the conservatives' banner, and again they declared the inviolability of slave property an insuperable obstacle to emancipation. State funds could not adequately compensate Virginia slaveholders. "Our treasury box," Brunswick delegate John Shell announced, is in a "state of . . . most grievous emptiness." Nor would slaveowners tolerate oppressive taxation to effect emancipation, since taxes would fall most heavily on slave property. Slaveholding Virginians, William O. Goode raged, would thus almost exclusively bear costs of compensation and colonization![59] Conservatives likewise rejected federal aid. Virginia's share of proceeds from sale of public lands could never finance the "Herculean task" of emancipation-colonization. Furthermore, Mecklenburg delegate Alex-

59. Richmond *Constitutional Whig,* February 16, March 28, 1832.

ander Knox warned, for Virginia to grant "federal jurisdiction over slave property" would not only violate her own states' rights doctrines but also imperil all slaveholding states. The "fanaticism of the age" would spread throughout the South, and egalitarian demagogues would proclaim the virtues of "universal emancipation." All that was "valuable" in the South's relationship to the Union would be "wrecked."[60] Emancipation-colonization was also physically impracticable, as no territory was available for huge numbers of Virginia freedmen. Liberia could accommodate only five hundred Virginia colonists annually. Thus race was another insuperable obstacle to abolition.[61]

Since Virginia could not accomplish emancipation, John Thompson Brown of Petersburg addressed antislavery delegates, why continue to demonstrate slavery's evils? He intended, the "Southside" conservative announced, to defend the institution. Brown seemed an improbable spokesman for the slaveholding east. Heretofore, he had represented the northwest Trans-Allegheny county of Harrison in the house of delegates. His 1828 address "To the People of Harrison" on the eve of Virginia's constitutional convention had proclaimed majority rule the essence of republican government, white population the only just basis of representation. Freehold suffrage, the Trans-Allegheny democrat had likewise contended, was "wholly anti-republican." Why, then, just four years later, did Brown champion an aristocratic white minority?[62]

Brown was neither by birth nor by life-style a member of Virginia's planter aristocracy. The son of a successful Lynchburg merchant, he had grown up in an essentially middle-class, urban environment. But early in life, Brown had aspired to transcend his background and to achieve "respectability." While a sophomore at Princeton, he had accumulated "urgent" debts by emulating the "extravagant" spending habits of wealthier friends, having forgotten, he wrote his father apologetically, "that my funds were not as large as theirs." Upon graduation from Princeton, Brown studied law and in 1824 settled in the Trans-Allegheny town of Clarksburg. His initial impressions of Clarksburg and Harrison

60. Richmond *Enquirer*, February 11, 1832.
61. Richmond *Constitutional Whig*, March 28, 1832.
62. *The Speech of John Thompson Brown, in the House of Delegates of Virginia, on the Abolition of Slavery* (Reprint; Richmond, 1860), 20; John Thompson Brown, "To the People of Harrison" (MS in Brown, Coalter, Tucker Papers, Earl Gregg Swem Library, College of William and Mary).

County were mixed. The territory was "first-rate grazing country," but the people were "wretchedly poor and lazy. . . . They seem to prefer a scanty subsistence by hunting, to the comforts and gains of husbandry." Perhaps when "my attainments have been made respectable," he wrote his brother, "I shall seek a more wealthy and populous district."[63]

A year later, Brown was more happily established and had acquired "some little reputation at the bar." In 1826, Clarksburg friends urged him to run for the state legislature. "I should value the office," he confided to his brother, "only as a stepping-stone to a more desirable one." After election to the house, he found it "gratifying" that "nearly all the most respectable men in the county" had supported his candidacy. Brown was reelected to the house of delegates in 1828 and 1829. "My next aim is for Congress," he informed his father in May, 1829. "My prospects two years hence are highly flattering. . . . I do not wish to continue long in political life, but am desirous of rising to a respectable height."[64]

His forthcoming marriage to the daughter of a prominent Petersburg family temporarily interrupted his political plans. He arrived in Petersburg in the spring of 1830 in the "manner expected" by his future in-laws, having purchased "some horses and a sulky" to avoid the "appearance of poverty and destitution." The wedding, he boasted, was a "large and splendid party." At age twenty-seven, Brown had achieved social and financial security.[65]

Social "respectability" failed to quench Brown's political ambitions. In 1831, he again sought and won a seat in the house of delegates, this time as a representative of "Southside" Virginia. The slavery debate offered sudden, new opportunities for fame. Petersburg constituents, Brown acknowledged, were "divided on the question of emancipation." Although located in the heart of Virginia's slaveholding plantation district, the town also contained important manufacturing and commercial interests, as well as numerous nonslaveholding white artisans and me-

63. John Thompson Brown to Henry Brown, May 8, 1818, and June 21, 1824, and John Thompson Brown to Henry Brown, Jr., August 20, 1824, all in Brown, Coalter, Tucker Papers.
64. John Thompson Brown to William Peronneau Finley, December 20, 1825, John Thompson Brown to Henry Brown, Jr., November 8, 1826, John Thompson Brown to Henry Brown, August 25, 1827, and May 8, 1829, all in Brown, Coalter, Tucker Papers.
65. John Thompson Brown to Henry Brown, March 18, 1830, and John Thompson Brown to Henry Brown, Jr., May 9, 1830, both in Brown, Coalter, Tucker Papers.

chanics. If Petersburg was "divided," however, its representative was not. Defense of slavery, Brown foresaw, would "generally . . . add much to my reputation" in east Virginia. "Lofty ambition" had transformed the Trans-Allegheny democrat into a "Southside" conservative.[66]

"In what code of ethics," Brown challenged abolitionists, "is it written that slavery is so odious?" Jesus Christ "came into this world to reprove sin. . . . Yet he rebuked not slavery." Shall this legislature, Brown chided, "affect a morality more pure and exalted" than that of the "Saviour?" He did not, the Petersburg conservative admitted, "advocate . . . slavery in the abstract"; he regretted its original introduction. Nevertheless, slavery as it now existed in Virginia was not "criminal or immoral." Virginia slaves enjoyed "more . . . comforts of life" than "four-fifths of the human family." They were free from the anxieties of hunger, sickness, and old age, and both public opinion and masters' "interests" protected them from cruel treatment. Freedom, Brown contended, was a "blessing only in name to a large majority of the human race. Man must be civilized, his mind enlightened, his feelings refined, before he is fitted for the enjoyment of liberty." Of all men, blacks were least capable of "elevation," and emancipation would not reverse this "doom of inferiority." Slaves would only become poor, ignorant "serfs . . . toiling anxiously for their daily bread." Nor would colonization promote slaves' happiness. Africa was an unknown, barbaric land. Habit and domestic affections bound blacks to Virginia; it was "their home—the only country they ever knew."[67]

If slaves' happiness did not justify emancipation, neither did Virginia's "interests." Contrary to abolitionists' views, the federal tariff, not slavery, was responsible for the state's economic "misfortunes." The "enormous" import duties that benefited the manufacturing North impoverished the agricultural South. Nor was slavery responsible for emigration of nonslaveholding yeomen, mechanics, and artisans. Virginia's white population had, admittedly, not kept pace with that of more recently settled western territories, but western migration had drawn whites from both nonslaveholding and slaveholding Atlantic states.

66. John Thompson Brown to Henry Brown, Jr., February 18, 1832, in Brown, Coalter, Tucker Papers. See Chapter VI, pp. 175–76, for evidence of antislavery sentiment among Petersburg white artisans and mechanics.

67. *The Speech of John Thompson Brown*, 20, 22–25.

During the past decade, Brown noted, increase of whites in Virginia had equaled that of most of the thirteen original states. This was the only "fair criterion" of comparison.[68]

Abolitionists further distorted slavery's dangers. True, from 1800 to 1810 the ratio of black-white increase in east Virginia was almost eleven to one. During the 1820–1830 decade, however, blacks and whites had increased at almost the same rate, a pattern that would persist. Deep South planters would always need Virginia slaves. Westerners' fears of surplus eastern blacks pouring over the Blue Ridge Mountains thus would prove unfounded, as would abolitionists' portrait of slaves as disaffected rebels. Southampton, Brown reiterated conservatives' position, was a "solitary calamity." This "single disaster" did not warrant overturning the "very foundations" of Virginia society. Neither moral, economic, nor social considerations, the Petersburg delegate insisted, demanded emancipation.[69]

Yet even the pragmatic Brown qualified his posture on *Virginia* slavery. While proclaiming the institution compatible with Christianity, economics, and public safety, the Petersburg conservative was equally persuaded of slavery's ultimate extinction in Virginia. Like fellow conservative James Gholson, Brown assumed that slave labor was only profitable in growing tobacco, cotton, rice, and sugar—staples that required a year-round work force. Based upon "calculation of interest," then, slavery would never spread "to any objectionable extent" to the Valley and Trans-Allegheny. West Virginians were graziers and farmers; they did not need slaves to attend cattle and sheep. Furthermore, rather than "owning a man," westerners would always prefer hiring seasonal white laborers to harvest wheat and corn. Slavery "disappeared from the eastern and middle states," Brown observed, "merely because slaves ceased to be profitable there. . . . Climate, habits . . . and pursuits" of western Virginia would similarly provide a "more effectual *cordon sanitaire*" against slavery than any "legislative art."[70]

"Interest," Brown further contended, would also abolish slavery in *east* Virginia. Expanding plantation agriculture in the lower South would increase demand for slave labor there. At the same time, growing num-

68. *Ibid.*, 26–27.
69. *Ibid.*, 29–31.
70. *Ibid.*, 13–14.

bers of Virginia slaveholders would abandon tobacco cultivation to raise wheat and corn. As slave labor became increasingly unprofitable, Tidewater and Piedmont slaveholders would sell surplus blacks to Deep South planters—a southward sale of Virginia slaves that would be voluntary and, above all, assure masters full compensation. Abolition would thus thoroughly protect slaveholders' rights.[71]

It was left to William O. Goode to develop the full implications of Brown's "abolitionism." Slave labor, Goode asserted, "will go to where it is most useful." This principle had already "banished" slavery from northern states, and a similar process would occur in Virginia. Slaveholders, like all men, were governed by economic interests. Already, Goode noted, east Virginia planters were "becoming farmers." Many who once "grew tobacco as their only staple" had begun to cultivate wheat, and as tobacco production declined, demand for slaves would also decline. With slave labor increasingly unprofitable in Virginia, ever greater numbers of blacks would be sold to the Deep South. Recent closings of southern markets to Virginia slaves, the "Southside" conservative insisted, was "only a temporary reaction to . . . the Nat Turner revolt." As cotton production expanded in the South and Southwest, planters there would require more and more slaves. Unlike Virginia, the geography, soil, and climate of Louisiana, Mississippi, and Alabama "constrained our southern brethren to continue planters." "Natural causes," then, would accomplish gradual, peaceful "removal of slavery from Virginia." Legislative emancipation, in contrast, would precipitate dismemberment of the state. Rather than jeopardize the commonwealth, Goode urged abolitionists, let the domestic slave trade abolish slavery.[72]

Thus even intransigents like Brown and Goode assumed that Virginia would someday be a free-soil state. While they denied the practicability of emancipation-colonization, conservatives affirmed that slaveholders' interest would accomplish what legislative action could not. Abolition by "natural causes" would avoid age-old obstacles of property and race. Slaveholders would receive full compensation, and slaves would be removed to the lower South. Conservatives seemed unconcerned that blacks would not be free.

Abolitionists from both sides of the Blue Ridge once more rejected

71. *Ibid.*, 28–29.
72. Richmond *Constitutional Whig*, March 28, 1832.

conservatives' notions of property rights and repeated William Ballard Preston's call for immediate antislavery legislation. The "safety of the people," western Piedmont delegate Samuel Garland declared, "is the supreme law . . . superior" to any constitutional or statutory guarantees of slave property. The Virginia legislature, this Amherst County abolitionist avowed, had an "inherent" duty to remove "dangerous or destructive" property.[73]

"Rights of private property and of personal security exist under every government," Valley representative James McDowell concurred, "but they are not *equal*." When private rights conflicted with the "life, liberty and happiness" of the community, laws protecting property must be repealed. Even "enemies of abolition," McDowell remarked, had acknowledged slavery's dangers. Descriptions of happy, harmless Virginia slaves belied conservatives' fears of public debate. So, too, efforts to ridicule the Southampton insurrection rang false. Requests for arms had poured into Governor Floyd's office, and panic was greatest in eastern counties where slaves outnumbered whites. Mr. Goode, the Valley abolitionist astutely noted, had termed the situation in Mecklenburg "critical if not perilous." Yet now he, and other "Southside" gentlemen, resisted measures to remove the peril. Nat Turner and his "drunken handful of followers," the Rockbridge County delegate stressed, had only furthered the "suspicion attached to every slave," the "withering apprehension" that an "insurgent" might lurk in any neighborhood, in any household. Slavery was always incompatible with whites' security.[74]

Slavery was similarly incompatible with blacks' happiness. Indifference to freedom, McDowell asserted, was "wholly unnatural." True, Virginia's slaves were well treated. But indulgence only fed slaves' disaffection. "Lift up the condition of the slave," and "you bring him nearer the liberty he has lost." Let Virginia slaveholders observe the "clothed and comforted and privileged condition of their slaves" and ask themselves, "is this safe?"[75] McDowell's trenchant analysis overturned conservatives' defense of Virginia paternalism. Kindness did not promote slaves' happiness; it inflamed their discontent. Virginia, it seemed, was an ideal setting for more Nat Turners!

73. Richmond *Enquirer*, April 17, 1832.
74. *The Speech of James McDowell, Jr.*, 14–15, 27–29.
75. *Ibid.*, 19–20.

While Garland and McDowell attacked slavery on grounds of public safety, other abolitionists restated its deleterious economic and moral effects. Slavery, Trans-Allegheny delegate George W. Summers charged, was the "fountain" of all Virginia's ills. The "anti-change," "anti-enterprise" spirit fostered by the "slave interest" had "crushed" efforts to develop a "wise and extensive system of internal improvements." By limiting growth of white population, slavery had also retarded general education. He would "blush" to compare the rate of Virginia white illiteracy with that of nonslaveholding states. Slavery also exercised "pernicious influence" on whites' "manners and character." Slaveholders' sons, aware of their superiority to "degraded negroes," entered the world with "miserable notions of self-importance" and "an unbridled temper." Slaveholders and nonslaveholders developed "habits of idleness" and "fondness for luxuries," and labor became "dishonourable" because associated with slaves. Industrious white workers accordingly abandoned the state; inefficient black laborers remained. No wonder Virginia's energies were paralyzed, her "political power waning," her "moral influence" gone. Her manufacturing, commerce, agriculture could not compare with that of northern states. For slavery, Summers concluded, blighted the "prosperity and happiness of the whole Commonwealth."[76]

Nor could the "curse of slavery" be confined to east Virginia. Conservatives knew "full well," northwest Trans-Allegheny delegate John Campbell challenged, that west Virginia's climate "accords but too well with the African constitution ever to operate as a bar." Even if westerners resisted buying blacks, easterners would still be compelled to purchase or rent lands in the Valley and Trans-Allegheny and send surplus slaves over the Blue Ridge under overseers' management. This system of absentee eastern ownership, the "Panhandle" abolitionist noted, had already been adopted, to some extent, in the southwest Trans-Allegheny. Westerners must not give another "inch to the advancing enemy." They must not allow Virginia's slaveholding minority exclusively to legislate on emancipation. This "same wretched compromise" by which, in 1830, Trans-Allegheny "freemen . . . suffered political disfranchisement" under "plea of necessary protection for slave property," Campbell warned conservatives, must not now bar west Virginians from

76. Richmond *Enquirer*, February 14, 16, 1832.

"participation" in a question of "vital . . . moment to the entire state." Slavery was the "real source of all sectional collision and sectional oppression" in Virginia. And abolition of this "evil" was essential to the "integrity of the Commonwealth," of which, the Brooke County delegate emphasized, "we . . . *as yet* . . . constitute a component part."[77]

Conservatives and abolitionists had now completed their principal arguments. As in the clash over political representation, their positions seemed irreconcilable. Conservatives defended private property; abolitionists defended public welfare. One group championed an aristocratic white minority, the other a democratic white majority. Rights and interests of blacks were of secondary concern. "Grounds of expediency" rather than the "injustice of slavery," Thomas Jefferson Randolph explained to his wife, better "suited . . . the public mind." Both groups further affirmed the disastrous economic and social consequences of their opponents' course. *Post-nati* emancipation, conservatives charged, would bankrupt east Virginia and endanger white lives. Continuance of slavery, abolitionists countered, would impoverish the entire commonwealth and jeopardize whites' safety.

If conservatives and abolitionists often disagreed about slavery, however, they also often agreed. Each acknowledged slaveholders' right to existent slave property; the controversy involved *post-nati*. No Virginia abolitionist heralded Garrisonian immediatism, and thus emancipation, if accomplished, would be gradual. Each also assumed that slavery was incompatible with an industrial-commercial economy and with non-plantation agriculture. Abolitionists urged general emancipation to promote a prosperous, enterprising, "Yankee-like" Virginia; conservatives linked slave labor to cultivation of staples and anticipated slavery's gradual demise as Tidewater and Piedmont planters shifted from tobacco to the wheat-and-corn farming of the Valley and Trans-Allegheny. No Virginia conservative in 1832 embraced George Fitzhugh's later vision of a vast industrial empire based on slave labor. Instead, all shared abolitionists' view that Virginia would someday be a free-soil state. Finally, both groups reflected the inveterate Negrophobia of Virginia's white community. Removal of slavery, all agreed, must also include removal of blacks. Abolitionists coupled general emancipation with African colo-

77. Richmond *Constitutional Whig*, March 16, 1832.

nization, whereas conservatives looked to the domestic slave trade to rid Virginia of blacks.

Abolitionists and conservatives clashed, then, over means, not ends. Abolitionists proposed to legislate uncompensated, *post-nati* emancipation and colonization. Conservatives declared legislative confiscation "unconstitutional," African colonization "impracticable," and instead urged slavery's "natural death." Yet ultimately, results of these divergent courses might prove the same. For as Thomas Jefferson Randolph had noted, and William Henry Brodnax had protested, *post-nati* proposals might induce slaveholders to consign black offspring to slavery in the Deep South rather than to freedom in Africa. Confronted with a set "hour of emancipation," masters would sell *post-nati* slaves southward at a faster rate than conservatives' "natural causes." In each instance, however, slaveholders' "interest" would abolish slavery in Virginia without emancipating a single black.

As conservatives and abolitionists debated *post-nati* compensation, threats of dismemberment mounted. Just as John Randolph had sounded the "tocsin of civil war" if the 1829–1830 convention approved majority rule, so now "Southside" Piedmont conservatives preferred to separate the state rather than surrender slave property. Northwest Trans-Allegheny abolitionists similarly urged division of Virginia at the Blue Ridge Mountains rather than submission to slaveholders' demands.

As the specter of state division stalked the house, moderates again advanced the Bryce preamble as a viable compromise on abolition. This declaration of eventual emancipation legislation, moderates insisted, more accurately reflected Virginia public opinion than either demands for immediate action or demands for perpetual inaction. The present legislature must openly proclaim slavery an "evil" and commence colonization of free blacks and manumitted slaves as a "first step." Once public opinion evolved to general emancipation, Tidewater moderate William Henry Roane avowed, a future legislature might "drive it up to *abolition*."[78]

Alarmed at recurrent drives for abolition, conservatives once more sought to gag debate. On January 25, "Southside" Piedmont delegate Vincent Witcher urged indefinite postponement of both the committee

78. Richmond *Enquirer*, February 4, 1832.

report and the Preston amendment. Moderates joined abolitionists to defeat the "gag" resolution 71 to 60. Immediately afterward, delegates voted on the "expediency" of immediate emancipation legislation as proposed by the Preston amendment. This time, moderates joined conservatives to defeat abolitionists' measure 73 to 58.[79] As in the 1829–1830 contest over political representation, neither conservatives nor abolitionists could carry their favorite slavery proposal.

Although voting on the Witcher resolution largely followed east-west lines, it more notably exposed schisms within all sections of Virginia except the Trans-Allegheny. Easterners, particularly, were not a united, conservative bloc. Twenty-five Tidewater and thirty-one Piedmont delegates approved indefinite postponement, but ten Tidewater and ten Piedmont delegates disapproved. West of the Blue Ridge, all thirty-one Trans-Allegheny representatives disapproved, whereas Valley delegates divided twenty to four against stifling slavery debate.

More than rigid sectionalism, alignments most closely mirrored reform-conservative patterns of the 1828 convention referendum and of the 1829–1830 constitutional convention itself. Just as Tidewater "reform" sentiment had centered in major cities and proximate counties, and in Accomack County on the "Eastern Shore," so now nine of ten Tidewater opponents of indefinite postponement represented the cities of, and counties near, Richmond and Norfolk; Spotsylvania and Stafford counties near Fredericksburg; and Accomack. More than other easterners, these Tidewater delegates came from regions whose manufacturing-commercial interests and nonslaveholding white artisans and laborers believed slavery inimical to a progressive, prosperous economy.

If proximity to urban-industrial centers influenced Tidewater attitudes toward slavery, proximity to the Blue Ridge Mountains affected Piedmont voting. Like their Tidewater counterparts, Piedmont opponents of indefinite postponement all came from regions supporting democratization of representation and suffrage at the 1829–1830 convention. Of these ten Piedmont delegates, eight represented the western and northwestern counties of Albemarle, Amherst, Goochland, and Loudoun; the other two represented Buckingham and Campbell, west-

79. Virginia, *Journal of the House of Delegates, 1831–32*, p. 109. All subsequent analysis of delegates' voting is from this source.

ern counties south of the James River. Unlike most of "Southside" Piedmont, however, Campbell included the tobacco-manufacturing town of Lynchburg.

West of the Blue Ridge, of the only four delegates voting *for* indefinite postponement, two represented Frederick, the northern Valley county casting the sole western vote for the "compromise" constitution during the 1829–1830 convention; and two were from the nearby northern Valley counties of Jefferson and Shenandoah. Slaves, significantly, comprised 30.9 percent of Jefferson's population, the highest percentage of any west Virginia county.

When the house turned from indefinite postponement to the "expediency" of immediate emancipation legislation, easterners were more resolute. Of the ten Tidewater delegates who had voted *against* Witcher's conservative resolution, only three voted *for* Preston's abolitionist amendment. One, John Drummond, represented the "Eastern Shore" county of Accomack. On this peninsula, where scarcity of land precluded plantation agriculture, nonslaveholding white fishermen and mechanics abounded. Slaves comprised only 27.9 percent of Accomack's total population, the lowest of any Tidewater county. The other two Tidewater abolitionists, Robert Mayo and Alexander Jones, represented counties near major cities. Mayo was a Richmond tobacco manufacturer, and Jones's constituents lived close to Norfolk, where interest in a "large and flourishing seaport" was strong.[80]

Of the ten Piedmont opponents of indefinite postponement, six favored immediate antislavery action. Three of these were from Loudoun, the populous northwestern county where slaves comprised only 24.4 percent of total residents, and where whites had long supported "western" demands for equal representation, internal improvements, and public education. The other three abolitionists—Samuel Garland, Thomas Jefferson Randolph, and Philip Bolling—represented Amherst, Albemarle, and Buckingham, all western Piedmont counties with large slave populations, but traditionally allied with reform.

Just as the urban Tidewater and parts of the "Eastern Shore" and

80. Robert, *Tobacco Kingdom*, 190; Norfolk and Portsmouth (Va.) *Herald*, March 2, 1832. The *Herald* attributed Virginia's lack of a major seaport to the "curse of slavery." Slavery, the urban Tidewater journal protested, inhibited growth of internal improvements and of white population.

western Piedmont deviated from the east Virginia majority in approving emancipation legislation, so the northern Valley diverged from the west Virginia majority in opposing immediate action. Of only six westerners voting against the abolitionist Preston amendment, one came from Shenandoah, one from Hardy, and two each from Jefferson and Frederick. Significantly, these two latter counties contained nearly one-third (32.8 percent) of all Valley slaves. With one-fourth of Valley delegates allied with the slaveholding east, on the issue of "expediency" the Alleghenies more sharply divided Virginians than did the Blue Ridge.

Throughout the commonwealth, county racial patterns most strongly influenced alignments on emancipation. Fifty-three of the fifty-eight abolitionists represented counties where slaves comprised *less* than 30 percent of the total population. Sixty-eight of the seventy-three delegates opposed to immediate antislavery legislation represented counties where slaves comprised *more* than 30 percent.[81]

Delegates' personal slaveholdings were a less significant influence. Opponents of Preston's abolitionist amendment admittedly owned three times as many slaves as proponents. But some intransigent conservatives owned no more slaves than intransigent abolitionists. "Southsiders" Alexander Knox and John Shell were nonslaveholders, as were Trans-Allegheny delegates William Ballard Preston and George Summers. John Thompson Brown and Charles James Faulkner each owned one slave. Conservative James Gholson owned twenty blacks, whereas abolitionist Thomas Jefferson Randolph owned thirty-six.[82] Both east and west of the Blue Ridge, constituents' interests preceded legislators' property. (See Appendix, Table VII.)

Had the house been apportioned on 1830 rather than 1820 white population, legislators would have come within one vote of declaring emancipation "expedient." Democratic representation would have allowed abolitionist Trans-Allegheny and Valley regions seven more delegates, and with these antislavery westerners voting "yes," Preston's proposed emancipation amendment would only have failed by the razor-thin margin of 66–65. Conservatives who in 1829–1830 had demanded and secured disproportionate power to protect slave property had, by that action, made Virginia's march toward emancipation more arduous.

81. U.S. Census Office, *Fifth Census*, Tables [10]–[13].
82. Virginia Personal Property Books, 1831.

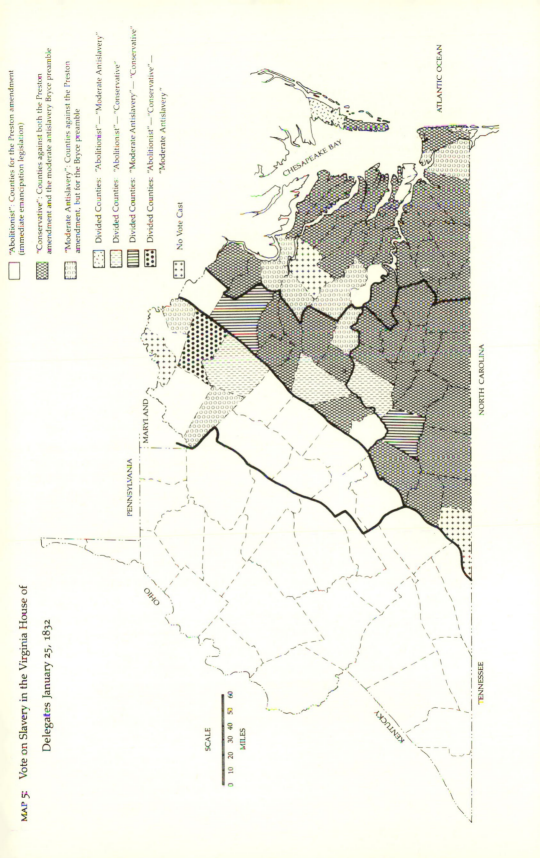

MAP 5: Vote on Slavery in the Virginia House of
Delegates January 25, 1832

"Abolitionist": Counties for the Preston amendment
(immediate emancipation legislation)

"Conservative": Counties against both the Preston
amendment and the moderate antislavery Bryce preamble

"Moderate Antislavery": Counties against the Preston
amendment, but for the Bryce preamble

Divided Counties: "Abolitionist" — "Moderate Antislavery"

Divided Counties: "Abolitionist" — "Conservative"

Divided Counties: "Moderate Antislavery" — "Conservative"

Divided Counties: "Abolitionist" — "Conservative" —
"Moderate Antislavery"

No Vote Cast

PENNSYLVANIA

MARYLAND

OHIO

KENTUCKY

TENNESSEE

NORTH CAROLINA

ATLANTIC OCEAN

CHESAPEAKE BAY

SCALE

0 10 20 30 40 50 60
MILES

Following defeat of Preston's immediate emancipation amendment, abolitionists fell back upon the milder, but still antislavery, Bryce preamble. For the house to declare slavery an evil and anticipate future emancipation, abolitionists almost unanimously agreed, was better than expressing no opposition to slavery. But conservatives again objected to adopting any antislavery amendment. The Bryce preamble, "Southside" Piedmont representative William Sims protested, contemplated "future measures on . . . abolition." Virginians had not sanctioned such action, and the house had no right to lead public opinion by proclaiming slavery an "evil."[83] A controlling coalition of moderates and abolitionists disagreed. Nine Tidewater, two Piedmont, and four Valley delegates who had voted against Preston's immediate emancipation now joined abolitionists to pass Bryce's antislavery compromise 67 to 60. Abolitionists divided 52–2, and moderates voted 15–0 *for* the Bryce preamble. Conservatives, equally staunch, opposed 58–0.[84] Such clear-cut ideological alignments indicated that, on this ultimate house resolution of the slavery issue, legislators of all persuasions, and from all sections of the state, upheld Archibald Bryce's own view of the preamble as Virginia's pledge of "final abolition," as a "first step" toward Thomas Jefferson's irrepressible dream.

Particularly for eastern and Valley moderates who unanimously cast the decisive votes proclaiming slavery an "evil," Bryce's compromise offered a "middle ground" between constituents' divided interests. All but one of the nine Tidewater moderates—Southey Grinalds of Accomack—represented areas where slaves comprised over 40 percent of the total population. At the same time, these eight also represented the cities of Richmond and Norfolk, or counties including or adjoining Richmond, Norfolk, and Fredericksburg. The two Piedmont moderates, Archibald Bryce, Jr., of Goochland, and William M. Rives of Campbell, likewise represented counties where slaves constituted, respectively, 55.1 percent and 46.7 percent of the total population. Concomitantly, extended canal routes linked Goochland commercially to Richmond, whereas Campbell included the tobacco-manufacturing town of Lynchburg.[85]

83. Richmond *Enquirer,* January 28, 1832.
84. Virginia, *Journal of the House of Delegates, 1831–32,* p. 110. Two Trans-Allegheny abolitionists, Jacob Helms of Floyd and Robert Gillespie of Tazewell, believed the Bryce preamble an inadequate antislavery declaration and thus voted "no" in protest.
85. U.S. Census Office, *Fifth Census,* Tables [10]–[13].

Three of the four Valley moderates represented the two counties—Jefferson and Frederick—with the highest slave percentages west of the Blue Ridge. Unwilling to sanction either hasty emancipation or perpetual slavery, this crucial moderate bloc instead affirmed the Jeffersonian view that abolition must reflect public opinion, and concurrently, the Jeffersonian faith that public opinion would, indeed, evolve to emancipation. In approving the Bryce preamble, the 1831–1832 house thus rejected the proslavery philosophy of the lower South and heralded Virginia's future as a free-soil state.

That a great majority of antislavery moderates, and even some abolitionists, resided within slaveholding bastions of east Virginia confirmed John Randolph's 1829 outcry against slaveholders' disloyalty to the "peculiar institution." So, too, the urban Tidewater-western Piedmont alliance with the Valley and Trans-Allegheny behind Bryce's antislavery compromise upheld Chapman Johnson's warning of nonslaveholders' hostility to slavery within the very "bosom" of eastern society.[86] Evidence of rifts within slaveholders' own ranks, and of class, not just sectional opposition to Virginia's slaveholding status quo—combined with the fact that a white-basis house already would have come within one vote of declaring emancipation "expedient"—alarmed conservatives within and without the general assembly as legislators moved toward adjournment.

The house concluded debate on slavery by passing the committee report with the Bryce preamble. Conservatives who had supported the original report as to the "inexpediency" of emancipation now voted solidly against the amended version. Abolitionists, in contrast, applauded house action. "Friends of abolition," T. J. Randolph affirmed, "have gained all that they asked." Emancipation had been brought to the "public mind" with the "view of further action. . . . You may rest assured," he wrote his troubled wife, "that a revolution has commenced which cannot go backward. . . . Silence was the strongest bulwark to slavery. Public opinion has broken this silence," and slavery is now "open to discussion."[87]

Newspapers on both sides of the Blue Ridge likewise acclaimed the

86. See Chapter III, pp. 60, 64–65, for Randolph's attack on eastern slaveholders and Johnson's warning of antislavery sentiment amongst eastern nonslaveholders.

87. Virginia, *Journal of the House of Delegates, 1831–32*, p. 110; Thomas Jefferson Randolph to Jane Randolph, January 29, 1832.

outcome of the house debate. "It appears to be a conceded point," the Valley Martinsburg *Gazette* declared, "that the West have come off conquerors . . . in the great debate" on slavery. "The East is nettled and goaded to desperation—we see frequent appeals to the people of Eastern Virginia, urging them to bring into the councils their most talented men. . . . It behooves the West to be up and doing. . . . She has talents. She has patriotism. Let her use them."[88]

The Richmond *Constitutional Whig* adopted a less strident tone in lauding legislators' course. Adoption of the committee report and Bryce preamble, the *Whig* happily informed, are *"deemed favourable to the cause of abolition."* A majority of the house had rejected perpetual slavery and proclaimed that "when public opinion is more developed . . . and means are better devised," Virginia "ought to commence a system of gradual" emancipation. "Many of the most decided friends of abolition," the *Whig* observed, "voted against the [Preston] amendment, because they thought public opinion not sufficiently *prepared.*" *Whig* editors agreed. "Habit" and "general bias" toward established institutions might "defer . . . public judgment . . . for years." Eventually, though, the "large slaveholder will be left alone to combat for slavery. . . . He will be the *only* person not convinced that slavery is a curse. The small slaveholder, the yeomanry, the mechanic, the merchant" from all sections of the commonwealth would unite to demand abolition. "These classes will not consent" to have their lives perpetually endangered, their economic rights perpetually denied. Hasty legislation, however, might "prejudice" abolitionists' cause. Legislators, *Whig* editors concluded, had acted wisely in "going no further" than the Bryce preamble "at this session."[89]

Virginians of all persuasions on slavery thus would have stoutly denied historians' latter-day view that the 1831–1832 house turned its back on Jefferson's dream of gradual emancipation and embraced instead the "pro-slavery" philosophy of John C. Calhoun and the Deep South. Far

88. Martinsburg (Va.) *Gazette,* February 16, 1832.
89. Richmond *Constitutional Whig,* January 21, 24, 26, 28, 1832. The Valley Charlestown *Virginia Free Press and Farmers' Repository,* February 16, 1832, and the Tidewater Norfolk and Portsmouth (Va.) *Herald* similarly commended the house for adopting only the moderate antislavery Bryce preamble at the present session. Unfortunately, to my knowledge, no copies of contemporary Trans-Allegheny newspapers have survived.

from revealing the strength of Virginia's commitment to the "peculiar institution," house debate dramatized slavery's tenuous status in a state with the largest slave population in the nation. Delegates from Virginia's vast Trans-Allegheny region, which already comprised 26.5 percent of the state's whites, unanimously demanded present emancipation. Although Valley representatives were somewhat less resolute, three-fourths urged immediate antislavery measures, and all but two favored future emancipation. East of the Blue Ridge, resistance to legislative emancipation was strongest in the Piedmont, with the "Southside" almost unanimously opposed to both the abolitionist Preston amendment and the moderate Bryce preamble. Yet even within Virginia's major slaveholding section, a considerable number of western Piedmont representatives deserted conservative ranks to endorse immediate and future abolition. Tidewater antislavery sentiment was still more widespread. There, though a large majority disapproved immediate emancipation, delegates from counties bordering east Virginia's two most populous cities—Richmond and Norfolk—approved Preston's amendment. Equally ominous to conservatives, a strong Tidewater minority from urban and "Eastern Shore" areas favored future antislavery legislation. Delegates voting for Bryce's antislavery compromise represented 394,067 whites, or 58 percent of Virginia's white population. Analyzed by sections, 100 percent of the Trans-Allegheny, 89.2 percent of the Valley, 35.3 percent of the Tidewater, and 17.5 percent of the Piedmont sanctioned eventual emancipation.[90] With the majority of an undemocratic house openly proclaiming slavery an "evil" and anticipating "final abolition," as Archibald Bryce, Jr., had defined his preamble's intent, antislavery Virginians of abolitionist and moderate persuasions might well regard the 1831–1832 legislative debate not as a repudiation of revolutionary hopes, but as a vigorous "fresh start" to the age-old dream of emancipation-colonization.

During the zenith of natural-rights fervor, Thomas Jefferson had determined that public opinion would not yet "bear" emancipation and, accordingly, had withheld his *post-nati* proposal. In 1796, the Virginia General Assembly had confirmed Jefferson's belief by tabling St. George

90. U.S. Census Office, *Fifth Census*, Tables [10]–[13]. Even though two Trans-Allegheny delegates voted "no" on the Bryce preamble, the Trans-Allegheny was 100 percent "abolitionist."

Tucker's abolition plan without discussion. Virginians' "general silence" on slavery, Jefferson had lamented in an 1814 letter to Edward Coles, was "unfavourable" to hopes for abolition.[91] Now, amidst public alarm occasioned by Nat Turner, Jefferson's grandson, Thomas Jefferson Randolph, had broken slavery's "seal of silence," and in so doing, the 1831–1832 house of delegates had linked Virginia's destiny more than ever to his grandfather's emancipationist dream.

Equally momentous, even delegates opposed to the antislavery declarations of the Bryce preamble did not approve the proslavery doctrines of the Deep South. Rather than permanent slaveholding allies, conservatives looked to Deep South planters as purchasers of Virginia slaves, as a means of ridding Virginia of both slavery and blacks. As Tidewater and Piedmont slaveowners shifted from single-crop to diversified agriculture, conservatives anticipated, slavery would push relentlessly southward and ultimately be confined to the cotton-sugar-rice plantations of the South and Southwest. No legislator in 1831–1832, then, assumed the perpetuity of *Virginia* slavery, or identified Virginia's interests with Louisiana, Mississippi, Alabama. Whereas the conservative minority expected "natural causes" to doom slavery, Virginia's antislavery majority hoped future legislators would effect emancipation.

A more radical antislavery stance would have precipitated a division of the state, since the large slaveholding interests of eastern Virginia would not have tolerated uncompensated, *post-nati* emancipation. In 1832, Virginians preferred compromise to dissolution. Abolitionists were willing to accept a partial victory rather than press for immediate action. As Charles J. Faulkner had declared, abolition would involve a "moral, physical, and political revolution."[92] For nearly two centuries, slavery had been deeply interwoven with Virginia's economic, political, and social structure. Few societies have overturned such basic institutions at a single legislative session. Revolutions so far-reaching are the work of time.

If the Bryce preamble were to prove more than a paper pledge, however, Virginia must begin to remove free blacks and manumitted slaves. Demonstration of the practicability of colonization, most antislavery del-

91. Ford (ed.), *The Writings of Thomas Jefferson*, X, 477–79.
92. *The Speech of Charles Jas. Faulkner*, 4.

egates believed, was crucial to continued action on emancipation. As the house turned to colonization, the ultimate meaning of the Virginia slavery debate was at stake. Would the declaration of future emancipation founder on dilemmas of race? Or would Virginia move forward gradually to "revolution"?

# VI / Dilemmas of Colonization

About "200 Free People of Colour" from "Southampton . . . and neighboring [Virginia] counties," a local American Colonization Society agent reported late in September, 1831, "are anxious to depart instantly." Although "innocent" and "unoffending," "these people and many more," John McPhail informed the society's national secretary, "are suffering severely in consequence of the late insurrection." Whites "of low character take advantage of the predjudice [sic] excited . . . against the colour" to "maltreat and abuse" free blacks. The American Colonization Society, the Norfolk agent urged, must "exert all their power" to afford Southampton emigrants "an opportunity of escaping to the land of their Fathers. . . . This is the time to strike."[1]

Just six weeks later, on December 9, 1831, the ship *James Perkins*, chartered by McPhail, set sail from Norfolk, bound for the American Colonization Society settlement, Liberia, on Africa's west coast. Of the 339 black emigrants aboard, the society's *African Repository* noted, "most . . . are from the lower part of Virginia . . . a very large proportion from Southampton." Many of these free blacks, the Norfolk and Portsmouth *American Beacon* elaborated, were "first rate Mechanics, including Blacksmiths, Carpenters, Tailors, Shoemakers, and Sawyers." Others were farmers. All, the *African Repository* proclaimed, had "high hopes of realizing in Africa, blessings which in this country could not be theirs."[2]

1. John McPhail to Ralph R. Gurley, September 23, 30, 1831, in American Colonization Society Papers.
2. American Colonization Society, *The African Repository and Colonial Journal*, VII, 320; *American Beacon* (Norfolk and Portsmouth, Va.), October 5, 1831.

Colonizationists from almost every region of Virginia were jubilant. Although all deplored the Southampton insurrection, most affirmed western Piedmont colonizationist John Hartwell Cocke's faith that a "beneficent Providence" would "overrule" this "tragedy" to the "ultimate ends of Justice and Mercy." "Excitement produced by the late insurrection," former Chief Justice John Marshall, now president of the Virginia Colonization Society declared, "makes this a favourable moment" to secure funds from state legislatures as well as laws to incline free blacks "to migrate." Proceeds from sale of public lands, the nationalistic Marshall unequivocally asserted, might also finance colonization.[3]

Marshall's more states' rightist friend, James Madison, likewise approved "territorial funds" for colonization. "A grant to Congress of the necessary authority," Madison echoed Thomas Jefferson's 1824 letter to Jared Sparks, could overcome the "Constitutional obstacle" to federal aid. As to emigrants' "new abode," Liberia was "peculiarly appropriate" and "prospects" there "highly encouraging." Present "circumstances" seemed to the aging revolutionary statesman to "brighten" hopes that the "dreadful calamity which has so long afflicted our Country . . . will be gradually removed" by the "just" and "peaceful" means of African colonization. Once adequate "asylums" and "pecuniary resources" made large-scale removal of blacks practicable, "private manumission . . . will increase" and the "great work" of emancipation proceed.[4]

Proponents of the American Colonization Society in "Southside" Virginia were more cautious. "If we are not imprudent," a society agent reported from Petersburg, "the recent massacre in Southampton will benefit our cause. It will certainly increase the disposition of . . . free people of colour to leave this state." Many whites "heretofore . . . neutral or opposed to us" would "no doubt" now favor legislative appropriations to remove free blacks. But, the Petersburg agent emphasized, "at this crisis" colonizationists must not allude to "*emancipation*." The "recent tragedy has excited the minds of *us all* in Southern Virginia to an unprecedented" degree of sensitiveness. "*A little thing* now, would prevent . . . the great progress" colonizationists "might otherwise hope for,

3. John Hartwell Cocke, Sr., to Ralph R. Gurley, October 17, 1831, in American Colonization Society Papers; John Marshall to Ralph R. Gurley, December 14, 1831, in Slaughter, *The Virginian History of African Colonization*, 59–60.
4. Gaillard Hunt (ed.), *The Writings of James Madison* (New York, 1910), IX, 468–70.

in Virginia." Should Virginia strongly endorse colonization, the Petersburg agent maintained, "No[rth] Carolina, will, very soon, and the other Southern States, ultimately follow her example. If Virginia should now be alienated," however, "my hopes for the C.S. [Colonization Society] would be extinct." The society's present "course" in Virginia's large slave-holding regions might determine "the destinies of two continents."[5]

Other "Southside" agents urged similar restraint. "I do not agree with you," a Dinwiddie County colonizationist wrote the society's national secretary, "as to the expediency of immediate efforts in this portion of Virginia. . . . Opposition to the Col. Soc. had been much greater" here than "you probably conceived." Whenever colonizationists have "publicly" pressed the society's "claims . . . senseless clamour about state rights & northern influence, etc., has at once been raised."[6] "Ultra slaveholders . . . south of the James River," another local agent concurred, "still" have "apprehensions . . . that colonizing will interfere" with slavery. In regions south and east of Richmond, it was consequently "most important to keep the two subjects" of colonization and emancipation "separate" so that "Southsiders" might support "liberal" legislative appropriations for "the cause."[7]

The Virginia Colonization Society followed such prudent path. Convening for the first time since 1828, colonizationists from every region of the commonwealth crowded into the Richmond capitol the evening of January 11, 1832. Among its diverse membership were prominent Virginians from both past and recent generations. John Marshall was president; vice-presidents included James Madison, John Tyler, former Virginia Governor James Pleasants, Abel P. Upshur (champion of 1829–1830 mixed-basis conservatives), and Philip Doddridge (champion of 1829–1830 white-basis reformers). Two outspoken members of Virginia's 1831–1832 house of delegates were also present. "Southside" moderate William Henry Brodnax, who would soon urge colonization as an "entering wedge, towards ultimate emancipation," and northwest Trans-Allegheny abolitionist John C. Campbell, who would demand immedi-

5. William Mayo Atkinson to Ralph R. Gurley, September 10, 1831, in American Colonization Society Papers.
6. John Grammer, Jr., to Ralph R. Gurley, December 14, 1831, in American Colonization Society Papers.
7. D. J. Burr to Ralph R. Gurley, December 24, 1831, April 16, 1832, in American Colonization Society Papers.

ate emancipation-colonization legislation to rid Virginia of slavery and blacks. If members differed on slavery, however, all hoped to secure widespread popular support for colonization. The Virginia society thus resolved to "confine its operations, to . . . removal of . . . free people of colour only, with their own consent."[8]

The "overflowing numbers" attending the society's meeting prompted the Richmond *Constitutional Whig* confidently to affirm that "African Colonization *has succeeded*. It has now received an impulse which cannot fail to carry it on to triumph." The annual report of the Virginia Colonization Society was similarly exuberant. Liberia, the report declared, had triumphed "over all incipient trials"; trade and agriculture showed "continued improvement"; civil, religious, and educational institutions were "well conducted." With the "practicability of African colonization" demonstrated, private citizens must now unite with the colonization society to secure larger state appropriations for this "flourishing" project.[9]

Public sentiment in most areas of Virginia echoed the call for vigorous action. Colonization petitions generally came from eastern, particularly Tidewater, counties having large numbers of free blacks. But several northern Valley counties also urged state and federal aid. Most memorials to the house of delegates reflected fears that free blacks were "incompatible" with whites' "safety and permanent tranquillity." Free blacks, Northumberland County petitioners charged, promoted a "spirit of discontent and insubordination among our slaves." Should "discontent" ripen into "insurrectionary movement," free blacks would be "master spirits . . . the most active promoters" of servile "rebellion." Slaves, Frederick County petitioners agreed, were "becoming more and more discontented by . . . continued contemplation of the (supposed) happy condition of free blacks, who live without the sweat of the brow." Virginia's free blacks, Northampton County petitioners elaborated, were an "anomalous population . . . standing in a middle position between the two extremes of our society. . . . Inferior to whites in intelligence; degraded by the stain . . . attached to their colour; excluded from many

8. Virginia Colonization Society Minute Book, 1823–1859, pp. 59–60; Richmond *Enquirer,* January 19, 1832.
9. Richmond *Constitutional Whig,* January 13, 1832; Richmond *Enquirer,* January 19, 1832.

civil privileges which the humblest white man enjoys," free blacks at the same time enjoyed a "personal freedom" that distinguished them from slaves. "Despairing of ever attaining . . . equality" with "higher" whites, free blacks "naturally connect themselves in feeling and interest with slaves" to whom all were "bound . . . by common complexion" and many by "domestic ties."[10]

Accompanying this portrait of free blacks as "inciters" of enslaved brethren was the equally common stereotype of free blacks as a "burden on the community." "Idle habits" and "want of regular employment," Fairfax County petitioners declared, made Virginia's free blacks a "profligate," "vicious," "degraded caste." Here, "they can never have the respect and intercourse . . . essential to rational happiness and social . . . improvement." Removed from the admittedly onerous Negrophobia of white Virginia, however, free blacks might become an "orderly . . . industrious, moral" population bringing to "barbarous," "benighted" Africa "blessings" of an "enlightened and Christian community." In Virginia, Northumberland County petitioners concurred, free blacks must remain "outcasts and vagrants." In Africa, "these people . . . will be placed upon a footing of liberty and equality" and "acquire rights . . . forever debarred" here. Colonization, white proponents believed, would benefit whites and blacks, Virginia and Africa.[11]

While colonization petitions portrayed free blacks as indolent and parasitical, other memorials relating to free black and slave laborers contradicted this stereotype. Demanding laws for "encouragement and protection of white mechanicks," petitioners from Culpeper County in the northwest Piedmont protested that "Mechanick trades and arts are fast falling into the hands of the black population." Already, slaves "almost exclusively carried on . . . the blacksmith's trade." Slaves and free blacks alike increasingly monopolized jobs as "stone masons, plasterers, painters, bricklayers, millers, carpenters and coopers" in Piedmont and Tidewater towns. Unable to compete with lower-paid blacks, the "white mechanick . . . east of the Blue Ridge" was consequently thrown "out of employ," his "profession . . . degraded," his "labour . . . depressed . . .

10. Virginia Legislative Petitions, Northumberland, Frederick, and Northampton Counties, 1831, Virginia State Library, Richmond. Petitions are arranged chronologically, by counties.
11. Virginia Legislative Petitions, Fairfax and Northumberland Counties, 1831, Virginia State Library, Richmond.

below its fair value." "Impoverished," he must finally abandon his "native state" and "find in the west an asylum" where his "honesty, industry, and ingenuity . . . will be appreciated." To stem migration of east Virginia's nonslaveholding whites, Culpeper memorialists urged legislation "prohibiting any slave, free negro, or mulatto" being apprenticed "to learn a trade or art."[12]

White mechanics from the "Southside" Piedmont town of Petersburg also decried "competition" of black "Carpenters, Masons, Coopers, Blacksmiths, etc." However, whereas Culpeper memorialists demanded proscription of all skilled black laborers, free and slave, Petersburg petitioners focused solely on slaves, particularly the practice of slave hiring. "As a sound rule of policy," nonslaveholding constituents of John Thompson Brown's insisted, "white men . . . ought to have . . . preference . . . in all vocations regarded as respectable, and . . . in which they are willing to embark." Slaves' "employments" should thus be "circumscribed within as narrow limits as possible," ideally "confined to agriculture and . . . menial offices." To "exclude" slaves from "mechanic arts" would allow "respectable and skilful" whites to find jobs "enough at fair and reasonable rates" so as to continue both their "trade" and their "residence." Substituting "white" for "coloured mechanics" would not only "promote . . . the interests and prospects" of skilled urban whites; it would also, Petersburg mechanics went beyond class concerns, benefit "society in general." Men who "constitute" Virginia's "bone and sinew" would no longer be "driven from a community to which," unlike slaves, "they are strongly attached and of which," they are "patriotic" citizens. Of equal concern to "public safety," slaves in "mechanic arts" enjoy a "comparative freedom . . . which may justly give rise to apprehension," whereas those in farm and domestic jobs "must ordinarily work in company with and under . . . control of white men."[13]

If the general assembly was not willing to bar "slaves altogether from mechanic arts," the course nonslaveholding Petersburg memorialists most favored, then legislators must at least "remedy" the "evils" of ur-

12. Virginia Legislative Petitions, Culpeper County, 1831, Virginia State Library, Richmond.
13. Virginia Legislative Petitions, Petersburg Town, 1831, Virginia State Library, Richmond. See Gavin Wright, *The Political Economy of the Cotton South* (New York, 1978), 123–27, for an interesting discussion of urban antislavery sentiment among white artisans and laborers.

ban slave hiring by imposing "limitations and restrictions" on slave-owners. To prevent slaves from carrying on "their trade as *master-work-men*, headmen, or contractors," masters must not allow bondsmen to establish mechanic shops unless "there be a white . . . *master-workman* or overseer . . . habitually labouring therein." With slaves laboring only as "underworkmen," white mechanics and artisans would no longer have to compete "with negroes, in offering proposals, fixing prices and making bargains for work." Moreover, slaves would no longer be "working alone," with "opportunity," as at present, "of fabricating . . . instruments of mischief . . . without observation." To further protect white artisans from slave "competition," and all whites from the dangers of black insurrectionary activity, slaves in towns must no longer be permitted to "go at large," hire themselves out, or pocket their earnings. Instead, Petersburg nonslaveholders advised, masters must arrange all slave contracts "in detail," and "receive" all "proceeds." Persons hiring slave mechanics and artisans must fully comply with aforementioned "limitations and restrictions." With slaveowners, slave employers, and slaves alike so "circumscribed," rights of nonslaveholding urban white laborers would be secure, and slavery in east Virginia towns would more closely mirror plantation and household patterns.

Chapman Johnson's 1829–1830 specter of antislavery allies in the very "bosom" of east Virginia society came to life in this 1831 memorial of Petersburg nonslaveholding white mechanics. Nonslaveholders' economic resentments reflected not just racial hostility toward blacks, but more ominous to slavery, class hostility toward whites who owned and hired out slaves. As the conservative John Thompson Brown had privately admitted, his Petersburg constituents were "divided on the question of emancipation." Urban antislavery sentiment, already evident in Brown's remark, in 1831–1832 legislative petitions, and in eastern delegates' alignments on the Bryce preamble, would intensify in post-1835 decades as slaves, especially hired slaves, became an ever larger part of the labor force in Tidewater and Piedmont towns. Slavery in Virginia was more than a sectional issue between east and west; it was also a class issue between slaveholding and nonslaveholding whites on both sides of the Blue Ridge.

Slaveholders' fear of free blacks as inciters of slave "brethren"; non-slaveholders' ire at black, especially slave, job competition; the deep-rooted Negrophobia of all white Virginians—such wide-ranging racial and economic perspectives suggested that whites of conflicting persuasions on slavery could support colonization. Conservatives could urge removal of just free blacks as a means of buttressing slavery. Abolitionists and moderates could endorse colonization of free blacks and slaves as an "entering wedge" to emancipation. Virginians who wished *all* blacks enslaved and those who wished *all* blacks removed thus could coalesce behind African colonization. With slaveholders and nonslaveholders both demanding action in the wake of Nat Turner, colonizationists expected vigorous legislative endorsement of their cause.

Legislators, too, seemed eager to commence. But a weighty obstacle obtruded. The house special committee, Tidewater member Charles Shirley Carter informed the American Colonization Society amidst initial debate on colonization, agreed as to the "expediency" of immediate measures to remove free blacks and manumitted slaves. Members disagreed, however, as to whether colonization of free blacks should be voluntary or compulsory. Although he was a "warm advocate" of African colonization, Carter acknowledged, coercion was a "painful part of the subject, for which I was not prepared." He hoped enough free blacks would *"apply* for emigration" to put the "scheme in motion."[14]

On January 27, 1832, eleven days after the committee had reported as to the "inexpediency" of abolition, chairman William Henry Brodnax presented members' conclusions on colonization. "Sound policy" as well as "enlightened philanthropy," the committee report declared, required that "all persons of colour . . . who are now free, or who may hereafter become free," be removed to Liberia or to other designated asylums outside the United States. As long as "sufficient numbers" of blacks "now free" were "willing to be transported," the report echoed Charles Carter's hopes, colonization would be voluntary. But if free blacks refused to emigrate, coercion "shall be resorted to." Males between the ages of sixteen and twenty-five, and females between fourteen and twenty-three, would be the "first class" forcibly deported. Males twenty-five to forty-five, "with their wives," and females twenty-three to forty, "having no husbands," would comprise the "second class." In an effort to mitigate such harsh policy, the report specified that

14. Charles Shirley Carter to Ralph R. Gurley, December 22, 1831, in American Colonization Society Papers.

sons under sixteen and daughters under fourteen would always accompany parents. So, too, no male over forty-five or female over forty would be colonized "without his or her consent."[15]

Colonization of "slaves hereafter emancipated" would, in all cases, be compulsory. Slaves whose owners financed transportation and "subsequent temporary support" would be removed "at the first convenient shipment of emigrants." Slaves whose masters did not would be "immediately hired out" until their labor defrayed estimated costs of removal. To implement "various purposes of this act," the special committee recommended appropriations of $100 thousand for 1833, $200 thousand annually thereafter.[16]

The house postponed consideration of the colonization bill until February 6. Outside the legislature, reaction was more immediate. "We pronounce this measure," the Richmond *Constitutional Whig* decried, "the most lawless, violent and despotic ever attempted in the United States. . . . We anxiously desire getting rid of . . . free negroes. . . . They are a nuisance and annoyance." They do not, however, pose such "danger to the public safety" as to "authorize . . . unqualified tyranny." During recent debate on abolition, the *Whig* chided, "Chairman Brodnax and others . . . challenged the constitutionality" of *post-nati* emancipation "as destroying" slaveowners' "vested right . . . to property in human beings . . . born years hence." Now those slaveholding gentlemen who "so passionately" defended "their own rights" would "cooly" abrogate free blacks' "constitutional *vested rights* to liberty and residence." To compel a "whole class . . . of free men . . . to leave the country of their nativity," *Whig* editors angrily reiterated, would "stain the Statute Book of Republican Virginia with a law which would disgrace Turkey." South of the James River, the Lynchburg *Virginian* likewise pronounced compulsory colonization "oppressive, tyrannical and unjust." To "*force* . . . free negroes to emigrate to Liberia or any where else" also contravened the voluntary principles of the American Colonization Society. Coercion, the "Southside" journal concluded, was "unnecessary." Once Liberia established a "good reputation," free blacks would willingly depart.[17]

15. Virginia, *Journal of the House of Delegates, 1831–32*, Bill No. 7, pp. 2–3.
16. *Ibid.*, 6–8.
17. Richmond *Constitutional Whig*, January 31, 1832; Lynchburg *Virginian*, February 2, 1832.

Similar opposition to compulsory colonization developed within the house of delegates. As open debate resumed, Trans-Allegheny representative John C. Campbell moved that emigration to Liberia depend on free blacks' "own consent." Coercion, the "Panhandle" abolitionist insisted, was unnecessary. Free blacks already willing to remove would absorb available state funds for two or three years. Furthermore, if Virginia commenced forcible deportation, the American Colonization Society could not cooperate. Its policy required voluntary removal of free blacks; Virginia must do the same.[18]

Committee chairman William Henry Brodnax rose to defend coercive removal. He knew, the "Southsider" began, that opponents of coercion thought themselves "sincere in their intention to remove free blacks." Nevertheless, voluntary colonization was "an absurdity," a "contradiction." The "gentleman from Brooke," Brodnax alluded to John C. Campbell, came from a part of Virginia where "there are comparatively" no free blacks. Delegates from counties with "great numbers" of free blacks could not "in truth" believe that "this class . . . is *willing*" to depart. Indeed, those who had had "opportunities of judging correctly" free blacks' "prejudices and opinions" knew that "out of about 50,000 free negroes in Virginia," no more than "1,000 could be found *really* willing to go in five years." The American Colonization Society could transport voluntary emigrants to Liberia. The committee bill provided for purchase of "additional territory" to colonize involuntary emigrants.

Coercion, Brodnax conceded, had for him "been . . . a subject of long and painful reflection." Nonetheless, he sincerely believed, "humanity and mercy are on my side." Should the general assembly adopt voluntary colonization, free blacks would still "sooner or later . . . be *forced* to leave." As Southampton reprisals had starkly revealed, nightly floggings, "lynch clubs," vigilance committees could "perpetrate" such "enormities" as to "induce" free blacks to emigrate. So, too, abrogation of free blacks' right "to hold property-obtain employment-rent residences, etc." would "make it impossible for them to remain." But surely, Brodnax protested, gentlemen could not prefer either "private or indirect compulsion" to "legal force." The former would be "arbitrary, unequal, unexpected,

18. Richmond *Enquirer*, February 14, 1832. All subsequent quotations from the colonization debate are from this source.

cruel," the latter "more general and uniform," "more just and impartial." Because free blacks would "know beforehand," legal coercion would allow time to "sell their little property and settle their affairs." In providing that husbands and wives, parents and children be colonized together, the committee bill further took "every precaution which humanity can dictate" to preserve the integrity of free blacks' domestic ties.

Just as practical and humanitarian considerations favored legal coercion, so, Brodnax argued, did Virginia's constitution. Free blacks had "many *legal* rights and privileges in Virginia, but no *constitutional* ones." They were not citizens, or members of the political community. All white citizens, the general affirmed, wished to remove free blacks. Delegates then must effect the "*constitutional* POWER which the State Government possesses" to forcibly and systematically deport "these people."

Northern Piedmont representative Thomas Marshall challenged Brodnax's view of compulsory colonization as comparatively "mild" and "humane." "Public sentiment," John Marshall's thirty-five-year-old son contended, would never "sanction" such "harsh," "inhuman" policy. Free blacks have "vested rights" here, rights which they "are entitled" to enjoy unless "forfeited . . . by misconduct." Provisions of the 1806 manumission act requiring emancipated slaves to emigrate had never been implemented, Marshall noted, because they "violated" Virginians' "feelings." Expulsion of free blacks would be similarly inoperative. If Virginia "resorted to compulsion," young Marshall further observed, the American Colonization Society could not settle these free blacks in Liberia. No other asylum presently existed. As many free blacks would consent to emigrate, the Piedmont delegate agreed with John Campbell, as state funds could presently finance and Liberia could presently receive. Let Virginia commence with voluntary removal of free blacks, then, lest she be "denounced" for "cruel" coercion.

"Eastern Shore" representative Miers Fisher defended Brodnax's contention that the great majority of Virginia free blacks would not willingly depart. Liberia, Fisher observed, could accommodate any voluntary emigrants "first removed," and additional territory could "later" be acquired for more numerous involuntary colonists. Free blacks, the Northampton County delegate declared, "form a pernicious association with our slaves." No "ties . . . bind" free blacks to "white men," nor do they "enjoy" white men's "rights." Only "personal liberty . . . raised" free blacks "above slaves," and that "liberty" results in "degradation," not "elevation" of free blacks' "character." Expunge legal coercion, Fisher repeated Brodnax's warning, and whites' "harsh treatment" would "force" free blacks to depart.

As Fisher concluded, Archibald Bryce, Jr., architect of compromise in the abolition debate, again proposed a "middle ground" between compulsory and voluntary colonization. Coercion, the western Piedmont delegate advanced, should apply to all blacks "freed hereafter" and to those, now free, who resided in Virginia contrary to mandatory emigration provisions of the 1806 manumission act. Blacks free before 1806, and thus legally entitled to residence, must consent to remove.

John C. Campbell again objected. Almost three-fifths of the state's free blacks, the Trans-Allegheny voluntarist noted, resided illegally. To compel these to emigrate would anger all blacks, free and slave, and increase the "danger" of servile insurrection. He agreed with Bryce that slaves "freed hereafter" must be forcibly colonized. But free blacks must consent.

In legislating to remove free blacks, the house thus could follow one of three possible paths. Colonization could be compulsory, voluntary, or a combination of the two. Removal of manumitted slaves, in contrast, presented no dilemmas. Delegates favoring state-financed colonization of blacks "freed hereafter" agreed that, "in all cases," freedmen would be forcibly deported.

Although voluntarists and coercionists each raised practical, constitutional, and moral objections to their opponents' course, neither side had adequately defended its principles. On practical grounds, voluntarists had the upper hand. Liberia was the only established black asylum, the American Colonization Society the only established agency available to transport and settle black emigrants. Coercionists maintained that "additional territory" could be "readily acquired" for blacks forcibly removed, but they did not specify how, where, or when such territory could be obtained. Would Virginia seek federal cooperation or attempt to organize a colony under state auspices? If the former, would other southern states tolerate national government involvement? If the latter, did Virginia have adequate funds to sustain this large-scale operation?

Lofty obstacles attended coercive removal; voluntarism followed a more traveled road.

On constitutional grounds, however, coercionists were more convincing. As Brodnax asserted, Virginia's constitution did not protect free blacks. Voluntarists' allusions to "vested rights" were markedly vague, elusive. Virginia laws recognized free blacks' personal liberty and their right to own landed property, yet the state's 47,349 free blacks were not citizens, but aliens, and thus *could* be forcibly colonized. Furthermore, as John C. Campbell had just noted, over half of Virginia's free blacks had been emancipated under the 1806 manumission act and thus already resided illegally. Virginia had only to enforce its own law to mock voluntarists' appeal to free blacks' legal rights.

Both sides deserted "humanity." Coercive colonization was inherently harsh and oppressive. Despite Brodnax's claims, such policy *would* tear husbands from wives, parents from children. Many free blacks were married to slaves, and manumission required slaveholders' consent; thus forcible deportation could not assure the integrity of black families. To remove an entire class, to force them to sell their property and migrate to unfamiliar, distant lands—this vision violated many Virginians' sense of benevolence. Even proponents found coercion a "painful subject." Their intentions were, in part, humane. Their means were not.

Voluntarists' means were equally dubious. Suppose Virginia's free blacks did not "consent" to remove? For colonization to succeed, would not some mode of indirect force then be necessary? Indiscriminate slaughter and harassment of blacks following the Southampton insurrection testified to whites' capacity for racial brutality. Continuous violence and extralegal oppression could ultimately drive free blacks to Africa, as emigrants aboard the ship *James Perkins* dramatized. But was colonization by involuntary consent any more "humane" than systematic, legal expulsion? Voluntarists side-stepped this grim possibility. Their course *required* that free blacks embrace white men's tainted dream of separate racial destinies.

After abbreviated debate, the house, on February 7, rejected both Brodnax's coercion and Bryce's compromise and by a strong majority of 71 to 54 adopted Campbell's voluntary colonization of free blacks, involuntary colonization of manumitted slaves. Although most westerners favored, and most easterners opposed voluntarism, alignments were less sectional than voting on emancipation.[19]

Patterns of racial distribution most directly influenced delegates' views. The Trans-Allegheny, where free blacks comprised only 0.8 percent of the total population and 3.4 percent of all Virginia free blacks, cast the highest percentage of votes—79 percent—for Campbell's voluntary colonization. The Valley, where free blacks comprised 2.7 percent of the total population and 10 percent of the state's free blacks, almost as resolutely endorsed voluntarism, with 76 percent of its delegates voting "yes." The Tidewater, in contrast, where free blacks represented 7.6 percent of the total population and a whopping 61.2 percent of all free blacks, cast the highest percentage of votes—66.6 percent—against voluntary removal. Of Virginia's major sections, only the Piedmont, where free blacks comprised just 2.7 percent of the total population but 25.4 percent of the state's free blacks, was markedly divided. With representatives from "Southside," western and northern counties all crisscrossing sides, twenty Piedmont delegates—or 49 percent—approved, whereas nineteen—or 51 percent—disapproved voluntary removal of free blacks. Where free blacks were least visible, then, legislators generally embraced the principle of "consent to remove." But where free blacks were a significant social component, legislators generally favored legal force to assure removal of this "anomalous" class.[20]

Although less weighty than racial demography, attitudes toward slavery also influenced alignments on voluntary versus coercive colonization of free blacks. Abolitionists who denied slaveholders' right to hold *post-nati* blacks in perpetual bondage generally denied white men's right to force free blacks to remove. Conservatives who upheld masters' right to enchain present and future slaves generally upheld white men's right to coerce all blacks, slave or free. Just as geographic alignments were somewhat blurred, however, so ideological alignments were quite often indistinct. Such intransigent abolitionists as Charles J. Faulkner, Samuel Garland, and Philip Bolling joined equally intransigent conservatives John Thompson Brown, William O. Goode, and Vincent Witcher in favor of coercive colonization of free blacks. Conversely, abo-

19. Virginia, *Journal of the House of Delegates, 1831–32*, pp. 136–37.
20. *Ibid.*; U.S. Census Office, *Fifth Census*, Tables [10]–[13].

litionists Thomas Jefferson Randolph, William Ballard Preston, and John Drummond allied with conservatives James Gholson, Charles S. Carter, and Southampton County representative Jeremiah Cobb in favor of voluntarism. A majority of Piedmont abolitionists and moderates approved voluntary colonization; a majority of Tidewater abolitionists and moderates disapproved.

Hodge-podge coalitions highlighted white Virginians' dilemma. Although all despised blacks, a majority of house members could not translate inveterate Negrophobia into support for forcible expulsion of *free* blacks. Slaves "freed hereafter" would be coerced, but to uproot an entire class of *free* men, even free black men, and treat them as white men's property smacked of slavery. Virginians denied free blacks' equality. Most could not so unabashedly disregard their liberty. With free blacks the major initial component of Virginia's colonization "experiment," voluntarism might well pose an unforeseen stumbling block to resolute action.

Following adoption of Campbell's voluntarist amendment, the house turned to financial matters. Members squabbled over appropriations for initial phases of colonization. Some proposed to halve the $100 thousand recommended by the special committee for 1833 on grounds that public opinion had not authorized such extensive operation. Others maintained that public opinion favored effectual colonization and would approve generous funding. Colonization, Trans-Allegheny abolitionist George Summers argued, not only intended to remove free blacks, but also to encourage voluntary manumissions as an "entering wedge" to emancipation. He hoped legislators would appropriate ample funds to "show the world" that "Virginia . . . was in earnest . . . in commencing" this momentous venture.[21]

Summers' bloc prevailed. The house, on February 15, approved $35 thousand for the remainder of 1832, $90 thousand for 1833. Immediately afterward, "Southsider" John Thompson Brown moved to delete provisions for blacks "freed hereafter" and, thereby, restrict colonization appropriations to blacks already free. Removal of free blacks, the Petersburg conservative contended, would absorb available state funds for

21. Richmond *Enquirer*, February 16, 1832. All subsequent quotations from the debate on colonization appropriations are from this source.

the next decade. Individual masters, not the Virginia legislature, should finance colonization of manumitted slaves.

Antislavery colonizationists of both abolitionist and moderate persuasions protested that Brown's amendment would discourage manumission. Many slaveholders willing to emancipate, "Panhandle" abolitionist John Campbell and "Southside" moderate William Henry Brodnax agreed, could not pay to colonize their slaves. Furthermore, Piedmont moderate Thomas Marshall noted, slaves manumitted without means for removal would be immediately hired out to defray colonization costs. Blacks "freed hereafter" thus would finance their own transportation to Liberia and would, in no instance, remain in Virginia. He urged those committed to antislavery provisions of the Bryce preamble to retain state-financed colonization of manumitted slaves.

A majority of the house concurred. Voting 60 to 41 against Brown's proposal, delegates resolved that state funds would remove free blacks *and* manumitted slaves.[22] Unfortunately, though total "ayes" and "noes" have survived, delegates' individual voting records have not. Preceding debate indicates, however, that abolitionists and moderates strongly opposed, and conservatives strongly supported, this attempt to quash state colonization of manumitted slaves. The vote on the Brown amendment must thus have been another vote on the Bryce preamble itself and, as such, was the key house statement on emancipation-colonization in 1831–1832. In defeating conservatives' last-ditch motion, the house defined colonization as indeed an "entering wedge" and reconfirmed Virginia's pledge of "final abolition."

The following day, the house passed the colonization bill by a lopsided majority of 79–41. The Tidewater unanimously approved; all other sections, in contrast, sharply divided. Twenty-four Piedmont delegates approved, but fifteen opposed. West of the Blue Ridge, the Valley voted 13 to 10 *for*, the Trans-Allegheny 16 to 12 *against*, state removal of free blacks and manumitted slaves. Ideological alignments were similarly confused. Delegates of abolitionist and conservative persuasions crisscrossed on both sides of colonization. Those who had earlier endorsed

22. *Ibid.* Although both the Richmond *Enquirer* and 1831–32 house *Journal* include total "ayes" and "noes," neither of these official sources lists individual votes on Brown's motion to expunge state colonization of manumitted slaves.

the Preston amendment's call for immediate emancipation legislation now divided 28 to 24 in favor of colonization. Tidewater and Piedmont abolitionists unanimously approved. Valley and Trans-Allegheny abolitionists voted respectively 9 to 8 *for*, and 16 to 12 *against*, state-financed removal.[23]

Delegates who had earlier opposed both the abolitionist Preston amendment and the moderate Bryce preamble now voted 36 to 16 for colonization. This seemingly more unified posture, however, disguised substantial disunity within conservative ranks. Tidewater conservatives, representing a section whose huge free black population led *all* delegates to favor removal, voted 20–0 for the 1832 colonization bill. However, Piedmont conservatives, representing a section with relatively fewer free blacks, but relatively more slaves, split 15–15. Having failed to expunge provisions for blacks "freed hereafter," uncompromising Piedmont conservatives now refused to endorse colonization as an "entering wedge." Valley conservatives followed their Piedmont counterparts in evenly dividing, 1–1, on colonization.

If abolitionists and conservatives crisscrossed alliances, moderates did not. Delegates who had earlier opposed Preston's immediate emancipation but approved Bryce's antislavery compromise now voted 15–1 for colonization. Removal of free blacks and manumitted slaves, the Bryce preamble affirmed, was a crucial first step. Ideologically consistent Tidewater, Piedmont, and Valley moderates resolutely sanctioned immediate colonization as an "entering wedge" to "final abolition."

That abolitionists and conservatives could coalesce on all sides highlighted contradictions inherent to colonization. Was removal of free blacks intended gradually to undermine slavery, or to strengthen the institution by ridding Virginia of an "anomalous population"? Abolitionists and conservatives alike seemed indecisive. Of the seventy-nine delegates approving colonization, abolitionists represented 35.4 percent, conservatives, 45.6 percent. Conversely, of the 41 "no" votes, abolitionists cast 58.5 percent, conservatives, 39.1 percent. Moderates, then, provided the crucial margin of support—19 percent—for the 1832 house colonization

23. Virginia, *Journal of the House of Delegates, 1831–32*, p. 158. Analysis of ideological alignments on colonization is based on delegates' earlier voting on the Preston amendment and the Bryce preamble. For these earlier divisions on slavery, see Chapter V, pp. 160–62, 164–65.

bill. Although conservatives were a strong minority, delegates favoring either present or future emancipation comprised a procolonization majority.

Amidst incongruous alignments, discernible patterns emerged. East of the Blue Ridge, the Tidewater and northern and western Piedmont soundly endorsed colonization, whereas the "Southside" Piedmont soundly opposed. Moving westward, most Valley counties bordering the Blue Ridge Mountains approved; most bordering the Alleghenies disapproved. The Trans-Allegheny cast the sole sectional majority against colonization, but voting here showed no marked regional divisions. Delegates from "Panhandle," central, and southwestern counties scattered on both sides of the issue. Statewide, then, anticolonization sentiment centered in Virginia's most extreme slaveholding *and* nonslaveholding bastions. Of the forty-one house members voting "no," two-thirds represented "Southside" Piedmont and Trans-Allegheny counties.

Although the "Southside" Piedmont had considerable numbers of free blacks, slaveholders there, as American Colonization Society agents had already reported, generally distrusted colonization as an abolitionist plot. As the heart of Virginia's slaveholding, plantation economy, this region south of the James River reflected attitudes, prevalent among Deep South planters, that removal of free blacks and manumitted slaves would culminate in government interference with slavery itself. "Southside" hostility to state colonization thus was ideologically consistent with earlier opposition to legislative emancipation. Intransigent conservatives may have identified Virginia's destiny with freedom—but slaveholders' interest, not government action, would abolish slavery.

Trans-Allegheny opposition to colonization, conversely, contradicted that section's definition of Virginia's long-run interests. Just three weeks earlier, Trans-Allegheny abolitionists had almost unanimously endorsed the Bryce preamble declaring slavery an "evil," and colonization a prelude to emancipation. Yet now, despite their belief that colonization of freedmen was integral to abolition, a majority of Virginia's most extreme antislavery ideologues resisted efforts to remove free blacks and manumitted slaves. If easterners would not commence abolition, these Trans-Allegheny ideologues seemingly reasoned, westerners would not approve state funds to remove free blacks, a class comprising only 0.8 percent of the total Trans-Allegheny population. This short-sighted,

provincial outlook confirmed fears expressed by a Richmond colonizationist before debate began that "the abolition party in our legislature
will not assist in removing . . . free negroes unless in conjunction with a
scheme for . . . total abolition of slavery." Preferring inaction to compromise, Trans-Allegheny anticolonizationists similarly ignored William
Henry Brodnax's plea that legislators not "refuse to do anything because
we cannot obtain all we desire." Such view of colonization as beneficial
only to eastern slaveholding interests paralleled conservatives' view of
emancipation as beneficial only to the nonslaveholding west and augured ill for Virginia's harmonious resolution of the slavery issue.[24]

If a majority of Trans-Allegheny abolitionists voted against colonization, a large, more consistent minority determined to carry out antislavery pledges of the Bryce preamble. Men like John C. Campbell, George
Summers, and William Ballard Preston who had led their section's drive
for immediate emancipation legislation now joined Valley and eastern
abolitionists and moderates to form an antislavery majority resolved to
take that initial step. Some, perhaps, regretted that so many conservatives embraced the dream of colonization. But at least Virginia would begin. And who could foretell whether that dream, once begun, might not
lead to "revolution"? Someday, antislavery colonizationists anticipated,
legislators might indeed record a tale of peaceful emancipation in Virginia's "book of fate."

For over two months, the house had debated the destiny of Virginia's
black population. Delegates had endorsed future emancipation of slaves
and voluntary colonization of free blacks, yet still the specter of Southampton lingered. Something more must be done *now*, delegates believed, to protect whites from other Nat Turners. As Governor Floyd had
urged in his annual message, laws governing slaves and free blacks
must effect "due subordination."[25]

Soon after passing the colonization bill, the house tightened existent
black codes and adopted harsh new regulations. Acting on widely held
beliefs that Negro preachers had sparked the Southampton insurrection, delegates barred all blacks, slave and free, from preaching, exhort-

24. Benjamin Brand to Ralph R. Gurley, January 23, 1832, in American Colonization
Society Papers; *The Speech of William H. Brodnax*, 29.
25. Virginia, *Journal of the House of Delegates, 1831–32*, pp. 9–10.

ing, or conducting religious meetings. Furthermore, unless accompanied by their "white family," slaves could not attend nighttime religious assemblages. Slaves could, however, receive spiritual instruction from masters.[26] Rather than inflammatory doctrines of equality, brotherhood, and natural rights, Virginia slaveholders presumably would inculcate the more "appropriate" Christian virtues of humility, loyalty, obedience.

As in the aftermath of Gabriel's aborted rebellion, legislators clamped down most severely on allegedly "dangerous" free blacks. Abrogating present rights to trial by jury, the 1832 "Police Bill" specified that "hereafter," free blacks would "be prosecuted, tried, convicted, and punished . . . by justices of oyer and terminer, in the same manner as slaves." Courts of "oyer and terminer," composed of county court justices, had heretofore been reserved for "speedy prosecution of slaves." Furthermore, the governor could sell and transport "free negroes" convicted of crimes punishable by death "as if" such person "were a slave."[27]

Along with denial of free blacks' civil rights, the "Police Bill" also proscribed free blacks' economic rights. Any free black "tradesman or mechanic" who refused "an opportunity" of state-financed "removing . . . to Liberia" could no longer practice "his trade or handicraft" in Virginia "except by special permission" of the local county court. So, too, "under no circumstances" could free black tradesmen or mechanics "hereafter . . . take apprentices . . . or . . . teach their trade or art to any other person." The bill exempted one group of free blacks from such restrictions. "Coloured barbers," a job long shunned by whites as "nigger work," could "take apprentices."[28]

A majority of the house had recently rejected compulsory colonization of free blacks as tyrannical and unjust. Yet, as Brodnax had feared, delegates now sanctioned rigid repression of free blacks who refused to depart. Indirect compulsion seemingly stirred fewer humanitarian qualms. Almost four decades earlier, St. George Tucker had similarly palled at coercive expulsion of Virginia freedmen but condoned oppressive measures to encourage "voluntary" emigration. Although

26. *Ibid.*, Bill No. 13, pp. 1–2.
27. *Ibid.*, 7.
28. *Ibid.*, 4–5.

the 1831–1832 house was willing to coerce manumitted slaves, most resorted to civil and economic proscription to rid the commonwealth of free blacks.

Outside the house, reaction to the "Police Bill" was unreservedly hostile. Newspapers east of the Blue Ridge declared denial of trial by jury "against liberty," a "recession toward despotism." While protesting "encroachments" upon free blacks' civil rights, however, the press particularly decried provisions barring free blacks from "handicrafts arts." Legislators, the Charlottesville *Virginia Advocate* remarked, had "very wisely and humanely" rejected coercive colonization. "They seem willing, however, to effect the same end" by means "infinitely more odious and barbarous. . . . Is this mercy to the free negro . . . to say . . . 'we shall not *force* you to go to Liberia, but *you shall not live here*'? . . . Open, avowed compulsion" was preferable to "cruel" economic coercion. The Richmond *Constitutional Whig* agreed. Although Virginia had declared "that she will not *directly* compel these people to leave," *Whig* editors objected, the house would "indirectly and insidiously . . . *compel*" free blacks "to fly to Africa . . . by prohibiting the exercise of mechanic arts. . . . A most Christian and Statesmanlike Bill," the *Whig* chided, "which our posterity will be proud of, as illustrating . . . our expanded views and comprehensive benevolence."[29]

Proscription of free black mechanics was not only inhumane; it was also, the Fredericksburg *Political Arena* charged, inexpedient. By converting the "respectable, industrious and useful portion" of free blacks into "degraded . . . idle . . . paupers," the "Police Bill" would "inflict . . . a most grievous injury . . . upon the whole community. . . . The citizens" of east Virginia "*Towns*," where free black tradesmen and mechanics abounded, would particularly suffer. Public opinion would never support such "suicidal legislation," and the bill would be a "dead letter from the day of its enactment."[30]

Passage of the colonization and police bills concluded house action on Virginia's black population. Senate approval was now necessary before either measure became law, and the upper body turned first to colonization. Controversy immediately developed over state-financed re-

29. Richmond *Constitutional Whig*, March 5, 1832; *Virginia Advocate* (Charlottesville), March 9, 1832.
30. *Political Arena* (Fredericksburg, Va.), March 6, 1832.

moval of manumitted slaves. Echoing his house counterpart, John Thompson Brown, "Southside" Piedmont Senator George C. Dromgoole moved to strike out this measure and, thereby, require individual slaveowners to pay for African deportation.[31]

The senate, on March 6, defeated Dromgoole's amendment by a 15–15 tie. All seven Trans-Allegheny senators opposed, whereas six of seven Tidewater senators approved restricting colonization appropriations to free blacks. Valley and Piedmont senators were less resolute. The Valley divided 3 to 2 against, the Piedmont 7 to 4 for deleting the Bryce preamble's provisions for manumitted slaves.[32]

Except for the Valley,[33] senate alignments on the Dromgoole amendment closely followed earlier house voting on slavery. The solidly abolitionist Trans-Allegheny solidly opposed diluted colonization. So, too, three of the four Piedmont opponents represented senatorial districts comprising the abolitionist or moderate counties of Loudoun, Goochland, and Fauquier. Likewise, five of seven Piedmont proponents represented the conservative "Southside." The sole Tidewater opponent of the Dromgoole amendment represented the senatorial district of Accomack-Elizabeth City-Warwick-Northampton. Delegates from these counties had cast two of three Tidewater votes for the abolitionist Preston amendment.

Antislavery senators enjoyed but a short-lived victory. On March 10, following a motion to reconsider, the senate passed Dromgoole's amendment 17 to 13. Two members absent on the initial vote—one from "Southside" Piedmont, one from the slaveholding Valley district of Jefferson and Frederick—allied with conservatives. Moreover, the sole "Southside" Piedmont senator formerly opposed now shifted to conservative ranks. Colonization funds, the senate resolved, would be restricted to free blacks who "consented to remove."[34]

Irate Trans-Allegheny senators quickly retaliated. Rather than taxing all Virginians, "Panhandle" Senator Charles Morgan resolved, let each

31. Virginia, *Journal of the Senate of the Commonwealth of Virginia, 1831–32* (Richmond, 1832), 148.

32. *Ibid.*

33. The two Valley senators voting for the Dromgoole amendment represented counties whose house representatives had unanimously approved both the abolitionist Preston amendment and the moderate Bryce preamble.

34. Virginia, *Journal of the Senate, 1831–32*, p. 166.

county finance colonization of its own free blacks. If conservative eastern and Valley members would quash state removal of manumitted slaves, Trans-Allegheny abolitionists would resist being taxed to transport free blacks.[35] The senate defeated Morgan's proposal 16 to 15. Alignments did not follow senate divisions on colonization of slaves but instead reflected house coalitions on colonization *per se*. Several Piedmont "Southsiders," hostile to any colonization as an emancipationist front, joined uncompromising Trans-Allegheny abolitionists to support county financing of free blacks. Conversely, several antislavery Valley and Piedmont senators, committed to effectual commencement of Virginia's "experiment," allied with conservative eastern colonizationists against Morgan's scheme.

Shortly before final voting on removal of free blacks, Tidewater Senator John Joynes, who had cast that section's only vote against the Dromgoole amendment, proposed that colonization be indefinitely postponed. The watered-down senate bill, Joynes believed, compromised the antislavery spirit of the Bryce preamble. Better to delay colonization than to begin without appropriations for manumitted slaves. The senate adopted Joynes' resolution 18 to 14. Alignments almost exactly paralleled those on county financing, with Trans-Allegheny and Valley abolitionists joining Piedmont anticolonizationists in favor of postponement, and three antislavery Piedmont senators joining six Tidewater, three Piedmont, and two Valley conservatives to urge present action. With help from representatives of Virginia's slaveholding bastions, the majority of antislavery senators succeeded in suspending further consideration of colonization by the 1831–1832 general assembly.[36]

Had apportionment reflected 1830 white population, conservative "Southside" Piedmont districts would have lost two senators and the abolitionist Trans-Allegheny would have gained two. If alignments had subsequently followed 1832 patterns, a republican senate would have defeated the Dromgoole amendment by a 16–16 tie. This senate could then have endorsed state colonization of manumitted slaves and thereby have committed Virginia to the voluntary emancipation policy already sanctioned by the house. Again, Virginia's undemocratic government

35. *Ibid.*, 167–69.
36. *Ibid.*, 169–70; Richmond *Constitutional Whig*, March 13, 1832.

obstructed action on slavery. Defeat of equal political representation at the 1829–1830 convention ultimately precluded action in 1832 on even the moderate antislavery provisions of the Bryce preamble.

During closing days of the session, senators took up the controversial "Police Bill." Members endorsed proscriptions against black preachers and religious assemblies and against free blacks' right to trial by jury. Before approving the new code, however, the senate expunged house-backed restrictions on free black mechanics. Humanitarian concerns may have prompted such action, or perhaps, following postponement of colonization, economic coercion no longer seemed expedient. As several legislative petitions had indicated, free blacks provided cheap skilled and unskilled labor in many areas of east Virginia. The amended "Police Bill" passed the house on March 15. Six days later, the tumultuous 1831–1832 Virginia General Assembly adjourned.[37]

As the final gavel sounded, legislators rose wearily from their seats and strode out of the capitol. Most stopped only to exchange genial farewells with departing friends; others looked quietly out over sun-drenched terrain of the James River Valley. Everywhere on this late-March morn, winter seemed to be giving way. Grassy slopes were slowly turning green. Tiny buds were sprouting on bushes and trees. Red-breasted robins scouted eagerly for worms amidst yellow and purple crocuses.

Yet as delegates lingered on Richmond's Capitol Square, some may have wondered whether nature's promise of rebirth was only an illusion, a taunting reminder of man's perennial hopes for a new beginning. For there also, glistening in the spring sunlight, stood the crumbling white facade of Virginia's capitol. This "city on a hill," too, once had augured a fresh start for mankind, a republic in which all men could escape Old World oppression and decay. Yet already Jefferson's edifice showed the erosions of time, and still his dream of universal freedom lay unfulfilled. Would man's quest for a better world prove always elusive? Must this dream, like promises of spring, inevitably yield to the cold, stark realities of winter? Was there no deliverance from Virginia's slaveholding past?

37. Virginia, *Journal of the Senate, 1831–32*, pp. 175–78; Virginia, *Acts Passed at a General Assembly, 1831–32*, Chap. XXII, 20–22. Senate debate on the "Police Bill" is, to my knowledge, unavailable. The act, in its final form, placed no restrictions on free blacks' pursuit of "mechanical arts." Virginia, *Journal of the House of Delegates, 1831–32*, pp. 200, 256.

No Virginian in the spring of 1832 could foresee the final outcome of Jefferson's long-elusive dream. None could determine the ultimate import of the angry confrontation between slaveholding and nonslaveholding whites. Those who wished to consummate the dream, though, took heart. Already, house debate had exposed widespread hostility to slavery. Over the years, abolitionists anticipated, Virginia's white nonslaveholding majority would prevail. The "march of time" was on their side.

Conservatives also believed that time favored abolitionists. Although an unrepublican house had staved off *post-nati* legislation, a majority had publicly proclaimed slavery an "evil" and committed Virginia to future emancipation. Delegates had also resolved to encourage private manumissions by approving immediate colonization funds for blacks "freed hereafter." The Virginia Senate, admittedly, had eliminated voluntary emancipationist policies of the Bryce preamble. Yet even in the more conservative upper house, antislavery senators had thwarted efforts to commence colonization without manumitted slaves. How much longer, conservatives fretted, could slaveholders resist majority will? In 1829–1830 conservatives had feared a white-basis house would erode slavery by oppressive taxation. Now, despite dilution of democracy in Virginia's 1830 constitution, threats to slave property appeared more imminent, direct. Led by representatives from the increasingly populous Trans-Allegheny, abolitionists on both sides of the Blue Ridge had demanded legislative confiscation of *post-nati* slaves.

The agitation of emancipation, conservatives determined, must cease, for silence was indeed the "strongest bulwark" to slavery. Silence, too, would best protect white lives. What could better "excite" a "spirit of rebellion" amongst "our slaves," Tidewater house member Thomas Smith wrote his brother shortly before the general assembly adjourned, than to know that "about one half of the white people wish to keep them in slavery, while the other half wanted to free them?"[38]

Ongoing abolition debate would not only jeopardize whites' safety; it would also, the conservative Smith echoed John Randolph's 1829 "tocsin of civil war," destroy the integrity of the commonwealth. Discussion of emancipation had aroused "more anger and unkind feelings than I have ever witnessed on any occasion. . . . At one time, I . . . almost doubted

38. Thomas Smith to William P. Smith, February 25, 1832, in William P. Smith Papers, Duke University Library, Durham, N.C.

whether" slaveholders had "any right to our property. If it be by the will of the western people," the Tidewater delegate declared, "it is by a very precarious tenure." Should abolition be "again agitated," slaveholders must "divide the State." This will be the "only means" by which slave property "can be secure." Hostile enslaved blacks and hostile non-slaveholding whites seemed everywhere to confront distraught Virginia conservatives.

With abolitionists confident and conservatives despondent about Virginia's future, blacks, too, might well have pondered their destiny. A month before the 1831–1832 general assembly adjourned, Southampton County free blacks aboard the ship *James Perkins* had disembarked on Liberia's distant shores.[39] As they stepped for the first time onto African soil, none could foresee what ventures lay ahead. Like whites who dreamed of a free-soil Virginia, these former Tidewater free blacks must also have hoped for a fresh start, a chance to escape the bigotry and oppression of white America. Whites' cruel harassment, not blacks' voluntary consent, had driven these emigrants from Virginia. But perhaps, as antislavery colonizationists anticipated, Liberia's advantages would prompt growing numbers of free blacks to set sail and, ultimately, lead to general emancipation. White and black men's dreams of liberty might thus slowly intertwine to rid Virginia of slavery and blacks.

Antislavery Virginians in 1832 did not view African colonization as a futile fantasy, but as an integral component of abolition. Although arduous, emancipation and deportation of Virginia's slaves, antislavery colonizationists believed, was *financially* and *physically* practicable. Virginians' insistence on voluntary removal of the largest initial group of emigrants, however, made free blacks the arbiters of colonization "experiments." Should a future general assembly endorse colonization and free blacks resist, would Virginians then sanction coercion to demonstrate the practicability of large-scale emigration? Or would emancipationist promises of the Bryce preamble prove forever stillborn? Just as the slave Nat Turner had sparked initial debate on abolition, so free blacks might well write the final contents of Virginia's "book of fate."

39. American Colonization Society, *The African Repository and Colonial Journal*, VIII, 44.

# VII / Free Blacks Foil the "Experiment"

As the Virginia house concluded debate on slavery late in January, 1832, not far from the capitol on Shockoe Hill, one of Richmond's most prominent residents took up his pen to decry abolitionists' "ill-timed . . . inflammatory" speeches.[1] Just as he had led conservative opposition to constitutional reform in years before 1829, and to white-basis representation within the 1829–1830 convention, so now Benjamin Watkins Leigh came forward to champion conservatives' crusade against emancipation.

"Who could have anticipated," Leigh exclaimed in his *Letter of Appomatox to the People of Virginia*, that "bloody horrors of Southampton" would "give birth to schemes of emancipation . . . instead of plans for stricter [slave] discipline?" Equally "extraordinary," who could have believed that Richmond newspapers would "publish and disseminate" abolitionists' "pernicious" doctrines? "Richmond!" Leigh protested, "the place of all others, where their influence is most likely to take effect on the minds of the blacks, and to spread." Neither "hallucinations of another Nat Turner" nor "incendiary writings of the *Liberator*" could better "incite servile rebellion" than "speeches delivered in our own legislature" and promulgated "by our own public journals."[2]

Turning from denunciations of open debate to attacks on antislavery measures proposed in the house, Leigh reiterated conservative notions of the inviolability of slave property, present and future, and of the im-

1. Mordecai, *Richmond in By-Gone Days*, 63–64; "Appomatox" [Benjamin Watkins Leigh], *The Letter of Appomatox to the People of Virginia* (Richmond, 1832), 21.
2. "Appomatox," *Letter of Appomatox to the People of Virginia*, 7, 20–21.

196

practicability of compensated emancipation-colonization. If "put to . . . actual experiment," *Appomatox* contended, Thomas Jefferson Randolph's *post-nati* scheme would "produce a general servile war" ending in "destruction of the negro race. . . . Parent slaves, seeing their children destined to . . . freedom, will think themselves entitled to participate in the blessing." So, too, young slaves, "with liberty . . . in prospect," will not "await patiently." As a final "objection to Mr. Randolph's plan," to "refer . . . emancipation to . . . qualified voters throughout the commonwealth" would "directly violate" provisions of the "new constitution" apportioning representation with "an especial view to . . . security of . . . slave property." Just "two short years" after the "great body" of easterners "insisted" on protection against "injurious" white-basis government, abolitionists proposed to "refer a plan for the violent abrogation of the rights of slave property" to persons having "little or no common interest."[3]

Just as Leigh decried T. J. Randolph's "liberation by abolition," he similarly protested Brodnax's "liberation by colonization." "This plan," Leigh declared, "also looks to ultimate" emancipation and to "removal" of all Virginia blacks, first of blacks "now free," then of manumitted slaves, and finally of slaves "purchased by the public at a fair price." Although Brodnax "professed . . . most sacred regard" for slaveholders' rights, his scheme would necessarily "impair the value" of slave property, or impose "additional," "burdensome . . . tax on slaves." Furthermore, by "continually engendering vague hopes in the slave population," colonization, like *post-nati* emancipation, would promote insurrectionary "projects . . . pernicious and dangerous" to both blacks and whites. Indeed, "no plan *for . . . abolition of slavery, and deportation*" of "the mass" of Virginia blacks, Leigh summarized his position, is "morally, politically, or physically . . . possible. . . . I have examined all . . . schemes . . . proposed in my time . . . and . . . found them all hopeless." Slavery in Virginia is a "*necessity imposed upon us by Providence; . . . and Providence, in its own good time, will dispose*" of slaves "according to its wisdom."[4]

In the interim before divine interposition, Leigh urged slaveholding Virginians to "*unite*" against both hostile black slaves and hostile white

3. *Ibid.*, 11–14.
4. *Ibid.*, 6, 24–26, 27.

nonslaveholders. To protect their "safety," the "people of eastern and southern Virginia" must purchase arms and ammunition, strengthen slave patrols, and organize well-equipped militia units ready to "meet and suppress servile rebellion . . . at a minute's warning." To protect their "property," slaveholding easterners must elect legislative representatives "openly" opposed to "all abolition projects, present or prospective" and to "all schemes for . . . *liberation of slaves* by colonization." Finally, easterners must "withdraw subscriptions . . . to papers of the Virginia *abolition presses.*" In resolving that "further action for . . . *removal of slaves should await . . . more definite development of public opinion,*" the house-passed Bryce preamble, Leigh objected, "intentionally kept alive . . . the question of abolition." Antislavery Virginians "obviously" planned to "*develop* . . . public sentiment" by continued discussion of emancipation "in public prints." Conservatives, in turn, must "promptly and vigorously . . . check" public opinion by "discouraging circulation" of "inflammatory" Virginia newspapers. "Let us pay no regard," the aristocratic Leigh concluded his *Letter of Appomatox,* "to claims for . . . independence of the press." Slaveholders, "in the exercise of our independence," have a "perfect right" to "suppress" such "injurious" writings.[5]

Rather than stifle debate, Leight's *Letter of Appomatox,* published anonymously in the February 4, 1832, Richmond *Enquirer,* touched off still wider discussion of abolition. For nearly three months after the general assembly adjourned, editorials, memorials, anonymous letters on both sides of the slavery issue filled the front pages of Virginia newspapers. Like William O. Goode's motion to gag house debate, Leigh's attempt to muzzle the press resoundingly backfired.

Newspapers of Leigh's own "eastern and southern Virginia" led the assault on "Appomatox." The Richmond *Enquirer,* Richmond *Constitutional Whig* and "Southside" Lynchburg *Virginian* denounced Leigh's call for a boycott of the press and urged all Virginians to weigh thoroughly arguments for and against emancipation. "Appomatox," the *Enquirer* chided, "uses the liberty of the Press for the purpose of extinguishing that liberty. . . . We will trust our cause to a cool jury of our countrymen." Appomatox's attempt to "intimidate" and "hold . . . *in terrorem* . . . the Virginia Press, particularly the Press of this City," the Richmond

5. *Ibid.*, 27–30.

*Constitutional Whig* charged, resembles "in principle" the infamous "sedition law" of 1798. "Why does not Mr. Leigh," the *Whig* echoed the *Enquirer*, "leave Public opinion to reach its own conclusions? . . . We shall go on as we have begun, to publish for the Public what is offered by that Public." In urging "the people" to "deliberately" examine house debate on slavery, the Lynchburg *Virginian* predicted that Leigh's effort to "shackle . . . the press" would only "rally" abolitionists "to their support." Rather than the "tempered and cautious language now employed," debate would become "broad and unmeasured," with "embittered feelings" on both sides. "Mr. Leigh . . . and others of the proscribing sect," the "Southside" journal advised, ought to "ponder" such consequences.[6]

Appomatox's view of slavery as a "necessity imposed . . . by Providence" drew similar editorial fire. The *Enquirer* acknowledged "that gentleman's abilities" and the "weight . . . his pen always carries," but rejected the notion that abolition of slavery in Virginia must await God's will. The *Whig* was markedly less deferential. "Mr. Leigh," the Richmond journal reproached, "belongs to that school which has fallen behind the world and will never again overtake it—that school which opposes . . . with inflexible obstinancy . . . all change in the Constitution of Societies." During the 1829–1830 constitutional convention, the Lynchburg *Virginian* astutely recalled, "Mr. Leigh" had termed Virginia slavery a "moral and political evil" and lamented its existence. Upon this same occasion, he had likewise declared that the "painful and heavy responsibility" of attending to blacks' "wants" and "distresses" made slavery a "greater evil to the master, than to the slave." No argument, the "Southside" journal asserted, could "more forcibly . . . show the necessity" of ridding Virginia of "unprofitable and vexatious" slave labor.[7]

Along with their own editorial volleys, leading eastern newspapers also printed numerous letters from anonymous Virginians denouncing the tenor and content of Leigh's *Letter*. The "*tone* and temper of 'Appomatox,'" a "Subscriber" protested, "is better suited to the arrogance of a Dictator than to the equality of a republican citizen. . . . The people are forbid to think, the press to speak, of abolition, because 'Appomatox,' in the plenitude of his wisdom, deems it impracticable. . . . Those who

6. Richmond *Enquirer*, February 4, 1832; Richmond *Constitutional Whig*, February 7, 1832; Lynchburg *Virginian*, February 9, 13, 1832.

7. *Ibid.* For Leigh's 1829–30 remarks on slavery, see Chapter III, p. 58.

look to the rights and . . . interests of the *whole* people," know that Virginia cannot have a "perfect community of interest . . . so long as our slave population remains." Does "Appomatox," a writer identified as "Jefferson" likewise taunted, subscribe to the "aristocratic principle" that only "rich" slaveholders have "any right to deal with abolition?" If so, it was "high time" for Virginia's "poorer and middling classes" to "assert their rights," to demonstrate that "this is a republic," not "an oligarchy." "Jefferson" accordingly urged "non-slaveholders" and "mechanics throughout the State" to "aid . . . this holy cause." Contrary to Appomatox's advice, Virginians must "read all" house speeches and "newspaper essays" on "both sides" of the slavery question. Furthermore, they must elect representatives sympathetic to "full inquiry" on abolition and "willing to vote for any *rational, practicable*" plan. Should a majority of whites "favor" emancipation, "Jefferson" proclaimed, Virginia's slaveholding minority must either "submit" or "quit the country."[8]

Consistent with their call for thorough public deliberation, the eastern press also published opinions supporting Appomatox. Abolitionists' "inflammatory speeches . . . delivered" in the house and "perpetuated in the public press," anonymous conservatives concurred, imperiled "property" and "lives." As Appomatox had avowed, abolition of slavery was financially impracticable, since state resources were "wholly inadequate" to compensate slaveowners for property worth almost $100 million. So, too, Virginia's constitution, protecting private property from "legislative usurpation," posed an "insuperable barrier" to uncompensated, "compulsory" emancipation. The people of Virginia, conservatives contended, had not sanctioned abolitionists' principle that the general welfare justified *post-nati* confiscation. Indeed, a "Correspondent" unabashedly affirmed, "offspring of a female slave belongs as much to her proprietor as his lambs, calves, pigs or colts" and cannot be wrested without "giving a fatal stab to our Constitution."[9]

East Virginians, conservatives renewed Appomatox's appeal, must arrest antislavery "agitation" so "disastrous" to Virginia's "future." No matter that the house had declared "present" abolition inexpedient. As Appomatox had noted in denouncing emancipationist tendencies of the

8. Richmond *Enquirer*, February 16, 1832.
9. *Ibid.*, February 9, 7, 1832.

Bryce preamble, legislators, conservatives emphasized, had "*not* set-tled" the slavery question. Should abolitionists continue to "rudely assail" slave property, "the days of our beloved and ancient Commonwealth shall be numbered."[10] Like house counterparts, then, conservatives outside the general assembly feared the Bryce preamble as an antislavery victory, the *start* of abolitionists' drive to rally Virginia's nonslaveholding whites behind legislative emancipation. Like white-basis representation, this "ruthless" crusade for compulsory abolition would, if unchecked, subvert minority rights and leave slaveholders no recourse but division of the state. To conservatives within and without the legislature, the 1831–1832 slavery debate seemed not to halt Virginia abolitionism, as latter-day historians assert, but rather to hasten Virginia's "hour of emancipation."

Early in April, 1832, amidst this journalistic fray, Virginians went to the polls to elect representatives to the forthcoming general assembly. Although abolitionist and conservative leaders had urged a popular referendum on slavery, both candidates and press largely sidestepped this explosive issue. In the western Piedmont counties of Albemarle and Buckingham, elections directly hinged on emancipation. After a hard-fought contest, Albemarle voters returned Thomas Jefferson Randolph by 95 votes. His support, Randolph affirmed, came primarily from "poorer" whites sympathetic to his "unflinching" abolitionism. South of the James River, conversely, Buckingham voters ousted outspoken abolitionist Philip Bolling in favor of a conservative.[11]

In most Virginia counties, national politics preempted state concerns. With a presidential election impending, newspapers reported legislative returns as a "complete triumph of National Republican candidates," a victory for "friends of Mr. Clay."[12] Rarely did the press cite a candidate's stand on slavery. Rather than a clear-cut plebiscite, the spring-1832 elections reflected once more the irresolution and drift of white Virginians.

With neither side obtaining a popular mandate, the slavery question, conservatives despaired, would revert to the legislature. Leigh's *Letter of*

10. *Ibid.*, February 9, 1832.
11. Thomas Jefferson Randolph to Nicholas J. Trist, April 4, 1832, in Nicholas J. Trist Papers, Library of Congress; Lynchburg *Virginian*, April 16, 1832.
12. Martinsburg (Va.) *Gazette*, April 19, 1832; Richmond *Constitutional Whig*, April 17, 1832; Lynchburg *Virginian*, April 26, 1832.

*Appomatox* had failed to disarm Virginia abolitionists. A more sweeping, philosophical defense seemed essential to protect slavery from internal assaults. Before the 1832–1833 general assembly convened, conservatives had found a new champion, a twenty-nine-year-old professor of political law at William and Mary College named Thomas Roderick Dew.

Thomas R. Dew was born December 5, 1802, on his family's large Tidewater plantation, Dewsville, in King and Queen County. Graduating from nearby William and Mary College in 1820, he received a master's degree there in 1824. Soon afterward, Dew journeyed to Europe in hopes of improving his health and, while abroad, visited England, Italy, and France. Returning to Virginia in 1826, he settled in Williamsburg and, in 1829, assumed the newly established professorship of political law at his alma mater.[13]

Unlike so many Tidewater gentlemen, Professor Dew actively supported state internal improvements. In July, 1828, he represented Williamsburg at the Charlottesville Convention on Internal Improvements. There delegates from thirty-nine Virginia counties—twenty-one eastern, eighteen western—as well as all major urban centers east of the Blue Ridge—Richmond, Norfolk, Petersburg, Lynchburg, Fredericksburg, and Williamsburg—petitioned the general assembly to finance extensive roads and canals "uniting the Ohio to the Chesapeake." Expansion of the James River Canal; improvement of the Potomac, Shenandoah, Roanoke, and Great Kanawha rivers; construction of roads linking the state's "political and commercial center" with the vast Trans-Allegheny—these projects, memorialists urged, would promote the "best interests" of all Virginians. Trade between Virginia and western states, and between now-disconnected sections of the commonwealth, would flourish. Agriculture, industry, white population would burgeon. Virginia, Charlottesville memorialists proclaimed in rhetoric foreshadowing 1831–1832 abolitionists, "cannot be stationary" while neighboring "sister states" are "advancing." By promoting "enlarged . . . Internal Improvement," she must regain "power . . . greatness, and wealth" within the nation, "unity" and "contentment" within the state.[14]

Support for "vigorous" state internal improvements was likewise

---

13. Stephen S. Mansfield, "Thomas Roderick Dew: Defender of the Southern Faith" (Ph.D. dissertation, University of Virginia, 1968), 2–24.

14. Virginia, *Journal of the House of Delegates, 1828–1829* (Richmond, 1829), 35–37, 45–49.

central to Thomas R. Dew's 1832 essay on slavery. Published first in the September *American Quarterly Review* and shortly thereafter in expanded pamphlet form, Dew's anonymous *Review of the Debate in the Virginia Legislature of 1831–1832* combined a specific analysis of slavery in Virginia with a general defense of the institution on historical-philosophical grounds. Historians have traditionally cited Dew's 1832 *Review* as a crucial watershed in Virginia history—a turning away from avowed antislavery principles of the revolutionary generation to adoption of a thoroughgoing "pro-slavery" philosophy. Whereas Thomas Jefferson had declared slavery an "evil" and looked forward to abolition, Thomas Dew allegedly pronounced slavery a "positive good" and assumed its perpetuity in Virginia.[15]

Dew's attempt to defend slavery did indeed represent a departure from Virginia's revolutionary heritage. Similarly, his repudiation of *postnati* emancipation and colonization diverged from traditional Jeffersonianism. But despite a more positive tone, Dew did not present a consistent proslavery ideology. More momentous, even as he decried *legislative* emancipation, Dew linked Virginia's destiny to the free-soil North, not to the slaveholding South.

Like Virginia conservatives within and without the house, Professor Dew affirmed the "impropriety" of public debate on slavery, particularly so soon after the Nat Turner insurrection. Since the "seal has now been broken," however, he would "boldly grapple" with abolitionists. Their arguments, the William and Mary professor protested, were "wild and intemperate," their principles "subversive of the rights of property, and the order and tranquillity of society." Furthermore, "every plan of emancipation and deportation" was "*totally* impracticable." Thomas Jefferson Randolph's *post-nati* scheme would trample property rights and endanger white lives. Blacks born before July 4, 1840, "doomed to servitude," would believe themselves "victims of injustice." Contemplating the future of "more fortunate" younger slaves, they would become "designing . . . desperate rebels."[16]

William Henry Brodnax's plan to deport the annual increase of Vir-

15. Moore, *Banner in the Hills*; Joseph C. Robert, *The Road from Monticello: A Study of the Virginia Slavery Debate of 1832* (Durham, N.C., 1941); and Ambler, *Sectionalism in Virginia*, represent some of the many traditional analyses of Thomas R. Dew as the father of Virginia's proslavery philosophy.

16. Thomas Roderick Dew, "Review of the Debate in the Virginia Legislature of 1831–1832," reprinted in *Pro-Slavery Argument* (Philadelphia, 1853), 290–92, 381–82.

ginia slaves was also "visionary." Slaveholders' interest would preclude large-scale voluntary manumissions. To purchase at full value and transport to Africa six thousand blacks would cost the state $1,380,000 annually—an intolerable burden. In addition, by substituting the government of Virginia as purchaser instead of Deep South planters, Brodnax's plan would check the current "salutary" flow of slaves southward and might ultimately increase the ratio of blacks to whites in Virginia! While high slave prices would encourage "negro raising," oppressive annual taxes would induce many whites to flee the state. Surely, Dew exclaimed, Virginians would not sanction this "absurdity!" Nor should Virginia seek national funds to compensate slaveowners. Federal involvement in master-slave relationships, Dew insisted, violated sacred states' rights principles.[17]

Compensation was not the only obstacle to legislative emancipation. African colonization was itself a "stupendous . . . folly." For over fifteen years, the American Colonization Society had been organizing Liberia, yet the colony presently had no more than twenty-five hundred settlers and could receive only five hundred new emigrants annually. Where, then, could Virginia acquire territory for six thousand blacks a year? Unhealthy climate, inadequate food, hostile African tribes—these also continued to blight Liberia. The "formidable fever" suffered by most newly arrived colonists, Dew observed, produced a mortality rate higher than that of the notorious "middle passage" of the African slave trade. Emancipation-colonization thus involved a "double impracticability." Full compensation to slaveowners and mass colonization of slaves were both impossible dreams.[18]

Having exposed financial and physical obstacles to legislative emancipation, Dew now undertook to refute abolitionists' moral attacks. Yet even as he turned to the Bible, to history, and to organic social theory to defend slavery, the Williamsburg professor adopted an apologetic, ambivalent tone.

Slavery in the abstract, Dew conceded, violated the "spirit of Christianity." However, the Bible nowhere suggested that slavery, "when once introduced," ought to be abolished, or that slaveholding was a sin. On the contrary, Jesus Christ exhorted "obedience and fidelity" toward mas-

17. *Ibid.*, 356–60, 370, 380, 418–19.
18. *Ibid.*, 405–16, 392–404.

ters. So, too, God's chosen people, the Israelites, owned slaves. Indeed, Dew observed, slavery had existed in some form throughout human history—from the ancient republics of Greece and Rome to modern-day Africa. Introduction of slavery in the United States, Dew further admitted, was "based upon injustice." The African slave trade, with its "wretched . . . middle passage," defied "principles of humanity." But England, not American colonies, had committed this "original sin." Virginia, particularly, had sought to prohibit black importation and should not be condemned for "an evil" now "intertwined and intertwisted with every fibre of society."[19]

Neither ought Virginia to be reproached for slavery's continuance. Challenging universalist assumptions of the eighteenth-century Enlightenment, Dew appealed instead to the Burkeian tenet that particular circumstances, not abstract principles, must govern political action. Virginia's circumstances, he insisted, precluded hasty alteration of black-white relations. Precipitous emancipation would be disastrous for slaveholders, slaves, and, especially, for nonslaveholders. Slaveholders would lose $100 million of property; slaves would lose the protection and support of kind, indulgent masters. "We have no doubt," Dew asserted, that Virginia's slaves, well fed and well treated, "form the happiest portion of our society."[20]

Nonslaveholders, that group of white Virginians who most boldly championed emancipation, would paradoxically suffer most from premature antislavery legislation. Playing on whites' racial antipathies and fears, Dew argued that only slavery protected nonslaveholding whites from hordes of degraded, dangerous blacks. The coincidence between color and caste inherent to slavery preserved white supremacy and black inferiority. Throughout slaveholding societies, "color alone . . . is the badge of distinction, the true mark of aristocracy." Legislate emancipation, Dew particularly addressed nonslaveholding mechanics, artisans, and laborers from east Virginia's slaveholding districts, and white ascendancy would be destroyed. Given the impracticability of mass colonization, Virginia slaves, freed from compulsory labor, would become "worthless drones . . . the very pests of society." Forced to mingle with inferior blacks, whites would descend "rapidly in the scale of civiliza-

19. Ibid., 451–52, 287, 342–54.
20. Ibid., 357, 457–60.

tion. . . . All history and experience show" that in "contact between . . . civilized and uncivilized man," the "former will sink to the level of the latter."[21]

Dew mustered additional arguments to blunt abolitionism's appeal to nonslaveholders. Again primarily addressing nonslaveholding whites within Virginia's slaveholding bastions, the Williamsburg conservative declared that slavery not only perpetuated white control, but also promoted equality and a "genuine spirit of liberty" among all whites. Throughout the South, racial stratification assured that "all who are white are equal" regardless of occupation. Concomitantly, just as "Aristotle and the great men of antiquity believed slavery necessary to keep alive . . . freedom," so "in modern times . . . liberty has always been more ardently desired by slaveholding communities."[22] Those who urged emancipation on pragmatic class grounds, Dew accordingly challenged abolitionists like Charles J. Faulkner and George Summers, dangerously distorted the true interests of nonslaveholding white Virginians.

Rejection of legislative emancipation-colonization did not, however, imply Dew's commitment to perpetual slavery. On the contrary, like other Virginia conservatives, the allegedly "pro-slavery" Dew assumed that Virginia would eventually be a free-soil state. Slave labor, he echoed house conservatives John Thompson Brown and William O. Goode, was best suited to the tropical climate and cotton-sugar-rice plantations of the Deep South. Virginia and Maryland, conversely, were "too far North" for slavery.[23]

Looking beyond the United States, Dew noted that in Western Europe development of an urban-commercial-industrial order had "gradually and silently effected . . . emancipation" of serfs. A "vigorous system" of state internal improvements would similarly "revolutionize" Virginia. He was "happy to see," Dew affirmed, that the 1831–1832 general assembly had incorporated a state agency to complete the James River and Kanawha projects. This vast commercial network, linking waterways of east and west Virginia, would increase the wealth and white population of the entire commonwealth. Its "first effect" would be to foster "larger towns" in eastern Virginia, towns that would attract both

21. *Ibid.*, 462, 443–44.
22. *Ibid.*, 461–62.
23. *Ibid.*, 482–84.

capital and white laborers from the North. Urbanization, higher population density, would, in turn, break up large-scale agriculture and substitute "garden for . . . plantation cultivation." Individual farming, Dew observed, would require "less slave and more free labor." Western Virginia, the William and Mary professor emphasized, would "particularly" benefit from canals, roads, railroads. Greater access to markets would transform the west from a sparsely settled "grazing country" to a populous, grain-growing region. Agricultural diversification and increased profits would check migration of nonslaveholding white Virginians to free-soil western states.[24]

Internal improvements thus would "diminish the evils of slavery" on both sides of the Blue Ridge. East of the mountains, an enterprising, middle-class, urban society would emerge. West of the mountains, prosperous, industrious yeomen would cultivate the soil. Throughout Virginia, white laborers would gradually replace black slaves. Commerce, manufacturing, agriculture all would flourish in this racially homogeneous, "Yankee-like" society. "Here then," Dew urged, "is the true ground for unity of action" between east and west Virginia. Rather than press for legislative emancipation, let Virginians join in "pushing forward" canals and railroads throughout the state. Such a policy would abolish slavery without violating property rights or destroying the financial and physical integrity of the commonwealth. Already, Dew applauded, "Baltimore is . . . by its mighty agency . . . fast making Maryland a nonslaveholding state." So, too, "time and internal improvements will cure all our ills" and accomplish a free-soil, white Virginia.[25]

Thus instead of inscribing slavery on Virginia's "book of fate," Thomas R. Dew kept alive the hope of peaceful abolition in "the march of time." Although the Williamsburg professor did not renounce Virginia's antislavery tradition, he did turn his back on Jefferson's dream of universal freedom. When liberated, Dew informed, white serfs of southern Europe were "gradually and imperceptibly absorbed" into the urban middle class. A "difference of color" would preclude any incorporation of Virginia's slaves. The "emancipated black . . . carries a mark which no time can erase; he forever wears the indelible symbol of his inferior condition." Since slaves could be neither incorporated nor colonized, Dew

24. *Ibid.*, 446–47, 478–80.
25. *Ibid.*, 478–81.

concluded that they would be sold to Deep South planters. As internal improvements revolutionized Virginia's economy, slaveholders' interest, joined to the domestic slave trade, would rid the commonwealth of unprofitable blacks. Rather than freedom in Africa, thousands of former Virginia slaves would remain in chains, doomed to perpetual bondage in America's lower South and Southwest.[26]

If Dew restated traditional antislavery formulas of Virginia conservatives, he also dramatically diverged in assigning the legislature an active role in "abolitionizing" the commonwealth. His call for "vigorous" internal improvements overturned conservatives' long-standing opposition to roads and canals as exclusively western projects. Instead, Dew affirmed, this indirect state promotion of abolition protected rights and interests of all white Virginians and thus offered a just, practicable alternative to unjust, impracticable emancipation-colonization.

Dew's categorical dismissal of both Randolph's *post-nati* and Brodnax's colonization schemes angered abolitionists, moderates, and colonizationists. Antislavery Virginians particularly resented his "outrageous" attack "upon the colony at Liberia." Without African deportation, abolitionists and moderates acknowledged, emancipation would falter. Dew's bleak portrait of Liberia, American Colonization Society officials furthermore feared, would discourage future general assembly appropriations. Nearly one-half of Liberia's settlers, the society's secretary noted, were from Virginia, and "many others are now awaiting to embark." However, he lamented, "we have exhausted our resources" and "incurred expenses far beyond our means." He "sincerely" hoped that the 1831–1832 Virginia legislature would provide at least "ten or twenty thousand dollars" to sustain this worthy cause. Before the general assembly convened, colonizationists determined, the society must "repel" Professor Dew's "slander."[27]

To answer the Williamsburg conservative, the American Colonization Society summoned another young Virginian, Jesse Burton Harrison. Like Thomas Dew, Jesse Harrison was descended from the colonial Tidewater aristocracy. Whereas Dew was born and raised on the family

26. *Ibid.*, 446–47, 361.
27. John H. Cocke, Sr., to Ralph R. Gurley, January 14, 1833, in American Colonization Society Papers; Ralph R. Gurley to John H. Cocke, Sr., February 15, 1833, in John Hartwell Cocke Papers.

plantation, however, Harrison grew up in an urban environment. And whereas Dew was educated entirely at nearby William and Mary, Harrison, after graduating from Hampden-Sydney College in "Southside" Virginia, journeyed to New England to attend Harvard Law School.[28]

Jesse's father, Samuel Jordan Harrison, had left home at age eighteen and established himself as a prosperous tobacco merchant in the western Piedmont town of Lynchburg. In 1809, four years after Jesse's birth, the elder Harrison purchased part of Thomas Jefferson's "Poplar Forest" estate in Bedford County, west of Lynchburg. This transaction began a close friendship between the two men, a friendship that later embraced Jesse Harrison as well. Following his graduation from Harvard in 1825, the young lawyer settled in Lynchburg and was a frequent, welcome visitor at Monticello until Jefferson's death.[29]

During this same period, young Harrison met and developed an equally strong friendship with his cousin, Henry Clay. More sympathetic to the nationalistic economic policies of Clay's "American System" than to Jefferson's states' rightist persuasions, Harrison also shared his cousin's active interest in African colonization. Jesse's July, 1827, address to the Lynchburg Colonization Society in praise of the American Colonization Society was published in the September, 1827, *African Repository*. Four months later, Harrison represented Lynchburg at the annual American Colonization Society meeting in Washington, D.C. Such activities, combined with a lively intelligence, soon made the young Virginian a well known, respected figure in colonization circles.[30]

In the summer of 1829, after unsuccessful attempts to secure teaching appointments at both the University of Virginia and the University of North Carolina, Harrison departed on a two-year tour of Europe. There he studied philosophy and classics, visited Europe's major cities, and met many prominent families and intellectuals. Returning to America in June, 1831, he found Virginia society dull and provincial. In search of a more cosmopolitan environment, he wrote Henry Clay as to possible cities in the rapidly expanding Southwest where a young lawyer might es-

28. Gurley to Cocke, February 15, 1833; Jesse Burton Harrison, "The Slavery Question in Virginia," in Fairfax Harrison (ed.), *Aris Sonis Focisque. The Harrisons of Skimino* (n.p., 1910), 3, 84–86.
29. J. Burton Harrison, "The Slavery Question in Virginia," 54–65, 88–89.
30. *Ibid.*, 93–101.

tablish a successful practice. Upon Clay's advice, Harrison, early in 1832, settled in New Orleans, a bustling commercial center whose diverse, refined population possessed a touch of European grace and elegance.[31]

Harrison was to remain in New Orleans until his death in 1841. Although he deserted his native state, however, Harrison never lost interest in the question of slavery in Virginia, nor in the American Colonization Society. When colonizationists asked him to refute Thomas Dew, the young lawyer readily agreed. His reply, Harrison explained, would "go to the bottom of the whole subject of abolition, as well as the defence of the Society." On the other hand, he would not "embrace the whole prospects of negro slavery in the United States." Since it was "hopeless to expect . . . Abolition of slavery in . . . South Western States," he would confine his arguments to Virginia. He intended to show that if Virginia were ever to prosper, she must replace slave labor with a "homogeneous population of freemen."[32]

As promised, Harrison's essay appeared "in exact time to act on the Virginia legislature."[33] Published first in the December, 1832, *American Quarterly Review* and soon afterward in pamphlet form, *The Slavery Question in Virginia* added little to prevailing antislavery doctrines. Reiterating familiar economic-racist arguments of 1831–1832 house abolitionists, Harrison declared that slavery retarded industrial-commercial development, agricultural improvement, and white population. By disposing whites to view manual labor as "menial and degrading," slavery destroyed values of enterprise and frugality essential to economic prosperity. Equally pernicious, contrary to Professor Dew's claim that slavery fostered white equality, "no property gives rise to greater inequalities" among whites than slave property. Economically, morally, politically, this "ruinous" institution sapped Virginia's white community.[34]

His indictment of slavery, Harrison emphasized, applied "very little" to South Carolina and Georgia and scarcely at all to Louisiana, Mississippi, and Alabama. Climate, soil, and cotton-sugar-rice cultivation of these Deep South and Southwest states all assured profitable use of slave labor. *"Virginia,"* in contrast, *"possesses scarcely a single requisite to*

31. *Ibid.*, 105–30.
32. Jesse Burton Harrison to Ralph R. Gurley, September 14, October 13, 1832, in American Colonization Society Papers.
33. Harrison to Gurley, September 14, 1832.
34. J. Burton Harrison, "The Slavery Question in Virginia," 344–48.

*make a prosperous slave-labour state."* Virginia had neither the oppressive tropical climate nor "inexhaustible rich soils" to *"put slaves on the vantage ground above whites."* Similarly, cultivation of her principal agricultural products did not demand "lives and labours baser than those of white men." Tobacco—the "only article which could justify the expense of slave labour in Virginia"—was grown successfully by white farmers in free-soil Ohio, Indiana, Illinois. Furthermore, Harrison noted, "wiser planters" in many areas of Virginia were abandoning tobacco culture for wheat and corn. These latter crops, requiring few laborers, could never be raised profitably with slaves.[35]

Virginia, the young lawyer reaffirmed, "is a land which should not have been stained by the tread of a slave." Worked by a "homogeneous race of freemen," she would soon become "one of the most flourishing. . . Atlantic States." Industrious white yeomen would renourish her impoverished soils, and an "extensive class of mechanics" would emerge. Establishment of an urban-manufacturing order would revive the commonwealth. Withdrawal of slave labor would everywhere allow Virginia to "fulfill her destiny" as a wealthy, productive member of the "glorious" Republic.[36]

Virginians pondering Harrison's reply to Dew may have noted considerable parallels between the two positions. Both cited geographic-climatic determinism to link Virginia's destiny to the temperate, free-soil North and to confine slavery to the tropical, plantation South. Slavery, each assumed, would always exist in the Deep South. But Virginia was "too far North" for profitable use of slaves. Accordingly, both Harrison and Dew looked forward to establishment of a prosperous, urban-industrial economy composed of enterprising, middle-class whites.

As Harrison's essay progressed, other similarities emerged. Although he favored abolition, Harrison declared, he deprecated hasty "legislative enactments." Viable antislavery must be "voluntary," not "compulsory." The "great majority" of Virginia "freemen" must be "convinced, persuaded, moved" to demand abolition. He thus equally opposed Thomas Jefferson Randolph's proposal for an immediate popular referendum and William Ballard Preston's proposal for immediate emancipation legislation. Like Dew, Harrison also denounced abolitionists'

35. *Ibid.*, 343, 348–52.
36. *Ibid.*, 358–59.

uncompensated emancipation. Although general welfare and public safety could, Harrison conceded, justify seizure of private property, the state must adequately compensate slaveholders for both present and *post-nati* blacks.[37]

If Harrison reiterated Dew's opposition to legislative emancipation, however, he rejected the professor's reliance on the domestic slave trade to rid the commonwealth of blacks. Those who "execrate the African slave trade," the young lawyer chided, ought not turn to a similarly "contaminated source" to abolish slavery in Virginia. Such immoral process would not only flout the "good name of the land of Washington and Jefferson" but would also require "some centuries" to accomplish. He hoped Virginians would not wait while the evil of slavery "ravages with increasing violence." Instead, let them effect a plan of gradual, voluntary emancipation consistent with interests of whites and blacks.[38]

Harrison's antislavery proposal mirrored the Brodnax-Bryce "middle ground." Dew had declared Brodnax's scheme financially "visionary," but Harrison maintained that Virginia could afford to colonize the annual increase of slaves. Challenging Dew's assumption that slaveholders' interest would preclude large-scale manumission, the former Virginian argued that "many masters" would "voluntarily and gratuitously" emancipate if the legislature provided funds for slaves' deportation. "A little virtue . . . a slight sense of justice . . . a grain of common honesty," these higher "moral forces" would increasingly triumph over "mere money speculation." If the state had only to finance removal of slaves, Harrison affirmed, surely this was no "insurmountable expense."[39]

Ample resources were also available, Harrison insisted, to purchase and remove slaves not freely manumitted. Even those with strict constitutional scruples could not rightfully oppose using proceeds from sales of public lands *"under the entire management of . . . State authorities."* Such confirmed states' righters as Jefferson and Madison had long urged applying these funds for colonization of blacks. Professor Dew to the contrary, compensation was not an insuperable obstacle to emancipation.[40]

Nor, Harrison countered Dew's assault on Liberia, was African colonization a "fanciful or impracticable" venture. Already Liberia offered a

37. *Ibid.*, 339-41, 367-68.
38. *Ibid.*, 353-54, 398.
39. *Ibid.*, 371-78.
40. *Ibid.*, 379-82.

congenial asylum for black emigrants. The climate was "mild and uniform . . . the process of acclimation gentle, fatal to comparatively few."
The soil required but "moderate labour" to grow a wide variety of crops.
At present, Liberia could admittedly accommodate no more than a thousand or fifteen hundred new colonists annually. But, Harrison informed,
"preparations are on foot for a vastly increased body of settlers." The
American Colonization Society had recently appropriated funds to build
a hospital and had also sent out "experienced physicians" and "supplies
of medicine." The society estimated that with generous expenditures on
housing and temporary subsistence, Liberia could receive ten thousand
new blacks per annum "at the end of five years."[41]

Rather than acquiesce in Thomas R. Dew's "ruinous fatalism," then,
let the "young men of Virginia" pledge their "future manhood and age"
to emancipation-colonization. Let Virginians remember that in 1618, the
eleven-year-old Jamestown colony was still a struggling outpost of six
hundred whites. Eleven years after Liberia's founding, the African
colony was a "self-supporting home" for twenty-four hundred blacks.
From Liberia's auspicious beginnings, Harrison proclaimed, an ever-
burgeoning community of "civilized black men" would one day "introduce polity, religion, morals, laws" and "plant the arts" throughout Africa. This fledgling black republic would also one day redeem Virginia
from the curse of slavery. Perhaps it would be best, the ardent colonizationist advised, to begin the "work of deliverance" with removal of Virginia's free blacks. This would involve only transportation costs and, if
successful, might persuade a large majority of slaveholding and nonslaveholding Virginians to commence emancipation and colonization of
slaves. "Public opinion once disposed to its success," Harrison re-
affirmed the cornerstone of mainstream Virginia abolitionism from
Thomas Jefferson to Archibald Bryce, the state could not fail to realize
the dream of freedom for all men.[42]

Virginians weighing abolition by the domestic slave trade, by *post-
nati* legislation, or by African colonization, first of free blacks, then of
manumitted slaves might have regarded Harrison's "middle ground" as
the most viable alternative. To allow "mere money speculation" to accomplish abolition would perpetuate slavery for "centuries," convert

41. *Ibid.*, 388–92.
42. *Ibid.*, 389–90, 370, 379, 394–96.

"gentlemanly" Virginia planters into sordid "negro-traders," and repudiate the revolutionary ideal of universal liberty. To compel slaveholders to
surrender *post-nati* blacks without compensation would most likely precipitate dismemberment of the state. To colonize free blacks, on the
other hand, might, as Harrison and other antislavery moderates anticipated, persuade growing numbers of slaveholders to manumit. Should
this latter course succeed, Virginia might then effect peaceful abolition
of slavery and universal freedom for slaves.

A more illustrious Virginian soon lent weight to young Harrison's
scheme. Early in February, 1833, in a further effort to assure continued
general assembly appropriations, the American Colonization Society
elected James Madison president of the national organization.[43] Anxious
to foil Dew's influence, the eighty-two-year-old Virginia patriarch readily accepted and, in a lengthy letter to the William and Mary professor, reiterated life-long faith in colonization. "It has appeared to me,"
the elderly Madison argued, that the "great difficulty [of emancipation-
colonization] . . . does not lie" in "expence," but in "attainment" of:
(1) "requisite asylums," (2) "consent of . . . individuals to be removed,"
and (3) "labor for the vacuum . . . created." Like Harrison and other Virginia moderates, Madison believed that "voluntary emancipations, increasing under the influence of example and the prospect of bettering
the lot of the slaves," would save "much" of the "expence" of colonization. "Gifts and legacies" from individual philanthropists, grants from
state legislatures, revenue from the sale of public lands "held in trust by
Congress" would finance purchase and removal of slaves not voluntarily
manumitted.[44]

Madison further confirmed Harrison's belief in the physical practicability of colonization. "Territory already acquired" in Africa, as well
as adjacent coastal and interior regions, he declared, offered a "flattering
prospect." Islands off the United States where the "colored population is
already dominant," or "where the wheel of revolution" might "produce
the like result," could also provide "new fields for colonising
enterprises."[45]

Although costs of emancipation-colonization could be surmounted
and adequate asylums acquired, the "known repugnance" of free blacks

43. Staudenraus, *The African Colonization Movement,* 183.
44. Hunt (ed.), *The Writings of James Madison,* IX, 498.
45. *Ibid.,* 499.

and slaves "to leave their native homes" posed a more difficult dilemma. Particularly among slaves, Madison noted, these "prejudices arise from . . . distrust" of whites' "favorable accounts" of Liberia. Once slaves and free blacks learned the "truth" from blacks already colonized, most would overcome "aversion to removal." As blacks departed, northern and European white laborers would fill Virginia. Such a process, the revolutionary patriarch conceded, "must be slow, uncertain, and attended with much inconvenience." But a "gradual remedy" was preferable to "torpid acquiescence in . . . slavery" or to abolition by "convulsions." Even "partial success," Madison concluded his letter to Dew, "will have its value; and . . . entire failure will leave behind a consciousness" of Virginia's "laudable" effort to effect emancipation by the "only mode" possible.[46]

As a final counter to Dew, the American Colonization Society again enlisted "Southsider" William Henry Brodnax to request general assembly appropriations for removal of free blacks. During opening days of the 1832–1833 house session, Brodnax reiterated Harrison's and Madison's call for continued commitment to African colonization. "At the time," the general however reported, "the legislature . . . was so much engrossed with *political* subjects" as to preclude consideration of "this matter."[47]

Of more pressing concern to Virginia legislators was South Carolina's angry defiance of federal authority. Less than a month before the general assembly met, a convention of the people of South Carolina had pronounced 1828 and 1832 tariffs unconstitutional and null and void within the state after February 1, 1833. Efforts to collect import duties by force, nullifiers had warned, would precipitate South Carolina's secession from the Union.[48] From the nation's capital, an equally resolute President Andrew Jackson trumpeted the doctrine of federal supremacy and announced his intent to enforce the laws against recalcitrant South Carolinians. Acting promptly to back up his threats, the irate old military hero sent reinforcements to federal forts in Charleston harbor and dispatched his leading general to oversee operations.

46. *Ibid.*, 500.
47. William Henry Brodnax to Ralph R. Gurley, February 14, 1833, in American Colonization Society Papers.
48. William W. Freehling, *Prelude to Civil War: The Nullification Controversy in South Carolina, 1816–1836* (New York, 1966), 1–2.

As tensions mounted and prospects of tariff compromise dimmed, civil war seemed imminent. Anxious to avert this "dreadful evil," the Virginia house, in mid-December, appointed a Committee on Federal Relations to devise "conciliatory" measures restoring national harmony.[49] Governor John Floyd, sounding Virginia's self-proclaimed role as mediator between federal and South Carolina governments, privately intoned delegates that "the future destiny of this republic . . . depends in . . . high degree . . . on you. It is for you to say whether the brand of civil war shall be thrown in the midst of these states . . . our fireside altars bathed in blood . . . or whether" sectional differences shall be "harmonized" and "impending calamity . . . averted."[50]

With the specter of disunion stalking the land, nullification, not colonization, riveted delegates' attention throughout December and January. "Ever since this committee on Federal relations was raised," Petersburg representative John Thompson Brown described house events, "we have had constant sessions commencing at 10 o'clock—suspended at dinner and resumed at 5 p.m. & so on 'till 10 o'clock at night." The committee, Brown noted, included "most of the *talkers* of the House & you may well suppose . . . we have had enough of debate." Despite such feverish activity, Tidewater committee member Thomas Smith despaired of Virginia's ability to resolve the national crisis. "I don't think it at all probable," the Gloucester County delegate privately avowed; "the people of South Carolina are literally mad on the subject and will not I believe abandon an inch of . . . ground. . . . Congress . . . no doubt will be equally firm in sustaining the tariff of the last session—under these circumstances, therefore, I cannot but believe that the inevitable consequences will be disunion, civil war, and all the attendant evils."[51]

Late in January, 1833, the Virginia House of Delegates and Senate adopted resolutions "entreating" South Carolina to "rescind" or "suspend" her nullification ordinance, and Congress to "modify . . . tariff acts." Although Virginia did not "sanction" nullification, the general assembly declared, she more strongly decried the president's Force Procla-

49. Thomas Smith to William P. Smith, December 14, 1832, in William P. Smith Papers.
50. John Floyd to the House of Delegates, December 13, 1832, in Executive Letter Book, Virginia State Library, Richmond.
51. John Thompson Brown to Mary Brown, December 21, 1832, in Brown, Coalter, Tucker Papers; Thomas Smith to William P. Smith, December 14, 1832.

mation as "in direct conflict" with "true" constitutional "doctrines of state sovereignty and states' rights. . . . Persuaded" that "our sister state . . . will listen willingly and respectfully to the voice of Virginia," legislators appointed Benjamin Watkins Leigh to communicate general assembly resolutions to South Carolina's governor.[52]

Virginia as North-South peacemaker foreshadowed her self-appointed role during the Secession Crisis almost three decades later and, in 1861, proved incompatible with her concurrent defense of state sovereignty against federal usurpations. So, too, Virginia's pose as protector of the Union belied events in both 1832 and 1861, as first, Henry Clay's tariff compromise resolved nullification, and later, Abraham Lincoln's coercion doctrine determined the nation's—and Virginia's—destiny.

With the national tempest temporarily becalmed by Henry Clay's intercession, Virginia legislators turned at last to state concerns. Early in February, 1833, the house reopened debate on Virginia's black population. Unlike in 1831–1832, colonization, not emancipation, was paramount. Although "some . . . western members" wished to "revive . . . the old subject of abolition,"[53] Tidewater conservative Thomas Smith reported, the house majority upheld 1831–1832 views as to the "inexpediency" of immediate antislavery legislation. Ongoing emancipation debate, most delegates also recognized, could only swell black discontent and aggravate white class and sectional divisions. Looking both to whites' safety and Virginia's integrity, then, the choice confronting the 1832–1833 legislature lay between acquiescing in slavery's status quo or commencing the colonization "experiment."

The house chose to commence, but to follow a more cautious path than that proposed by last session's Bryce preamble. On February 14, the special house committe recommended "appropriating __ thousand dollars for five years" for removal of free blacks and manumitted slaves. William Henry Brodnax optimistically informed the American Colonization Society that "this bill will pass, and . . . the blank will be filled with $20,000. We are afraid to ask more," he declared, "but I have no doubt that if the experiment proceeds happily . . . it will be greatly increased

---

52. Virginia, "Preamble and Resolutions on the Subject of Federal Relations," in *Acts Passed at a General Assembly of the Commonwealth of Virginia, 1832–1833* (Richmond, 1833), 201–203.
53. Thomas Smith to William P. Smith, December 14, 1832.

long before the five years have expired and continued as long as individuals can be found for it to operate on."[54]

Brodnax's prediction proved only partially correct. On February 27, the house rejected "Southside" Piedmont conservative William Sims's motion for indefinite postponement of colonization. Instead members voted, 72 to 48, to appropriate $18,000 annually for five years to remove free blacks and manumitted slaves. Immediately afterward, however, delegates upheld "Southside" Piedmont conservative James Gholson's motion to reconsider. A third "Southside" Piedmont conservative, John Thompson Brown of Petersburg, then proposed, as he had in 1831–1832, to restrict state colonization funds to free blacks. Having rebuffed "Southside" Piedmont conservatives' favorite scheme to postpone colonization, the house now approved Brown's amendment, 68 to 51. Twenty-six abolitionists and fourteen moderates joined twenty-eight conservatives to endorse state removal of free blacks only. Twenty-seven abolitionists, one moderate, and twenty-three conservatives opposed.[55]

As at the previous house session, colonizationists crisscrossed sectional and ideological lines. West of the Blue Ridge, the Valley, which in 1832 had voted 13–10 for colonizing free blacks *and* manumitted slaves, now approved the more restrictive 1833 policy 14 to 8. Overall, Valley alignments reflected a shift of just 1 vote, as moderates divided 4–0, rather than 3–1, in favor of colonization. The Trans-Allegheny, which in 1832 had disapproved colonization 16–12, now disapproved 16–13. With an additional Valley moderate and Trans-Allegheny abolitionist voting "yes" in 1833, a colonization policy ostensibly discouraging emancipation paradoxically attracted two more antislavery westerners than the openly promanumission version of 1832.

If antislavery westerners were a bit more partial to colonization in 1833, conservative easterners were markedly less so. The Tidewater, approving the 1833 bill, 25–5, again cast the highest percentage of procolonization votes. But whereas a year earlier, *all* Tidewater delegates had endorsed state removal of free blacks and manumitted slaves, now four conservatives and one moderate voted against removing just free blacks.

54. Brodnax to Gurley, February 14, 1833.
55. Virginia, *Journal of the House of Delegates of the Commonwealth of Virginia, 1832–1833* (Richmond, 1833), 226–28. All subsequent analysis of voting alignments is from this source.

Piedmont disaffection was far more striking. There in 1832, delegates had sanctioned colonization 24–15; now, *disapproving* 22–16, they cast the highest percentage of "no" votes of any section of the commonwealth. Although four Piedmont abolitionists joined anticolonization ranks, the most striking shift occurred among Piedmont conservatives. Piedmont conservatives in 1832 had split 15–15 on colonizing free blacks and freed slaves. In 1833, they divided 18–11 against removing just free blacks. Taken together, 70 percent of all eastern conservatives had endorsed colonization in 1832; by 1833, only 55.1 percent did so, with the Tidewater alone of *all* Virginia sections retaining a conservative, procolonization majority.

With Tidewater and Piedmont conservatives more opposed, and antislavery delegates as favorable to colonization as in 1832, the 1833 house bill cannot be labeled an attempt to buttress slavery by removing free blacks. Despite provisions against state deportation of manumitted slaves, abolitionists and moderates cast 58.8 percent of the "yes" votes— higher than the 54.4 percent antislavery vote of 1832. State-financed removal of blacks "freed hereafter," an issue crucial to 1832 antislavery colonizationists, seemed less so to their 1833 house counterparts. Western abolitionists, especially, appeared more willing to compromise, to adopt a more pragmatic posture. Antislavery ideologues like Valley delegate Charles J. Faulkner and Trans-Allegheny "Panhandler" John C. Campbell, who a year before had led their sections' drive for immediate emancipation, now approved restricting colonization funds to free blacks. Perhaps they recalled William Henry Brodnax's earlier advice not to "peril everything" by "attempting too much" nor to "refuse to do nothing because we cannot obtain all we desire." Jesse Burton Harrison had more recently recommended a similar course. Let Virginia commence with removal of free blacks, these antislavery moderates proposed, in hopes that initial "experiment" might become an "entering wedge." To "deport free negroes first" would require only transportation costs and would not so excite slaveholders' sensitivities. "Happy" accomplishment of such preliminary venture might persuade masters to manumit and legislators to colonize emancipated slaves. For antislavery delegates in 1833, a modest beginning seemed preferable to indefinite postponement.

Although antislavery ideologues were readier to compromise, conservative counterparts were more intransigent. Like Deep South planters, growing numbers of slaveholding easterners, particularly Piedmont "Southsiders," seemed to view colonization—even gradual removal of free blacks—as indeed an "entering wedge," an ominous first step toward state interference with slaves. Far better to tolerate Virginia's free blacks, conservative anticolonizationists reasoned, than to so jeopardize slavery's status quo.

The Virginia Senate, having voted to postpone colonization in 1832, now passed the 1833 bill. In initial debate, senators mirrored house action by rejecting both a "Southwide" Piedmont conservative's motion for indefinite postponement and a Trans-Allegheny abolitionist's motion to also colonize manumitted slaves. A coalition of seven Tidewater, four Piedmont, four Valley, and one Trans-Allegheny senator then approved state removal of just free blacks by a razor-thin margin of 16–15. One Tidewater, six Piedmont, two Valley, and six Trans-Allegheny senators opposed. Sectional and ideological alignments generally followed house patterns. Both east and west Virginia split apart, with the Tidewater and Valley majority voting for, the Piedmont and Trans-Allegheny majority voting against, colonization. Conservative Tidewater and Valley senators together provided almost two-thirds—62.5 percent—of the positive votes. "Southside" Piedmont conservatives, hostile to any colonization, and Trans-Allegheny abolitionists, opposed to removing only free blacks, together furnished almost three-fourths—73.3 percent—of the negative votes.[56]

Of the total general assembly votes for colonization in 1833, forty-one were abolitionist or moderate, forty-three conservative. If legislators disagreed as to colonization's ultimate intent, however, most agreed that removal of free blacks must be voluntary. Whites' irresolution, their paradoxical regard for free blacks' "vested rights," would empower an "anomalous population" to control Virginia's initial "experiment."

Soon after the legislature adjourned, the central Board of Commissioners, established to administer colonization, requested county courts to provide information after "due and diligent enquiry" concerning "free persons of colour . . . willing to emigrate to . . . Africa." From every district came a similar reply. "I could not find one that . . . have the most

56. Virginia, *Journal of the Senate of the Commonwealth of Virginia, 1832–1833*, 168–69.

distant idea of leaving their native land to go to Liberia or elsewhere unless compelled," reported a Piedmont court clerk. "None willing to go unless compelled," echoed a Tidewater official. "The free people of colour in this country are hostile in the extreme to the project," a Trans-Allegheny clerk recorded. "Not one free person of colour willing to emigrate," a Valley official confirmed. "Not fifty free people have been found throughout the state," a local agent informed the American Colonization Society in November, 1833, "to express a desire to go."[57]

Virginia colonizationists blamed northern "abolition societies" for fostering free blacks' hostility.[58] Garrison and other Yankee "incendiaries," colonizationists protested, repeatedly indicted the American Colonization Society as a tool of slaveholding interests. "In this place," a Lynchburg colonizationist accordingly explained, "free negroes generally regard the whole scheme as a plot of the whites, whom they look upon as hereditary enemies, to seduce them to a barren soil and sickly climate, anxious only for their departure from among them, and indifferent whether they afterwards prosper."[59]

Coupled with assaults on African colonization, "fanatical" northerners also "raised expectations . . . that in the course of time," free blacks in America "will enjoy equal privileges with . . . whites. That opinion," though it "can never be realised," a Norfolk colonizationist observed, has nonetheless "gained some ground among . . . free coloured people in this quarter" and greatly enhanced the "difficulty of obtaining emigrants."[60]

Although conceding that 1833 legislative appropriations "will not all be expended," Virginia colonizationists generally believed that free blacks' "prejudices" against African emigration could be overcome. Free blacks, colonizationists agreed, must "have some more satisfactory mode of acquiring information" about Liberia.[61] "Agents and members

57. "An Act for the Transportation of Free Negroes, 1833–36," in Auditor's #153, Virginia State Library, Richmond; D. J. Burr to Ralph R. Gurley, November 5, 1833, in American Colonization Society Papers.

58. John McPhail to Ralph R. Gurley, October 15, 1833, in American Colonization Society Papers.

59. Richard H. Foler to Ralph R. Gurley, August 22, 1833, in American Colonization Society Papers.

60. McPhail to Gurley, October 15, 1833.

61. Charles Dresser to Ralph R. Gurley, July 25, 1833, in American Colonization Society Papers.

of Colonization Societies" must dispel "false stories . . . circulated against" the settlement. Much more influential than whites' accounts, however, blacks already colonized in Africa might, "by their representations," convince "brethren" to emigrate.[62]

Virginians of more immediate antislavery persuasion did not so "regret" free blacks' opposition to African colonization. If free blacks' resistance continued, these whites anticipated, the general assembly might then "extend" colonization "provisions . . . to emancipated slaves."[63] County clerks and private citizens alike had informed the Board of Commissioners that several local slaveholders would manumit, "provided" freedmen "could be transported . . . to Liberia" with state "monies."[64] Deportation of slaves would, in all cases, be compulsory and once begun might more readily dispose the commonwealth toward emancipation. "On this account," a Richmond colonizationist reasoned, "I am less anxious that there . . . be a numerous emigration [of free blacks] . . . just now."[65]

If most antislavery Virginians in 1833 accepted yet another postponement of the colonization "experiment," at least one determined to commence. For John Hartwell Cocke, a large western Piedmont slaveholder and proponent of emancipation-colonization, the moment seemed opportune to begin his own "experiment" in colonizing manumitted slaves.

Born September 19, 1780, in Surry County, just across the James River from Jamestown, Cocke was the eldest son of a prominent Tidewater tobacco planter. His father, John Hartwell Cocke, Sr., belonged to "The Hundred," a title accorded Virginia's largest land- and slaveowning families. Orphaned at age eleven, Cocke, upon reaching twenty-one, inherited his father's vast Tidewater and Piedmont plantations. In 1809, he sold the Tidewater holdings to his sister and brother-in-law and settled on more fertile lands at Bremo, an upcountry western Piedmont estate on the James River in Fluvanna County. There, Cocke soon became the

62. Foler to Gurley, August 22, 1833.
63. D. J. Burr to Ralph R. Gurley, September 21, 1833, in American Colonization Society Papers.
64. "An Act for the Transportation of Free Negroes, 1833–36"; William M. Rives to Ralph R. Gurley, October 16, 1833, Richard H. Foler to Ralph R. Gurley, October 3, 1833, both in American Colonization Society Papers.
65. D. J. Burr to Ralph R. Gurley, November 5, 1833, in American Colonization Papers.

prototype of the progressive Virginia planter, engaged in diversified agriculture and committed to commercial-industrial growth.[66]

Like many slaveholding Virginians, Cocke viewed slavery as a "curse upon our land." Unlike so many fellow slaveholders, however, he refused to succumb to "that fatal indolence" which, he noted, stemmed from widespread belief in slavery's intractability. Slavery, Cocke rebutted, was not "an evil without a remedy." Admittedly, abolition in Virginia must be "so slow as to preclude . . . any one generation from the honor of its accomplishment." Only our "faithful domesticks" and skilled "mechanicks," who "form a separate caste from the common herd of slaves," were "sufficiently advanced in moral and intellectual improvement to be useful members of a free community." The "great mass" of field slaves were "in such a state of abject ignorance as would sink them below the lowest grade of menial servants in any free and enlightened" society. Before these "common working negroes" were ready for emancipation, Cocke insisted, they must be instructed in reading and writing, in Christian religion, and in mechanical trades. Only then would they "possess . . . suitable qualifications for Citizenship in the embrio Republic" of Liberia, "destined to be a blessing to the two Continents of Africa and America."[67]

Acting upon his beliefs, Cocke provided intellectual, mechanical, and religious instruction for Bremo's slaves. Before the 1830–1831 Virginia legislature prohibited such practices, Cocke hired white teachers, usually northern ladies, to tutor slaves in reading and writing. Local white artisans also trained Bremo blacks as carpenters, bricklayers, stonemasons, blacksmiths. To "improve" slaves' "moral character," Cocke, himself a zealous member of the American Temperance Society, successfully urged many of his black "family" to abstain from alcoholic drink. His devout wife, Louisa, instructed slaves in the Bible and general Christian philosophy.[68] Concern with slaves' education, Cocke acknowledged, contravened attitudes of most Virginia masters. Contrary

66. Martin B. Coyner, Jr., "John Hartwell Cocke of Bremo: Agriculture and Slavery in the Antebellum South," (Ph.D. dissertation, University of Virginia, 1961), 1–27, 153–56, 179, 260.

67. John Hartwell Cocke, Sr., to [?], December, 1833, John Hartwell Cocke, Sr., to [?], September 23, 1831, John Hartwell Cocke, Sr., to John H. Cocke, Jr., December 31, 1832, all in John Hartwell Cocke Papers. The first two, both drafts of letters, provide excellent summaries of Cocke's views on Virginia slavery and on emancipation-colonization.

68. Coyner, "John Hartwell Cocke of Bremo," 24, 323–48.

to popular opinion, however, he believed a "higher degree of intelligence" would "show" slaves the folly of "insurrectional attempts" as well as prepare them for "civil liberty under a government of their own." In the period before emancipation, educated slaves would thus be less "dangerous and ungovernable."[69]

To the ever fervent Cocke, legislative debate on emancipation following Nat Turner's insurrection heralded Virginia's "future redemption." At last Virginians had the "moral courage" to attack slavery in "our public councils. . . . I trust and hope," he wrote his daughter, that abolition "will ultimately . . . become the settled course and policy of our State government." As William Henry Brodnax had "clearly shown," Virginia could, "for the moderate tax of 30¢ a tythe, export . . . to Africa . . . the whole annual increase of [our] free colored and slave population. . . . Combine this" with abolitionists' "equally tenable . . . principle" of declaring the "annual increase of slave property . . . a nuisance," and the state could forego compensation. Such plan could, "by the self-same operation," accomplish the "double blessing of removal of slavery from Virginia and Christianizing and civilizing benighted Africa."[70]

The general assembly endorsement of colonization at the following session reinforced Cocke's buoyancy. The 1833 colonization bill, he elatedly wrote the American Colonization Society secretary, indicated that "Professor Dew's elaborate efforts against our cause have failed." Rather than acquiesce in the "deep depravity of the slave trade" to accomplish abolition, Virginia had determined to promote the "wise . . . and Christian enterprise" of African emigration. "For some time past," Cocke continued, "I have been looking among my people for some suitably qualified to aid . . . so moral and Religious and every way respectable a community . . . as Liberia. I have now fixed upon my first emigrant. He is a stone mason by trade, a professor of Christianity, a member of the Temperance reformation. . . . He has a wife and six children the oldest about 12—all of whom" will accompany him.[71]

Cocke chose as his first African colonist a thirty-three-year-old favor-

---

69. John Hartwell Cocke, Sr., to Henry Smith, October 1, 1833, John Hartwell Cocke, Sr., to [?], December, 1833, both in John Hartwell Cocke Papers.
70. John Hartwell Cocke, Sr., to Sally Cocke, March 4, 1832, in John Hartwell Cocke Papers.
71. John Hartwell Cocke, Sr., to Ralph R. Gurley, March 31, 1833, in American Colonization Society Papers.

ite slave named Peyton Skipwith. In October, 1833, he issued Skipwith and his family a deed of emancipation and arranged for their immediate departure aboard the ship *Jupiter*. He preferred, the paternalistic Cocke explained, that his "faithful servant" arrive in Liberia "after the rainy season has passed" so as to reduce risk of fever and assure his success as a citizen of a "free, Christian community." Skipwith's happy establishment "in the land of . . . his forefathers" might convince other Virginia slaveholders of the feasibility of colonization and, equally important, Cocke avowed, influence "our" now unwilling "House servants" to "accept . . . freedom on . . . condition of going to Africa."[72]

Skipwith's advent in Liberia flouted Cocke's benevolent design. In his first letter from Africa, Skipwith reported that after "fifty six days on the ocean," he and his family had "all landed safe on New Year's Day." During their first weeks in the colony, however, all "hav . . . had the fever" and his daughter, Felicia, had died. Although the rest of the family were now "in moderate health . . . myself and wife," Skipwith asserted, "are dissatisfied in this place."

"As . . . respects farming," Cocke's former slave elaborated, "their is no chance." The soil "is a solid body of stones." And "when we ought to put in our grain it rains so hard that we dare not be out." Stonemasons, he noted, "can get a good price" to "put up" houses. But "the sun is so hot that the people from America can not stand it in the dry season and in the wet it rains too much. . . . I want you to write to me by the first opportunity," the disheartened Skipwith asked Cocke, "and let me no on what terms I can come back. . . . For," he insisted, "I intend coming back as soon as I can."[73]

Cocke disregarded Skipwith's request to return to Virginia. During the next decade, although conditions in Liberia improved, Cocke's black settlers remained generally discontent. In a March 6, 1835, letter to his former master, Skipwith reported that his wife had died six months after their arrival, and that he was currently suffering from a "blindness of nights so that I cannot see." Skipwith's blindness, an American Colonization Society official wrote Cocke, resulted from excessive exposure

72. John Hartwell Cocke, Sr., "Certification of Emancipation for Peyton Skipwith," October, 1833, in John Hartwell Cocke Papers; Cocke to Gurley, March 31, 1833, Cocke to [?], September 23, 1831.
73. Peyton Skipwith to John Hartwell Cocke, Sr., February 10, 1834, in John Hartwell Cocke Papers.

to the "glaring heat and light of the sun" while working as a stone-mason. He is "still anxious to return to Virginia," the agent admitted, "yet . . . appeared less dissatisfied . . . with Liberia than formerly."[74]

Almost a year later, Skipwith himself declared, "I feel satisfied with my present home and desire no other." His health had improved, his blindness disappeared, and two of his children now regularly attended school. However, Skipwith's daughter, Diana, writing to "Mistress Louisiana" in May, 1838, remarked that her father still "talks of coming back." He had, at present, a bad wound, "but . . . if his wound ever get well and if he can get money enough, he will come back, for he want to come back bad. . . . I was happy to hear," Diana revealed her own affections for Virginia, "that Master has bild a Church for the cullard people. I know that they injoy therselves better than they would hear."[75]

Skipwith's youngest son died in 1839. That same year, Skipwith complained to Cocke that the American Colonization Society seemed to have "entirely foresaken us. We have continual wars" with neighboring African tribes. The "natives are very savage when they think they have the advantage." "It is something strange to think," the discouraged emigrant wrote the following year, "that those people of Africa are called our ancestors. In my present thinking if we have any ancestors they could not have been like these hostile tribes in this part of Africa."[76]

As Liberia developed better schools, churches, and agricultural techniques, Skipwith's disaffection waned. By September, 1844, he affirmed that "I am as well satisfied as I can be in this little community." Our farmers are "rapidly" expanding production of "rice, potatoes, plantains, corn." The "U.S. Fleet . . . on the coast of Africa . . . has subdued the natives," so that "peace and harmony" now prevails "among us." "I must thank you," Skipwith wrote Cocke, for teaching me "a trade" and sending "me to this country." Here, "I can speak for myself like a man and show myself to be a man, so far as my ability allows me."[77]

In a similarly buoyant letter to his mother in June, 1846, Skipwith

74. Peyton Skipwith to John Hartwell Cocke, Sr., March 6, 1835, George P. Todson to John Hartwell Cocke, Sr., May 25, 1835, both in John Hartwell Cocke Papers.
75. Peyton Skipwith to John Hartwell Cocke, Sr., April 27, 1836, Diana Skipwith to "Mistress Louisiana," May 8, 1838, both in John Hartwell Cocke Papers.
76. Peyton Skipwith to John Hartwell Cocke, Sr., May 20, 1839, April 22, 1840, both in John Hartwell Cocke Papers.
77. Peyton Skipwith to John Hartwell Cocke, Sr., September 29, 1844, in John Hartwell Cocke Papers.

urged other Virginia blacks to "come to this country. . . . I think the people would go over," he observed, "if they were not affraid of the fever." But Liberia's climate "should not be an obstacle." Colonists had "learned what to do in regard to the fever." After nearly thirteen years in Africa, Skipwith proclaimed, "my health is . . . very good. . . . My efforts have been crowned with success from on high . . . and my confidence in the Lord is as bright now as . . . when I first left—if anything more so."[78]

Peyton Skipwith died in 1849, still reconciled to Liberia, still an ardent "professor of Christianity."[79] For his surviving children, however, the colonization "experiment" proved, at best, ambivalent. Throughout the 1850s, reports of "hard times" filled their letters to Cocke, accompanied by repeated requests for food, clothing, books. Some years, torrential rains destroyed crops; others, persistent drought "parched up" the soil. Colonists at times warred with native blacks; at other times they lived in harmony.[80] The fever, Skipwith's daughter Matilda wrote in 1854, is "not as bad . . . as . . . some years back." My "three daughters" are all in school. "I have been a member of the Baptist Church for eighteen years and of the Daughters of Temperance for four," she wrote again in 1857. Yet since the death of her husband and her brother, Nash, in 1851, she found Liberia a "lonsum country" and longed to see her family and friends in Virginia.[81]

Others of Cocke's manumitted slaves, colonized in Liberia during the 1850s, were more enthusiastic. "I am please with the country so far as I have seen," Solomon wrote Cocke in August, 1857. "But," he conceded, "it wants men of money to make it a land of plenty." "I have enjoyed som of the privileges of a free man," James Skipwith, a relative of Peyton's, affirmed. "I have served my country as Grand Jury and as Petty Jury and also as voting, something strange to me. . . . I have had the pleasure also," this "sabbath school teacher" applauded, of converting thirty-one black emigrants to Christianity. Already "Liberia is doing her part in the

78. Peyton Skipwith to Lucinda Nicholas, June 27, 1846, in John Hartwell Cocke Papers.
79. John H. Faulcon to John Hartwell Cocke, Sr., November 22, 1849, in John Hartwell Cocke Papers.
80. Matilda Lomax to John Hartwell Cocke, Sr., September 30, 1850, Nash Skipwith to John Hartwell Cocke, Sr., May 15, 1851, Matilda Lomax to John Hartwell Cocke, Sr., January 27, 1852, and April 20, 1853, all in John Hartwell Cocke Papers.
81. Matilda Lomax to John Hartwell Cocke, Sr., June 20, 1854, Matilda Richardson to John Hartwell Cocke, Sr., August, 1857, both in John Hartwell Cocke Papers.

great work of improving human affairs. . . . I believe Liberia will yet stand with . . . other parts of the Civilized World." This country, James Skipwith wrote his brother in May, 1860, is "the best for the black man on the face of the Earth. God intended Africa for the black race."[82]

Like white Virginians, Cocke's former slaves were thus divided and ambivalent as to the feasibility of African colonization. Some regretted emigration from Virginia, whereas others, as Cocke had hoped, achieved a greater human dignity as free and equal citizens of Liberia.

Virginia's free blacks were not irresolute. Although the general assembly, in 1850 and 1853, again appropriated generous colonization funds, free blacks remained unwilling to remove. Dismal accounts of famine, destitution, disease; escalating northern attacks on the American Colonization Society as a proslavery agency; growing demand for free black laborers in Virginia—all these stiffened free blacks' resistance to African emigration after 1833. In the end, then, free blacks themselves undermined the Brodnax-Bryce-Harrison antislavery compromise. Their refusal to emigrate voluntarily, coupled with whites' compunctions against coercion, aborted colonization as an "entering wedge." Free blacks' identification with America, not Africa, as their native land, ironically would seal the fate of slaveholding white Virginia.

But not all white Virginians regarded perpetual slavery as a sealed "book of fate." While growing numbers succumbed to that "fatal indolence"[83] in the 1840s and 1850s, many others continued to press for emancipation. Renewed abolition agitation west of the Blue Ridge, mounting attacks on slaveholders' political power and tax privileges, final dissolution of the commonwealth and formation of the free-soil state of West Virginia—such recurrent internal debate over slavery in post-1833 decades would belie historians' traditional portrait of white Virginia as a "closed," proslavery society committed to the "positive good" philosophy of the Deep South.

82. Solomon to John Hartwell Cocke, Sr., August 19, 1857, James P. Skipwith to John Hartwell Cocke, Sr., August 20, 1859, James P. Skipwith to Edwards Skipwith, May 31, 1860, all in John Hartwell Cocke Papers.
83. Cocke to [?], December, 1833.

# VIII / "Whither Will Virginia Go?"

As Virginia conservatives struggled to defend slaveholders' political and economic hegemony against internal assaults during the years 1829–1833, external attacks on the South's "peculiar institution" also intensified. Besieged by demands for majority rule and *post-nati* emancipation within the commonwealth, Virginia slaveholders concurrently confronted an increasingly virulent northern abolitionist crusade. Already in 1830, following discovery of David Walker's *Appeal* circulating among Richmond free blacks, Governor William B. Giles had urged legislators to counter "increasing" dissemination of "insurrectionary pamphlets and speeches." A year later, Governor John B. Floyd had held Walker, William Lloyd Garrison, and other "Northern incendiaries" partly responsible for the Nat Turner insurrection. Now, just four years after Southampton, Floyd's successor, Governor Littleton W. Tazewell, informed the 1835–1836 Virginia General Assembly that "since the last adjournment" of the legislature, "citizens from northern and eastern states" had organized "numerous societies" to effect "immediate emancipation of our slaves." To promote their "mischievous schemes," these "fanatics" had disseminated "seditious and incendiary materials" through the federal mails. Moreover, they had "boldly" petitioned Congress to abolish slavery in the District of Columbia and to prohibit its "future introduction" in all United States territories. The slaveholding South, Governor Tazewell insisted, must not tolerate such "direct interference" with "our property." Virginia and other slaveholding states must demand that northern governments adopt "prompt . . . efficient means to suppress" all abolition societies "within their limits."[1]

Several weeks after the governor's address, in February, 1836, both houses of the general assembly resolved that "this commonwealth only has the right to control or interfere with . . . domestic slavery" and called upon nonslaveholding states to prohibit "all abolition societies." As a further curb on meddling Yankees, legislators ordered the fine and imprisonment of any person who "shall come into this state" to advocate emancipation or to deny slaveholders' property rights. Persons writing, printing, or circulating incendiary doctrines would, if slave or free black, be punished by deportation and sale outside the United States, if white by two to five years in jail. Abolitionist tracts arriving at Virginia post offices would be immediately burned.[2]

Virginia abolitionists joined conservatives in denouncing northern extremists. Vituperation of slaveowners, attacks on African colonization, demands for immediate emancipation—such antislavery tenets contravened the gradualist tradition of Virginia abolitionism. Emancipators in 1831–1832 had affirmed the *benevolence* of Virginia slaveholders, the *mildness* of Virginia slavery. All had preferred black bondage to incorporation of freedmen. Most had recognized, as the Bryce preamble proclaimed, the need for "temperate discussion" of slavery to persuade "whites of all classes" of the superiority of free white labor and of the practicability of *gradual* abolition. "Satisfy our people on these points," antislavery Virginians affirmed, "and you will have thousands of converts to emancipation." The "violent tirades," "abuses," "threats" of "northern antislavery presses," conversely, "paralize our efforts . . . and rivet with a double bolt, the bonds they are intended to loosen." No "friend of emancipation . . . cares to open his mouth . . . for fear of being branded . . . an ally of Garrison."[3] Rather than promoting the cause, Yankee "fanatics" had driven slaveholders "almost en masse half a century back of the late advancement of liberal public sentiment" and strengthened the "hands of ultra-slavists amongst us." If northerners

1. Virginia, *Journal of the House of Delegates of the Commonwealth of Virginia, 1835–36* (Richmond, 1836), 6–7.
2. Virginia, *Acts Passed at a General Assembly of the Commonwealth of Virginia, 1835–36* (Richmond, 1836), 44–45, 395–96.
3. Edward Colston to Ralph R. Gurley, July 9, 1833, in American Colonization Society Papers.

would "only let us manage this affair in our own way," Virginia abolitionists grumbled, "the question will be agitated with much greater probability of success."[4]

If antislavery Virginians found their task more arduous after 1835, few abandoned their course. Indeed, as "temporary patchworks" of the 1829–1833 period proved increasingly objectionable to Virginia's nonslaveholding majority, internal attacks on slavery and on slaveholders' power escalated.

The most publicized attempt to promote emancipation was the Reverend Henry Ruffner's 1847 *Address to the People of West Virginia*.[5] Ruffner was a descendant of those hardy German yeomen who had first settled the Valley of Virginia in the early eighteenth century. President of Washington College in the town of Lexington in Rockbridge County, Ruffner was also a Presbyterian minister and a small slaveholder. His abolition scheme appeared in pamphlet form in September, 1847, and a month later in serial form in the local Lexington *Gazette*.[6]

Ruffner's abolitionism drew largely upon gradualist principles long espoused by Thomas Jefferson and rekindled by Jefferson's grandson, Thomas Jefferson Randolph, during the 1831–1832 slavery debate. Let slaves "born after a certain day," Ruffner proposed, "be emancipated at an age not exceeding 25 years" and, after laboring a year or two to defray transportation costs, be colonized in Liberia. In reviving *post-nati* emancipation, however, the reverend showed greater humanitarian concern for blacks than had Jefferson's grandson. Whereas Randolph's 1832 plan had allowed masters to sell after-born slaves out of Virginia up to the very "hour of emancipation," Ruffner's scheme prohibited "exportation" of *post-nati* children over "five years old" and specified that those under five be "exported" only with their families. This "restriction" on masters' rights, Ruffner explained, "is intended to prevent slaveholders from defeating the benevolent intentions of the law, by selling into slavery those entitled to freedom." Furthermore, to prepare "heirs of emancipation" for freedom, Ruffner's plan required masters to have slave children

4. John Hartwell Cocke, Sr., to Edward C. Delavan, July 24, 1837, in John Hartwell Cocke Papers.

5. Henry Ruffner, *An Address to the People of West Virginia* (Reprint; Bridgewater, Va., 1933).

6. William Gleason Bean, "The Ruffner Pamphlet of 1847: An Antislavery Aspect of Virginia Sectionalism," *Virginia Magazine of History and Biography*, LXI (1953), 260–82.

taught "reading, writing and arithmetic," and "churches and benevolent people" to provide "religious instruction."[7]

Ruffner's antislavery proposal differed from Randolph's and those of other 1831–1832 Virginia abolitionists in another crucial regard. Although he deplored slavery's retarding effect on white population, manufacturing, commerce, agriculture, and education in all sections of the commonwealth, Ruffner nevertheless acknowledged the impracticability of emancipation in east Virginia. Echoing arguments of 1831–1832 house conservatives, he cited huge numbers of Tidewater and Piedmont slaves, and an eastern "slave interest" that "overrules and absorbs everything" as insurmountable obstacles. West of the Blue Ridge, in contrast, where slaves comprised "only one-eighth of the population" and slaveholders "less than one-eighth of the whites," the predominant "free interest" could abolish slavery gradually without "inconvenience . . . to society in general, or to slaveholders in particular."[8]

"Intimately connected" with westerners' antislavery drive, Ruffner resolved, was the "vital . . . republican principle that *the majority shall rule*." Once west Virginians "obtain . . . just weight in the government," the general assembly could no longer resist Valley and Trans-Allegheny demands for "an emancipation law." The "momentous struggle for political power," Ruffner proclaimed, would enter a "critical period" when the new federal census revealed considerable white majorities west of the Blue Ridge. "When the crisis of 1850 shall arrive," let the West "adhere inflexibly" to the "white basis, *without compromise*," to "insure success" of that "equally momentous . . . cause" of gradual abolition.[9]

Without westerners' "united stand," Ruffner resurrected the racist-economic warnings of 1831–1832 Valley abolitionist Charles J. Faulkner, this "lovely land" of "white freemen" would be increasingly "blackened" with "loathsome dregs of Eastern Virginia." As declining cotton prices depressed Deep South demand for Tidewater and Piedmont blacks, aristocratic eastern planters would "come with their multitude of slaves to settle upon the fresh lands of West Virginia." Deprived of southern outlets, easterners would also send "thousands" of surplus slaves to a "market" in West Virginia. With "Negroes . . . dog cheap," "many" Valley

7. Ruffner, *An Address to the People of West Virginia*, 38–40.
8. *Ibid.*, 10–11.
9. *Ibid.*, 5–6.

and Trans-Allegheny "people will buy them." "Delay not then," Ruffner "beseeched" westerners, lest slavery "shed its black streams through every gap of the Blue Ridge and pour over the Allegheny," and your "population . . . be as motley as Joseph's coat of many colors."[10]

In urging west Virginians to press first for political equality and then for gradual emancipation, Ruffner also sought to assure east Virginians that neither majority rule nor abolition west of the Blue Ridge would jeopardize eastern "security." A constitutional amendment, the Valley abolitionist insisted, could "easily" protect slave property "against all unjust legislation arising from the power or the anti-slavery principles of the West." Furthermore, if easterners allowed the Valley and Trans-Allegheny *post-nati* emancipation, ongoing agitation for "separation" of the state would disappear. Just as the free-soil North and slaveholding South had lived "peacefully . . . under one Federal Government" for fifty-eight years, so Virginia could be "harmoniously" composed "partly of free, and partially of slaveholding territory."[11]

Ruffner's portrait of a harmonious Union belied mounting national tensions during post-1835 decades, as North and South squared off over slavery. So, too, his vision of peaceable coexistence between a commonwealth half-slave and half-free ignored recurrent clashes between slaveholding and nonslaveholding Virginians over "intimately connected" questions of white-basis representation and slavery. As dramatized during the 1829–1830 convention, eastern conservatives had repeatedly dismissed constitutional guarantees for slave property as "paper pledges" and insisted on disproportionate power to protect slaveholding interests. Renewed demands for political equality and for abolition west of the Blue Ridge only confirmed conservatives' long-standing fears of western disloyalty to slavery and raised the specter of eventual statewide action by a nonslaveholding white majority actively committed to emancipation. With the Mexican War and 1848 presidential election threatening to exacerbate North-South divisions over slavery, Virginia slaveholders were particularly intolerant of internal dissent. Although Ruffner dissociated his antislavery scheme from northern "ultra-abolitionism"[12] and decried northern free-soil politicians, Tidewater and

10. *Ibid.*, 36–38.
11. *Ibid.*, 10–11.
12. *Ibid.*, 8.

Piedmont conservatives linked "Ruffnerism" with "Garrisonianism" under the single, despised category of "abolitionist."[13]

Ruffner had hoped to spark formation of a newspaper and party in western Virginia dedicated to gradual emancipation. Instead, the hostility of local Valley conservatives led him to resign as president of Washington College in June, 1848, and, soon afterward, to carry his antislavery cause westward to Kentucky. "Most . . . Valley editors and politicians," Ruffner reported in a letter to the Trans-Allegheny *Kanawha Republican,* "objected to our movement as ill-timed, while northern abolitionism was raging." They further declared emancipation "an enterprise of doubtful success." Although the pamphlet was "better received west of the Allegheny," still, without Valley "concurrence," Ruffner lamented, "we must fail."[14]

If Ruffner's insistence on a "harmonious" Union and commonwealth, part-slave, part-free, belied events, so his hopes for a "united" antislavery west Virginia overlooked the disparate "slave interest" of the Trans-Allegheny and Valley. As Ruffner noted, slaves *did* comprise "only one-eighth of the population" west of the Blue Ridge by the late 1840s. This ratio, however, represents the average for *both* sections, not slave percentages within *each* section. Computed separately, the "critical" 1850 federal census would reveal that the Trans-Allegheny's 24,443 slaves comprised just 6.8 percent of that section's total population, whereas 38,792 Valley slaves comprised 18.8 percent of that section's total. West of the Alleghenies, thirty-nine of forty-nine counties had *less* than 10 percent slaves, with most northwestern and northern counties having fewer than 2 percent. Significantly, of the ten Trans-Allegheny counties with more than 10 percent slaves, all were either in or bordering the salt-mining Kanawha Valley, or in southwestern regions near slaveholding Tennessee and North Carolina. Of nineteen Valley counties, in contrast, only four had less than 10 percent slaves, whereas seven, including Ruffner's own Rockbridge, had more than 25 percent. Admittedly, the Valley's overall slave ratio (18.8 percent) fell far short of the Piedmont's 50.5 percent and the Tidewater's 44.5 percent. So, too, total numbers of Valley slaves (38,792) in no way approximated the Piedmont's 233,069 or

13. Bean, "The Ruffner Pamphlet of 1847," 275, 281–82.
14. *Ibid.,* 275–77.

the Tidewater's 176,224. Yet with almost three times the slave pecentages and 14,349 more slaves than the vast Trans-Allegheny, the Valley by 1850 had a more extensive "slave interest" than Ruffner portrayed.[15] (See Appendix, Table VIII.)

Ruffner's call for white-basis representation also dramatized the divisions between Virginia's western districts. White population had swelled west of the Blue Ridge in the years since adoption of the 1830 constitution, but with Trans-Allegheny increases far outstripping the Valley's. During these two decades, the Trans-Allegheny had gained 147,137 whites—a growth rate of 80 percent—; the Valley, in contrast, had gained 27,759 whites—a 20.6 percent increase. East of the Blue Ridge, the Tidewater had gained 21,660 whites—a 13 percent increase, while the Piedmont, with but 3,942 new whites, had grown just 1.9 percent. Valley white population gains from 1830 to 1850 thus approximated that of the Tidewater and Piedmont combined, whereas the Trans-Allegheny accounted for 73.4 percent of Virginia's total white population increase.[16] (See Appendix, Table IX.)

As Trans-Allegheny whites multiplied, discontent with the state's "patchwork" constitution intensified. The 1830 constitution, apportioning the house on 1820 white population and the senate on arbitrary districts, had authorized the general assembly to reapportion representation after 1841 if two-thirds of each house approved. Thus, when the 1840 census revealed a more than 2,000 white majority west of the Blue Ridge, and the eastern-dominated legislature refused to act, Trans-Allegheny ire quickened. As in the 1820s, angry reformers looked to a constitutional convention as the sole redress against slaveholders' rule.[17]

The convention movement gained ground in the late 1840s as growing numbers of east Virginians, particularly urban residents, joined reform ranks. Eastern disaffection centered not on legislative representation, but on complex, ambiguous, and undemocratic suffrage requirements.[18] Amidst statewide clamor, the general assembly in March, 1850,

15. U.S. Census Office, *The Seventh Census of the United States: 1850* (Washington, D.C., 1853), 256–57.
16. U.S. Census Office, *Fifth Census*, Tables [10]–[13]; U.S. Census Office, *Seventh Census*, 256–57.
17. Ambler, *Sectionalism in Virginia*, 251–56.
18. Moore, "Slavery as a Factor," 57; Neely, "Development of Virginia Taxation," 331–32.

finally agreed to submit the convention issue to popular referendum. However, desertion of several Valley legislators from the white basis enabled conservatives to secure their long-cherished mixed basis of white population and taxation combined as the apportionment principle for the proposed convention. Such unrepublican organization, allowing one delegate for every 13,151 whites and one for every $7,000 paid in taxes, would give the Tidewater and Piedmont thirty-eight representatives each, the Valley twenty-four, the Trans-Allegheny thirty-five. Apportionment on 1850 white population alone, in contrast, would give the Tidewater twenty-nine, the Piedmont thirty-two, the Valley twenty-four, and the Trans-Allegheny fifty representatives. The Valley, with 18.2 percent of all Virginia whites in 1850, would thus have 17.8 percent of convention delegates under either the mixed or white basis. If representation of both persons and property allowed Valley whites full political power, however, this principle would reduce Trans-Allegheny strength from 37 percent of convention delegates under the white basis to just 25.9 percent. Equally outrageous to white-basis reformers, mixed-basis apportionment would assure east Virginia, which in 1850 contained only 44.9 percent of the state's whites, majority power, whereas the Valley and Trans-Allegheny together, with a 92,282 white majority, would have a convention minority.[19]

Virginians at the spring-1850 elections endorsed the constitutional convention 46,327 to 20,668. Voting exposed a sharp schism, not between east and west Virginia, but between the Trans-Allegheny and the rest of the commonwealth. East of the Blue Ridge, all but two counties voted "yes." Valley counties unanimously approved. Conversely, more than two-thirds of Trans-Allegheny counties opposed, preferring no convention to the proposed mixed-basis assemblage.[20] With Virginia's populous nonslaveholding region already so hostile, the convention that opened in the hall of the house of delegates on October 14, 1850, promised even stormier clashes between reformers and conservatives than had occurred during the more illustrious 1829–1830 assemblage.

19. U.S. Census Office, *Seventh Census*, 256–57; James C. McGregor, *The Disruption of Virginia* (New York, 1922), 56–57; Francis P. Gaines, "The Virginia Constitutional Convention of 1850–1851: A Study in Sectionalism" (Ph.D. dissertation, University of Virginia, 1950), 88–92.

20. Gaines, "The Virginia Constitutional Convention of 1850–51," 93–106; McGregor, *The Disruption of Virginia*, 56.

Following appointment of several special committees, the convention adjourned until January 6, 1851, to await results of the 1850 federal census. These returns, confirming the huge increase of whites west of the Alleghenies, bolstered Trans-Allegheny demands for legislative reapportionment. By 1850, the Trans-Allegheny boasted 37 percent of Virginia's whites but, under the 1820 population basis of the state's constitution, had only 23.1 percent of house, and 21.9 percent of senate, members. Moreover, western Virginia, with 55.2 percent of total whites, controlled only 41.8 percent of the house and 40.7 percent of the senate. Having been defeated in the 1829–1830 convention, white-basis reformers determined to make a "final and decisive effort" to wrest political power from slaveholding conservatives.[21]

For four months, the convention deadlocked on the representation issue, with arguments largely echoing those of 1829–1830. But confronted now with the *reality* of a white majority west of the Blue Ridge, reformers and conservatives alike sounded a more strident note. Abstract appeals to natural rights and to Jeffersonian political tenets more often gave way to pragmatic references to population statistics and tax returns. The struggle for control of Virginia's government became more naked, threats of state dismemberment more bellicose.

Underlying such an ominous stand-off was the irrepressible question of slavery. Declare that Virginia cannot have "republican government . . . because of negro slavery," Trans-Allegheny reformers reiterated Chapman Johnson's 1829–1830 warning, and you strike the "deadliest blow at the institution itself." To graft the principle that "money is power" upon the "altar of freedom" would "array classes against each other" throughout the commonwealth. Nonslaveholding white mechanics, artisans, and laborers east of the Blue Ridge would join nonslaveholding western farmers, miners, and laborers to oppose government by that most "odious and detestable" of all aristocracies—a "monied aristocracy." Statewide "war" against slaveholders' rule would escalate, white-basis delegates stressed, as suffrage democratization enfranchised ever larger numbers of nonslaveholding Virginians.[22]

Why, then, reformers challenged, did conservatives demand repre-

21. U.S. Census Office, *Seventh Census*, 256–57; Ruffner, *An Address to the People of West Virginia*, 5.
22. Richmond *Enquirer*, March 12, 1851, Supplement 16; June 17, 1851, Supplement 43.

sentation for property? Contrary to conservatives' fears, westerners were not "cutthroats" or "robbers" bent on destroying slavery. The Valley was a slaveholding region and would generally "unite with the east" on legislation affecting slave property. If eastern slaveholders would only grant the white majority equal political rights, western "fidelity" to slavery would be "forever secure." However, westerners could not "ardently support" an institution that allowed a "negro aristocracy" disproportionate power and reduced nonslaveholding whites to political "slaves." We prefer immediate division of the state, white-basis reformers resolved, to further compromise of our democratic rights.[23]

Conservatives faced a difficult dilemma. To yield the white basis would assure western control of the general assembly and, thereby, conservatives had long assumed, expose slave property to oppressive taxation and to emancipation legislation. Yet to resist majority rule, they concomitantly recognized, would deepen nonslaveholders' antipathy both to slaveholders and to slavery and would, in all probability, sever the state. Confronted with such dire alternatives, conservatives once again chose to resist, to shield slave property from democracy.

To "surrender legislative control to a majority of mere numbers," conservatives echoed 1829–1830 stalwarts Benjamin Watkins Leigh and John Randolph, would endanger "that great and sensitive property . . . congregated in one quarter of the state." The east was not willing to subject an "immense interest" of 400,000 slaves, worth $150 million, to the "absolute dominion" of "those whose rights and interests" might require its "destruction." Westerners' 1831–1832 support for *post-nati* emancipation, conservatives noted, mocked present assurances of "fidelity" to slavery. So, too, belligerent demands for white-basis apportionment "array nonslaveholders against . . . slaveholders" within Virginia and, in so doing, "direct the attention of distant enemies to the point of weakness in slaveholding communities." In a bifurcated society like Virginia's, "every great interest" must "assent" to legislation. Only the mixed-basis representation of property and numbers could protect the state's slaveholding white minority from the "tyranny" of the nonslaveholding white majority.[24]

23. *Ibid.*, March 5, 1851, Supplement 14.
24. *Ibid.*, March 8, 1851, Supplement 15; June 4, 1851, Supplement 40; June 21, 1851, Supplement 45.

As in the 1829–1830 convention, intransigent reformers could not carry their favorite plan of a white-basis house and senate, nor intransigent conservatives their long-sought mixed-basis apportionment for both legislative branches. Instead, amidst mounting Trans-Allegheny threats to sunder the state, delegates, late in May, 1851, finally adopted a compromise apportioning a 152-member house on qualified voters and a 50-member senate on existing district representation.[25] This plan, proposed by Piedmont delegate Samuel Chilton of Fauquier County, reflected the moderate reform tradition long characteristic of the western Piedmont, of major Tidewater and Piedmont cities, and of part of the "Eastern Shore"—a tradition embodied in the 1829–1830 convention by William Fitzhugh Gordon and, in the 1831–1832 slavery debate, by Archibald Bryce, Jr. Whereas Gordon's apportionment had favored conservative interests, however, Chilton's now favored reform. Democratic principles particularly triumphed in the house, where, following delegates' sweeping endorsement of universal white manhood suffrage in July, 1851, the qualified voters' basis effected white-basis representation. Accordingly, house apportionment almost precisely mirrored 1850 white population, with the Tidewater having 21.1 percent of house seats, or thirty-two members; the Piedmont 24.3 percent, or thirty-seven members; the Valley, 17.8 percent, or twenty-seven members; and the Trans-Allegheny, 36.8 percent, or fifty-six members. With a present western majority of fourteen in the lower house as well as provision for future house reapportionment in 1865 and every ten years thereafter, Virginia's new constitution at last incorporated, in one legislative branch, the principle of equal political rights for white men.

If white-basis reformers triumphed in the house, they fared less well in the senate. Here, Chilton's compromise simply continued arbitrary district representation of the 1830 constitution, giving the Tidewater 26 percent of senate seats, or thirteen members; the Piedmont 34 percent, or seventeen members; and the Valley and Trans-Allegheny alike 20 percent, or just ten senators each. Even with the senate's democratic shortcomings, however, west Virginia had a general assembly majority of 4 on joint ballots. Furthermore, unlike 1830 representation provisions, Virginia's 1851 constitution authorized senate reapportionment in 1865,

25. Gaines, "The Virginia Constitutional Convention of 1850–51," 214–27; Neely, "Development of Virginia Taxation," 346–47.

with the possibility of extending the universal white manhood suffrage basis to both houses of the general assembly. Jubilant over democratization of the house and of suffrage, and anticipating future legislative re-apportionment, white-basis reformers in 1851 did not steadfastly oppose Virginia's unrepublican senate. Indeed, when the convention added popular election of Virginia's governor, lieutenant-governor, judges, and Board of Public Works commissioners to already-approved representation and suffrage clauses, reform delegates hailed the 1851 constitution as a momentous victory for democracy.[26] Although unbending eastern conservatives resisted, moderates preferred incorporation of most long-standing reform principles to probable separation of the commonwealth. Except for senate representation, then, Virginia's 1851 mixed-basis convention overturned conservative-oriented compromises of 1829–1830 in all three government branches.

Unable to stave off majority rule in the house and on joint general assembly ballots, conservatives countered defeat of mixed-basis representation with insistence on special tax privileges for slave property. Acting on traditional assumptions as to slavery's "peculiar" vulnerability to democracy, conservatives demanded, and received, constitutional guarantees protecting slaves from "oppressive" taxation by Virginia's western majority. While declaring that "all other property . . . throughout the Commonwealth . . . shall be taxed in proportion to its value," the 1851 constitution specifically exempted slaves under twelve years of age from any taxation and imposed a *fixed* per capita value of $300 on slaves over twelve. The *ad valorem* principle, culminating Virginia's decades-old effort to achieve "equal and uniform taxation,"[27] would thus apply to all property, real and personal, of nonslaveholding white farmers, mechanics, laborers, merchants—but not to the "peculiar property" of Virginia slaveholders. Elated over newly acquired political power, western reformers objected to, but did not relentlessly oppose, slaves' privileged tax status. But as slave prices soared ever upward after 1851, such concession to conservative interests would become the principal source of antagonism between nonslaveholding and slaveholding Virginians.[28]

26. Gaines, "The Virginia Constitutional Convention of 1850–51," 223–25, 279–83; Neely, "Development of Virginia Taxation," 347.

27. Neely, "Development of Virginia Taxation," 349, 373.

28. Ambler, *Sectionalism in Virginia,* 267–68; Moore, "Slavery as a Factor," 62.

The convention on July 30, 1851, passed the revised constitution by a decisive 75–35 majority. Three months later, Virginia voters ratified the new government by an even greater majority of 75,784 to 11,063. Every Valley and Trans-Allegheny county approved. East of the Blue Ridge, though public opinion was more divided, all but five counties—two Piedmont and three Tidewater—returned positive majorities. Leading newspapers in all sections of the commonwealth likewise endorsed the 1851 constitution. Valley and Trans-Allegheny journals particularly applauded house apportionment on qualified voters and predicted 1865 senate reapportionment on this same democratic suffrage basis. The Richmond *Whig* and *Enquirer,* the Lynchburg *Virginian,* the Norfolk and Portsmouth *Herald,* all initially favoring mixed-basis representation, nevertheless by August, 1851, were staunch advocates of both the apportionment compromise and of the state's more republican constitution.[29] Virginians' internal harmony, however, proved short-lived. For as the decade progressed, the Trans-Allegheny would increasingly resent eastern control of the senate and, above all, unequal taxation of slaves.

Virginia's failure to forge commercial bonds between slaveholding and nonslaveholding regions contributed to the growing alienation, and isolation, of the populous Trans-Allegheny. The post-1851 decade saw rapid expansion of state-financed internal improvements designed to promote Virginia's internal unity as well as southern economic independence from the north. By the late 1850s, short-run railroad lines crisscrossed east Virginia, connecting the major cities of Richmond, Lynchburg, Petersburg, and Norfolk. A longer line, the Virginia Central Railroad, extended from Richmond through the Blue Ridge Mountains to Staunton, linking the grain and livestock economy of the central Valley to eastern markets. The Virginia and Tennessee Railroad, completed from Lynchburg to Memphis in 1857, likewise opened up trade between east Virginia, the southwest Trans-Allegheny, and the cotton South. While railroads provided the principal commercial impetus, work also gradually proceeded on the James River and Kanawha canal, long Virginia's major internal improvements project. By late 1851, the canal extended 196½ miles from Richmond through the Blue Ridge Mountains to

29. Gaines, "The Virginia Constitutional Convention of 1850–51," 220–22, 277–86; Ambler, *Sectionalism in Virginia,* 271.

Buchanan, allowing continuous water transportation between east Virginia and the southern Valley.[30]

Neither railroads nor canals, however, consummated the age-old dream of joining the distant northwest Trans-Allegheny with the rest of the commonwealth. Instead, completion of the Baltimore and Ohio Railroad to the burgeoning industrial city of Wheeling in 1853 directed the trade of the northwest Trans-Allegheny and northern Valley to Baltimore, not Richmond, whereas the Cleveland-Pittsburgh-Wheeling and Central Ohio railroads connected Wheeling's economy to nonslaveholding Pennsylvania, Ohio, Indiana, and Illinois.[31] As the specter of disunion stalked the nation, commercial, manufacturing, and agricultural interests of Virginia's predominantly nonslaveholding northwest thus were more closely tied to the free-soil North than to the slaveholding South.

Virginia's improved transportation and market facilities in turn fostered rapid industrial growth on both sides of the Blue Ridge during the 1850s. By the end of the decade, large-scale tobacco factories, flour mills, iron works dotted Richmond's landscape, making Virginia's capital city the nation's foremost tobacco manufacturing center, and the South's leading industrial center. Although processing industries predominated, Richmond also had seventy-seven iron-manufacturing establishments in 1860. The largest, the Tredegar Iron Works, was the South's principal iron-making enterprise, producing locomotives and other railroad equipment, cannons, guns, ship iron, and sundry heavy machinery and tools. Not far from Richmond, the "Southside" cities of Petersburg and Lynchburg likewise expanded tobacco manufacturing and flour milling in the 1850s and, with railroad connections to the cotton South, also established several cotton mills. Petersburg, by 1860, further boasted a locomotive factory and seven iron works.[32] Outside the slaveholding east, the "Panhandle" city of Wheeling ranked second to Richmond as the state's principal manufacturing center. Heavy, not processing, industries

30. Goldfield, *Urban Growth in the Age of Sectionalism*, 182–89; Dunaway, *History of the James River and Kanawha Company*, 156–57.

31. Goldfield, *Urban Growth in the Age of Sectionalism*, 188, 246, 266; Milton Reizenstein, *The Economic History of the Baltimore and Ohio Railroad, 1827–1853*, Johns Hopkins University Studies in History and Political Science, Series 15, VII–VIII (Baltimore, 1897), 33–38, 62–71.

32. Goldfield, *Urban Growth in the Age of Sectionalism*, 192–95; Robert, *Tobacco Kingdom*, 181–89.

dominated Wheeling's economy, with the city's two largest iron foundries producing more railroad iron than Richmond's Tredegar Works. Nail and glass manufacture were also important Wheeling enterprises.[33]

As slaveholding and nonslaveholding Virginia concurrently pursued industrialization, however, a crucial difference existed. East of the Blue Ridge, slaves manufactured tobacco, iron, and constructed railroads. Throughout the northwest Trans-Allegheny, whites, including growing numbers of northern and New England immigrants, manned manufacturing and mining pursuits.

To meet escalating labor needs in Tidewater and Piedmont towns, urban entrepreneurs increasingly turned to slave hiring, a practice which had long existed in east Virginia communities, but which burgeoned amidst industrial-commercial expansion of the 1850s. Rather than owning slaves, tobacco and iron manufacturers, as well as internal improvements contractors, annually hired blacks from local plantations to work in both skilled and unskilled jobs. To urban entrepreneurs, slave hiring avoided costly capital investment in buying blacks and also allowed a more flexible labor force for busy and slack periods. To large rural slaveholders who typically supplied hired blacks, this system assured a profitable return on surplus plantation hands. With city and country elite alike benefiting, adaptation of slave labor to industrial-commercial growth strengthened bonds between east Virginia's urban and rural economies as the 1850s progressed.[34]

Although Tidewater and Piedmont "gentlemen" generally applauded slave hiring, east Virginia's urban white mechanics and artisans did not. Echoing the 1831–1832 memorial of Petersburg's nonslaveholding white craftsmen, Norfolk and Portsmouth counterparts petitioned the 1851–1852 general assembly to give "white men the exclusive privilege of the mechanic arts."[35] To prohibit slave mechanics would remove the "great cause of jealousy which exists between nonslaveholders and slaveholders." On the other hand, should legislators refuse to limit slave com-

33. Goldfield, *Urban Growth in the Age of Sectionalism*, 19; Moore, *Banner in the Hills*, 3.
34. Starobin, *Industrial Slavery in the Old South*, 15–23, 135; Goldfield, *Urban Growth in the Age of Sectionalism*, 130–37; Wade, *Slavery in the Cities*, 30–38.
35. Virginia Legislative Petitions, Portsmouth City, February 25, 1851, and Norfolk City, November 12, 1851, Virginia State Library, Richmond. See Chapter VI, pp. 175–76, for discussion of the 1831–32 Petersburg memorial.

petition, urban Tidewater petitioners cautioned, "the day is not far distant, when mechanics and nonslaveholders, generally, will demand . . . total expulsion of . . . negroes from our state."

Recurrent images of class divisions between east Virginia's nonslaveholding and slaveholding whites, fresh warnings of heightened abolitionist sentiment among nonslaveholding white laborers in Tidewater and Piedmont towns—such ongoing evidence of internal disloyalty to slavery, a "Southern Man" protested in an anonymous letter to the June 6, 1856, Richmond *Enquirer*, was "more to be feared" than the "*Anti-Nebraskaism*" or "Black Republicanism" of northern abolitionists. To "prevent . . . employment of slave labor in . . . mechanic arts" like "Moulding and Iron manufacture," as the white mechanics' association "called the *Mechanic Union*" intends to do all "over Virginia," is "living, practical abolitionism . . . in our very midst." Indeed, this correspondent angrily reiterated, for Virginia's white mechanics and artisans to so band together and refuse to "work in any establishment where slave labor is employed . . . is as much at war with Southern rights, and as much subversive of slavery as the Wilmot Proviso, or any other scheme which gives a Northern man rights . . . withheld from Southern." Unless Virginia slaveholders countered efforts of "Southern anti-slavery men" to declare that "another and another trade shall be sacred from the touch of polluted slavery," a "Southern Man" concluded, "we must be forced at last to basely surrender, because slavery has become a burden too heavy to be borne."

A "Southern Man's" fear of "internal foes," of "this spirit of Southern abolitionism" embodied in the Mechanic Union's drive against urban slave laborers, suggests the impracticability of the dream of Virginia's George Fitzhugh and other 1850s southern nationalists to build a vast industrial order on slavery. As Gavin Wright has argued in *The Political Economy of the Cotton South*, nonslaveholding white laborers'—skilled and unskilled—resentment of slave competition would most likely have precluded "drastic reallocation of slave labor"[36] from plantation agriculture to urban manufacturing. Paradoxically, then, assumptions of 1831–1832 Virginia conservatives as to the long-run incompatibility of slavery and industrialization might well have been valid, not because slaves

36. Wright, *Political Economy of the Cotton South*, 127. For Chapman Johnson's warning of class abolitionism, see Chapter III, p. 60.

would prove unprofitable in nonplantation pursuits, as conservatives believed, but because nonslaveholders would not tolerate large-scale transfer of blacks from country to city. Burgeoning reliance on slaves, as the slave-hiring system allowed, perhaps would have so antagonized Tidewater and Piedmont nonslaveholding white laborers as to realize Chapman Johnson's foreseen coalition of eastern and western abolitionists determined to oust slaveholders, slavery, and slaves.

Widespread demand for slave laborers not only aggravated white class divisions within east Virginia during the 1850s. By inflating slave prices, it also heightened sectional tensions between Virginia's principal slaveholding and nonslaveholding regions. As slave prices soared ever upward after 1851, Trans-Allegheny resentment of slaves' privileged tax status intensified, making slavery an ever more explosive issue within the commonwealth as the nation veered toward disunion. Just like expansion of internal improvements, industrial growth divided, rather than united, Virginia's whites.

More important than internal demand in inflating slave values, though, was the accelerating sale of Virginia blacks to the Deep South. There, expansion and boom in cotton production prompted planters to purchase ever larger numbers of border South, particularly Virginia, slaves. By the mid-1850s, Virginia was exporting approximately twenty thousand blacks annually to the cotton South, making the domestic slave trade a major component of Virginia's economic prosperity and assuring substantial profits to Tidewater and Piedmont slaveholders. Brisk demand without, coupled with brisk demand within, led to serious labor shortages in urban east Virginia by the late 1850s. With labor scarce, slave prices soared, so that a young adult black male valued at $700–$800 in the early 1850s cost $1500 by 1860.[37] Despite spiraling values, Virginia continued to tax slaves over twelve years of age at the fixed $300 rate specified by the 1851 constitution.

At the same time that the domestic slave trade increased Virginia slave prices, continuing southward exportation decreased the *relative* size of Virginia's slave population during the 1850–1860 decade. In 1850, 472,528 slaves comprised 33.2 percent of Virginia's total population. By 1860, despite an *absolute* increase, 490,865 slaves comprised 30.7 per-

37. Goldfield, *Urban Growth in the Age of Sectionalism*, 119–22; Frederick Bancroft, *Slave Trading in the Old South* (Baltimore, 1931), 291, 383, 406.

cent of Virginia's total population. Relative slave losses occurred in all sections of the commonwealth, most notably in the Tidewater where slaves dropped from 44.5 percent to 41.9 percent of the total population. Piedmont slave ratios, in contrast, remained almost constant, decreasing from 50.5 percent to 50.2 percent. West of the Blue Ridge, Trans-Allegheny slave ratios declined from 6.8 percent to 5.7 percent, Valley ratios from 18.8 percent to 17.1 percent. The Valley also lost absolute numbers of slaves from 1850 to 1860, the only section to experience overall relative *and* absolute declines. In the decade before the Civil War, then, slavery was relatively receding from Virginia, marching slowly but inexorably southward from the border slaveholding states—Maryland, Delaware, Virginia, Kentucky, Missouri—to the Deep South states of Alabama, Arkansas, Georgia, Mississippi, and Texas.[38] (See Appendix, Table X.)

Just as slavery marched ever southward within the nation, so slavery generally receded from northern to southern regions within Virginia. Many northern Tidewater and all northern Valley counties lost relative and absolute numbers of slaves from 1850 to 1860. Slavery's southerly drift was particularly discernible, however, in the Piedmont and Trans-Allegheny, respectively Virginia's principal slaveholding and nonslaveholding sections. Whereas slaves decreased both relatively and absolutely in the northwestern Piedmont county of Loudoun, the "Southside" Piedmont, long the state's tobacco-growing, slaveholding bastion, experienced the greatest relative slave gains of any region of the commonwealth. By 1860, slaves in Amelia and Nottoway comprised over 70 percent of the total population; in Brunswick, Cumberland, Lunenburg, Mecklenburg, Pittsylvania, and Prince Edward, all "Southside" Piedmont counties with relative slave increases since 1850, slaves comprised over 60 percent of the total population. West of the Alleghenies, of the twenty-five counties with *absolute* slave losses during the 1850–1860 decade, the overwhelming majority were in the "Panhandle," northwestern, and western regions bordering nonslaveholding Ohio and Pennsylvania. Counties like Brooke, Ohio, Tyler, Monongalia, Hancock, and Preston had less than 1 percent slaves by 1860. Conversely, of

38. U.S. Census Office, *Seventh Census,* 256–57; U.S. Census Office, *Population of the United States in 1860; Compiled from the Original Returns of the Eighth Census* (Washington, D.C., 1864), 516–18.

the thirteen Trans-Allegheny counties with relative slave gains, eleven were in southwestern areas near Tennessee or in southeastern areas near the Blue Ridge Mountains. By 1860, counties like Washington and Tazewell in the southwest Trans-Allegheny, and Montgomery and Pulaski in the southeast, had, respectively, 15.1 percent, 12.1 percent, 20.9 percent, and 29.3 percent slaves. During the 1850–1860 decade, then, slavery strengthened its hold on the "Southside" Piedmont, made significant inroads in the southern Trans-Allegheny, but virtually "withered away" in Virginia's populous northwest.[39] (See Appendix, Table VIII.)

As in previous "chapters" on the 1829–1830 convention, the 1831–1832 house debate, the 1850–1851 convention, Virginia in the years immediately preceding disunion thus recorded an irresolute "middle ground" in slavery's "book of fate." On the one hand, the interstate slave trade was slowly, silently ridding the commonwealth of blacks, narrowing slavery's base, and confining it to that region of Virginia traditionally akin to the Deep South. On the other hand, despite ongoing southward exportation, absolute numbers of Virginia slaves slightly increased from 1850 to 1860, so that on the eve of the Civil War, Virginia still had the largest slave population of any state in the nation. Heightened external demand also enhanced the profitability of both slaves and slave-breeding within the commonwealth, adding to slavery's resilience. Whether, someday, the domestic slave trade would, as Thomas R. Dew and other 1831–1832 Virginia conservatives had unanimously affirmed, abolish slavery by "natural causes" must therefore remain ambivalent.

Another development, not foreseen in 1831–1832, cast a shadow on Dew's dream of slavery's "natural death." Dew had assumed that urban-industrial growth, fostered by state internal improvements, would make slave labor increasingly unprofitable in Virginia and, accordingly, prompt slaveholders to sell surplus blacks southward. Instead, as slaveholding Virginia extended railroads, built factories, diversified agriculture in the 1850s, demand for slave labor increased and slave values soared. With nonslaveholding white laborers hostile to slave competition, slavery's resilience may well have proved shortlived. Still, the mounting threat of class abolitionism fostered by urban-industrial growth augured not a

39. *Ibid.*

gradual, peaceful exodus of slaveholders' "peculiar property" from Virginia, as Dew had anticipated, but rather a convulsive internal confrontation between the state's nonslaveholding and slaveholding whites.

If 1850s Virginia conservatives seemingly heralded a prosperous, industrial economy based on slave labor, the state's proslavery polemicists nevertheless continued to display ambivalences characteristic of their 1831–1832 counterparts like Dew, William O. Goode, and John Thompson Brown. Even as national tensions over slavery intensified, the dream that Virginia would someday be rid of both slavery and blacks cropped up in most unlikely places. Nathaniel Beverly Tucker, who was at once St. George Tucker's son, John Randolph's half-brother, William and Mary law professor, and Virginia's most notorious disunion conspirator, urged secession to accomplish emancipation! Addressing the Nashville Southern Convention in 1850, the quixotic Tucker proposed that an independent southern Confederacy establish a colony in Latin America and there teach freedmen responsibilities of citizenship. After such training, southern blacks "will be in condition to go forth from this normal school, and settle colonies of their own on all the coasts of Africa." Tidewater conservative Henry Wise, who in late antebellum years was Virginia's most successful proslavery politician, shared Tucker's dream of emancipation-colonization. "*Slavery on this continent,*" Wise affirmed, "is the gift of Heaven to Africa. . . . Africa gave to Virginia a *savage* and a *slave;* Virginia gives back to Africa a *citizen* and a *Christian.*" [40]

Indeed, Virginia's proslavery professors and writers in the late antebellum period were not often committed to perpetual bondage. Albert T. Bledsoe of the University of Virginia pronounced "absurd" the view that blacks should remain enslaved once they were "fit for freedom." Bledsoe concomitantly termed Virginia slavery a providential "school of correction," and though he did not directly propose that slaves one day graduate to Africa, he praised a fellow Virginia colonizationist who did so urge. President William A. Smith of Randolph-Macon College similarly declared slavery "the *natural,* the only *safe,* and ultimately the *effectual* means of the intellectual and moral elevation of the African." Like Bled-

40. Nathaniel Beverly Tucker, *Prescience. A Speech Delivered by Hon. Beverly Tucker, of Virginia, in the Southern Convention, Held at Nashville, Tennessee, April 13, 1850* (Richmond, 1862), 30–32; Barton H. Wise, *The Life of Henry A. Wise of Virginia, 1806–1876* (New York, 1899), 156–62. For evidence of Wise's similar views in the 1850s, see Henry Wise to Nehemiah Adams, August 22, 1854, in Richmond *Enquirer,* October 19, 1854.

soe, Smith looked forward to the "remote, distant," but inevitable demise of the "peculiar institution." So, too, Virginia's best-known proslavery writer, George Fitzhugh, publicly called for development of an industrial economy based on slave labor but privately conceded, "I am no friend of slavery or the slave trade." Although he saw "great evils in slavery," Fitzhugh acknowledged, "in a controversial work I ought not to admit them."[41]

The prevalence of such antislavery notions among proslavery Virginians in the 1850s caused Edmund Ruffin, one of the state's very few advocates of perpetual black bondage, to spend much time attacking African colonization. Virginia's irrepressible, time-worn distaste for slavery also troubled more committed proslavery forces in the lower South. Although emancipation was for 1850s Virginia conservatives an ill-defined, often veiled aspiration, simply their anticipation of future abolition aggravated Deep South fears of border South disloyalty to slavery.[42]

Contradiction, irresolution, drift continued to mark Virginia's course. The historic attachment to the Union, the narrowing base of slavery, the Baltimore and Ohio Railroad—these pulled Virginia toward the freesoil North. The still-buoyant "slave interest," and extensive industrial-commercial ties to the Cotton Kingdom pulled Virginia toward the slaveholding South. With election of the Republican presidential candidate, Abraham Lincoln, in November, 1860, Virginia's "middle ground" would prove increasingly untenable. For the secession of the lower South, precipitated by Lincoln's victory, would force Virginians at last to take a stand.

Lincoln had received only a smattering of votes (1,929) in Virginia, these almost entirely from "Panhandle" counties around Wheeling, and from Fairfax County bordering Washington, D.C.[43] Still, public opinion in nearly all sections of the commonwealth opposed secession in the im-

41. Albert Taylor Bledsoe, *An Essay on Liberty and Slavery* (Philadelphia, 1857), 139–40, 292, 299; William A. Smith, *Lectures on the Philosophy and Practice of Slavery as Exhibited in the Institution of Domestic Slavery in the United States: with the Duties of Masters to Slaves* (Nashville, 1856), 236; George Fitzhugh to George Frederick Holmes, April 11, 1855, in George Frederick Holmes Papers, Duke University Library, Durham, N.C.; George Fitzhugh to Jeremiah Black, May 6, 1857, in Jeremiah Black Papers, Library of Congress.

42. Edmund Ruffin, *African Colonization Unveiled* (Washington, D.C., 1858). For evidence of Deep South fears of Virginia's disloyalty, see George H. Reese (ed.), *Proceedings of the Virginia State Convention of 1861* (4 vols.; Richmond, 1965), I, 62–75.

43. Henry T. Shanks, *The Secession Movement in Virginia 1847–1861* (Richmond, 1934), 116–17.

mediate aftermath of his election. Most Virginians hoped to avert civil war, to restore sectional harmony by additional compromises on slavery. Moreover, moderates were confident that Virginia, with her historic prestige and still-powerful influence among both southern and northern states, could indeed accomplish peaceable reconstruction of the Union on terms more favorable to slaveholding interests. Yet if most Virginians opposed disunion, a large majority also opposed federal coercion. Should compromise efforts fail, the North had no right to force seceded states to remain in the Union.

The special session of the general assembly called by Governor John Letcher to deal with the secession crisis mirrored Virginia public opinion. Convening January 7, 1861, house and senate quickly affirmed the right of peaceful secession and rejected the doctrine of federal coercion. A week later, without submitting the bill to popular referendum, legislators called for a state convention to determine what the state should do. When electing delegates on February 4, voters were also to decide whether convention actions required popular approval. The general assembly further resolved on January 21 that if North-South reconciliation faltered, Virginia should join the slaveholding Confederacy.[44]

Although Virginians had not authorized a state convention, most approved the general assembly's call. The northwest Trans-Allegheny particularly sought to use this emergency forum to secure *ad valorem* taxation of slaves and a white-basis senate. Already, in hopes of weakening Trans-Allegheny resistance to secession, conservative legislators had approved a white-basis convention.[45] Perhaps amidst national crisis over slavery, Trans-Allegheny nonslaveholders would finally achieve full democratic rights within Virginia.

Elections to the convention represented no victory for Virginia secessionism. Of the 152 delegates who assembled in Richmond on February 13, less than one-third were "precipitationists," or proponents of immediate secession. The over two-thirds opposed to precipitous secession, however, divided into two distinct groups. Most were moderate, or conditional, Unionists who looked to sectional compromise to restore the

44. Richard Orr Curry, *A House Divided: A Study of Statehood Politics and the Copperhead Movement in West Virginia* (Pittsburgh, 1964), 28–29; Virgil A. Lewis (ed.), *How West Virginia Was Made* (Charleston, W.Va., 1909), 8–9.
45. Moore, *Banner in the Hills*, 38.

Union and opposed federal coercion of seceded states. A smaller bloc of "extreme" or "ultra-Unionists" also favored resolute efforts to reconstruct the Union. But unlike moderates, "ultra-Unionists" uncompromisingly opposed Virginia's secession, preferring separation of the state to alliance with the southern Confederacy.[46]

As in the past, moderates held the balance of power at the 1861 Virginia convention, and, as before, they urged compromise, postponement, drift. Intertwined strategies of securing further northern guarantees for slavery, or seceding in the event of federal coercion, committed Virginia's destiny to the hands of the Lincoln administration. "Whither Will Virginia Go?," "Will We Go North, or Will We Go South?," "What Will Virginia Do?," echoed through the convention hall during the latter weeks of February. "Await the course of events," moderates replied; avoid hasty action; determine first the policy of the "veiled" man who will soon assume the presidency.[47]

As the convention "awaited," delegates debated the "interests" of Virginia. All hoped to avert civil war. Each argued that his course alone would accomplish this overriding "interest" and also protect Virginia's "rights" and "honor."

Delegates from the "Southside" Piedmont and coastal Tidewater, joined by a few from the southwest Trans-Allegheny, led the fight for immediate secession. Virginia's "institutions," "habits," "religion," and family ties, "precipitationists" insisted, were "homogeneous" with "sister states" of the lower South. Slavery was the "foundation" of the "whole" North-South "difficulty." Virginians, these representatives of the state's slave citadels proclaimed, were "all . . . vitally concerned in the preservation of the institution of African" bondage. Virginia's "ancient fame," abundant resources, and strategic location, "precipitationists" appealed to Virginians' historic pride of leadership, would all assure her "position at the head of the Southern column." Secede now, and the other slaveholding "border states will wheel quickly into line." A united South, with "old Virginia" at the fore, could then achieve either "just and honourable" reconstruction of the Union with "proper guarantees" for slavery, or "peaceable and final separation."

46. Moore, *Banner in the Hills*, 39; Granville D. Hall, *The Rending of Virginia* (Chicago, 1901), 142–45; Reese (ed.), *Proceedings of the Virginia State Convention*, III, 352.
47. Reese (ed.), *Proceedings of the Virginia State Convention*, I, 194–97.

Continued delay, "hope against hope" for compromise, in contrast, would place Virginia at the "tender mercies of Mr. Abraham Lincoln." "What would be our fate," secessionists challenged, in a confederacy of "nineteen Black Republican nonslaveholding states" and only eight border slave states? Heretofore, with the seven Deep South slave states "united with us," the South was unable to "maintain our equal rights" within the Union. Now, with the Deep South seceded, the eight border South states "will be, to all intents and purposes, disfranchised in the Government." Our "Northern masters," who condemn the "right of property in slaves" and bar slavery from public territories, "will decide" our destiny. Was "noble Virginia" willing, by her languid "slumbering between the two sections," so to "lower her proud banner and . . . pass under the yoke of Northern abolition?"[48]

Commissioners from Mississippi, Georgia, and South Carolina seconded "precipitationists'" call for immediate secession to uphold Virginia's "rights" and "honor." Addressing the convention on February 18 and 19, representatives from the already-seceded Deep South cited Virginia's "identical" interests with, and historic ascendancy among, slaveholding states as irresistible grounds for alliance with the southern Confederacy. With Virginia the "leader," the South could secure additional guarantees for slavery within the Union, or a peaceable separation. The North would not use force against a united, powerful South. Should an independent Confederacy ensue, Virginia, free from shackles of northern competition, would become the industrial capital of the South, a "great manufacturing empire." United with the antislavery North, Virginia would "sink much lower than you now stand."[49]

Along with traditional appeals to pride and interest, Deep South commissioners interjected another pressing motive for secession not common to Virginia "precipitationists." "I fear that the day is not distant," Georgia's representative observed, "when the Cotton States will be the only slave states. . . . Some of our own slave States are becoming free States already." The slave population of Delaware and Maryland was "actually" declining, and in other border South states slaves were decreasing "relative" to whites. As slavery disappeared from the border

48. *Ibid.*, 186, 194–200.
49. *Ibid.*, 71–74.

South, it would "go down lower and lower, until it all gets to the Cotton States—until it gets to the bottom." Then, when the ever larger bloc of free states abolished slavery by constitutional amendment, the Deep South, with its huge slave population, would have "black governors, black legislatures, black juries, black everything." Whites would be "completely exterminated." Since "this is Abolition to the Cotton States," Deep South commissioners concluded, Lincoln's election left no recourse but secession. The cotton states could not remain in the Union to "wait for Abolition" by a "permanent" northern "majority" publicly hostile to slavery and bent on its "ultimate extinction." To avert "destruction" of southern "institutions," "noble" Virginia must now "take her place" at the head of the slaveholding Confederacy. Rather than "submit" to continued northern "domination," she must "take her own destiny into her own hands."[50]

Even as Deep South commissioners looked to slavery to rally Virginians behind secession, they ironically separated, not linked, the long-run destinies of Virginia and the cotton states. If Virginia had not "actually" lost slaves as had Delaware and Maryland, blacks there had decreased *relative* to whites in every decade since 1810, and most notably since 1830. While slave populations had steadily declined, either absolutely or relatively, in Maryland, Delaware, Kentucky, Missouri, and Virginia in post-1830 decades, slave populations of Alabama, Arkansas, Georgia, Mississippi, Texas, and South Carolina had, either absolutely or relatively, increased. The gradual erosion of border South slavery, that region's growing identity with the free-soil North, the final holocaust of constitutional abolition—inherent to all such Deep South fears was the assumption of slavery's "peculiar" adaptability to cotton cultivation. In their claustrophobic vision of slavery's ultimate confinement to the lower South, Deep South commissioners thus inadvertently confirmed Thomas R. Dew's 1832 view that Virginia was "too far North" for slavery and, in so doing, identified the state's "interests" with freedom.

If Deep South commissioners unwittingly severed Virginia from the cotton states, "ultra-Unionist" delegates did so intentionally. Uncompromising Unionists, generally from the northwest Trans-Allegheny and northern Valley, denied "precipitationists'" claim that Virginia's "in-

50. *Ibid.*, 53–54, 62–66, 87–88.

stitutions," "habits," "interests" were "homogeneous" with the lower South. Indeed, northwesterners argued, neither the "social system" nor the "interests" of North and South were "so diverse," the "conflict" so "irrepressible," as to justify secession. If "Old Virginia" remained within the Union, the seven seceded states would "soon return." Then North and South together might "construct a government that will . . . enable them to live . . . in peace."

Secession, in contrast, was not a "peace measure" as "precipitationists" presumed. Although "war may be avoided for a time, sooner or later" the South would "become engaged" in bloody conflict with the North. Once civil war began "North-Western Virginia" would be "swept from the face of the earth." "Cut off" from the rest of the commonwealth by the "impassable . . . Allegheny mountains," and with "450 miles of hostile border" on the "powerful States" of Pennsylvania and Ohio, northwest Virginia would be the "weakest point of a Southern Confederacy, and, therefore, the point of attack." Were "gentlemen of Eastern Virginia," who had long opposed "enough legislative aid to transpierce these mountains" and connect east and west, now willing to "expose our wives and children to the . . . ravages of civil war . . . to convert our smiling valleys into slaughter pens?" "Look at the geography of Virginia," "ultra-Unionists" urged, before "dragging" the state into "some miserable Southern Confederacy."

Secession not only meant North-South war and ensuing "desolation" of Virginia's isolated northwest. It also meant Virginia's "repudiation" of the "principle that political power resides in the people." The "Congress at Montgomery," "ultra-Unionists" charged, was a "totally new government . . . formed without . . . popular sanction." Furthermore, this "Congress" had "appointed a President and Vice-President without any popular election or ratification." Such "policy," "ultra-Unionists" warned, "foreshadows . . . oligarchy . . . monarchy, or military despotism." And, contrary to secessionists' portrait of Virginia as "head" of a southern Confederacy, cotton states would "always have the balance of power." Would Virginia so forsake her republican heritage? Would she abandon this "glorious . . . experiment of . . . Union" to join an oligarchic, "weak" Confederacy? The "Union," northwesterners reiterated, is "not yet dissolved. . . . It still lives, and will live while Virginia stands firm. Let Old Virginia," then, "stand fast where she ever stood" and be "true" to her "glorious destiny."[51]

While "precipitationists" proposed Virginia's unilateral withdrawal from, and "ultra-Unionists" Virginia's unilateral allegiance to the Union as the path to peaceable reconstruction, moderates urged Virginia's co-operation with other slaveholding border states to effect North-South compromise or, should compromise fail, "concurrent" secession. Moderate, or conditional, Unionists represented almost all regions of the commonwealth outside the "Southside" Piedmont and northwest Trans-Allegheny. Some were from the Tidewater and Piedmont, especially urban areas, some from the Valley, and some from the southwest Trans-Allegheny. All declared Virginia's "interests" separate from both the seceded lower South and the *existent* federal Union. But none offered a unified policy, a definite course of action to resolve the sectional crisis. Some suggested a border South conference to achieve an "undivided front" amongst not-yet-seceded slave states. Others proposed actual formation of a "Middle Confederacy" of border slave and northern free states outside New England to stand as a neutral buffer between the nation's extreme slaveholding and nonslaveholding sections. Counseling calm, compromise, delay to reconcile North and South, moderates counted above all on the success of the Washington Peace Conference, and on Lincoln's opposition to federal coercion.[52]

Failure of the Washington Peace Conference to secure slavery compromise, and its subsequent adjournment on February 28, sounded the initial "death-knell" of conditional unionism. Just a few days later, Lincoln's March 4 Inaugural Address, with its doctrine of federal supremacy and implications of coercion against seceded states, dealt Virginia moderates a second, more lethal blow. Although most moderates still counseled delay and opposed adoption of a secession ordinance unless Lincoln actually coerced the lower South, the convention mood abruptly shifted, and fiery secessionist appeals mounted.[53]

Amidst heightened national tension, Trans-Allegheny delegates interjected the explosive state issue of *ad valorem* taxation of slaves. While

51. *Ibid.*, 364–72.
52. *Ibid.*, 173–76, 182–83, 206, 212–14, 219.
53. Shanks, *The Secession Movement in Virginia*, 171–78.

Virginia worked for "national conciliation," northwesterners contended, it would also be "wise . . . to remedy . . . causes of difficulty and strife at home." For almost a decade, the "odious distinction or unequal burthens" imposed upon nonslaveholders by the 1851 constitution had produced "contention and complaint." Virginia's "free white men" now looked to this convention to remove the "yoke of inequality and oppression . . . riveted upon their necks" by the state's slaveholding minority.[54]

*Ad valorem* taxation of slaves, northwesterners insisted, was not entirely a "sectional question," but rather a "question between the non-slaveholding and . . . slaveholding portions of the people of Virginia." Because "we are peculiarly sensitive upon this subject of equality," the northwest Trans-Allegheny admittedly was "more interested . . . than any other quarter of the state." Nevertheless, "nonslaveholding taxpayers" comprised a "large majority" of whites in all four sections of the commonwealth. Why should the man who "toils . . . for his daily bread" continue to "groan and groan under taxation," while "opulent slaveholders, resting upon pampered wealth and fortune, own a valuable property . . . wholly . . . or virtually exempted from taxation?"

"Nonslaveholding tax-payers in Eastern Virginia," northwesterners reiterated, had as "much right to be heard upon this floor as . . . nonslaveholding tax-payers West of the Blue Ridge." If something was not done to make "taxation equal and uniform," this would become a "question between classes." "Before long," Virginia would have a "dire and awful conflict," not between the "people of the sea-coast and of the mountains," but an "irrepressible conflict between the laboring man and the slaveowner."[55]

Their people, northwesterners asserted, were not "Abolitionists" bent on destruction of slavery. They did not desire, as conservative easterners had repeatedly charged, to "oppress" slaveholders by "harsh" or "unreasonable" taxation. If east Virginia refused to assess the "negro interest" at "full value," however, such short-sighted obstinance *would* arouse "unkind feelings" toward slavery and "abolitionize" the northwest.

Equal taxation of slaves thus "involves the integrity of the state." Just

54. Reese (ed.), *Proceedings of the Virginia State Convention*, I, 765–66; II, 3–4, 61, 126–27.
55. *Ibid.*, I, 766; II, 15, 64, 135, 507; III, 3–5.

as slaveholding east Virginia demanded "equality of rights" to preserve the Union, so the nonslaveholding northwest insisted upon its "just rights" to preserve the "peace of Virginia." At this moment of national crisis, Virginia must be "one and indivisible in sentiment and feeling." Let us accordingly "reform our organic laws," northwesterners urged, so as to "consolidate" the slaveholding and nonslaveholding peoples of the commonwealth.[56]

"Precipitationists" likewise called upon Virginians to "stand . . . shoulder to shoulder, to confront a common peril." Why then, they angrily demanded, did northwesterners hurl this "fire-brand . . . into our midst?" Rather than compose "internal strife," debate on *ad valorem* taxation of slaves would so divide Virginians as to preclude any unified action against common northern aggressors. When Virginia "adopted a constitution upon a compromise" in 1851, "precipitationists" reminded northwesterners, "the people agreed" that articles governing slave taxation and senate representation would not be touched until 1865. The issue thus was not whether slaves "ought to be" equally taxed, but whether northwesterners should "press" for *ad valorem* principles at a time "when Governments [are] dissolving around us. . . . Let us postpone," secessionists doggedly resolved. Before considering state matters, "let us unite" to settle the more urgent "subject of Federal Relations.'"[57]

Although debate on taxation continued, delegates avoided definite action. More than a month after Lincoln's inaugural, Virginia had resolved neither her national nor her domestic destiny. To arrest the drift in federal relations, the convention determined on April 8 to send three commissioners to Washington to ascertain Lincoln's intentions toward seceded states. Before Virginia's commissioners returned to Richmond, delegates received official news of the firing on Fort Sumter. The following day, amidst reports of Lincoln's call for 75,000 federal troops to quash the Deep South rebellion, the convention voted 80 to 43 to go into secret session. There in the hall of the house of delegates where in 1832 he had demanded immediate emancipation legislation, an aging William Ballard Preston now introduced an ordinance of secession proposing Virginia's alliance with the slaveholding Confederacy.[58]

56. *Ibid.*, II, 6, 14–15, 61–65, 71, 126, 253; III, 3.
57. *Ibid.*, II, 132–34.
58. *Ibid.*, III, 350–51, 678, 730, 736–41; IV, 24–25.

Northwestern delegates denounced this "hasty measure" and re-affirmed unbending loyalty to Union. Adoption of the secession ordinance, they warned, would dissolve the commonwealth and place the northwest Trans-Allegheny in "an attitude of revolution and resistance." Some moderates also opposed immediate, unilateral action, urging instead cooperative secession or a border state Confederacy. But with the tocsin of civil war sounded and Richmond's streets crowded with fiery disunionists, most conditional Unionists joined "precipitationists" on April 17 to approve Virginia's secession 88 to 55. Tidewater delegates voted 23 to 6, Piedmont delegates 32 to 4, *for* immediate secession. Valley delegates divided 17 to 10, Trans-Allegheny delegates 28 to 23, *against* secession.[59]

If most easterners approved and most westerners opposed Virginia's alliance with the lower South, voting alignments nevertheless exposed sharp regional differences within each major section.[60] The ten easterners disapproving secession represented southwestern Piedmont counties of Franklin and Henry near the Blue Ridge, the Loudoun-Fairfax district near Washington, D.C., Accomack County on the "Eastern Shore," and counties proximate to, or including, the major Tidewater cities of Norfolk and Richmond. All these antisecession areas had lower slave percentages than the 45–70 percent ratios characteristic of other eastern counties. During struggles over representation and suffrage in 1829–1830, 1850–1851, and over emancipation in 1831–1832, all had supported "reform" and antislavery interests, whether abolitionist or moderate. By 1860, all but the southwest Piedmont counties had developed flourishing trade connections with the North. Furthermore, proximity to the North and to the United States Navy Yard made most of these east Virginia regions particularly vulnerable to attack.

West of the Blue Ridge, slavery, economics, and geography likewise affected delegates' attitudes toward secession. The northwest Trans-Allegheny, with its tiny slave population, its Baltimore and Ohio Railroad, its borders on Pennsylvania and Ohio overwhelmingly disapproved disunion. The southwest Trans-Allegheny, with its considerable slave population, its railroad connections to Tennessee and east Virginia,

59. *Ibid.*, IV, 52–53, 88–89, 123–24, 144–46; Shanks, *The Secession Movement in Virginia,* 205–208.

60. Shanks, *The Secession Movement in Virginia,* 205–10.

its borders on Kentucky and Tennessee conversely approved secession as strongly as the Tidewater and Piedmont. In the Valley, northern counties served by the Baltimore and Ohio Railroad, and central counties having fewer slaves and bordering the Allegheny Mountains generally opposed secession. Conversely, southern Valley counties, and central counties having higher slave ratios and bordering the Blue Ridge generally approved.

Following adoption of the secession ordinance, many northwesterners bolted the convention and returned home to rally support for union. Those who remained renewed demands for *ad valorem* taxation of slaves —demands easterners continued to resist. Virginia slaveholders, several "Southside" Piedmont delegates protested, could not pay an "*ad valorem* tax upon negroes, of all ages and all conditions." This principle, though "not so intended by the West," was an "abolition measure in disguise." Four days before the convention adjourned, however, easterners at last surrendered. Bent on preserving northwestern allegiance to Virginia, slaveholders approved *ad valorem* taxation of their "peculiar property."[61]

But slaveholders' concession came too late and had little, if any, influence on northwestern attitudes. Secession, not taxation, was northwesterners' paramount concern. Even before the Richmond convention adopted *ad valorem* slave taxes, nonslaveholders had held mass meetings throughout northwest Virginia to protest alliance with the Confederacy. Such course, northwesterners generally agreed, represented the culmination of minority tyranny. For decades, eastern slaveholders had thwarted equal representation, internal improvements, public education, equal taxation. Now in severing Virginia's ties to the Union, slaveholding aristocrats had exposed the northwest to military and economic havoc. Secession, northwesterners resolved, was the final usurpation. No longer would the nonslaveholding Trans-Allegheny be "tyrannized over, and made slaves of" by "haughty . . . Eastern Despots." If the people of Virginia ratified the ordinance, the northwest would call a "General Convention" to determine its "interests" in this "fearful emergency." Never, "under any circumstances," would northwesterners yield the "rich legacy of Freedom . . . inherited from our fathers."[62]

61. Reese (ed.), *Proceedings of the Virginia State Convention*, IV, 296–300, 312–15, 545–46.
62. Lewis (ed.), *How West Virginia Was Made*, 33–34, 62–64, 72–75.

On June 11, 1861, three weeks after Virginia voters ratified the seces-sion ordinance, delegates from thirty-two northwestern counties con-vened in Wheeling. Although a few urged immediate division of the commonwealth, most declared present dismemberment inexpedient. After short debate, the Wheeling convention voted almost unanimously to establish the "Re-Organized Government of Virginia." Once the Lin-coln administration recognized this as Virginia's *de jure* representative, such reconstructed, Unionist government would then legally authorize separate statehood.[63]

Lincoln, on July 4, 1861, declared this pro-Union government the offi-cial organ of Virginia. A month later, northwesterners reassembled to consider independent statehood. Following debate on proposed bound-aries and on timing of separation, delegates adopted a Dismemberment Ordinance calling for establishment of a new state to consist of thirty-nine designated counties, with provision for inclusion of additional counties bordering the thirty-nine. If a majority of voters in each of these counties endorsed independence, their representatives would convene in November, 1861, to draft a state constitution.[64]

Throughout preliminary sessions, northwesterners had deliberately avoided debate on slavery. Abolitionist agitation, most feared, would alienate the region's small slaveholding population and thereby jeopar-dize the new-state movement. Furthermore, many delegates hoped to incorporate northern Valley counties containing the Baltimore and Ohio Railroad. This vast commercial artery, traversing a Valley area with con-siderable numbers of slaveholders, was deemed vital to the welfare of the proposed new state.[65]

Such overriding concerns again prompted delegates to gag abolition debate during the first West Virginia Constitutional Convention. Dele-gates repeatedly tabled resolutions, introduced by a small group of Methodist ministers, to incorporate *post-nati* emancipation in the new state's constitution. Emancipation provisions, opponents ironically res-urrected arguments of 1831–1832 east Virginia conservatives, were un-necessary and "inexpedient." West Virginia's geography, climate, soil,

63. *Ibid.*, 78–80, 107–109, 132; Curry, *A House Divided*, 69–72.
64. Lewis (ed.), *How West Virginia Was Made*, 183–90.
65. Moore, *Banner in the Hills*, 143; Charles H. Ambler, *Waitman T. Willey* (Huntington, W.Va., 1954), 62.

economic pursuits would all preclude profitable use of slaves. Rather than allow controversial emancipation laws to endanger statehood, let "time" and "interest" together abolish slavery.[66]

If delegates rejected *post-nati* emancipation, they overwhelmingly approved, 48 to 1, a second Methodist resolution barring further entry of slaves and free blacks into West Virginia as permanent residents. While so proscribing both slavery and blacks, the first West Virginia convention concurrently endorsed sweeping equality for whites. The new state constitution, adopted unanimously in February, 1863, met long-standing Trans-Allegheny demands for white-basis representation in house *and* senate, for universal white manhood suffrage, for *ad valorem* taxation of *all* property, and for statewide public education.[67]

Uncompromising insistence on white men's equality contrasted with northwesterners' expediential posture toward black men's freedom. Such dichotomy, like past struggles for control of Virginia's government, indicated that nonslaveholding westerners objected more to slaveholders' flouting of democracy than to the institution of slavery *per se*. Yet, practicably, the two were inseparable. For democracy and slavery, slaveholders had long contended, could not coexist. Slave property required unequal power, unequal protection, to withstand assaults by a nonslaveholding majority. Demands for equal representation, equal taxation, conservatives had angrily protested in 1829–1830, 1850–1851, 1861, were but abolitionism "in disguise."

West Virginia's acceptance of compulsory emancipation could only have confirmed slaveholders' assumptions as to nonslaveholders' disloyalty. Whereas northwesterners had looked to geographic-economic forces, combined with constitutional bans on further slave entry, to accomplish abolition, the United States Senate required *post-nati* emancipation as a condition for Union admission. The West Virginia Constitutional Convention accordingly reassembled in February, 1863, and, following debate over state versus federal compensation to slaveowners, unanimously endorsed the *post-nati* amendment. Delegates also unanimously approved compensation for slaveholders loyal to the Union and, prior to adjournment, requested a $2 million federal appropriation

66. Lewis (ed.), *How West Virginia Was Made*, 218–25, 269–73; Hall, *The Rending of Virginia*, 415–16; Moore, *Banner in the Hills*, 143–45.
67. Moore, *Banner in the Hills*, 144–45; Ambler, *Waitman T. Willey*, 64.

for such purposes. As a final compliance with congressional demands, the West Virginia convention expunged restrictions on free black emigration to the new state.[68]

On March 26, 1863, West Virginia voters overwhelmingly ratified the amended state constitution. Three weeks later, President Lincoln proclaimed West Virginia's admission to the Union, effective June 20, 1863. At that time, northwest Virginia officially severed its "unnatural connection" with the rest of the commonwealth and entered the Union under a free-soil government.[69]

The dream of an united, free Virginia espoused by eastern and western abolitionists alike in 1831–1832 lay forever shattered. Whereas the new-born state of West Virginia would approach the "hour of emancipation" by peaceful, gradual means, for most of Thomas Jefferson's beloved commonwealth, the process would be violent and abrupt.

Values, interests, demography combined to promote such separate destinies. Although northwest Virginians upheld private property, most did not share easterners' states' rights convictions. West Virginia accordingly looked to the federal government to provide compensation funds. Furthermore, the insignificant *numbers* of slaves and slaveholders west of the Alleghenies lessened costs of compensation, assured the predominance of the nonslaveholding interest, and, above all, removed dilemmas of race. Without convulsing white society, West Virginia could effect compensated, *post-nati* emancipation *and* incorporate an almost invisible black population.

Outside the northwest, resistance to federal aid, a powerful "slave interest," and, most importantly, a huge slave population drove Virginia's "revolution" backward to secession. State revenue was inadequate, uncompensated emancipation impracticable, and incorporation of more than 470,000 slaves "unthinkable." With the "experiment" of African colonization ever stillborn, the perennial dilemma of "what to do with hordes of freed blacks" dashed prospects for general emancipation throughout Virginia's major slaveholding regions.

Yet if slavery proved incompatible with state integrity, neither east nor west Virginians ultimately resolved this conflict. For more than three decades, each preferred compromise to decision, postponement to ac-

68. Hall, *The Rending of Virginia,* 505; Moore, *Banner in the Hills,* 203.
69. Ambler, *Waitman T. Willey,* 101–102; Moore, *Banner in the Hills,* 205–206.

tion, drift to mastery. This irresolution, step by step, allowed outsiders to dictate Virginia's destiny. Nat Turner's insurrection aroused whites from "apathetic security" and provoked demands for abolition. Free blacks' resistance to African colonization aborted plans for future emancipation and deportation of slaves. Abraham Lincoln's strategy of federal coercion prompted slaveholding Virginia to secede. Secession, in turn, led the northwest Trans-Allegheny to stand with the Union and sever its ties with the rest of the commonwealth. Yet only when the United States Senate required *post-nati* emancipation did West Virginia adopt a free constitution.

Virginia's resolution of conflicting loyalties paralleled actions throughout the upper South. Just as secession split Virginia in two, so remaining slave states outside the Deep South opted for diverse destinies. Like newborn West Virginia, the northernmost tier of slave states —Delaware, Maryland, Kentucky, and Missouri—sided with the Union, whereas the middle tier of North Carolina, Arkansas, and most of Tennessee followed secessionist Virginia southward to Montgomery. Again like West Virginia, the border slave states that fought against the Confederacy initially balked at compulsory emancipation. But, as had Trans-Allegheny whites, border southerners ultimately preferred Union and abolition to secession and slavery. Virginia, leader and symbol of the northern half of the antebellum South, never ceased to mirror the contradictions and ambiguities which, in 1861, tore an allegedly monolithic, proslavery bloc apart.

Secessionists and Unionists alike in 1861 portrayed Virginia as a mighty power whose course would control the nation's destiny. Instead the Old Dominion, ever Hamlet-like, proved unable to control her own. Buffeted by the exigencies of civil war, Virginia's white peoples followed two separate roads, one "from Monticello" southward to slavery, the other "to Monticello" and Jefferson's dream of universal freedom.

# Appendix

## TABLES FOR CHAPTER II

### Table I: Virginia Population by Counties in 1830

| County | Whites | Slaves | Free Blacks | % Slaves to Total Population | % Free Blacks to Total Population |
|--------|--------|--------|-------------|-----------------------------|-----------------------------------|
| *A. Tidewater* | | | | | |
| Accomack | 9,458 | 4,654 | 2,544 | 27.9 | 15.3 |
| Caroline | 6,499 | 10,741 | 520 | 60.5 | 2.9 |
| Charles City | 1,782 | 2,957 | 761 | 53.8 | 13.8 |
| Chesterfield | 7,709 | 10,337 | 591 | 55.5 | 3.2 |
| Elizabeth City | 2,704 | 2,218 | 131 | 43.9 | 2.6 |
| Essex | 3,647 | 6,407 | 467 | 60.9 | 4.4 |
| Fairfax | 4,892 | 4,001 | 311 | 43.5 | 3.4 |
| Gloucester | 4,314 | 5,691 | 603 | 53.6 | 5.7 |
| Greensville | 2,104 | 4,681 | 332 | 65.8 | 4.7 |
| Hanover | 6,526 | 9,278 | 449 | 57.1 | 2.8 |
| Henrico | 5,716 | 5,932 | 1,089 | 46.6 | 8.5 |
| Isle of Wight | 5,023 | 4,272 | 1,222 | 40.6 | 11.6 |
| King and Queen | 4,714 | 6,514 | 416 | 55.9 | 3.6 |
| King George | 2,475 | 3,635 | 287 | 56.8 | 4.5 |
| King William | 3,155 | 6,310 | 347 | 64.3 | 3.5 |
| Lancaster | 1,976 | 2,632 | 193 | 54.8 | 4.0 |

| County | Whites | Slaves | Free Blacks | % Slaves to Total Population | % Free Blacks to Total Population |
|---|---|---|---|---|---|
| Mathews | 3,994 | 3,481 | 189 | 45.4 | 2.5 |
| Middlesex | 1,868 | 2,138 | 116 | 51.9 | 2.8 |
| Nansemond | 5,143 | 4,943 | 1,698 | 41.9 | 14.4 |
| New Kent | 2,586 | 3,530 | 342 | 54.7 | 5.3 |
| Norfolk (City) | 5,130 | 3,756 | 928 | 38.3 | 9.5 |
| Norfolk County | 8,184 | 5,838 | 970 | 38.9 | 6.5 |
| Northampton | 3,574 | 3,734 | 1,333 | 43.2 | 15.4 |
| Northumberland | 4,029 | 3,357 | 567 | 42.2 | 7.1 |
| Petersburg (City) | 3,440 | 2,850 | 2,032 | 34.2 | 24.4 |
| Prince George | 3,069 | 4,598 | 700 | 55.0 | 8.4 |
| Prince William | 5,127 | 3,842 | 361 | 41.2 | 3.9 |
| Princess Anne | 5,025 | 3,734 | 343 | 41.0 | 3.8 |
| Richmond (City) | 7,755 | 6,349 | 1,956 | 39.5 | 12.2 |
| Richmond County | 2,975 | 2,630 | 450 | 43.4 | 7.4 |
| Southampton | 6,573 | 7,756 | 1,745 | 48.3 | 10.9 |
| Spotsylvania | 6,384 | 8,053 | 697 | 53.2 | 4.6 |
| Stafford | 4,713 | 4,164 | 425 | 44.5 | 4.5 |
| Surry | 2,865 | 3,378 | 866 | 47.5 | 12.2 |
| Sussex | 4,118 | 7,736 | 866 | 60.8 | 6.8 |
| Warwick | 633 | 910 | 27 | 58.0 | 1.7 |
| Westmoreland | 3,710 | 3,839 | 847 | 45.7 | 10.1 |
| York | 2,129 | 2,598 | 627 | 48.5 | 11.7 |
| James City | 1,283 | 1,983 | 572 | 51.7 | 14.9 |
| Totals | 167,001 | 185,457 | 28,980 | 48.6 | 7.6 |

B. *Piedmont*

| County | Whites | Slaves | Free Blacks | % Slaves to Total Population | % Free Blacks to Total Population |
|---|---|---|---|---|---|
| Albemarle | 10,455 | 11,679 | 484 | 51.6 | 2.1 |
| Amelia | 3,293 | 7,523 | 220 | 68.2 | 2.0 |
| Amherst | 5,883 | 5,925 | 263 | 49.1 | 2.2 |
| Bedford | 11,123 | 8,782 | 341 | 43.4 | 1.7 |
| Brunswick | 5,397 | 9,758 | 612 | 61.9 | 3.9 |
| Buckingham | 7,177 | 10,929 | 245 | 59.6 | 1.3 |

| County | Whites | Slaves | Free Blacks | % Slaves to Total Population | % Free Blacks to Total Population |
|---|---|---|---|---|---|
| Campbell | 9,995 | 9,496 | 859 | 46.7 | 4.2 |
| Charlotte | 5,583 | 9,433 | 236 | 61.8 | 1.5 |
| Culpeper | 12,046 | 11,415 | 565 | 47.5 | 2.4 |
| Cumberland | 4,054 | 7,309 | 327 | 62.5 | 2.8 |
| Dinwiddie | 5,215 | 7,506 | 858 | 55.3 | 6.3 |
| Fauquier | 12,950 | 12,523 | 613 | 48.0 | 2.3 |
| Fluvanna | 4,223 | 3,795 | 203 | 46.2 | 2.5 |
| Franklin | 9,728 | 4,988 | 195 | 33.5 | 1.3 |
| Goochland | 3,857 | 5,716 | 796 | 55.1 | 7.7 |
| Halifax | 12,918 | 14,528 | 590 | 51.8 | 2.1 |
| Henry | 4,058 | 2,868 | 174 | 40.4 | 2.5 |
| Loudoun | 15,497 | 5,363 | 1,079 | 24.4 | 4.9 |
| Louisa | 6,468 | 9,382 | 301 | 58.1 | 1.9 |
| Lunenburg | 4,479 | 7,233 | 245 | 60.5 | 2.0 |
| Madison | 4,289 | 4,876 | 71 | 52.8 | 0.8 |
| Mecklenburg | 7,471 | 12,117 | 889 | 59.2 | 4.3 |
| Nelson | 5,186 | 5,946 | 122 | 52.8 | 1.1 |
| Nottoway | 2,965 | 6,942 | 223 | 68.5 | 2.2 |
| Orange | 6,456 | 7,983 | 198 | 54.5 | 1.4 |
| Patrick | 5,496 | 1,782 | 117 | 24.1 | 1.6 |
| Pittsylvania | 14,694 | 10,999 | 341 | 42.2 | 1.3 |
| Powhatan | 2,661 | 5,472 | 384 | 64.2 | 4.5 |
| Prince Edward | 5,039 | 8,593 | 475 | 60.9 | 3.4 |
| Totals | 208,656 | 230,861 | 12,026 | 51.1 | 2.7 |

C. *Valley*

| County | Whites | Slaves | Free Blacks | % Slaves to Total Population | % Free Blacks to Total Population |
|---|---|---|---|---|---|
| Alleghany | 2,197 | 571 | 48 | 20.3 | 1.7 |
| Augusta | 15,257 | 4,265 | 404 | 21.4 | 2.0 |
| Bath | 2,797 | 1,140 | 65 | 28.5 | 1.6 |
| Berkeley | 8,323 | 1,919 | 276 | 18.2 | 2.6 |
| Botetourt | 11,798 | 4,170 | 386 | 25.5 | 2.4 |
| Frederick | 17,361 | 7,420 | 1,265 | 28.5 | 4.9 |

| County | Whites | Slaves | Free Blacks | % Slaves to Total Population | % Free Blacks to Total Population |
|---|---|---|---|---|---|
| Hampshire | 9,796 | 1,330 | 153 | 10.0 | 1.4 |
| Hardy | 5,408 | 1,167 | 223 | 17.2 | 3.3 |
| Jefferson | 8,435 | 3,999 | 493 | 30.9 | 3.8 |
| Morgan | 2,519 | 153 | 22 | 5.7 | 0.8 |
| Pendleton | 5,752 | 496 | 23 | 7.9 | 0.4 |
| Rockbridge | 10,465 | 3,398 | 381 | 23.9 | 2.7 |
| Rockingham | 17,814 | 2,321 | 548 | 11.2 | 2.6 |
| Shenandoah | 16,869 | 2,423 | 458 | 12.3 | 2.3 |
| Totals | 134,791 | 34,772 | 4,745 | 19.9 | 2.7 |

D. *Trans-Allegheny*

| County | Whites | Slaves | Free Blacks | % Slaves to Total Population | % Free Blacks to Total Population |
|---|---|---|---|---|---|
| Brooke | 6,774 | 228 | 39 | 3.2 | 0.6 |
| Cabell | 5,267 | 561 | 56 | 9.5 | 1.0 |
| Giles | 4,760 | 465 | 49 | 8.8 | 0.9 |
| Grayson | 7,161 | 462 | 52 | 6.0 | 0.7 |
| Greenbrier | 7,782 | 1,159 | 65 | 12.9 | 0.7 |
| Harrison | 13,887 | 771 | 64 | 5.2 | 0.4 |
| Kanawha | 7,533 | 1,717 | 76 | 18.4 | 0.8 |
| Lee | 5,830 | 612 | 19 | 9.5 | 0.3 |
| Lewis | 6,056 | 172 | 13 | 2.8 | 0.2 |
| Logan | 3,511 | 163 | 6 | 4.4 | 0.2 |
| Mason | 5,776 | 713 | 119 | 10.9 | 1.8 |
| Monongalia | 13,575 | 362 | 45 | 2.6 | 0.3 |
| Monroe | 7,033 | 682 | 83 | 8.7 | 1.1 |
| Montgomery | 10,224 | 2,026 | 56 | 16.5 | 0.5 |
| Nicholas | 3,224 | 121 | 1 | 3.6 | 0.03 |
| Ohio | 15,029 | 360 | 195 | 2.3 | 1.3 |
| Pocahontas | 2,298 | 227 | 17 | 8.9 | 0.7 |
| Preston | 4,988 | 129 | 27 | 2.5 | 0.5 |
| Randolph | 4,626 | 259 | 115 | 5.2 | 2.3 |
| Russell | 6,002 | 679 | 33 | 10.1 | 0.5 |
| Scott | 5,378 | 330 | 16 | 5.8 | 0.3 |

| County | Whites | Slaves | Free Blacks | % Slaves to Total Population | % Free Blacks to Total Population |
|---|---|---|---|---|---|
| Tazewell | 4,911 | 820 | 18 | 14.3 | 0.3 |
| Tyler | 3,991 | 108 | 5 | 2.6 | 0.1 |
| Washington | 12,785 | 2,568 | 261 | 16.4 | 1.7 |
| Wood | 5,501 | 877 | 51 | 13.6 | 0.8 |
| Wythe | 9,952 | 2,094 | 117 | 17.2 | 1.0 |
| Totals | 183,854 | 18,665 | 1,598 | 9.1 | 0.8 |

Source: U.S. Census Office, *Fifth Census*, Tables [10]–[13].

## Table II: Virginia Population in 1830—A Summary

| Section | Whites | % of All Va. Whites | Slaves | % of All Va. Slaves | Free Blacks | % of All Va. Blacks |
|---|---|---|---|---|---|---|
| Tidewater | 167,001 | 24.1 | 185,457 | 39.5 | 28,980 | 61.2 |
| Piedmont | 208,656 | 30.0 | 230,861 | 49.1 | 12,026 | 25.4 |
| Valley | 134,791 | 19.4 | 34,772 | 7.4 | 4,745 | 10.0 |
| Trans-Allegheny | 183,854 | 26.5 | 18,665 | 4.0 | 1,598 | 3.4 |
| Totals: | 694,302 | | 469,755 | | 47,349 | |

Source: U.S. Census Office, *Fifth Census*, Tables [10]–[13].

## TABLES FOR CHAPTER III

### Table III: Virginia's White Population, 1790–1830

| Section | 1790 | % of All Whites | 1810 | % of All Whites | 1820 | % of All Whites | 1830 | % of All Whites |
|---|---|---|---|---|---|---|---|---|
| Tidewater | 154,471 | 34.9 | 158,555 | 28.2 | 161,075 | 26.1 | 167,001 | 24.1 |
| Piedmont | 164,674 | 37.3 | 190,403 | 33.9 | 195,220 | 31.7 | 208,656 | 30.0 |
| Valley | 88,740 | 20.1 | 108,185 | 19.3 | 123,631 | 20.1 | 134,791 | 19.4 |
| Trans-Allegheny | 34,230 | 7.7 | 104,391 | 18.6 | 136,296 | 22.1 | 183,854 | 26.5 |
| Virginia | 442,115 | | 561,534 | | 616,222 | | 694,302 | |

Source: U.S. Census Office, *Fifth Census*, Tables [10]–[13].

### Table IV: Apportionment of Delegates to 1829–1830 Convention

| Section | Actual Number of Delegates | % of All Delegates | Delegates if had been by White Basis | % of All Delegates if had been by White Basis |
|---|---|---|---|---|
| Tidewater | 28 | 29.2 | 23 | 23.9 |
| Piedmont | 32 | 33.3 | 28 | 29.2 |
| Valley | 16 | 16.7 | 19 | 19.8 |
| Trans-Allegheny | 20 | 20.8 | 26 | 27.1 |

Source: Virginia, *Acts and Resolutions of the General Assembly of the Commonwealth of Virginia, 1828–1829*, pp. 17–21.

**Table V: Proposed Representation in House of Delegates (134 Members)**

| Basis of Apportionment* | Tidewater | | Piedmont | | Valley | | Trans-Allegheny | |
|---|---|---|---|---|---|---|---|---|
| | No. of Delegates | % of Delegates | No. of Delegates | % of Delegates | No. of Delegates | % of Delegates | No. of Delegates | % of Delegates |
| Equal County | 47 | 35.0 | 37 | 27.6 | 17 | 13.1 | 33 | 24.3 |
| Mixed Basis | 41 | 30.6 | 46 | 34.3 | 24 | 17.9 | 23 | 17.2 |
| White Basis | 32 | 23.9 | 40 | 29.8 | 26 | 19.4 | 36 | 26.9 |
| Federal Numbers | 38 | 28.4 | 48 | 35.8 | 21 | 15.7 | 27 | 20.1 |
| Gordon Plan | 36 | 26.9 | 42 | 31.3 | 25 | 18.7 | 31 | 23.1 |

Source: Virginia, *Proceedings and Debates of the Virginia State Convention of 1829–1830*, pp. 341–42.
*Numbers of delegates under each basis are adjusted to reflect the 134-member house ultimately incorporated in Virginia's 1830 constitution.

**Table VI: Proposed Representation in Senate (32 Members)**

| Basis of Apportionment* | Tidewater | | Piedmont | | Valley | | Trans-Allegheny | |
|---|---|---|---|---|---|---|---|---|
| | No. of Senators | % of Senators | No. of Senators | % of Senators | No. of Senators | % of Senators | No. of Senators | % of Senators |
| 1776 Constitution 1817 | 16 | 50.0 | 10 | 31.2 | 3 | 9.4 | 3 | 9.4 |
| Reapportionment | 9 | 28.1 | 10 | 31.2 | 7 | 21.9 | 6 | 18.8 |
| Mixed Basis | 10 | 31.2 | 11 | 34.4 | 6 | 18.8 | 5 | 15.6 |
| White Basis | 8 | 25.0 | 10 | 31.2 | 6 | 18.8 | 8 | 25.0 |
| Federal Numbers | 9 | 28.1 | 11 | 34.4 | 5 | 15.6 | 7 | 21.9 |
| Gordon Plan | 8 | 25.0 | 11 | 34.4 | 6 | 18.8 | 7 | 21.9 |

Source: Virginia, *Proceedings and Debates of the Virginia State Convention of 1829–1830*, pp. 341–42.
*Numbers of senators under each basis are adjusted to reflect the 32-member senate ultimately incorporated in Virginia's 1830 constitution.

# TABLE FOR CHAPTER V

## Table VII: Taxable Slaveholdings and Voting Records of 1831–1832 House Members[1]

| County | Delegate | No. of Taxable Slaves Owned | Vote on Indefinite Postponement (Conservative) | Vote on Preston Amendment (Abolitionist) | Vote on Bryce Preamble (Moderate Antislavery) |
|---|---|---|---|---|---|
| *A. Tidewater* | | | | | |
| Accomack | Drummond, John P. | 4 | No | Yes | — |
|  | Grinalds, Southey | 5 | Yes | No | Yes |
| Caroline | Dickinson, William W. | 43 | — | — | — |
| Charles City-New Kent | Halyburton, James D. | 10 | Yes | No | No |
| Chesterfield | Patteson, William A. | 6 | Yes | No | No |
| Elizabeth City-Warwick | Jones, Alexander | 4 | No | Yes | Yes |
| Essex | Ritchie, Archibald | 26 | Yes | No | No |
| Fairfax | Ball, Spencer | 0 | Yes | No | No |
| Gloucester | Smith, Thomas | 41 | Yes | No | No |
| Greensville | Spencer, Thomas | 36 | Yes | No | No |
| Hanover | Roane, William | 28 | No | No | Yes |
| Henrico | Mayo, Robert A. | 11 | No | Yes | Yes |
| Isle of Wight | Jordan, James | 9 | Yes | No | No |
| King and Queen | Harwood, Archibald | 19 | Yes | No | No |

| County | Delegate | | | | |
|---|---|---|---|---|---|
| King George | Hooe, John | 5 | Yes | No | Yes |
| King William | Dabney, Benjamin | 7 | Yes | No | No |
| Mathews & Middlesex | Hudgins, Houlder | 16 | Yes | No | No |
| Nansemond | Webb, Richard | 3 | Yes | No | No |
| Norfolk (City) | King, Miles | 5 | No | No | Yes |
| Norfolk County | Chandler, John | 4[2] | No | No | Yes |
| | Leigh, John P. | 13[3] | No | No | Yes |
| Northampton | Fisher, Miers | 3 | Yes | No | No |
| Northumberland | Harvey, Thomas | 8 | Yes | No | No |
| Petersburg (City) | Brown, John T. | 1 | Yes | No | No |
| Prince George | Shands, William | 9 | Yes | No | No |
| Prince William | Carter, Charles S. | 21 | Yes | No | No |
| Princess Anne | Land, Jeremiah | 15[4] | Yes | No | No |
| Richmond (City) | Rutherfoord, John C. | 5 | No | No | Yes |
| Richmond-Lancaster | Carter, Robert W. | 52 | Yes | No | No |
| Southampton | Cobb, Jeremiah | 14 | Yes | No | No |
| Spotsylvania | Powell, Robert D. | 1 | No | No | Yes |
| Stafford | Moncure, Thomas | 2[5] | No | No | Yes |
| Surry | Crump, John C. | 22 | Yes | No | No |
| Sussex | Hargrave, Jesse | 9 | Yes | No | No |
| Westmoreland | Newton, Willoughby | 29 | Yes | No | No |
| York-James City-Williamsburg | Shield, Robert | 15 | Yes | No | No |
| Tidewater Totals | | 501 | 25   10 | 3   32 | 11   23 |

| County | Delegate | No. of Taxable Slaves Owned | Vote on Indefinite Postponement (Conservative) | Vote on Preston Amendment (Abolitionist) | Vote on Bryce Preamble (Moderate Antislavery) |
|---|---|---|---|---|---|
| *B. Piedmont* | | | | | |
| Albemarle | Randolph, Thomas J. | 36 | No | Yes | Yes |
| | Wood, Rice | 5 | No | No | No |
| Amelia | Booker, Richard | 9 | Yes | | No |
| Amherst | Garland, Samuel | 1[6] | No | Yes | Yes |
| Bedford | Campbell, Robert | 12 | Yes | No | No |
| | Pate, Edmund | 5 | Yes | No | No |
| Brunswick | Gholson, James | 20 | Yes | No | No |
| | Shell, John E. | 0 | Yes | No | No |
| Buckingham | Bolling, Philip A. | 16 | No | Yes | Yes |
| | Patteson, William N. | 6 | Yes | No | No |
| Campbell | Daniel, William, Jr. | 0 | Yes | No | No |
| | Rives, William M. | ? | No | No | Yes |
| Charlotte | Richardson, John | 26 | Yes | No | No |
| Culpeper | Broadus, Edmund | 5 | Yes | No | No |
| | Pendleton, John S. | 5 | Yes | No | No |
| Cumberland | Wilson, Allen | 25 | Yes | No | No |
| Dinwiddie | Brodnax, William H. | 26 | Yes | No | No |
| Fauquier | Chilton, Mark | 10[7] | Yes | No | No |
| | Marshall, Thomas | 45 | No | No | No[8] |
| Fluvanna | Stillman, George | 0 | Yes | No | No |
| Franklin | Hale, Samuel | 16 | Yes | No | No |

| County | Delegate | No. | | | | | | |
|---|---|---|---|---|---|---|---|---|
| Goochland | Woods, Wyley | 3 | Yes | | | No | | No |
| | Bryce, Archibald, Jr. | 20 | | No | | No | Yes | |
| Halifax | Bruce, James C. | 69 | Yes | | | No | | No |
| | Sims, William D. | 1 | Yes | | | No | | No |
| Henry | Gravely, Peyton | 0 | Yes | | | No | | No |
| Loudoun | Caldwell, Samuel | 2[9] | | No | Yes | | Yes | |
| | Cordell, Presley | 3 | | No | Yes | | Yes | |
| | McIlhaney, James | 5[10] | | No | Yes | | Yes | |
| Louisa | Poindexter, Nicholas J. | 11 | Yes | | | No | | No |
| Lunenburg | Street, John | 12 | Yes | | | No | | No |
| Madison | Banks, Linn | 21 | Yes | | | No | | No |
| Mecklenburg | Goode, William O. | 7 | Yes | | | No | | No |
| | Knox, Alexander | 0 | Yes | | | No | | No |
| Nelson | Cabell, Joseph C. | 47 | Yes | | | No | | No |
| Nottoway | Anderson, Hezekiah | 14 | Yes | | | No | | No |
| Orange | Davis, Thomas | 13 | Yes | | | No | | No |
| Patrick | Adams, Isaac | 10 | — | | — | | — | |
| Pittsylvania | Swanson, William | 13 | Yes | | | No | | No |
| | Witcher, Vincent | 10[11] | Yes | | | No | | No |
| Powhatan | Miller, Thomas | 22 | Yes | | | No | | No |
| Prince Edward | Dupuy, Asa | 28 | Yes | | | No | | No |
| **Piedmont Totals** | | 579 | 31 | 10 | 6 | 35 | 8 | 33 |

C. *Valley*

| County | Delegate | No. | | | | | | |
|---|---|---|---|---|---|---|---|---|
| Alleghany | Persinger, John | 0 | | No | Yes | | Yes | |
| Augusta | Brooke, Robert S. | ? | | No | Yes | | Yes | |
| | McCue, John C. | 4 | | No | Yes | | Yes | |
| Bath | Cameron, Andrew | 20 | | No | Yes | | Yes | |

| County | Delegate | No. of Taxable Slaves Owned | Vote on Indefinite Postponement (Conservative) | Vote on Preston Amendment (Abolitionist) | Vote on Bryce Preamble (Moderate Antislavery) |
|---|---|---|---|---|---|
| Berkeley | Faulkner, Charles J. | 1 | No | Yes | Yes |
| Botetourt | Good, William | 2[12] | No | Yes | Yes |
|  | Anderson, William | 0 | No | Yes | — |
|  | Wilson, George | 0 | No | Yes | Yes |
| Frederick | Bryce, James G. | ? | Yes | No | Yes |
|  | Smith, John B. D. | 3 | Yes | No | No |
|  | Wood, William | 1 | No | Yes | Yes |
| Hampshire | Carskadon, Thomas | 2[13] | No | Yes | Yes |
|  | Poston, Elias | 0 | No | Yes | Yes |
|  | Mullen, John | 5 | No | No | Yes |
| Hardy | Berry, Henry | 3 | No | No | Yes |
| Jefferson | Gallaher, John S. | 1 | Yes | No | Yes |
| Page | Robertson, William M. | 1[14] | No | Yes | Yes |
| Pendleton | Hiner, Harmon | 0 | No | Yes | Yes |
| Rockbridge | McDowell, James | 4 | No | Yes | Yes |
|  | Moore, Samuel McD. | 0 | No | Yes | Yes |
| Rockingham | Cline, Joseph | 3 | No | Yes | Yes |
|  | McMahon, William | 6 | No | Yes | Yes |
| Shenandoah | Bare, Samuel | 0 | No | Yes | Yes |
|  | Carson, William | 3 | Yes | No | No |
| Valley Totals |  | 59 | 4   20 | 18   6 | 21   2 |

## D. Trans-Allegheny

| County | Name | | | | |
|---|---|---|---|---|---|
| Brooke | Campbell, John C. | 0 | No | Yes | Yes |
| Cabell | Spurlock, William | 0 | No | Yes | Yes |
| Floyd | Helms, Jacob | 11 | No | Yes | No[15] |
| Giles | Snidow, William | ? | No | Yes | Yes |
| Grayson | Hail, Lewis | 5 | No | Yes | Yes |
| Greenbrier | Erskine, Henry | 7 | No | Yes | Yes |
| Harrison | Johnson, William | 0 | No | Yes | Yes |
|  | Williams, George | 0 | No | Yes | Yes |
|  | Summers, George | 0 | No | Yes | Yes |
| Kanawha | Allen, James | 1 | No | Yes | Yes |
| Lee | Hays, Samuel | 1 | No | Yes | Yes |
| Lewis | Lawson, Anthony | 1 | No | Yes | Yes |
| Logan | Smith, Nehemiah | 0[16] | No | Yes | Yes |
| Mason & Jackson | Billingsly, Francis | 0 | No | Yes | Yes |
| Monongalia | Henry, William G. | 1 | No | Yes | Yes |
|  | Vawter, John H. | 0 | No | Yes | Yes |
| Monroe | Preston, William B. | 0 | No | Yes | Yes |
| Montgomery | Stephenson, John | 0 | No | Yes | — |
| Nicholas & Fayette | Fitzhugh, Samuel | 0 | No | Yes | Yes |
| Ohio | Parriott, John | 0 | No | Yes | Yes |
|  | Gilliland, John | 0 | No | Yes | Yes |
| Pocahontas | Zinn, William B. | 0 | No | Yes | Yes |
| Preston | Hart, Joseph | 1 | No | Yes | Yes |
| Randolph | Jessee, Archer | 0 | No | Yes | Yes |
| Russell | Kilgore, Hiram | 0 | No | Yes | Yes |
| Scott | Gillespie, Robert | 0 | No | Yes | No |
| Tazewell | McCoy, John | 1 | No | Yes | Yes |

| County | Delegate | No. of Taxable Slaves Owned | Vote on Indefinite Postponement (Conservative) | Vote on Preston Amendment (Abolitionist) | Vote on Bryce Preamble (Moderate Antislavery) |
|---|---|---|---|---|---|
| Washington | Keller, John | 0 | No | Yes | Yes |
| | McCulloch, Thomas | 0 | No | Yes | Yes |
| Wood | Morris, Isaac | 0 | No | Yes | — |
| Wythe | Crockett, Charles | 7 | No | Yes | Yes |
| Trans-Allegheny Totals | | 36 | 0    31 | 31    0 | 27    2 |

1. Unless otherwise noted, the number of taxable slaves (those twelve years of age and older) owned by each Tidewater, Piedmont, Valley, and Trans-Allegheny delegate is from Virginia Personal Property Book, 1831, Virginia State Library, Richmond. Delegates' voting records are all from Virginia, *Journal of the House of Delegates of the Commonwealth of Virginia, 1831–32,* pp. 109–10.
2. From 1830 Personal Property Book.
3. From 1830 Personal Property Book.
4. Listed in 1831 Personal Property Book as "Land, Peter and son Jeremiah."
5. From 1829 Personal Property Book.
6. Garland also listed twelve taxable slaves as "Trustee" of the estate of Catherine Pendleton, deceased.
7. Chilton also listed three taxable slaves as "Trustee" for the children of Nathaniel Griggs.
8. Although Marshall initially voted "no" on the Bryce preamble, he later voted "yes" on the committee report with the Bryce preamble and thus must be considered an antislavery moderate.
9. McIlhaney owned the five slaves jointly with Aaron Scatterday.
10. Caldwell owned the two slaves jointly with William Hough.
11. Listed as property of "Vincent Witcher & Son."
12. Listed as property of "Wm. Good & Son."
13. From 1832 Personal Property Book.
14. From 1832 Personal Property Book.
15. Two Trans-Allegheny abolitionists, Jacob Helms of Floyd and Robert Gillespie of Tazewell, voted against the Bryce preamble as an inadequate antislavery declaration. See Chapter V, n. 84.
16. From 1830 Personal Property Book.

**TABLES FOR CHAPTER VIII**

Table VIII: Virginia's White and Slave Population by Counties—1850, 1860

| County | 1850 | | | 1860 | | |
|---|---|---|---|---|---|---|
| | Whites | Slaves | % Slaves to Total Population | Whites | Slaves | % Slaves to Total Population |
| *A. Tidewater* | | | | | | |
| Accomack | 9,608 | 4,987 | 29.2 | 10,661 | 4,507 | 24.2 |
| Alexandria (City) | 7,217 | 1,382 | 13.8 | 9,851 | 1,386 | 11.0 |
| Caroline | 6,891 | 10,661 | 57.8 | 6,948 | 10,672 | 57.8 |
| Charles City | 1,664 | 2,764 | 53.2 | 1,806 | 2,947 | 52.5 |
| Chesterfield | 8,406 | 8,616 | 49.3 | 10,019 | 8,354 | 43.9 |
| Elizabeth City | 2,341 | 2,148 | 46.8 | 3,180 | 2,417 | 41.7 |
| Essex | 3,035 | 6,762 | 66.5 | 3,296 | 6,696 | 64.0 |
| Fairfax | 6,835 | 3,250 | 30.4 | 8,046 | 3,116 | 26.3 |
| Gloucester | 4,290 | 5,557 | 54.2 | 4,517 | 5,736 | 52.4 |
| Greensville | 1,731 | 3,785 | 67.1 | 1,974 | 4,167 | 65.4 |
| Hanover | 6,539 | 8,393 | 55.4 | 7,482 | 9,483 | 55.1 |
| Henrico | 23,826 | 16,109 | 37.0 | 37,985 | 20,041 | 32.5 |
| Isle of Wight | 4,710 | 3,395 | 36.3 | 5,037 | 3,570 | 35.8 |
| James City | 1,489 | 1,868 | 46.5 | 2,167 | 2,586 | 44.6 |
| King and Queen | 4,094 | 5,761 | 55.9 | 3,801 | 6,139 | 59.4 |
| King George | 2,301 | 3,403 | 57.0 | 2,510 | 3,673 | 55.9 |
| King William | 2,701 | 5,731 | 65.3 | 2,589 | 5,525 | 64.8 |

|  | 1850 | | | 1860 | | |
|---|---|---|---|---|---|---|
| County | Whites | Slaves | % Slaves to Total Population | Whites | Slaves | % Slaves to Total Population |
| Lancaster | 1,802 | 2,640 | 56.1 | 1,981 | 2,869 | 55.7 |
| Mathews | 3,642 | 2,923 | 43.5 | 3,865 | 3,008 | 42.4 |
| Middlesex | 1,903 | 2,342 | 53.3 | 1,863 | 2,375 | 54.4 |
| Nansemond | 5,424 | 4,715 | 38.4 | 5,732 | 5,481 | 40.0 |
| New Kent | 2,222 | 3,410 | 56.2 | 2,146 | 3,374 | 57.3 |
| Norfolk | 20,329 | 10,400 | 31.5 | 24,420 | 9,004 | 24.9 |
| Northampton | 3,105 | 3,648 | 48.7 | 2,998 | 3,872 | 49.4 |
| Northumberland | 3,072 | 3,755 | 51.1 | 3,870 | 3,439 | 45.7 |
| Prince George | 2,670 | 4,408 | 58.0 | 2,899 | 4,997 | 59.4 |
| Prince William | 5,079 | 2,498 | 30.7 | 5,690 | 2,356 | 27.5 |
| Princess Anne | 4,280 | 3,130 | 40.8 | 4,333 | 3,186 | 41.3 |
| Rappahannock | 5,642 | 3,844 | 39.3 | 5,018 | 3,520 | 39.8 |
| Richmond | 3,463 | 2,277 | 35.3 | 3,570 | 2,466 | 36.0 |
| Southampton | 5,940 | 5,755 | 42.6 | 5,713 | 5,408 | 41.9 |
| Spotsylvania | 6,894 | 7,481 | 50.2 | 7,716 | 7,786 | 48.4 |
| Stafford | 4,415 | 3,311 | 41.2 | 4,922 | 3,314 | 38.7 |
| Surry | 2,215 | 2,479 | 43.7 | 2,334 | 2,515 | 41.0 |
| Sussex | 3,086 | 5,992 | 61.0 | 3,118 | 6,384 | 62.7 |
| Warwick | 599 | 905 | 58.5 | 662 | 1,019 | 58.6 |
| Westmoreland | 3,376 | 3,558 | 44.0 | 3,387 | 3,704 | 44.7 |
| York | 1,825 | 2,181 | 48.9 | 2,342 | 1,925 | 38.9 |
| Totals: | 188,661 | 176,224 | 44.5 | 220,448 | 183,017 | 41.9 |

*B. Piedmont*

| | | | | | |
|---|---|---|---|---|---|
| Albemarle | 11,875 | 13,338 | 51.9 | 12,103 | 13,916 | 52.3 |
| Amelia | 2,785 | 6,819 | 69.8 | 2,897 | 7,655 | 71.3 |
| Amherst | 6,352 | 5,953 | 46.9 | 7,167 | 6,278 | 45.7 |
| Appomattox | 4,209 | 4,799 | 52.2 | 4,118 | 4,600 | 51.7 |
| Bedford | 13,556 | 10,061 | 41.8 | 14,388 | 10,176 | 40.6 |
| Brunswick | 4,885 | 8,456 | 60.9 | 4,992 | 9,146 | 61.8 |
| Buckingham | 5,426 | 8,161 | 59.0 | 6,041 | 8,811 | 57.9 |
| Campbell | 11,533 | 10,866 | 46.8 | 13,588 | 11,580 | 44.2 |
| Charlotte | 4,615 | 8,988 | 64.4 | 4,981 | 9,238 | 63.8 |
| Culpeper | 5,112 | 6,683 | 54.4 | 4,959 | 6,675 | 55.3 |
| Cumberland | 3,082 | 6,329 | 64.9 | 2,946 | 6,705 | 67.3 |
| Dinwiddie | 10,942 | 10,880 | 43.3 | 13,678 | 12,774 | 42.3 |
| Fauquier | 9,875 | 10,350 | 49.6 | 10,430 | 10,455 | 48.2 |
| Fluvanna | 4,539 | 4,737 | 49.9 | 5,093 | 4,994 | 48.2 |
| Franklin | 11,638 | 5,726 | 32.9 | 13,642 | 6,351 | 31.6 |
| Goochland | 3,863 | 5,845 | 56.5 | 3,814 | 6,139 | 57.6 |
| Greene | 2,667 | 1,699 | 38.6 | 3,015 | 1,984 | 39.5 |
| Halifax | 10,976 | 14,452 | 55.7 | 11,060 | 14,897 | 56.2 |
| Henry | 5,324 | 3,340 | 38.0 | 6,773 | 5,018 | 41.5 |
| Loudoun | 15,081 | 5,641 | 25.6 | 15,021 | 5,501 | 25.3 |
| Louisa | 6,423 | 9,864 | 59.1 | 6,183 | 10,194 | 61.0 |
| Lunenburg | 4,314 | 7,187 | 61.5 | 4,421 | 7,305 | 61.0 |
| Madison | 4,456 | 4,724 | 50.6 | 4,360 | 4,397 | 49.7 |
| Mecklenburg | 7,256 | 12,462 | 60.4 | 6,778 | 12,420 | 61.8 |

|  | 1850 | | | 1860 | | |
| County | Whites | Slaves | % Slaves to Total Population | Whites | Slaves | % Slaves to Total Population |
| --- | --- | --- | --- | --- | --- | --- |
| Nelson | 6,478 | 6,142 | 48.8 | 6,649 | 6,238 | 47.9 |
| Nottoway | 2,234 | 6,050 | 71.7 | 2,270 | 6,468 | 73.2 |
| Orange | 3,962 | 5,921 | 58.8 | 4,553 | 6,111 | 56.3 |
| Patrick | 7,187 | 2,324 | 24.2 | 7,158 | 2,070 | 22.1 |
| Pittsylvania | 15,263 | 12,798 | 44.4 | 17,105 | 14,340 | 44.7 |
| Powhatan | 2,513 | 5,282 | 64.6 | 2,580 | 5,403 | 64.4 |
| Prince Edward | 4,177 | 7,192 | 60.7 | 4,037 | 7,341 | 62.0 |
| Totals: | 212,598 | 233,069 | 50.5 | 226,800 | 245,180 | 50.2 |

*C. Valley*

|  | 1850 | | | 1860 | | |
| County | Whites | Slaves | % Slaves to Total Population | Whites | Slaves | % Slaves to Total Population |
| --- | --- | --- | --- | --- | --- | --- |
| Alleghany | 2,763 | 694 | 19.7 | 5,643 | 990 | 14.6 |
| Augusta | 18,983 | 5,053 | 20.5 | 21,547 | 5,616 | 20.2 |
| Bath | 2,434 | 947 | 27.6 | 2,652 | 946 | 25.7 |
| Berkeley | 9,566 | 1,956 | 16.6 | 10,589 | 1,650 | 13.2 |
| Botetourt | 10,746 | 3,736 | 25.1 | 8,441 | 2,769 | 24.0 |
| Clarke | 3,614 | 3,614 | 49.2 | 3,707 | 3,375 | 47.2 |
| Frederick | 12,769 | 2,294 | 14.4 | 13,079 | 2,259 | 13.7 |
| Hampshire | 12,379 | 1,433 | 10.2 | 12,478 | 1,213 | 8.7 |
| Hardy | 7,927 | 1,260 | 13.3 | 8,521 | 1,073 | 10.9 |
| Highland | 3,837 | 364 | 8.6 | 3,890 | 402 | 9.3 |
| Jefferson | 10,476 | 4,341 | 28.3 | 10,064 | 3,960 | 27.2 |

| | | | | | |
|---|---:|---:|---:|---:|---:|
| Morgan | 3,431 | 123 | 3.5 | 3,614 | 94 | 2.5 |
| Page | 6,332 | 957 | 12.6 | 6,875 | 850 | 10.5 |
| Pendleton | 5,443 | 322 | 5.6 | 5,870 | 244 | 4.0 |
| Roanoke | 5,812 | 2,511 | 29.6 | 5,250 | 2,643 | 32.8 |
| Rockbridge | 11,484 | 4,197 | 26.2 | 12,841 | 3,985 | 23.1 |
| Rockingham | 17,496 | 2,331 | 11.5 | 20,489 | 2,387 | 10.2 |
| Shenandoah | 12,565 | 911 | 6.6 | 12,827 | 753 | 5.4 |
| Warren | 4,493 | 1,748 | 26.5 | 4,583 | 1,575 | 24.4 |
| Totals: | 162,550 | 38,792 | 18.8 | 172,960 | 36,784 | 17.1 |

*D. Trans-Allegheny*

| | | | | | | |
|---|---:|---:|---:|---:|---:|---:|
| Barbour | 8,670 | 113 | 1.3 | 8,728 | 95 | 1.1 |
| Boone | 3,054 | 183 | 5.7 | 4,681 | 158 | 3.3 |
| Braxton | 4,123 | 89 | 2.1 | 4,885 | 104 | 2.1 |
| Brooke | 4,923 | 31 | 0.6 | 5,425 | 18 | 0.3 |
| Buchanan | — | — | — | 2,762 | 30 | 1.1 |
| Cabell | 5,902 | 389 | 6.2 | 7,691 | 305 | 3.8 |
| Calhoun | — | — | — | 2,492 | 9 | 0.4 |
| Carroll | 5,726 | 154 | 2.6 | 7,719 | 262 | 3.3 |
| Clay | — | — | — | 1,761 | 21 | 1.2 |
| Craig | — | — | — | 3,103 | 420 | 1.2 |
| Doddridge | 2,718 | 31 | 1.1 | 5,168 | 34 | 0.7 |
| Fayette | 3,780 | 156 | 4.0 | 5,716 | 271 | 4.5 |
| Floyd | 6,001 | 443 | 6.9 | 7,745 | 475 | 5.8 |
| Giles | 5,858 | 657 | 10.0 | 6,038 | 778 | 11.3 |
| Gilmer | 3,403 | 73 | 2.1 | 3,685 | 52 | 1.4 |

| County | 1850 | | | 1860 | | |
|---|---|---|---|---|---|---|
| | Whites | Slaves | % Slaves to Total Population | Whites | Slaves | % Slaves to Total Population |
| Grayson | 6,142 | 499 | 7.5 | 7,653 | 547 | 6.6 |
| Greenbrier | 8,549 | 1,317 | 13.1 | 10,500 | 1,525 | 12.5 |
| Hancock | 4,040 | 3 | 0.1 | 4,442 | 2 | 0.1 |
| Harrison | 11,213 | 488 | 4.2 | 13,176 | 582 | 4.2 |
| Jackson | 6,480 | 53 | 0.8 | 8,240 | 55 | 0.7 |
| Kanawha | 12,001 | 3,140 | 20.5 | 13,785 | 2,184 | 13.5 |
| Lee | 9,440 | 787 | 7.7 | 10,195 | 824 | 7.5 |
| Lewis | 9,620 | 368 | 3.7 | 7,736 | 230 | 2.9 |
| Logan | 3,533 | 87 | 2.4 | 4,789 | 148 | 3.0 |
| Marion | 10,439 | 94 | 0.9 | 12,656 | 63 | 0.5 |
| Marshall | 10,050 | 49 | 0.5 | 12,911 | 29 | 0.2 |
| Mason | 6,841 | 647 | 8.6 | 8,750 | 376 | 4.1 |
| McDowell | — | — | — | 1,535 | 0 | 0.0 |
| Mercer | 4,018 | 177 | 4.2 | 6,428 | 362 | 5.3 |
| Monongalia | 12,092 | 176 | 1.4 | 12,901 | 101 | 0.8 |
| Monroe | 9,062 | 1,061 | 10.4 | 9,536 | 1,114 | 10.4 |
| Montgomery | 6,822 | 1,471 | 17.6 | 8,251 | 2,219 | 20.9 |
| Nicholas | 3,889 | 73 | 1.8 | 4,471 | 154 | 3.3 |
| Ohio | 17,612 | 164 | 0.9 | 22,196 | 100 | 0.4 |
| Pocahontas | 3,303 | 267 | 7.4 | 3,686 | 252 | 6.4 |
| Pleasants | — | — | — | 2,925 | 15 | 0.5 |
| Preston | 11,562 | 87 | 0.7 | 13,200 | 67 | 0.5 |
| Pulaski | 3,613 | 1,471 | 28.7 | 3,814 | 1,589 | 29.3 |

| | | | | | | |
|---|---|---|---|---|---|---|
| Putnam | 4,693 | 632 | 11.9 | 5,708 | 580 | 9.2 |
| Raleigh | 1,729 | 23 | 1.3 | 3,291 | 57 | 1.7 |
| Randolph | 5,003 | 201 | 3.8 | 4,793 | 183 | 3.7 |
| Ritchie | 3,886 | 16 | 0.4 | 6,809 | 38 | 0.6 |
| Roane | — | — | — | 5,307 | 72 | 1.3 |
| Russell | 10,866 | 982 | 8.2 | 9,130 | 1,099 | 10.7 |
| Scott | 9,322 | 473 | 4.8 | 11,530 | 490 | 4.1 |
| Smyth | 6,898 | 1,064 | 13.0 | 7,732 | 1,037 | 11.6 |
| Taylor | 5,130 | 168 | 3.1 | 7,300 | 112 | 1.5 |
| Tazewell | 8,807 | 1,060 | 10.7 | 8,625 | 1,202 | 12.1 |
| Tucker | — | — | — | 1,392 | 20 | 1.4 |
| Tyler | 5,456 | 38 | 0.7 | 6,488 | 18 | 0.3 |
| Upshur | — | — | — | 7,064 | 212 | 2.9 |
| Washington | 12,369 | 2,131 | 14.6 | 14,096 | 2,547 | 15.1 |
| Wayne | 4,564 | 189 | 4.0 | 6,604 | 143 | 2.1 |
| Webster | — | — | — | 1,552 | 3 | 0.2 |
| Wetzel | 4,261 | 17 | 0.4 | 6,691 | 10 | 0.1 |
| Wirt | 3,319 | 32 | 1.0 | 3,728 | 23 | 0.6 |
| Wise | — | — | — | 4,416 | 66 | 1.5 |
| Wood | 9,008 | 373 | 4.0 | 10,791 | 176 | 1.6 |
| Wyoming | 1,583 | 61 | 3.7 | 2,795 | 64 | 2.2 |
| Wythe | 9,618 | 2,185 | 18.2 | 9,986 | 2,162 | 17.6 |
| Totals: | 330,991 | 24,443 | 6.8 | 427,203 | 25,884 | 5.7 |

Source: U.S. Census Office, *Seventh Census*, 256–57; U.S. Census Office, *Population of the United States in 1860*, 516–18.

**Table IX: Virginia's White Population in 1830, 1850, 1860—A Summary**

| Section | 1830 Whites | 1830 % of All Whites | 1850 Whites | 1850 % of All Whites | 1860 Whites | 1860 % of All Whites |
|---|---|---|---|---|---|---|
| Tidewater | 167,001 | 24.1 | 188,661 | 21.1 | 220,448 | 21.0 |
| Piedmont | 208,656 | 30.0 | 212,598 | 23.7 | 226,800 | 21.7 |
| Valley | 134,791 | 19.4 | 162,550 | 18.2 | 172,960 | 16.5 |
| Trans-Allegheny | 183,854 | 26.5 | 330,991 | 37.0 | 427,203 | 40.8 |
| Virginia | 694,302 | | 894,800 | | 1,047,411 | |

Source: U.S. Census Office, *Fifth Census*, Tables [10]–[13]; *Seventh Census*, 256–57; *Population of the United States in 1860*, pp. 516–18.

**Table X: Virginia's Slave Population in 1830, 1850, 1860—A Summary**

| Section | 1830 | | | 1850 | | | 1860 | | |
|---|---|---|---|---|---|---|---|---|---|
| | Slaves | % Slaves to Total Pop. | % of All Va. Slaves | Slaves | % Slaves to Total Pop. | % of All Va. Slaves | Slaves | % Slaves to Total Pop. | % of All Va. Slaves |
| Tidewater | 185,457 | 48.6 | 39.5 | 176,224 | 44.5 | 37.3 | 183,017 | 41.9 | 37.3 |
| Piedmont | 230,861 | 51.1 | 49.1 | 233,069 | 50.5 | 49.3 | 245,180 | 50.2 | 49.9 |
| Valley | 34,772 | 19.9 | 7.4 | 38,792 | 18.8 | 8.2 | 36,784 | 17.1 | 7.5 |
| Trans-Allegheny | 18,665 | 9.1 | 4.0 | 24,443 | 6.8 | 5.2 | 25,884 | 5.7 | 5.3 |
| Virginia | 469,755 | 38.7 | | 472,528 | 33.2 | | 490,865 | 30.7 | |

Source: U.S. Census Office, *Fifth Census*, Tables [10]–[13]; *Seventh Census*, 256–57; *Population of the United States in 1860*, pp. 516–18.

# Bibliography

PRIMARY SOURCES: UNPUBLISHED

**Manuscripts**

Duke University, Durham, N.C.
    Campbell, David. Papers.
    Clark, Henry. Papers.
    Dromgoole, George C. Papers.
    Faulkner, Charles James. Papers.
    Holmes, George Frederick. Papers.
    Kilby, John Richardson. Papers.
    McDowell, James. Papers.
    Rutherfoord, John C. Papers.
    Smith, William P. Papers.
Library of Congress, Washington, D.C.
    American Colonization Society Papers.
    Black, Jeremiah. Papers.
    Floyd, John. Papers.
    Rives, William Cabell. Papers.
    Trist, Nicholas P. Papers.
University of North Carolina, Southern Historical Collection, Chapel Hill
    Brodnax, John W. Papers.
    Dromgoole, Edward. Papers.
    Hubard, Edmund W. Papers.
    Kimberly, John. Papers.
    McDowell, James. Papers.
    Trist, Nicholas P. Papers.
    Trist. Family Papers
University of Virginia, Alderman Library, Charlottesville
    Cabell, Joseph C. Papers.

Cocke. Family Papers.
Cocke, John Hartwell. Papers.
Coolidge, Ellen Wayles. Correspondence, 1829–1833.
Edgehill-Randolph Papers.
Harrison, Gessner. Papers.
Virginia Historical Society, Richmond
Brodnax, William Henry. Papers.
Doddridge, Philip. Letter to Constituents, March 1, 1830. Manuscript 2D6615al.
Dupuy. Family Papers.
Leigh, Benjamin Watkins. Papers.
Virginia Colonization Society. Minute Book, 1823–1859.
Virginia State Library, Richmond
Auditor's #153. Unbound Material on the Southampton Insurrection, Condemned Slaves, Transportation of Free Negroes.
Council Journal, 1831–1832.
Executive Communications, Box 37.
Floyd, John. Executive Letter Book, 1830–1834.
———. Executive Papers, 1830–1834.
———. Slave and Free Negro Letterbook, 1831–1832.
Southampton County Minutebook, 1830–1835.
Tazewell. Family Papers.
Virginia Legislative Petitions, 1786, 1831–1832, 1851.
Virginia Personal Property Books, 1830–1833.
West Virginia University, Morgantown
Faulkner, Charles James. Papers.
Summers, George. Papers.
Summers, Lewis. Papers.
William and Mary College, Earl Gregg Swem Library, Williamsburg, Va.
Brodnax, William Henry. Papers.
Brown, Coalter, Tucker Papers. John Thompson Brown Correspondence.
Dew. Family Papers.
Harrison, Francis Burton. Papers.
Tucker-Coleman Papers. St. George Tucker Correspondence.


## PRIMARY SOURCES: PUBLISHED

### Manuscript Collections

Ambler, Charles H., ed. *The Life and Diary of John Floyd*. Richmond: Richmond Press, 1918.
Betts, Edwin Morris and James Adam Bear, Jr., eds. *The Family Letters of Thomas Jefferson*. Columbia: University of Missouri Press, 1966.

Boyd, Julian P., ed. *The Papers of Thomas Jefferson.* Vol. II. Princeton: Princeton University Press, 1950.

Clarke, John Henrik, ed. "The 1831 Text of the Confessions of Nat Turner." In *Ten Black Writers Respond.* Boston: Beacon Press, 1968.

Coleman, Mary H., ed. *Virginia Silhouettes: Contemporary Letters Concerning Negro Slavery in the State of Virginia.* Richmond: Dietz Press, 1934.

Ford, Paul Leicester, ed. *The Writings of Thomas Jefferson.* Vols. I, IV, VIII, IX, X, XII. New York: G. P. Putnam's Sons, 1905.

Hamilton, Stanislaus M., ed. *The Writings of James Monroe.* Vol. III. New York: G. P. Putnam's Sons, 1903.

Hunt, Gaillard, ed. *The Writings of James Madison.* Vol. IX. New York: G. P. Putnam's Sons, 1910.

Tragle, Henry I. *The Southampton Slave Revolt of 1831: A Compilation of Source Material.* Amherst: University of Massachusetts Press, 1971.

Tucker, St. George. "Queries Relating to Slavery in Massachusetts." In *Collections of the Massachusetts Historical Society.* Vol. III (1877), 373–442.

### Contemporary Books, Pamphlets, and Speeches

American Colonization Society. *The African Repository and Colonial Journal.* Vol. VII. Washington, D.C.: James C. Dunn, 1831.

Bledsoe, Albert Taylor. *An Essay on Liberty and Slavery.* Philadelphia: J. B. Lippincott, 1857.

Cabell, Margaret C. *Sketches and Recollections of Lynchburg.* Richmond: C. H. Wynne, 1858.

Doddridge, Joseph. *Notes on the Settlement and Indian Wars of the Western Parts of Virginia and Pennsylvania from 1763 to 1783, inclusive, together with a Review of the State of Society and Manners of the First Settlers of the Western Country.* Reprint. Parsons, W.Va.: McClain, 1910.

Harrison, Fairfax, ed. *Aris Sonis Focisque. The Harrisons of Skimino.* N.p., 1910.

Howe, Henry. *Historical Collections of Virginia.* Charleston, S.C.: W. R. Babcock, 1852.

Howison, Robert R. *A History of Virginia, From Its Discovery and Settlement by Europeans to the Present Time.* Vol. II. Richmond: Drinker and Morris, 1848.

Jefferson, Thomas. *Notes on the State of Virginia.* Ed. William Peden. Chapel Hill: University of North Carolina Press, 1954.

Kercheval, Samuel. *A History of the Valley of Virginia.* 2nd ed. Woodstock, Va.: John Gatewood, 1850.

[Leigh, Benjamin Watkins.] *The Letter of Appomatox to the People of Virginia.* Richmond: Thomas W. White, 1832.

Little, John P. *History of Richmond.* Reprint. Richmond: Dietz, 1933.

Martin, Joseph, ed. *A New and Comprehensive Gazeteer of Virginia, and the District of Columbia.* Charlottesville: J. Martin, 1836.

Mordecai, Samuel. *Virginia, Especially Richmond, in By-Gone Days: Being Reminis-*

cences and Last Words of an Old Citizen. Richmond: West and Johnston, 1860.

Randolph, Sarah. The Domestic Life of Thomas Jefferson. New York: Harper and Brothers, 1871.

Ruffin, Edmund. African Colonization Unveiled. Washington, D.C.: n.p., 1858.

Ruffner, Henry. An Address to the People of West Virginia. Reprint. Bridgewater, Va.: Green Bookman, 1933.

Slaughter, Philip. The Virginian History of African Colonization. Richmond: Macfarlane and Fergusson, 1855.

Smith, William A. Lectures on the Philosophy and Practice of Slavery as Exhibited in the Institution of Domestic Slavery in the United States: with the Duties of Masters to Slaves. Nashville: Stevenson and Evans, 1856.

The Speech of Henry Berry (of Jefferson) in the House of Delegates of Virginia, on the Abolition of Slavery. Richmond: Thomas W. White, 1832.

The Speeches of Philip A. Bolling (of Buckingham), in the House of Delegates of Virginia, on the Policy of the State in Relation to Her Colored Population. Richmond: Thomas W. White, 1832.

The Speech of William H. Brodnax (of Dinwiddie) in the House of Delegates of Virginia, on the Policy of the State with respect to Its Colored Population. Richmond: Thomas W. White, 1832.

The Speech of John Thompson Brown, in the House of Delegates of Virginia, on the Abolition of Slavery. Reprint. Richmond: Charles H. Wynne, 1860.

The Speech of John A. Chandler (of Norfolk County) in the House of Delegates of Virginia, on the Policy of the State with respect to Her Slave Population. Richmond: Thomas W. White, 1832.

The Speech of Charles Jas. Faulkner (of Berkeley) in the House of Delegates of Virginia, on the Policy of the State with respect to Her Slave Population. Richmond: Thomas W. White, 1832.

The Speech of James McDowell, Jr. (of Rockbridge) in the House of Delegates of Virginia, on the Slave Question. Richmond: Thomas W. White, 1832.

The Speech of Thomas Marshall, in the House of Delegates of Virginia, on the Abolition of Slavery. Richmond: Thomas W. White, 1832.

The Speech of Thomas J. Randolph, in the House of Delegates of Virginia, on the Abolition of Slavery. Richmond: Thomas W. White, 1832.

Tucker, Nathaniel Beverly. Prescience. A Speech Delivered by the Hon. Beverly Tucker, of Virginia, in the Southern Convention, Held at Nashville, Tennessee, April 13, 1850. Richmond: Colin, Baptist, and Nowlan, 1862.

Tucker, St. George. A Dissertation on Slavery with a Proposal for the Gradual Abolition of It, in the State of Virginia. Philadelphia: Mathew Carey, 1796.

Tucker, St. George ["Sylvestris"]. Reflections on the Cession of Louisiana to the United States. Washington, D.C.: Samuel Harrison Smith, 1803.

Wiltse, Charles M., ed. David Walker's Appeal in Four Articles; Together with a Preamble to the Colored Citizens of the World, but in Particular, and Very Expressly, to those of the United States of America. New York: Hill and Wang, 1965.

## Contemporary Articles

Dew, Thomas Roderick. "Review of the Debate in the Virginia Legislature of 1831–1832." Reprint. *Pro-Slavery Argument.* Philadelphia: Lippincott, Grambo, 1853.

Grigsby, Hugh Blair. "Sketches of Members of the Constitutional Convention of 1829–1830." *Virginia Magazine of History and Biography,* LXI (July, 1953), 319–32.

———. "The Virginia Convention of 1829–30." *Virginia Historical Reporter,* I (1854), 15–116.

"Memorial of the Staunton Convention to the Legislature of the State of Virginia." *Niles' Weekly Register,* XI (September 7, 1816), 17–25.

Pleasants, Hugh R. "Sketches of the Virginia Convention of 1829–30." *Southern Literary Messenger,* XVII (1851), 147–54, 297–304.

"Virginia Convention." *Niles' Weekly Register,* II (March 15, 1824), 179.


## Government Documents

Catterall, Helen, ed. *Judicial Cases Concerning American Slavery and the Negro.* Vol. I. Washington, D.C.: Carnegie Institution, 1926.

Hening, William W., ed. *Virginia Statutes at Large, 1619–1792.* Vols. VI, IX, XI, XII. Richmond: George Cochran, 1823.

Lewis, Virgil A., ed. *How West Virginia Was Made.* Charleston, W.Va.: Tribune Printing, 1909.

Palmer, William P., Sherwin McRae, and H. W. Flournoy, eds. *Calendar of Virginia State Papers and Other Manuscripts Preserved in the Capitol at Richmond.* Vol. IX. Richmond: H. W. Flournoy, 1890.

Peterson, Merrill D., ed. *Democracy, Liberty, and Property: The State Constitutional Conventions of the 1820's.* Indianapolis: Bobbs-Merrill, 1966.

Reese, George H., ed. *Proceedings of the Virginia State Convention of 1861.* 4 vols. Richmond: Virginia State Library, 1965.

Shepherd, Samuel, ed. *The Statutes at Large of Virginia, from October Session 1792, to December Session, 1806, Inclusive.* Vol. III. Richmond: Samuel Shepherd, 1836.

Swem, Earl Gregg and John W. Williams. *A Register of the General Assembly of Virginia and of the Constitutional Conventions.* Richmond: Virginia State Library, 1918.

U.S. Census Office. *Fifth Census; or Enumeration of the Inhabitants of the United States, 1830. To Which is Prefixed a Schedule of the Whole Number of Persons Within the Several Districts of the United States, Taken According to the Acts of 1790, 1800, 1810, 1820.* Washington, D.C.: Duff Green, 1832.

———. *Population of the United States in 1860; Compiled from the Original Returns of the Eighth Census.* Washington, D.C.: Government Printing Office, 1864.

———. *The Seventh Census of the United States: 1850.* Washington, D.C.: Robert Armstrong, 1853.

Virginia. *Acts and Joint Resolutions of the General Assembly of the Commonwealth of Virginia, 1815–1829.* Richmond: Thomas Ritchie, 1816–1829.

———. *Acts Passed at a General Assembly of the Commonwealth of Virginia, 1830– 1836.* Richmond: Thomas Ritchie, 1831–1836.

———. *Journal, Acts and Proceedings of a Convention Held in the Commonwealth of Virginia, 1829–1830.* Richmond: Thomas Ritchie, 1830.

———. *Journals of the House of Delegates of the Commonwealth of Virginia, 1801– 1802, 1820–1821, 1828–1836.* Richmond: Thomas Ritchie, 1821–1836.

———. *Journal of the Senate of the Commonwealth of Virginia, 1831–1832.* Richmond: John Warrock, 1832.

———. *Journal of the Senate of the Commonwealth of Virginia, 1832–1833.* Richmond: Thomas Ritchie, 1833.

———. *Proceedings and Debates of the Virginia State Convention of 1829–1830.* Richmond: Thomas Ritchie, 1830.

Virginia Board of Immigration. *Virginia: A Geographical and Political Summary.* Richmond: R. F. Walker, 1876.

## Newspapers

Charlestown *Virginia Free Press and Farmers' Repository,* 1831–32.
Charlottesville *Virginia Advocate,* 1832.
Fredericksburg (Va.) *Political Arena,* 1831–32.
Lynchburg *Virginian,* 1831–32.
Martinsburg (Va.) *Gazette,* 1831–32.
Norfolk and Portsmouth (Va.) *American Beacon,* 1831–32.
Norfolk and Portsmouth (Va.) *Herald,* 1831–32.
Richmond *Argus,* 1806.
Richmond *Constitutional Whig,* 1831–33.
Richmond *Enquirer,* 1831–33.
Richmond *Enquirer Supplements,* March–June, 1851.
Wellsburg (Va.) *Gazette,* December, 1831–March, 1832.

## SECONDARY SOURCES

### Books

Abernethy, Thomas P. *Three Virginia Frontiers.* Reprint. Gloucester, Mass.: Peter Smith, 1962.

Adams, Alice D. *The Neglected Period of Anti-Slavery in America, 1808–1830.* Boston: Ginn, 1908.

Ambler, Charles H. *Sectionalism in Virginia from 1776 to 1861*. Reprint. New York: Russell and Russell, 1964.

——. *Thomas Ritchie. A Study in Virginia Politics*. Richmond: Bell Book and Stationery, 1913.

——. *Waitman T. Willey*. Huntington, W.Va.: n.p., 1954.

Ambler, Charles H. and Festus P. Summers. *West Virginia: The Mountain State*. Englewood Cliffs, N.J.: Prentice-Hall, 1958.

Anderson, Dice Robins. *William Branch Giles: A Study in the Politics of Virginia and the Nation from 1790 to 1830*. Menasha, Wis.: George Banta, 1914.

Aptheker, Herbert. *American Negro Slave Revolts*. New York: International Publishers, 1963.

Ballagh, James Curtis. *A History of Slavery in Virginia*. Baltimore: Johns Hopkins University Press, 1902.

Bancroft, Frederick. *Slave-Trading in the Old South*. Baltimore: J. H. Furst, 1931.

Berlin, Ira. *Slaves Without Masters: The Free Negro in the Antebellum South*. New York: Pantheon, 1974.

Boorstin, Daniel J. *The Lost World of Thomas Jefferson*. Boston: Beacon Press, 1948.

Bouldin, Powhatan. *Home Reminiscences of John Randolph of Roanoke*. Danville, Va.: Powhatan Bouldin, 1878.

Brown, Robert E. and B. Katherine. *Virginia 1705–1786: Democracy or Aristocracy?* East Lansing: Michigan State University Press, 1964.

Bruce, Kathleen. *Virginia Iron Manufacture in the Slave Era, 1800–1860*. New York: Century, 1931.

Bruce, William Cabell. *John Randolph of Roanoke, 1773–1833*. New York: G. P. Putnam's Sons, 1922.

Chandler, Julian A. C. *The History of Suffrage in Virginia*. Johns Hopkins University Studies in Historical and Political Science. Series 19, VI–VII. Baltimore: Johns Hopkins University Press, 1901.

——. *Representation in Virginia*. Johns Hopkins University Studies in Historical and Political Science, Series 14, VI–VII. Baltimore: Johns Hopkins University Press, 1896.

Cobban, Alfred. *Edmund Burke and the Revolt Against the Eighteenth Century*. London: Allen and Unwin, 1960.

Coleman, Mary H. *St. George Tucker: Citizen of No Mean City*. Richmond: Dietz Press, 1938.

Craven, Avery O. *Edmund Ruffin Southerner: A Study in Secession*. Baton Rouge: Louisiana State University Press, 1953.

——. *The Growth of Southern Nationalism, 1848–1861*. Baton Rouge: Louisiana State University Press, 1953. Vol. VI of Wendell Holmes Stephenson and E. Merton Coulter, eds., *A History of the South*.

——. *Soil Exhaustion as a Factor in the Agricultural History of Virginia and Maryland, 1606–1860*. University of Illinois Studies in the Social Sciences, XIII. Urbana: University of Illinois Press, 1926.

Curry, Richard Orr. *A House Divided: A Study of Statehood Politics and the Cop-perhead Movement in West Virginia.* Pittsburgh: University of Pittsburgh Press, 1964.

Davis, David Brion. *The Problem of Slavery in the Age of Revolution, 1770–1823.* Ithaca: Cornell University Press, 1975.

Davis, Richard Beale. *Intellectual Life in Jefferson's Virginia 1790–1830.* Chapel Hill: University of North Carolina Press, 1964.

Dodson, E. Griffith. *The Capitol of the Commonwealth of Virginia at Richmond.* Richmond: n.p., 1938.

Drewry, William S. *Slave Insurrections in Virginia.* Washington, D.C.: Neale, 1900.

Dulaney, Paul S. *The Architecture of Historic Richmond.* Charlottesville: University of Virginia Press, 1968.

Dunaway, Wayland F. *History of the James River and Kanawha Company.* Columbia University Studies in History, Economics, and Public Law, CIV. New York: Columbia University Press, 1922.

Eaton, Clement. *The Freedom-of-Thought Struggle in the Old South.* Revised ed. New York: Harper and Row, 1964.

Foner, Eric. *Free Soil, Free Labor, Free Men: The Ideology of the Republican Party Before the Civil War.* New York: Oxford University Press, 1970.

Fox, Early Lee. *The American Colonization Society 1817–1840.* Johns Hopkins University Studies in Historical and Political Science, Series 38, III. Baltimore: Johns Hopkins University Press, 1919.

Freehling, William W. *Prelude to Civil War: The Nullification Controversy in South Carolina, 1816–1836.* New York: Harper and Row, 1966.

Gaines, William H., Jr. *Thomas Mann Randolph.* Baton Rouge: Louisiana State University Press, 1966.

Garland, Hugh A. *The Life of John Randolph of Roanoke.* New York: D. Appleton, 1860.

Gewehr, Wesley. *The Great Awakening in Virginia, 1740–1790.* Durham, N.C.: Duke University Press, 1930.

Goldfield, David R. *Urban Growth in the Age of Sectionalism: Virginia, 1847–1861.* Baton Rouge: Louisiana State University Press, 1977.

Gordon, Armistead C. *William Fitzhugh Gordon. A Virginian of the Old School: His Life, Times and Contemporaries (1787–1858).* New York: Neale, 1909.

Gray, Lewis C. *The History of Agriculture in the Southern United States to 1860.* 2 vols. Washington, D.C.: Carnegie Institution, 1933.

Green, Fletcher M. *Constitutional Development in the South Atlantic States, 1776–1860.* Chapel Hill: University of North Carolina Press, 1930.

Guild, June P. *Black Laws of Virginia: A Summary of the Legislative Acts of Virginia Concerning Negroes from Earliest Times to the Present.* Richmond: Whittet and Shepperson, 1936.

Hall, Claude H. *Abel Parker Upshur Conservative Virginian, 1790–1844.* Madison: Wisconsin Historical Society, 1964.

Hall, Granville D. *The Rending of Virginia.* Chicago: n.p., 1901.

Jackson, Luther P. *Free Negro Labor and Property Holding in Virginia, 1830–1860*. New York: D. Appleton-Century, 1942.

Jenkins, William Sumner. *Pro-Slavery Thought in the Old South*. Reprint. Gloucester, Mass.: Peter Smith, 1960.

Johnson, F. Roy. *The Nat Turner Slave Insurrection*. Murfreesboro, N.C.: Johnson, 1966.

Jordan, Winthrop D. *White Over Black: American Attitudes Toward the Negro, 1550–1812*. Chapel Hill: University of North Carolina Press, 1968.

Kirk, Russell. *John Randolph of Roanoke. A Study in American Politics*. Chicago: Henry Regnery, 1964.

Koch, Adrienne. *Jefferson and Madison: The Great Collaboration*. New York: Knopf, 1950.

———. *The Philosophy of Thomas Jefferson*. New York: Columbia University Press, 1943.

Lewis, Virgil A. *West Virginia: Its History, Natural Resources, Industrial Enterprises, and Institutions*. Charleston, W.Va.: Tribune Printing, n.d.

Locke, Mary S. *Anti-Slavery in America from the Introduction of African Slaves to the Prohibition of the Slave Trade (1619–1808)*. Boston: Ginn, 1901.

McColley, Robert. *Slavery and Jeffersonian Virginia*. Urbana: University of Illinois Press, 1964.

McGregor, James C. *The Disruption of Virginia*. New York: Macmillan, 1922.

McIlhany, Hugh. *Some Virginia Families*. Staunton, Va.: Stoneburner and Prufer, 1903.

Maddox, William A. *The Free School Idea in Virginia Before the Civil War*. New York: Teachers College, Columbia University, 1918.

Miller, John Chester. *The Wolf by the Ears: Thomas Jefferson and Slavery*. New York: Free Press, 1977.

Moore, George E. *A Banner in the Hills: West Virginia's Statehood*. New York: Appleton-Century-Crofts, 1963.

Morgan, Edmund S. *American Slavery, American Freedom: The Ordeal of Colonial Virginia*. New York: W. W. Norton, 1975.

———. *Virginians at Home: Family Life in the Eighteenth Century*. Williamsburg, Va.: Colonial Williamsburg, 1952.

Mullin, Gerald W. *Flight and Rebellion: Slave Resistance in Eighteenth-Century Virginia*. New York: Oxford University Press, 1972.

Munford, Beverly B. *Virginia's Attitude toward Slavery and Secession*. New York: Longmans, Green, 1909.

Peterson, Merrill D. *Thomas Jefferson and the New Nation*. New York: Oxford University Press, 1970.

Pinchbeck, Raymond B. *The Virginia Negro Artisan and Tradesman*. Richmond: William Byrd Press, 1926.

Porter, Albert O. *County Government in Virginia, A Legislative History, 1607–1904*. New York: Columbia University Press, 1947.

Reizenstein, Milton. *The Economic History of the Baltimore and Ohio Railroad,*

*1827–1853.* Johns Hopkins University Studies in History and Political Science, Series 15, VII–VIII. Baltimore: Johns Hopkins University Press, 1897.

Risjord, Norman K. *The Old Republicans: Southern Conservatism in the Age of Jefferson.* New York: Columbia University Press, 1965.

Robert, Joseph C. *The Road from Monticello: A Study of the Virginia Slavery Debate of 1832.* Durham, N.C.: Duke University Press, 1941.

————. *The Tobacco Kingdom: Plantation, Market, and Factory in Virginia and North Carolina, 1800–1860.* Durham, N.C.: Duke University Press, 1938.

Russell, John H. *The Free Negro in Virginia 1619–1865.* Johns Hopkins University Studies in Historical and Political Science, Series 31, III. Baltimore: Johns Hopkins University Press, 1913.

Shanks, Henry T. *The Secession Movement in Virginia 1847–1861.* Richmond: Garrett and Massie, 1934.

Starobin, Robert S. *Industrial Slavery in the Old South.* New York: Oxford University Press, 1970.

Staudenraus, Philip J. *The African Colonization Movement 1816–1865.* New York: Columbia University Press, 1961.

Sydnor, Charles S. *The Development of Southern Sectionalism, 1819–1848.* Baton Rouge: Louisiana State University Press, 1948. Vol. V of Wendell Holmes Stephenson and E. Merton Coulter, eds., *A History of the South.*

————. *Gentlemen Freeholders: Political Practices in Washington's Virginia.* Chapel Hill: University of North Carolina Press, 1952.

Wade, Richard C. *Slavery in the Cities: The South, 1820–1860.* New York: Oxford University Press, 1964.

Wayland, John W. *The German Element of the Shenandoah Valley of Virginia.* Charlottesville: Michie, 1907.

Weeks, Stephen B. *Southern Quakers and Slavery.* Baltimore: Johns Hopkins University Press, 1896.

Wertenbaker, Thomas J. *Norfolk: Historic Southern Port.* Durham, N.C.: Duke University Press, 1931.

Whitfield, Theodore M. *Slavery Agitation in Virginia 1829–1832.* Baltimore: Johns Hopkins University Press, 1930.

Williamson, Chilton. *American Suffrage from Property to Democracy 1760–1860.* Princeton: Princeton University Press, 1960.

Wilstach, Paul. *Tidewater Virginia.* Indianapolis: Bobbs-Merrill, 1929.

Wise, Barton H. *The Life of Henry A. Wise of Virginia, 1806–1876.* New York: n.p., 1899.

Wise, Harvey. *George Fitzhugh. Propagandist of the Old South.* Reprint. Gloucester, Mass.: Peter Smith, 1962.

Wright, Gavin. *The Political Economy of the Cotton South.* New York: W. W. Norton, 1978.

Wright, Louis B. *The First Gentlemen of Virginia: Intellectual Qualities of the Early Colonial Ruling Class.* San Marino, Calif.: Huntington Library, 1940.

Zilversmit, Arthur. *The First Emancipation. The Abolition of Slavery in the North.* Chicago: University of Chicago Press, 1967.

## Articles

Batten, J. M. "Governor John Floyd." *John P. Branch Historical Papers of Randolph-Macon College,* IV (June, 1913), 5–49.

Bean, William Gleason. "The Ruffner Pamphlet of 1847: An Antislavery Aspect of Virginia Sectionalism." *Virginia Magazine of History and Biography,* LXI (July, 1953), 260–82.

Bradford, S. Sydney. "Negro Iron Workers in Antebellum Virginia." *Journal of Southern History,* XXV (1959), 194–206.

Bruce, Kathleen. "Virginia Agricultural Decline to 1860: A Fallacy." *Agricultural History,* VI (January, 1932), 3–13.

Eaton, Clement. "A Dangerous Pamphlet in the Old South." *Journal of Southern History,* II (1936), 323–34.

————. "Henry Wise: A Study in Virginia Leadership, 1850–61." *West Virginia History,* III (April, 1942), 187–204.

Freehling, William W. "The Founding Fathers and Slavery." *American Historical Review,* LXXVII (February, 1972), 81–93.

Largent, Robert J. "Virginia Takes the Road to Secession." *West Virginia History,* III (January, 1942), 120–47.

Moore, George E. "Slavery as a Factor in the Formation of West Virginia." *West Virginia History,* XVIII (October, 1956), 5–89.

Pole, J. R. "Representation and Authority in Virginia from the Revolution to Reform." *Journal of Southern History,* XXIV (1958), 16–50.

Robinson, Morgan P. "Virginia Counties: Those Resulting from Virginia Legislation." *Bulletin of the Virginia State Library,* IX (1916), 123–59.

Schmidt, Frederika Teute and Barbara Ripel Wilhelm. "Early Proslavery Petitions in Virginia." *William and Mary Quarterly,* XXX (1973), 138–41.

Shryock, Richard H. "British Versus German Traditions in Colonial Agriculture." *Mississippi Valley Historical Review,* XXVI (June, 1939), 39–54.

Spengler, J. J. "Malthusianism and the Debate on Slavery." *South Atlantic Quarterly,* XXXIV (April, 1935), 170–89.

Stampp, Kenneth M. "An Analysis of Thomas R. Dew's 'Review of the Debates in the Virginia Legislature.'" *Journal of Negro History,* XXVII (October, 1942), 380–87.

————. "The Southern Refutation of the Proslavery Argument." *North Carolina Historical Review,* XXI (January, 1944), 35–45.

Turner, H. F. "General William Henry Brodnax." *John P. Branch Historical Papers of Randolph-Macon College,* III (June, 1909), 14–26.

Wyatt, Edward A. "Rise of Industry in Antebellum Petersburg." *William and Mary Quarterly,* 2nd Series, XVII (January, 1937), 1–36.

## Theses and Dissertations

Coyner, Martin B., Jr., "John Hartwell Cocke of Bremo: Agriculture and Slavery in the Antebellum South." Ph.D. dissertation, University of Virginia, 1961.

Gaines, Francis P. "The Political Career of James McDowell." M.A. thesis, University of Virginia, 1947.

————. "The Virginia Constitutional Convention of 1850–1851: A Study in Sectionalism." Ph.D. dissertation, University of Virginia, 1950.

Hickin, Patricia. "Antislavery in Virginia, 1831–1861." Ph.D. dissertation, University of Virginia, 1968.

McVeigh, Donald R. "Charles J. Faulkner, Reluctant Rebel." Ph.D. dissertation, West Virginia University, 1954.

Mansfield, Stephen S. "Thomas Roderick Dew: Defender of the Southern Faith." Ph.D. dissertation, University of Virginia, 1968.

Neely, Frederick. "The Development of Virginia Taxation, 1776–1860." Ph.D. dissertation, University of Virginia, 1953.

Sutton, Robert P. "The Virginia Constitutional Convention of 1829–1830: A Profile Analysis of late–Jeffersonian Virginia." Ph.D. dissertation, University of Virginia, 1967.

Tanner, Carol M. "Joseph C. Cabell, 1778–1856." Ph.D. dissertation, University of Virginia, 1958.

Turrentine, Percy W. "The Life and Works of Nathaniel Beverly Tucker." Ph.D. dissertation, Harvard University, 1950.

Vance, Joseph C. "Thomas Jefferson Randolph." Ph.D. dissertation, University of Virginia, 1957.

# Index